Strategy & Soul

a campaigner's tale of fighting billionaires, corrupt officials, and Philadelphia casinos

Daniel Hunter

Read about this campaign, including original documents and a reader's guide:
www.strategyandsoul.org

Visit the author's website: www.danielhunter.org

Cover art © 2013 Kaytee Riek, KayteeRiek.com.
Cover photos of Philadelphia City Hall © Jose Gill 2013. Used under license from
Shutterstock.com.
Cover photo of Daniel Hunter (left) and Jethro Heiko © Chris Meck Photo,
ChrisMeck.com

ISBN-10: 0-9885508-0-6
ISBN-13: 978-0-9885508-0-3

Printed in the United States of America

First edition: February 2013

STRATEGY & SOUL

a campaigner's tale of fighting billionaires,
corrupt officials, and Philadelphia casinos

Contents

Acknowledgements

Writers warned me that writing a book would mean many hours alone. They knew I'd face my own demons, worrying over the what-if's and if-we-only-had's—not to mention reliving my embarrassing mistakes or moments when I failed to live up to my own values. But they completely failed to mention that writing is also community-building.

Friends pitched in by letting me read to them for hours at a time—thank you Clarissa Rogers, Maurice Weeks, Shandra Bernath-Plaisted, Kaytee Riek, Lunden Abelson, Sadie Forsythe, Nico Amador, Stephanie Alarcon, Matthew Armstead, Terrill Thompson, and Leigh Seeleman. Shout-out to my heart school peeps, who helped get me in the emotional shape to be honest and reflective: Ingrid Lakey, Pamela Haines, Lunden Abelson, and George Lakey.

I'm honored that organizers from Colombia to New Zealand, from Boston, Massachusetts to Richmond, Indiana, provided feedback and a listening ear. I'm grateful to you all, including Andrea Parra, Tanya Newman, Maureen White, and my mom and sister. Thanks to the zillions of people who offered tidbits about writing, especially Waging Nonviolence's Nathan Schneider, Pluto Press's David Shulman, and my writers' group: Antje Mattheus, Maurice Eldridge, George Lakey, and Niyonu Spann. Thanks to researcher Elowyn Corby, Les Bernal of Stop Predatory Gambling for technical advice, and Matthew Armstead for helping me find the right title. Thanks to my fabulous copy editor, Suzy Subways, and to Kaytee Riek for her beautiful cover.

Above all, I must thank everyone who was part of Casino-Free Philadelphia, Philadelphia Neighborhood Alliance, and our many allies—you all are inspiring. I hope the book captures my love and respect for each of you, even as I strove to write honestly of the tense and difficult times. If there's a moment in the book where I fail to show how much respect I have for you, I beg your forgiveness. I could not possibly cram into a book all the stories of the movement, so I must also ask your pardon for the stories absent in this book. My deep admiration and gratitude to all of you.

Special appreciation for Casino-Free Philadelphia's executive team for your openness, transparency about our own tensions, and the wisdom you gave to the rest of us. I love you all very much.

Introduction

OUR MOVEMENT WAS OUTSPENT by hundreds of millions of dollars. Every local official resisted us. Newspapers chastised us. The governor derided us. Private investigators were hired against us. Thugs threatened and even attacked us. And the state supreme court suspiciously and consistently sided against us.

On a good day, we had confidence we could win—even with the odds against us.

This conviction tells you something about our movement against two unwanted casinos in Philadelphia. We believed in people power. We had faith in folks' ability to organize and overcome long-shot odds. That we were able to make huge wins shows our correctness in thinking David can beat Goliath, even when Goliath has deep pockets and overwhelming political support.

What that conviction doesn't show is the strategy. The uncertainty. The skills. The mistakes. The heart. The soul. It doesn't show you how we organized or used direct action to feed our success (which, though substantial, was not complete).

I want you to see all that—which is why I wrote this book.

One of the leaders of Casino-Free Philadelphia, Shirley Cook, often pulled me aside and urged me to write about our movement, saying, "Other people need to learn how to do what we did. We rallied thousands of people when everyone thought it was hopeless, and when there was so much corruption. Lots of people can learn from us."

Yet as I began writing, I didn't want to essentialize our movement into lists of what a good organizer does, or reduce our story into bite-sized vignettes that prove my points about what makes for good organizing. I wanted to invite you into the real deal, where you can see our glories, our inventiveness, our mistakes, and join us in assessing what makes for good strategy. It's risky business, because it'd be much safer to give you a list that we could both pretend is the whole story. You then wouldn't see my flaws, our missteps, or our shortcomings so clearly. But I didn't want to sell you a dream.

Instead, this book is a narrative of real bare-knuckles, on-the-ground organizing. I bring you into our fervent worrying in late-night meetings, yelling matches behind church benches, and last-minute action planning outside judges' chambers. The nuances of strategy come to life in those moments. You get to wrestle with us over our choices—*Do we publicly humiliate the judges who screwed us, or do we show traditional decorum because they will rule on future lawsuits?*

It's a faithfully recreated narrative, showing the grand arc of a movement. I meticulously went through tens of thousands of emails, thousands of articles, and hundreds of meeting notes to portray events accurately. I wanted to avoid the pitfalls of other historical movement narratives—often written by people outside the movement—which had left me shaking my head, not believing the activists had *really* seen something coming, knowing it had never *really* happened that way, or frustrated that the movement's loss (or win) was foreshadowed as if its outcome were inevitable. I tried to be honest about the personal struggles in the movement, even while striving to respect the dignity of all of the people involved. I even kept names real, as much to honor the work of everyone involved as to keep the sense of authenticity.

Though it's a story of a movement, it's not written to be a comprehensive story of Philadelphia's anti-casino movement. It's my story, with plenty of interesting moments that have never been publicly aired: threats to destroy our offices, our strong-arming councilmembers to support our shadow election, private brokering with the governor, and behind-the-scenes arguments with senators. But there are plenty of other stories left out and people who deserve more credit than could fit in this book. I hope folks will pardon me for that.

As I wrote, it became important to make this more than just a reflection on our methods and tactics. A mentor, Antje Mattheus, challenged early drafts of the book, saying, "It reads great, but *you're* not present in the narrative." Her words struck me as if she had accused me of lying—because to my mind, it would be dishonest to separate the part of the journey that relates to soul. I needed to reveal my sense of hopelessness when the supreme court screwed us, the high, elated feeling after successful direct actions, and my love and affection for our team when we were in the groove. I had to bring in the heart and the emotional journey, a too-often ignored dimension of campaigning.

The result is that you'll get the feel and passion of campaigning alongside the challenges and art of strategizing.

You'll see many traditional lessons of activism applied—as well as us bending or even breaking those rules. On this point, I'm remembering the first direct action training I attended, almost two decades ago, where I was taught that when dealing with the media we should always be succinct, stick to our talking points, and be courteous. It's generally good advice. But in the grind of the campaign, we sometimes became wordy, waded far from our talking points, and even yelled at a reporter! And you can see how we made those moments work for us.

Therefore, this book is not a single set of rules, but stories to help you better understand the logic behind effective strategy. Even when we created rules, we sometimes broke them—like when we abandoned our agreement to never do a march or rally. You'll see why we made that rule, and how it helped us create vibrant new tactics like the *public filibuster, shadow election, document search,* and *we-are-not-scared-of-stunts* actions. Then, when we break the rule and organize a rally, you'll see how the timing is right and it makes sense.

You may want to just read this page-turner as a political thriller or historical novel, but if you want to get the most out of the strategy lessons, it'll be helpful to keep asking yourself what you might have done in our situation, or how you would analyze the current political terrain, or how you might make a better decision. I'll be delighted if you come up with better answers.

Either way, you'll learn how we responded to the strategic challenges before us. When things go well, you'll see the often hidden ingredients that got us to that point. You'll see how important it was for me to show empathy for our opponents, even when they attacked us. That's another part of the dimension of soul in this book, using that core value of empathy—what I refer to as high-ground organizing—to stay on the offensive and be more savvy campaigners.

It all adds up to giving you more skill in the art of strategizing, organizer tricks and techniques, reflections on the personal journey of campaigning, and even a few facilitation tools and theories of social change along the way. By exploring these levels all at once, you'll gain skill in doing what organizers need to do: weigh multiple options and juggle many balls simultaneously.

It'll be a fun ride. Enjoy learning about both strategy *and* soul.

CHAPTER 1
The Phone Call

FEBRUARY 3, 2004 — OCTOBER 13, 2006

a sneaky bill brings me into the campaign • a classic organizer ask •
organizing in the present, not with scripts • recruiting with strategic questions

ON FEBRUARY 3, 2004, a tiny, thirty-three-line bill was introduced into the Pennsylvania House of Representatives. It was a quiet, one-page bill about background checks in the horse-racing industry. It followed the uneventful procedural motions of a first, second, and third reading in the House and Senate, then sat abandoned for four months.

This book has nothing to do with that bill.

Instead of passing that bill intact, in early July, the Pennsylvania State Senate stripped the thirty-three lines from the bill and discreetly added a 146-page amendment. In three whirlwind days, the reengineered bill circumvented legal requirements for public readings because—so it was argued with merciless bureaucratic technicality—the bill had already been publicly read three times. At 3:30 A.M., the bill blasted past shocked opponents in the Senate and House and was passed.

As Philadelphians headed toward the riverfront to watch fireworks and celebrate another year of US independence, the bill reached Governor Ed Rendell's desk. Even for him, the passage was masterful orchestration. To gain support, the bill dripped with a medley of pork-barrel giveaways, backed generously by well-connected political donors. With colleague and co-conspirator State Senator Vince Fumo at his side, the Governor signed the bill into law the same day.

The bill was Act 71, the single largest introduction of casino gambling in American history: 61,000 slot machines at fourteen casinos and racetracks across Pennsylvania, including two slated for Philadelphia with up to 5,000 slots each. It had moved through the legislative process without a single public debate, no public scrutiny, and a nearly complete media blackout.

This book has a lot to do with *that* bill.

That bill had sufficient support from powerful politicians and businesses to earn the designation of "done deal." In the well-worn rut of Philadelphia's top-down politics, the assumed bill's storyline was to end with local communities begrudgingly accepting the imposition of two massive casinos. Respected civic association leaders know that the rulebook for "good" community organizations is to rock the boat just enough to tip a few kickbacks into their community.

But that was not to be. Instead a movement rose above the safe waters of grumbling acquiescence and broke the rules of polite negotiation.

This book has *everything* to do with that movement.

Like most Philadelphians back in 2004, I didn't notice when the bill passed. Our media coverage was lax and hardly made an issue out of it. So I continued living my life, running activist training courses on how to facilitate workshops and meetings with Training for Change. For more than two years, I remained oblivious to the state setting up the Pennsylvania Gaming Control Board (PGCB); five casino applicants applying for two casino licenses in Philadelphia; the PGCB creating shockingly complex applications to speak at public hearings, with strict, three-minute-per-person limits; and the PGCB's flat refusal to put impact studies online. I missed all of that—until a friend called me on October 11, 2006.

Jethro Heiko's voice was absent of doom and despondency. That surprised me, because if someone were putting a casino across the street from me, I'd feel desperate. He was self-possessed as he laid out how a group he founded, Neighbors Allied for the Best Riverfront (NABR), had at first merely opposed the four casino proposals along the Delaware River. But that left them competing with the fifth neighborhood in East Falls/Nicetown—who didn't want a casino either. NABR refused to sink into a politics of division and established a loose formation to oppose all five casino proposals: Casino-Free Philadelphia (CFP).

I tried to imagine a casino's glaring signs, five-story parking garages, twenty-four-hour foot traffic, and road congestion across from Jethro's tiny, one-way street. It didn't make sense, it didn't seem right, and I didn't see what could be done about it.

He spoke with a slow rhythm, like the chanting of a monk. "My neighbors feel angry, discouraged, and hopeless. Some people are talking about moving if SugarHouse casino does get selected and built on the December 20 licensing. I moved here to try to get *away* from community organizing, to get a sabbatical, and look what they do! My wife and I are not going to move. I know we can stop these, but I don't know what we can do in three months to stop the licensing."

I wondered if I was overly detached from my friend's emotions. All I could think was, *Good luck... You're gonna need it.* But he was an experienced organizer and wasn't telling me all this just so I could buck him up. He was gearing up for an ask.

"Everyone says this is over, just because every city and state elected official is backing these projects. But you have to get a sense of these things. They're not just any big-box development. They offer free, unlimited drinks. There are 5,000 slot machines, more than in any casino in Atlantic City or Las Vegas. They're gigantic—and all proposed in residential neighborhoods."

Wait for it. It's coming...

"And I could really use your help."

My mind jump-started a list of reasons not to help: I had a job that kept me busy. I didn't see any way a handful of citizens could win against seemingly every politician across the spectrum. It was not an issue I cared about. I was not opposed to gambling or casinos. I knew nothing about development issues.

Before I could begin, he continued, "I know you're good at helping groups plan strategy and direct action. You're creative, and we need that. We need a strategy not just for my neighborhood fighting SugarHouse, but for all five neighborhoods. Everyone's worried their casino will get selected at the licensing. It makes people fearful and easily divided. Can you help me think through strategy?"

To my own wonder and mild horror, "No, thanks" or "I'm too busy" did not escape my lips. His request wasn't just for him or his own community, but for neighborhoods across the city. My refusal was held back by something about responsibility or guilt.

I have been moved by duty ever since I was little. I still feel an echo of responsibility for a stranger's broken coffee cup from when I was five years old. My family had come across the man in the wheelchair on a sidewalk—carrying books, a backpack, a coffee mug—and trying to wheel himself up a steep incline. My mom asked if he needed a hand. He gratefully handed my mom his books and my sister the backpack and let my dad push him up. I thought about taking the coffee cup but didn't, out of shyness or fear I'd offend him.

When we got to the top, he thanked us. My mom and sister handed his belongings back to him. But in the transition, the coffee cup shattered on the ground, spilling coffee that seeped back down the hill. My only thought was: *I could have done something, and I didn't.* It was a major recurring nightmare from my childhood.

Jethro asked again, "I don't know how you can best help. We need new ideas. Me and my neighbors are so worried that we're not thinking well."

I broke my silence. "Okay, let's meet and see if I can help somehow."

Days later, Jethro ambled into my house in West Philadelphia, sat across from me, and politely accepted some tea. In the few years I had known him, he always had short stubble on his wide bald head, with jeans and a loose button-down shirt. He often wore a serious expression that barely covered his grinning, laughing personality. He had come down from Boston after leaving his job as a community organizer. This was our longest uninterrupted conversation to date.

Quickly I saw that Jethro had a very special way about him. If I were to divide the world of community organizers into two types, one would be the type schooled in rigorous, technical approaches to building organizations. They use written, scripted "raps" to recruit people, employing regimens of proven track records with ruthless discipline.

Jethro was the other kind. He was in the present moment, more attentive to people than scripts, like an organizer mixed with yoda. "Thanks, the mint tea smells wonderful," he said as he inhaled it and let it sit on his tongue. Yes, he would like to have a seat. Yes, he understands that I don't have the time to commit long-term. Yes, he'd love to give me background.

He was moved by instinct, schooled in a belief that if you dig at what other people want and their role in making it happen, then you'll build a movement. Throughout his explanation, he peppered me with questions: What did *I* think of the process of Act 71 passing? How does someone convince others to be roused and angry enough to do something about it? What would a better process have looked like? What values were being violated?

He was as unlike the first type of organizer as the rough agitation of a spinning dryer is unlike the breezy act of dropping clothes onto a line and letting the sun do the work. His presence shone, helping my ideas air out.

I quickly agreed that building massive casinos in neighborhoods without consultation is wrong. "It's wrong that you got thousands of pages dumped on you with only a few days to read them. And there should have been more than two days of public hearings. And it's wrong that now the PA Gaming Control Board is letting the casinos make major changes that you can't see. But the problem is structural. By design, you've been excluded from the very process. The PGCB is a politically appointed body with no community representation. It's all an insider process."

"Yes, *exactly*!" exclaimed Jethro, like a child learning a delightful new word. It couldn't be his first time making this connection, but he reveled in the specific way I framed it. "Act 71 was deliberately crafted so that unlike in other states, citizens have no say in where casinos will be located. There's no public referendum, no public debate. Giving us two minutes to speak in public hearings held during work hours isn't meaningful input. The whole bill was purposely written by the governor, State Senator Fumo, and the casino lobby—all to limit public resistance so they could railroad this through."

Even as I nodded, I held internal reservations. The impact may have been excluding public opinion, but I wasn't certain of the purpose. I grew up in a small town where even when I disagreed with the mayor on one thing, I might agree on another. It meant there are always at least two sides, and it's important to me to understand and be empathetic to all of them.

I asked Jethro to describe the tactics they have used and how they thought they could win.

"I was part of forming Neighbors Allied for the Best Riverfront with a vision for the *best* riverfront, without empty lots and residents cut off by fences," he said. "We want a lush, green waterfront that's accessible and pedestrian-friendly, with attractive local and small businesses. Casinos completely contradict that vision. They violate nearly every core planning principle. Instead of an accessible riverfront, their business model puts people inside big boxes as long as possible. They want to create a casino strip malls filled with hotels and big-box development."

"That's all fine," I said. He wove a tapestry of values and background into his speech—but I wanted to cut to the chase. "What have you *done*? Is there a plan of action?"

Jethro breathed heavily into what was a sore point. "You have to understand that at first we just paid attention to the four proposed casinos on the riverfront. But that's the not-in-my-backyard, NIMBY, way of thinking. Why should we argue for a casino to be put anywhere? That's their job. Ours is to oppose it wherever neighbors don't want it. That's why we birthed Casino-Free Philadelphia."

Jethro described CFP's first action, a rally on the first of June, almost two years after Act 71 was passed. It featured street theater with a giant slot machine, drawing a crowd of diverse ages and races from all five neighborhoods.

"So not much," I sighed.

In response to Jethro's questioning look, I added, "The political significance of one-time rallies is overestimated, because pro-casino folks are content to ignore it and move on. Unless it's coupled with ongoing pressure, it does little to effect change, even if it feels good."

"You're right," he said without a trace of defensiveness. "You have to remember that Councilman Frank DiCicco, my councilman, is the protégé of the same guy who co-wrote the casino bill, Senator Fumo. Small wonder then that DiCicco says he's just being 'realistic' when he tells civic groups there's no hope and they should make deals with the casinos before the licensing happens. What else? We have almost zero press allies. The few who did cover us, I wish they didn't. The *City Paper* reinforced the storyline that it's inevitable, while the *Philadelphia Inquirer...*" Anger flashed on his face. "They wrote a scathing editorial, chiding us and saying it was all a done deal and we should give up now." He steamed.

"Fine to be mad at them," I said. "But what alternative story have you given them to tell? Rallies are boring, ritualistic." Jethro's request for me to help weighed on me, making me want to be insightful or challenging. "You've got to get on the offensive and pick some tactics that are creative."

"We tried one other thing," said Jethro, and launched into a story of their singular confrontation with the PGCB—the only other public action of Casino-Free Philadelphia to date.

At the end of June, Jethro had gone to a hearing of the PGCB in Harrisburg. The NABR activists arrived in the swank judicial chambers, with deep wood veneer and a large chandelier hanging from the ceiling.

The PGCB officials—all political appointees by the legislature or governor—moved through their agenda, interspersed with relaxed banter with the casino applicants. The public was absent—except the ten-person Casino-Free Philadelphia crew. As the chairwoman moved to the next item on the agenda, Jethro stood up.

"I was really nervous," he admitted with ease. "I swear, I was shaking all over, my knees almost buckled. I said as loudly as I could, 'Madam Chairwoman, sorry to interrupt.' *That* got everyone's attention. People's heads turned toward me and the chairwoman quickly gaveled, 'Do not interrupt me.'

"I cited Pennsylvania law, trying to get them to register our objection. Our larger hope was to convince them to extend their licensing dates, or at least give us some time for public testifying, so our communities could digest the complex plans they had given us." Jethro's voice rose. "In any other public hearing in the state of Pennsylvania, the public would be offered at least a cursory opportunity to have its say at every hearing. But not this board. It has what's called 'quasi-judicial status,' which means they interpret, sign, seal, and rewrite their own rules. They are virtually above state law."

The chairwoman gaveled Jethro down. Then Matt Ruben got up. He was likewise gaveled down. Then Anne Dicker stood up and got the same treatment. The chairwoman called a recess.

"The police then swarmed us!" Jethro grinned widely. "Matt Pappajohn was amazing. He's a big Fishtown guy and not scared of anything. He held the police back, barking questions about what law we had broken—but the police ordered us out, even though they admitted we hadn't broken any laws.

"That was their biggest mistake, 'cause then reporters created a second perimeter surrounding them, trying to get the story of what was happening. We got some decent coverage. I mean... the articles were not very good, since everyone keeps saying it's a done deal. But it was something." Jethro slouched back in his chair, stretching his jeans out and sipping some more tea. "But it didn't get us an extension of time, and everyone's now nervous about the December 20 licensing, when they'll select the two licenses."

"Anything else?" I asked.

He shook his head. "Casino-Free Philadelphia is basically a shell organization with no plans or clear leadership, but we're all open to whatever good ideas emerge. So what advice can you give us?"

"Well," I paused and sat quietly for a moment, unsure where to begin. "First off... you're stuck on their timeline. It's gripping you, as if you're going to win or lose on the day of licensing. As long as you're on their timeline, you are going to lose."

"Uh-huh," encouraged Jethro, as uncertain about where I was going as I was.

Warming to the strategic considerations, I continued, "You don't have a plan, and that's a problem. Your opposition clearly does. Though direct action can help, it's not a cure-all without a strategy. Right now, a good 80% of Philadelphians want casinos—of course, all they've heard is jobs and revenues, no debate on neighborhood development." I paused. "To win, you need more people on your side—and that means you need to find a value bigger than one that's just about casinos. You need to tap core values. Unfortunately, your actions have all been routine and don't do that. Rather than rallying or marching, could we organize bold, courageous actions, like a big anti-casino carnival or something?"

The conversation flowed into possible ideas, but Jethro knew he had found my values and hooked into them, even if we still had no plan. He smiled broadly. "You're using 'we' language. Welcome to Casino-Free Philadelphia."

CHAPTER 2

Operation Transparency

OCTOBER 14, 2006 — NOVEMBER 13, 2006

breaking out of defeatism • rulers cannot govern without consent •
cutting unwinnable issues into a campaign • heads we win, tails you lose •
making each one-on-one meeting fruitful • being bold attracts attention •
the first rule of online organizing • no more marches or rallies

CASTING A SHADOW ON OUR COFFESHOP TABLE, an older, seasoned organizer stopped by to give us some paternal advice. He looked down at Jethro. "I live right next to the proposed casino in South Philly, so it's personal for me. I'm worried about a casino bringing crime so close to my family. But you gotta let this issue go. It's a done deal."

Inside, I recoiled. "Done deal" was an excuse for low expectations—for birthing only small dreams.

His eyes flickered toward me as he continued, "The casinos spent millions cutting these deals. I wish you could win, but you can't."

It was like the voice of my guidance counselor telling me I was another black man who couldn't make it to college. That had just fueled my fire to drop out of his high school, enroll directly in college, and show him up by graduating with honors. Statements of impossibility only make me want to prove them wrong—but this was Jethro's fight. I was just helping out. I gazed over at Jethro.

"Of course, you're right," Jethro said with his deep voice, handling each word with care. "People in this city are *convinced* we're defeated. They're *so used* to losing that nobody expects the government to protect them." His fingers moved in rhythm to his punctuated words. "But if we convince people to hold high expectations and believe it's not over, then it's not."

Our friend opened his mouth to disagree, then paused. Everything Jethro said was true, except...

"That's not a strategy," the organizer half-shouted. "You can lobby the state house all you want, but they're not going to change their minds. They cashed their checks long ago."

"I know," said Jethro defensively. "But community and civic groups are going to find out soon that the PGCB doesn't care what their traffic experts say and that local officials are only pretending to be on their side. I'm not begging the state house, I'm talking about activating ourselves. You know that when I wrote the letter to the editor challenging Senator Fumo for passing Act 71, it was the first one published against him?"

"It was gutsy." The organizer smiled.

"No, it wasn't gutsy. That's the problem. People told me to keep my head down. Someone even said I should hire a bodyguard. We don't need that kind of fear. Our defeatist mentality is killing this city and needs fixing."

The older organizer shrugged and shook his head slowly. "I'm sorry, but you're running up against city officials, state legislators, the governor, and powerful monied interests. I've run lots of campaigns in this city. You just can't win this one."

It was like he was passing his trauma onto us. *Stay small! Be cautious!* It grated on my skin, making me feel I *must* join the campaign to prove him wrong. I didn't have any particular beef with casinos, but people deserved control in their neighborhoods. Besides, even if we lost, working with Jethro would teach me a lot.

I sipped my tea, realizing I had reached a decision. The organizer turned to leave, crying out as a parting shot, "It's David versus Goliath. Except it's a whole bunch of Goliaths."

"Exactly," Jethro said back, tilting his head and smiling broadly. "But remember who wins?"

Unfortunately, like David before he picked up a sling, we didn't have a plan. In truth, David headed into the fight against Goliath only after ignoring his friends' advice. After earning reluctant support from the king, David rejected the king's offer of conventional weapons. A shepherd, he did not accept the brass helmet, coat of mail, or sword. He picked up what made sense to him: a slingshot.

Likewise, our Goliaths were too big to be taken down by conventional responses. Despite some residents' optimism, Jethro and I knew that they would not be halted by South Philly's hiring traffic experts, or East Falls/Nicetown's tough negotiations, or political appeals from civic groups in Northeast Philly. The casinos had too much sway with the PGCB and politicos. Our Goliaths could easily withstand those strategies—just as they could ignore actions that merely protested against them or expressed our outrage, like marches or rallies. We needed a slingshot. And we needed it fast.

A week later, I pulled together a gathering of friends and activists in West Philly. There, I introduced Jethro to the smartest strategist I knew, Philippe Duhamel, who was visiting from Montreal. The year before, Philippe and I had run a campaign with the Canadian Union of Postal Workers. The union faced a powerful adversary backed by a hostile government and big business.

"Explain the arc of the campaign you designed," I told Philippe.

Jethro took a chair nearby and slumped heavily from a full day's work.

"You can't win if you're stuck reacting," said middle-aged Philippe, waving his hands energetically. "That's the first lesson of campaigning. But the union was stuck in a defensive posture, suffering from death by a thousand cuts and closings. They needed a way to get on the offensive and not just talk about individual plant closings, but the government's large-scale plan to dismantle the union and privatize the industry."

Jethro nodded, perking up.

"They needed a campaign to seize the initiative by appealing to an unassailable value, one that all but the most hostile person could agree with. I thought to myself, 'What's a widely shared value here that's being violated?' And then it hit me: transparency. The government is closing all these plants without giving any reason or explanation. All their plans are secret—and that's not right."

Philippe pulled out his computer, balancing it on his lap. He pulled up a PowerPoint presentation of the postal workers' campaign, Operation Transparency. Its goal was straightforward: force the government to release all strategic planning documents related to the plant closings.

"The campaign uses the value of transparency like a fulcrum, to pull people to our side of the debate. Instead of defensively responding to plant closings, we're on the offensive."

"How does that help us with casinos?" asked Jethro, clearly stimulated.

"You can't win a debate framed as casinos or no casinos," I said. "With the city's current sentiments, we'd lose right away. We need to speak to a higher value to tilt people to our side... Philippe, talk about the actions you designed."

Philippe skipped to a slide of the campaign timeline. It started with a public ultimatum asking for the release of all documents and continued with cute, media-friendly actions, like an Easter Egg Hunt, during which union members searched the plant for planning documents to emphasize the point. One local had a member dress up in a white bunny rabbit suit armed with a magnifying glass.

"For three months we used actions to build a media presence and our base, all the while giving our opponents time to do the right thing," Philippe said. "Since any worthy goal needs a way to carry it out, our tactics escalated to a culminating action I've used before: the nonviolent search and seizure, where we go to their offices and liberate the plans."

Jethro chuckled and grinned, "Your action was your message."

Philippe clapped, "Exactly! We weren't going to wait for Canada Post to sit on its hands, ignoring our requests or rallies. We were creating a dilemma demonstration, where no matter the outcome, we win. If Canada Post releases the documents, we win. If they don't, we do the document search. Then, either we successfully liberate the documents and win—or they look bad arresting citizens who are exemplifying transparency, and they lose. Heads we win, tails you lose."

I knew that for Philippe and me, the document search wasn't a stunt. It was the *direct action* approach—what I had learned ever since I was eight. Back then, I got it into my head that it was blasphemous to use God's name in the Pledge of Allegiance. Associating God with country seemed to me taking God's name in vain. My teacher insisted that I join the rest of the class in its recitation—and then began threatening me with detention when I steadfastly refused.

While my parents eventually talked her down on the principle that I was allowed my form of religious expression, I withstood days of the teacher's taunts. It was there that I first learned: Nobody can *make* you do anything. There might be consequences, but my choices are my own, and nobody can force me do something against my will. That changed my relationship to every boss, teacher, and police officer ever since.

And it made it easy for me to join the direct action way of thinking. Instead of thinking that teachers, bosses, or CEOs carry the most power, Philippe and I saw the world through a lens that showed us power resides in the bottom, in the workers and the governed. Most people picture power as residing up at the top and flowing downward. But we saw those at the bottom as having great power via their consent or refusal to do what those at the top ask. That's the heart of a direct action philosophy.

The direct action group Otpor, who overthrew a dictator with a nonviolent revolution, explained it succinctly, "By themselves, rulers cannot collect taxes, enforce repressive laws and regulations, keep trains running on time, prepare national budgets, direct traffic, manage ports, print money, repair roads, keep food supplied to the markets, make steel, build rockets, train the police and the army, issue postage stamps or even milk a cow. People provide these services to the ruler through a variety of organizations and institutions. If the people stop providing these skills, the ruler cannot rule."

That was the heart of the document search — ending citizen passivity by challenging an abusive organization.

But I wasn't sure Jethro was ready for all of that. So I simply said, "Casino-Free Philadelphia can design a campaign like this. We model transparency by laying out our complete timeline, to help get people off the PGCB's timeline and put citizens back in the driver's seat. That gives the media time to cover us and time for your neighbors and others to digest our bold dilemma demonstration. Because we can't win if this is just about casinos. We need to use a dramatic action to carry our framing."

For the next hour, Jethro flooded Philippe with questions about the mechanics, the framing, and the use of a public timeline. It was going better than I had hoped.

We talked late into the night, long after the others had departed. By the time I locked up the house for the night, Jethro and I had a sketch of plans.

On a rainy October day, Jethro and I sloshed into Sahara Grill, a Middle Eastern restaurant in Center City. We tossed our umbrellas in a corner and dripped on our booth. I nervously smoothed out draft flyers of Operation Transparency, wishing our draft was perfect. I wanted our best foot forward with Ed Goppelt for our first one-on-one meeting to share the campaign.

With permission, Jethro and I extracted large chunks of Philippe's design. We took the goal of releasing documents and the culminating citizens' search-and-seizure action, but developed new actions and adapted the framing to our context. We debated replacing "search-and-seizure action" with a less confrontational name. Jethro's view prevailed, that his brand-new-to-activism neighbors would be turned off by sounding too combative, and offered "document search."

Jethro had suggested enlisting endorsements from ally groups, starting with Ed Goppelt of the independent city watchdog group Hallwatch.org, a site so effective even government insiders used it to read upcoming City Council bills and access public tax records. Ed had ripped into the secrets of the casino licensing process, filing dozens of right-to-know requests (all turned down). He was the first journalist to show that the riverfront casinos needed public land known as "riparian land"—which had been historically submerged when the waterline was higher—in order to build their plans. Ed poured any shred of PGCB documents onto his website.

Right at twelve, lanky Ed opened the door and strode to our table, warmly greeting us. After short pleasantries, he whipped out a pen and began a barrage of razor-sharp questions. "Exactly which documents do you want?" His thin body leaned forward, his tie nearly dripping into his food.

"All the casino-related planning documents, like site plans," I said.

"The casinos published their original site plans long ago. But most of them have radically shifted their plans and we have not been able to see them. For example, I heard TrumpStreet's casino proposal added twelve more acres to its site. It's the updated documents you're seeking?"

TrumpStreet in East Falls/Nicetown was the casino proposed by Donald Trump, located across from a school. And in a twist of deep cynicism, was placed just a block from a local addiction treatment center. Like all the casinos, it was placed within blocks of people's homes.

"Yes," I said. "We're trying to make an ask that makes sense to anyone. Shouldn't people get to see updated plans of a massive casino building across from their house?"

Ed looked at us with great intensity. "Why stop at updated site planning documents? Why not revenue planning projections?"

"We did not know about those," I said.

"Those would be good, too," Jethro said.

Ed skimmed the flyer. "If you get the documents released, what then?"

"We expect the documents to stand on their own as an argument to slow the process down for more consideration," said Jethro. "They cannot have seriously addressed site plans, environmental plans, or social impacts. SugarHouse still claims they are not in a residential neighborhood."

"So you go to Harrisburg, do the action. If you get arrested, what will you do then?"

"Create headlines," I said. "Delegitimize the PGCB and the licensing process. Build momentum against whichever casinos get selected or, in the best case, make enough obstacles so the PGCB can't go through with the licensing."

"These other little actions on the timeline? What do they do?"

"They give us time to organize," I said. "Our campaign needs an arc, time to raise the issue in the public's eye and get into people's consciousness. Plus, we need time to build pressure on the PGCB."

His questions continued on and on. Under the scrutiny of Ed's mind, the campaign lost its glamour. "The ultimatum page is excellent," he concluded. "The rest"—the tactics and direct action, apparently—"seems sketchy." Thanking us for our ideas, he grabbed his umbrella and bade us a spritely goodbye, leaving Jethro and me sitting at the booth.

I felt sulky that Hallwatch would not run the campaign with us. "He was our most likely ally and probably won't even endorse it?"

Jethro's savvy organizing experience made him see it differently. He knew organizing is about starting wherever people are, using their core values to move into action for social change. "Ed gave us a lot of important information. We know more about what parts we have to tighten up, especially explaining the point of the direct action. It's not a failure, it's just more information on how to bring Ed a step closer. If Ed won't get arrested with us or even endorse us, I bet he'll tighten up our document demands."

Jethro was right. Ed helped hone our vague demands into eight core requests: case files for each of the casinos; social, environmental, and crime impact studies; hearing presentations; revenue projections; updated site plans; updated traffic plans; architectural drawings; and a complete history of casinos' past commitment to communities—all kept secret by the PGCB.

It was the first time—but far from the last—that I saw Jethro's brilliance at making even "unsuccessful" meetings count, by giving everyone a chance to help the campaign, no matter where they were.

After hundreds of emails, dozens of phone calls, and a handful of one-on-one meetings, nobody else had endorsed the campaign. Most just weren't interested in casinos as an issue. I couldn't motivate housing advocates, union leaders, or good government groups. At best, they admitted that neighbors were being mistreated and locked out from the process. However, most unhelpfully repeated that the deals were already struck. With no sense of irony that *they* were in losing movements themselves, they advised that since we couldn't win, it wasn't worth trying.

I wrote to Philippe in frustration. "*Are we crazy?* We're up against a multibillion dollar industry and don't even have money for copies. What's wrong with us?"

Casino-Free Philadelphia was a shell of an organization, with no institutional support or structure. Jethro received moral support from NABR, but members were focused on broader planning and internal issues. He had to beg to get our flyer copied. Meanwhile, I tossed together a bare-bones website hosted on a friend's server, with an email listserve of only fifteen people.

Philippe wrote back quickly, "Yes, you are out of you mind. And that's why I love you. Remember to breathe, and laugh at the whole mess!"

It felt silly to take a deep breath in front of my computer, but I tried. I had been so caught up in creating something new, I forgot that most new campaigns suffer this moment: testing whether the campaign's vision and organization is strong enough to weather forces outside of the womb.

It felt crazy. Our capacity was so tiny that to carry out the campaign we absolutely *had* to grow. Yet that's exactly what a campaign *should* do. The goal should be inspiring and bold enough that its capacity needs to grow and expand. Our wildly ambitious timeline and zany actions were part of what made the campaign interesting; when people saw them, they'd want to join—or so I hoped.

Convinced that the campaign was ready, Jethro and I emailed our listserve and five media contacts. The day before Halloween, we would deliver our ultimatum.

*   *   *

On October 30, five of us gathered under a bright blue sky. Our tiny group was dwarfed by the shadow of massive City Hall, the largest masonry building in the nation. It's what I expected for our maiden voyage, but I couldn't help but feel concern. *Are we really going to go through with this?*

Journalists from independent media dribbled in first, led by Ed Goppelt. At the stroke of noon, two journalists arrived from the mainstream daily newspapers: Jeff Shields for the *Philadelphia Inquirer* and Chris Brennan for the *Philadelphia Daily News*. Adding to their numbers were mainstream radio stations, including KYW and WHYY.

Nervously I turned to Caryn Hunt, one the four NABR activists who showed up to support CFP's new campaign. "Do you see this? We have more reporters than participants!" My heart began racing. She patted my arm supportively.

I was of two minds. One was proud our press calls had convinced skeptical reporters that we were serious and would offer a dramatic storyline. Most reporters couldn't help but ask, "If they don't give you the documents, are you *seriously* going to walk into their offices and just take the documents?" I would grin widely and silently point to our document, which laid out everything.

But I hadn't been this nervous before an action for years. It wasn't only my anxiety about leading a confrontational action. What weighed most heavily was that we were promising everyone an escalating, two-month campaign—but we didn't have the organizational resources to back it up.

Consciously, I chose to act from a place of confidence. I had been a trainer for years, which had taught me that I had a choice on how to present. Inside I'd still often worry that *this* time I wouldn't be useful, but outside I'd project confidence—something I'd do so smoothly few people would know my own internal dialogue.

To the crowd, Jethro read from the ultimatum, "People have a right to see plans of what is being built in this city. If these documents are not made public by December 1 at high noon, we will be forced to search for the documents ourselves. We are prepared to go the full lengths of nonviolent civil disobedience to assert our right as citizens for this information, including carrying out a Document Search on the Pennsylvania Gaming Control Board's offices in Harrisburg, where we will liberate the texts that have not been given to us."

I moved to the front of our huddle, steadying my voice. "Now, we're going to head in and up to the mayor's office to try faxing a copy of the ultimatum to Tad Decker, head of the PA Gaming Control Board. We'll also send it to Governor Rendell."

I led the contingent up to the mayor's office. Halfway through, I discretely pulled Jethro to help lead the way—I didn't even know where the mayor's office was! I chided myself, and my stomach churned at my naïveté and all I did not know.

At the mayor's fourth-floor office, we were confronted by a stiff, balding official. "How can I help you?" he asked, glancing suspiciously at the small crew and reporters in tow.

I stuttered through our request, amazed at how poorly I was remembering what I had been editing for weeks. "We're just wanting to use the mayors' fax to send out... uh... a note to Chairman Decker and also to Governor Rendell letting them know that we're wanting ... uh... to get documents... uh... the casino applications, traffic and site plans, etc."

The gentleman made no eye contact with me as he read our ultimatum. "So you want to use our fax machine?"

Well, it was *our* fax machine—our taxpayer dollars had paid for it, a point made to us earlier by Ed Goppelt.

The stiff official glanced at the video cameras, then reluctantly ushered us into the mayor's communications office. "They're going to just use the fax for a minute," he told the wide-eyed staff.

Dazed, I stood at the fax machine awkwardly entering first Decker's, then Rendell's fax numbers. Minutes later, the fax machine printed a confirmation that the letter had been sent. Success! Our ultimatum was delivered and the campaign officially launched.

I turned to Jethro, "With five reporters covering us, I think its safe to say this is the most highly covered fax transmission in Philly history!" We passed out "trick-or-treat bags" to the mayor's communications staffers—and later to councilmembers two floors lower. Unlike the casino industry, we did not have any money to buy off politicians, so we offered them what we could afford: chocolate coins. I had added magnifying glasses, so they could help us search for the documents, and some Tastykakes, because it was rumored that Tasty Baking Company might close its doors if Trump's casino were built, costing the city hundreds of jobs.

The action was cute, funny, and fairly well-executed—but not earth-shattering, with PGCB merely a non-participative fax recipient. Still, with an action each week until the December 1 ultimatum, we would get them engaged.

The next morning, I ran downstairs and tore open the pages of the *Inquirer* to find the first press of the campaign. The *Philadelphia Inquirer* is a Pulitzer Prize-winning newspaper, generally well-regarded for its reporting.

I had to turn several pages to find the article. I scanned for my quote. When I found it, a familiar thrill at seeing one's name in print ran through my body. "'If the documents are not made public by that date, we're going to have to take them ourselves,' said Daniel Hunter of West Philadelphia, a member of Casino-Free Philadelphia."

Reading more closely, I noted that the *Inquirer* ignored our drama with the mayor's fax machine. It did mention our demands for "documents the board has not released" and referred to us as "residents from throughout the city." Not activists—*that's good*, I thought to myself. Even though I *am* an activist, the "activist" framing has been contaminated with images of undirected outrage or random violence, not the high-ground action by citizens that we were modeling.

But the debate was poorly framed. Rather than transparency versus government secrecy, the article's framing was about confidentiality and proper procedure. Responding to our requests for documents, the *Inquirer* wrote, "PGCB officials say it may be privileged." Spokesperson Doug Harbach dismissed our accusations, saying, "We're not running away from releasing information that the public can obtain—we're doing this by the book, and the book is Act 71."

It was barely a rebuttal, sidestepping entirely the accusation that his organization was operating behind a veil of secrecy. That the reporter had let that slide meant we had not increased the pressure enough. But it was a start.

*　　　*　　　*

All around Jethro's dining room lay scattered lumber and sawdust. He kept an undampened hope his stairwell, attic, and bedroom would be finished soon, despite numerous contractor delays. Nothing seemed to get in the way of his buoyancy.

Jethro cocked his head, showing his pronounced chin, "You know I've never gotten arrested before?"

My eyes grew wide in disbelief at this cavalier revelation. *He never did direct action before? Yet he's happy, even confident, in leading people outside his own comfort zone?*

"I haven't," he said, not noticing my reaction. "I know community organizing, and you know direct action. We're a great match. But everything about doing a document search is totally new for me. What's gonna happen? People are asking me about what happens if we're arrested. I don't know what to tell them."

"If we are arrested doing the document search, police can hold us in jail for up to seventy-two hours. It's an early morning action on a weekday, not a high-volume time for arrests. So we're unlikely to have a queue of people in front of us being booked. Unless they decide to play hardball with us, I bet we could be out by later that afternoon."

"Can they stop us from going into the building?"

"Yes, they could set up some barricade. Then we just do the action there. We go as far as we can to legitimately carry out a document search."

"Could they arrest us before we do the action?"

"It's *possible*," I said slowly. "I've seen them do that in Philadelphia before, during the Republican National Convention. They arrested protestors—even snatching cardboard puppets—only to release them after the event. But that's real unlikely. It's a pretty obscene violation of our rights, and we're not perceived as much of a risk."

Inside my head, I brainstormed other scenarios: *What if an angry spectator tries to start a brawl? What if they let us up, but all the doors are locked? What if they let us search but plant false evidence? How do we make it joyous if people are getting handcuffed?* It was like a giant puzzle—and I like solving puzzles.

Jethro sat back, smiling. "People need this information to combat their fears. They've never done anything like this, and it's hard to get them totally psyched. NABR is supportive, but they're not pushing it as hard as I hoped."

I said nothing. If he couldn't recruit people for the action, then it wasn't going to happen.

"Including us, only four people have signed up so far," he said, his body sagging slightly. "You have any more?"

I shook my head. "We've got sixty people on our email list. But no commitments for the document search."

He downed the last of the coffee. "How many people do we need at minimum?"

"Maybe double-digits. Too few and we look completely marginal."

He stared at his empty cup. I waited.

His head snapped up, some internal decision made. "Then let's get ten."

It was certainty in his voice, borne from years of organizing people. The act of setting goals set him in motion. Definite numbers freed his energy. He ran upstairs. "Grab your coat!"

I grabbed my coat off a chair and put it on. Jethro returned swiftly, and I followed him out of the house and four houses down. Jethro banged loudly on the door.

A loud, gruff shout carried from deep inside the house, "WHO IS IT?"

"It's Jethro."

A large man with a big trucker belly filled the doorway. He swaggered like a man who knew his way around a bar fight. "Jethro!" He lit up excitedly and clutched Jethro's extended hand.

After introductions and small talk, Jethro wheeled on Ed Verral. "The document search can make a big impact. It's not over—it's just barely begun."

Ed hated the idea of a casino across from his house, enough to give his name to CFP's long-shot legal challenge and deliver a Halloween ultimatum. But that didn't mean he was going to do something stupid.

"I've never been arrested before," he said.

"Me either," said Jethro. "It'll be fun to do together. I want to do it with you."

Ed looked skeptical, as if his mind were swirling with exaggerated fears of jail or losing a job due to an arrest record.

"What do you worry might happen?" I asked him. "What is the worst thing that might happen?"

"It's just..." Ed stared at me for the first time. His face showed a deeper fear than bad food in cold jail cells—something about being on the wrong side of the law. "It's just not *right*."

Cigarette smoke from his jacket crawled into my nose. I wanted to challenge him: his Teamsters union had a history of using direct action to win rights. Words flashed in my mind from Dr. Martin Luther King about unearned suffering being redemptive to society. But it was too early in our relationship to push it.

Jethro leaned in. "It's not right to put gigantic casinos with giant parking garages and 24/7 neon lights across from our houses. It's not right to stomp on our say, to hide documents from us. When they've left us no options, taking actions into our hands is the right thing to do."

Ed nodded with respect, but said nothing.

"So will you do it with us?"

"I just don't think—"

Jethro cut him off. "I hope you'll come to the action, even if you decide not to risk arrest. But please consider it before saying no, because it would be fun to be arrested with you. Don't decide now."

Jethro and I shot quick, nervous glances to each other—the same glances we'd share at a dozen more houses.

"So," said Jethro, "will you at least come to the action next week?"

"You bet," said Ed. "It sounds like fun!"

So next week we squeezed a two-hour trek to the PGCB's offices into our packed schedule. Ed Goppelt wanted confirmation that the PGCB—despite its public face— wasn't sharing the information we sought, and Jethro sold the action as a chance to re-launch Operation Transparency to the rest of the state. I wanted to make sure it wasn't a boring press conference, so I made sure we brought along some "supplies."

When we arrived in Harrisburg, Pennsylvania's capital, our little troop, twelve-strong, meandered into Strawberry Square, a 1,000,000-square foot office and mall complex across the street from the capitol building. I bantered with Ed, feeling none of the anxiety from last week's action. With the campaign commitment made, it was just follow-through.

After stepping through the mall's entrance, we took an immediate right through large glass doors and walked up to a security desk. If the PGCB didn't release the documents by our due date, we might do our action there in a month.

Unlike other government offices, where you could walk right in, we had to sign in with security and wait for a PGCB "escort" up to their office. Eyeing us with suspicion, our escort took us to the twelfth floor and into a dark, cramped room with a few folding tables and little air.

PGCB staff hauled boxes of files into the room. Left alone, we quickly learned their strategy: bore us to death with unrelated files. Most were generic public corporation filings, others were heavily redacted with hundreds of entirely blacked-out pages. We waded for hours, searching knee-deep for any scrap of useful information. Nothing.

When the clock hit one, we headed back down to the mall. We huddled just past the glass doors, beyond the PGCB security desk, and unveiled our "supplies." We donned bright-yellow miner hats and headlamps, then waited for members of the press to arrive to our scheduled 1:30 P.M. press conference.

Four or five arrived, stealing multiple glances at our costumes.

Anne Dicker stepped forward, wearing a giant headlamp. "We are data miners," she said, "and have come searching for any plans from the Gaming Control Board." The Harrisburg-based journalists from several statewide newspapers smiled, perhaps wondering if their story was "Crazy Activists Wear Funny Clothes Outside of PGCB Office."

Silly or not, it was that hook—plus the general arc of the campaign—that got them to show up. Who would show up to a press conference called "Philadelphia Citizens Ask for Documents and Don't Get Them"?

We described the shreds of information the PGCB offered us, as reporters scribbled notes furiously, peppering us with questions in our informal "Data Miners' Report Session."

Cheered that *something* had come from our full-day trip, we took off our hats and crammed back into our cars for the ride home. While we were still on the road, a *Pittsburgh Tribune* reporter called the PGCB to find out why so few documents were available. "We have opened our offices for review of this information and welcome the public during normal business hours to inspect these records," PGCB spokesman Doug Harbach told him, again side-stepping the issue.

Days later, a Pittsburgh state representative, Jake Wheatley, saw the *Tribune's* headline piece and unexpectedly became the first politician to sign on to our campaign. Hearing that, a reporter from the *Pittsburgh Post-Gazette* posted a half-week-old story about our data-mining action and asked Doug a new round of questions.

Doug switched his tune, saying that architectural renderings are confidential because they might reveal the locations of security cameras or vaults. He "wasn't sure why" community groups were denied site plans but said impact studies and reviews would be available "once licensing hearings are complete." It was a tacit acknowledgement of secrecy—and the beginnings of a crack in their talking points.

Half-an-hour ahead of a NABR meeting in the low-ceilinged Old Brick Church in Fishtown, I plopped down breathlessly next to Jethro.

I started to talk, but Jethro launched into his frustrations about NABR not giving him as much support as he wished. Normally, I would have listened patiently, but I was too excited and waved him off.

This was big. "Doug Harbach just called me!"

Jethro halted quickly and looked at me in disbelief. "Doug called you?"

My heart was still pounding. I squealed in excitement, "Yes!"

"You mean Doug Harbach? *From the PGCB?*"

"Yes, yes," I said. "He asked what documents we wanted. Wait, no. First, he said he heard we were having trouble getting some documents—"

"Because of him!"

"Yeah," I said hurriedly, "so I gave him the list of documents we wanted. He told me he'd try to get them on the PGCB website quickly. He didn't apologize or anything. But he sounded serious." I took my first full breath since the call. "He just called up out of the blue. I started to tell him I hoped they'd restart community hearings, but he hung up. I'm gonna send a follow-up to him and Chairman Decker." I second-guessed myself, hoping Jethro thought I did a good job. *He* would have built a personal relationship with Doug... or recruited him... or something...

"This is big," said Jethro. "We have to let our people and reporters know about this. We're getting to the PGCB."

I nodded, my heart still thudding in my chest. "That's what our timeline does, it creates pressure. They would have ignored a one-time rally or direct action, waiting until the heat blew over. But the timeline builds pressure. Press are referencing our December 1 demands and our document search threat—"

"Except Philadelphia press," said Jethro curtly.

"In turn, that creates pressure as more politicians are signing on to our campaign—"

"Except Philadelphia politicians."

"The point is," I said, "this is the result—the PGCB is nervous about *our* deadline!"

It was a marked contrast from other groups I had worked with, who raced from action to action on the belief that time was against them and they had to act *now*. They'd plan an action, execute it, and then do it all again—the activist version of "rinse, lather, repeat." But it rarely worked.

Instead, we made an ally out of time. We transparently announced our direct action far in advance. That gave time for our opponents to worry about what was coming, and it gave us time to publicly escalate pressure on our opponent—with a clear escape route for them: Release the documents.

"Of course, if that's the case, maybe the PGCB will give us the documents." Jethro looked at me expectantly, then added, "Or it could all just be a bluff, hoping we'll call it off. Or they'll release a portion. Either way, we have to be ready."

I nodded and asked, "Any more people sign up for the document search?"

We were now in well-traversed terrain. We'd called every person on our small listserve—several times now.

"Only six people," he said. "You have any?"

"I'm not having success getting any statewide groups."

"Ha, that's okay. Everyone's so paralyzed. Up North, people talk about their fears about having maybe two casinos in their vicinity. But does that make them want to take bold direct action? No. Instead, civic leaders are telling people to negotiate and beg politicians to save us."

"But I'm not even getting to *talk* to people statewide."

"Why not?"

"Well," I said. "I emailed Diane *again* to send Operation Transparency flyers to her list. She hasn't replied to me. And she won't give me lists of statewide contacts."

A one-woman show overseeing the statewide anti-casino organization, Diane Berlin was a wealth of information, distributing clippings of every newspaper article and report to her extensive statewide and nationwide list.

"Then you must follow the first rule of online organizing," Jethro said.

I waited for him to say more. When he didn't, I asked, "Which is?"

"The first rule of online organizing: Stop being online. Stop emailing her, and give her a call. You'll only make up stories about each other that are probably not true."

I sighed. He was right. As much as I tried to tell myself that maybe she just missed my email or it got lost in a spam filter, my nagging fear returned that she was sticking it to us for a reason. There was already so much statewide tension set up in the divide-and-conquer strategy of how Pennsylvania brought in casinos. Because locations were competitive, it easily turned each locality against each other. Gettysburg people hoped it would be built in Bethlehem, who hoped it would be built in Allentown. It was the same divisive design in Philadelphia. Yet just as Operation Transparency was designed to bring together all citywide groups, I hoped it could do the same with the statewide groups.

"Call me if it doesn't work out," said Jethro, as NABR members started to assemble for their meeting. He turned to chat up members about the good news from the campaign, before turning back and whispering, "And that call with Doug... You did great, really great."

I exhaled and beamed.

A week later, I jumped off the bus with my boombox blaring *Mission Impossible*'s theme song. A half-dozen supporters followed me to the State Museum auditorium in Harrisburg. The first-ever mock document search was on.

In the chilly mid-November air, I projected confidence, despite my own discomfort with the oddness of the street theater we were about to do. "This mock search is a practice session for our nonviolent document search. It is playful, but we are serious. The future of our city is at stake. What are they hiding? Let's see if we can find out!"

The PGCB's penchant for secrecy had been confirmed days earlier. Their advertisements for "public" hearings reminded us there would be no chance for public testimony—and avoided saying *where* they would be held. After a flurry of fruitless emails with equally puzzled reporters, I finally called Doug Harbach to obtain the location. It was as if they didn't want us there.

To the tune from *The Pink Panther*, we each picked up a magnifying glass and started scouring the entrance, looking under bushes and outside the doors for the documents. It was awkward silliness, until people started arriving.

Lawyers, architects, casino investors, and other professionals headed in to listen or give testimony. Surprising them, we thrust magnifying glasses in their faces asking, "Do you have the Philadelphia casino planning documents?" Most muttered "No" and scurried off.

I was good-naturedly envious of NABR activist Lena Helen's boldness as she casually strolled up, with dollar-store magnifying glass held aloft, and asked authoritatively, "Can we search you for any casino planning documents?" One lawyer-type gripped his briefcase as if we might run off with it and weakly shot back, "No, I never saw them!" He fled into the auditorium.

A few reporters meandered through, and we half-heartedly replayed our searches on them. Most more-or-less playfully responded, "Haven't seen them either. But when you find them, let us know."

We used it as a chance to strengthen relationships with reporters; for example, taking aside a reporter for the Associated Press. As a national distributor, the AP gets news stories placed into thousands of newspapers and TV stations across the state and country. Jethro introduced the AP reporter to his neighbor, 60-year-old Joanne Sherman, who had lived in Fishtown for decades, while I countered the latest that Doug had been saying, urging the reporter to get tough with him.

We continued for about half an hour, with a dozen people playfully, and some nervously, holding up magnifying glasses—to the tune of a dozen spy-related songs. When we turned the music off, it was time for the hearings to begin. I felt dumbfounded: how to close this kind of action? "Well," I said awkwardly, thrusting my hands into my jeans. "We successfully did the first-ever mock document search! Congrats! And, uh, let's go inside."

We headed inside to the low-ceilinged, darkly lit auditorium of the hearings. Here, casinos would show videotaped messages of support from Bruce Willis, Sylvester Stallone, Michael Jordan, Quincy Jones, and others, each vying to be selected for the coveted Philly licenses. When the Casino-Free Philadelphia crew found seats, I scuttled out. I couldn't stand being cooped up listening, helplessly, to casino investors drone on. I'd planned legislative visits, while everyone else wanted to glean what they could from the hearings.

Alone, I headed toward the capitol building, immediately running into an anti-casino activist from Pittsburgh. She was a freelance, independent lobbyist.

Concerned as I was about messing up my first attempts at lobbying, I asked if she would join. She readily agreed, and together we entered the offices of State Representative Jake Wheatley for an unannounced meeting. Butterflies fluttered in my stomach as Jake invited us to his couch and offered us soda. He lowered himself behind his imposing desk and kindly asked us why we were there.

"We're here to know... you see, to find out if..." I collected myself. "You signed on to our campaign. We thank you. And I wanted to hear more about why you did that."

As an African-American representing Pittsburgh's predominantly African-American Hill District, he reiterated the same statements he had given to the press. "The fact that many in the public don't have access to the most updated changes in these proposals is problematic. How can the public determine the impact on their neighborhoods and communities if they are not seeing the constant changes being made to the plans?"

I agreed excitedly, only to be interrupted by my colleague, who demanded it was not enough to be anti-process—he must be anti-casino, too. For several minutes he politely nodded as she dictated to him, until he cut her off to strenuously disagree. "I'm not anti-casino," he said, staring at us. "I think we need jobs."

This was not going well. Instead of trying to bring him one step closer, she was giving ideological purity tests.

"We, uh, represent different organizations," I said. "Though we are against casinos, the campaign I'm involved in is specifically about good process. We think we'd never have these casinos without a bad process. That's why we're asking for transparency from the PGCB, as a first step. We'll be back on December 11 to fight for that goal, which we share. Would you come and be part of our rally?"

He nodded tenuously, as if looking for the catch. "Of course it's an important issue. I'll talk to my scheduler about it."

Later, I realized I should have pressed. This was a politician's polite form of no. One shouldn't leave a politician's office without a hard confirmation, but I was vaguely proud of not doing anything tragically wrong. It gave me more confidence in meeting additional representatives—but without my one-note colleague.

At lunchtime, I headed across the street to a dive of a restaurant, where Gene Stilp introduced me to a few of his activist colleagues. They were part of his statewide tour with his signature fifteen-foot-high inflatable pig, protesting legislative pork and a controversial pay raise by state legislators. A year after Act 71 introduced casinos, legislators used the same 2 A.M. process without public review to give themselves and judges a pay raise of up to one-third. Horrified by their blatant disregard for process and the people, Gene took to the streets.

Like many others, he believed the inclusion of judges in the pay raise was likely in exchange for their support for casinos. But though his passion on the issue was evident, I wasn't sure how we could help each other. He was as noncommittal about coming to our action as I was about his. I persisted, trying to find a way to bring him and his good government activists into our movement. I didn't need a conversion, I just needed him to move one step closer to us. "You must have some local experience from your high-profile actions," I said. "One thing we need is to prepare for possible scenarios for the day and scout the location for our document search."

His eyes lit up. "I know the place—and know all the police very well." He jumped up from the table. "Come on, let's go scouting!" He swept out of the restaurant, leaving me hurrying behind.

Back at Strawberry Square, he pointed to the Commonwealth of Pennsylvania lobby, saying, "These are public facilities, so Capitol Police would arrest you here."

"But PGCB's offices are on that side," I pointed to the other side of the entrance, toward Verizon Tower.

"No way," he said. "All the government offices are here, because it's public property." He watched me continue to point. "You sure?"

He looked surprised and sought out a local state police officer. "Excuse me, who owns that tower?" He pointed at Verizon Tower.

"It's private," the officer said.

"So any arrests there would be by local Harrisburg police?"

The officer raised an eyebrow. "Yes, I guess so."

"Well, that would be Randy King's jurisdiction," Gene said, rattling off from memory the contact of the Harrisburg communications director. "He's a decent guy."

Gene continued to spew information until he glanced at his watch and excused himself.

Alone in the lobby, I tried to envision our action.

The lobby is public, so here we can gather from the cold to get warm and collect ourselves. We'll go through the front doors, instead of the back entrance. We're not trying to sneak past them. Then we'll gather at the security desk where everyone can cheer us on and press can go stand by the wall for good pictures. Then those willing to risk arrest will press on, through the glass doors, up the elevators, and as far as we can go to liberating the documents.

So what's likely to go wrong? If they lock the doors, we'll go as far as we can to carry out the action. What if the person at the security desk freaks out?

I walked over to a bored woman with Securitas insignia and introduced myself, hoping to imprint my face on her memory. Maybe she would be working when — *if* — we did the document search.

After a few more moments standing in imagination, I headed back to the auditorium to join my bleary-eyed colleagues for one last event. They emerged looking stunned by the slick presentations, each casino boasting of its plans for a half-a-billion investment to build the first phase, with second and third phases including larger parking garages, restaurants, hotels, and amenities. None trumped community support, because none had it.

To close the day, we headed over for a short, statewide protest arranged by statewide allies. It was a classic rally, with signs wafting from the capitol steps as hand-chosen people followed each other to drone on a lectern.

I had nothing to say until Jethro and I were back on the bus, heading home. By then, we had learned that our first Associated Press story was spreading across the state. Doug had reiterated that releasing documents was unacceptable, because it might reveal the "location of security cameras," but looked weak in the face of Jethro's neighbor tenaciously fighting nightclubs only to be facing the prospect of SugarHouse casino within 500 feet of her home, who said simply, "We're a nice and quiet neighborhood, we all stick together. A casino doesn't belong in a residential neighborhood." Even so, Doug yielded part-way, offering that more documents *should* be disclosed during the hearings.

"See, Jethro, despite our small numbers, we're getting noticed by doing something unusual, something to report on. Press don't cover issues. They cover *news stories*, so, to earn press we must be *new* and a *story*, not just a litany of problems... Plus, it helps to show up where media were already coming!" I smiled and leaned toward him closely. "But Jethro, promise me we'll keep doing things like the document search and not bland rallies."

"You mean because no press showed up at the afternoon rally?" he asked.

"No, because the entire action was commonplace. People walked past us without a second glance. Promise me we'll only use fresh actions—mock document searches, data mining, or the most highly covered fax transmission in Philly history."

"Sure... No boring rallies or marches for us."

"Promise?"

"I promise," he said, smiling broadly at me.

I leaned back in my seat. Over the winding months, our commitment would force us to stay creative and generative, rather than defaulting to actions that are the lowest common denominator. We couldn't slay Goliath with conventional weapons. We had found our slingshot: direct action.

CHAPTER 3
The Document Search

NOVEMBER 14, 2006—DECEMBER 11, 2006

*empathizing with media's needs • the second rule of online organizing •
teasing the story to reporters • dealing with civil affairs •
the threat terrifies more than the act • rejections can radicalize •
choreographing actions to relieve tension and reveal secrecy • showing, not telling*

BUILDING PRESS MOMENTUM takes effort and time. I had conscientiously sent press releases two days before the action and again the day before, and then followed up with calls to each reporter. On a good week, I'd even call after actions or to chat up reporters with campaign updates. But lately, I felt ground down, guilty at dropping the extra effort.

Jethro was likewise stressed. "People don't get it! They're telling me the action is a waste of time, but they're blindly writing to the PGCB, giving the PGCB credibility, feeding the beast," he spat during one exasperated conversation. "They don't see how Operation Transparency delegitimizes the PGCB's process... I don't know if I can get enough people to pull off the document search by December 1." He sighed heavily. "We'll get it. But we need to cancel next week's action just to focus on recruitment."

I was empathetic, but as a country boy, I felt that your word was your bond. It felt like lying to not follow through. I translated that in strategic language. "We may be stretched, but our opponents will accurately sense weakness if we don't pull off *everything* we said we would. Our word gives us credibility. And right now getting into media *helps* with recruitment." A smile crept over my face. "Besides, our flyer never said *which* PGCB office it would be!"

So on Monday, we drove two cars to the PGCB's eastern Pennsylvania satellite office in Conshohocken, a mere twenty minutes from Philadelphia instead of a two-hour trek to Harrisburg. Volunteer Tommy Bendel pulled out supplies from his trunk to help the PGCB become more transparent—by washing their office windows. Out came red buckets with bright yellow and orange signs saying "Transparency" and "Ingredients: 100% Respect, Democracy, and Openness." Jethro added soap to the buckets, boasting stickers: "Now with people power" and "For a secrecy-free shine."

Equipped with squeegees, we approached the building complex where the PGCB sequestered its offices, this time to the tune of Rose Royce's "Car Wash." I could find no window-washing songs.

Jethro organized the outside window-washing team, while I headed inside with Mike Seidenberg, a real estate agent and our first Republican supporter. An elderly security guard asked us where we were going, peering around us but failing to notice the outside window washers.

"We're here to drop off some petitions for the PA Gaming Control Board," I said. He wearily waved us in and returned to his newspaper.

Too worried about being kicked out, we didn't ask for directions and explored the far reaches of the office complex until finding the PGCB's offices. It was locked. We knocked. Nobody answered. We knocked again. Silence.

The lights were off. "Did they close down because we were coming?" I asked.

Mike peered between the slats. "There's no furniture at all. The PGCB hasn't even set up their office!"

Unexpectedly, I felt relief. We could end the action there, without confrontation. But embarrassment overtook my relief. *What an anti-climax!*

I pulled out my cell phone and called the PGCB. "Yeah, I'm a citizen standing outside your offices in Conshohocken trying to deliver petitions."

A snippy voice responded on the other end of the line, "But nobody is at those offices."

"*I know,*" I said. "I can see that."

"Sir, that office isn't open yet." Her crisp voice conveyed both annoyance and bureaucratic haughtiness. "If you have a message, you *should* come to Harrisburg. That address isn't public."

"We got it from *your* website," I said. "We're leaving our petitions here at your office. Please have someone come and pick them up." I hung up before she could reply.

I dropped a heavy stack of petitions on the ground. A few pages were Operation Transparency's petition for public documents. But realizing those thin papers would look insignificant, I had requested citywide and statewide allies to add their petitions to the mix. It brought us closer with South Philly leaders, who were united against the Foxwoods proposal in their neighborhood. Passyunk Square leader Chris Meck submitted a massive stack of anti-Foxwoods signatures, her first step toward us. Others around the state added until it became a sizable pile—but without any from Diane Berlin, who, strangely, refused my requests.

I made a mental note to mail copies of the petitions later, so they could go through the formal process of being ignored, added to the meaningless record of "public input" by the PGCB.

Mike and I stared awkwardly at the petitions, then shrugged and left.

Downstairs, the security guard blocked our exit and interrogated us—perhaps now realizing nobody came to the PGCB offices or alerted to our presence by a call from the PGCB. We answered his questions, trying to avert our eyes from our supporters wiping the front with squeegees and bright yellow towels. Thankfully, he didn't turn around as we proceeded outside.

Once outside, we wanted to share our story, but the crew was far more fascinated with polishing the surprisingly clean office complex windows. Volunteer Marj Fulmer pointed out with delight how clean she had made the filthy corners.

A *Daily News* photographer, the only attending press, staged "candid" shots. The twenty-minute drive was too far for frazzled reporters, he explained. We were lucky *any* news outlet covered us. I learned my lesson: reporters are so busy they needed to be handed the story—including making the event easy for them to attend.

As the photographer finished his snapshots, the security guard blundered out of the offices and ordered us to leave. We cheerily obliged and headed back to our cars, only to be stopped by a Whitemarsh Township police car cutting us off.

"What are you doing here?" asked the police officer, leaning out his window.

"Cleaning windows," one of us joked.

"*What?*"

Jethro stepped forward and explained.

"Look, I agree with what you're doing here." The officer looked torn. "We know casinos will result in a lot more crime. But we can't allow you to... um... wash anybody's windows." He paused awkwardly, trying to regain control of the situation. "It's trespassing, since they don't want you here. I'm sorry, I have to ask you to leave."

We left, smiling and laughing.

Hallwatch.org and independent media gave generous coverage of the window-washing action. The Philadelphia Student Union, environmentalists in Columbus, and dozens of other groups later used the tactic. The window-washing action was simple, repeatable, and carried a clear message. Reporters from Gettysburg and Pittsburgh covered it with tough articles featuring tense interviews with the PGCB. As an apparent result, the PGCB conceded a piece of our demand and quietly released complete meeting transcripts. "A one-eighth victory," we crowed in our next press release.

The rest of the state covered the action in detail, but Jethro and I scratched our heads, observing that of all the Philly press, the *Daily News* merely printed a photo with caption buried deeply in the newspaper. Philadelphia press were proving hard to crack.

Research from Hallwatch.org's Ed Goppelt uncovered one hypothesis. The owner of the two Philly dailies—the *Philadelphia Inquirer* and the *Daily News*—was a major investor in TrumpStreet casino. If TrumpStreet were selected, the owner would invest $5 million, nearly equivalent to his investment in the two newspapers, and become an active manager in the casino. It was a small wonder, then, that the *Inquirer* editorial page—which reported directly to him—and the news sections seemed cold, if not openly hostile to us.

Which made our first big break with Philadelphia press all the more impressive.

At first, I couldn't believe it. I shouted into the phone at Jethro. "He's going to *what?*"

I could hear Jethro grin. "It's true, after your press releases to him, Anne Dicker reached out and... well... you see the article."

After a beat, Jethro added, "He calls it his 'Thanksgiving Valentine' to us."

It was hard to believe that Bruce Schimmel would go though with it. That Bruce was an idiosyncratic reporter was no question. After founding the *Philadelphia City Paper* in

1981 with lofty civic goals, he sold it for millions in 1996, earning a permanent emeritus editorial. Now, in the bitingly sharp, hipster-styled weekly, he could rise above the daily grind that most reporters faced and connect the dots across issues. His article, in the hands of about a 250,000 Philadelphians, was a breath of fresh air.

> *I love Philly's anti-casino activists. For me, this battle casino royale pits pranksters against power brokers. And I think the pranksters are winning.*
>
> *Though you won't know it from the Inquirer. Editorial page editor Chris Satullo essentially buried the anti-casino activists. Buried them alive. In his column, "That Train Done Gone and Left the Station," Satullo writes that "[t]o me, the sight of such an intelligent, roused citizenry is always stirring." But then laments that, "this time [it is] depressing." Because for Satullo, the casinos are "a done deal."*
>
> *Satullo penned that epitaph in mid-September. By Thanksgiving, Satullo might have found solace when his "roused citizenry" won local control of casino zoning. When state Sen. Vince Fumo made an abrupt about-face. And when Councilman Frank DiCicco and the mayor signed off on an independent riverfront panel that views casinos with fresh skepticism.*
>
> *I see momentum building.*

He chronicled our "pranks"—the halloween trick-or-treat, data mining, and window-washing actions. "Apparently, clever tweaking of politicians' noses isn't newsworthy," he jabbed at his media competitors.

The article was great, and Jethro and I had immediately planned a strategy to get the *City Paper* further on board, convincing them to set up a section of their website devoted to the casino issue. But Bruce Schimmel had gone much further.

Jethro's voice lilted with excitement. "It's true. This framing of transparency aligns with media's values, too—they need information for their jobs. So on December 11, he'll be there for the document search!"

"*If* we do the action," I said.

"Of course," said Jethro. After a pause, he wondered aloud, "Think the PGCB will release them all?"

"If I were them, I would. But they're a wild organization, untamed by any regulation. They are flying by the seat of their pants, stretching to their fullest to get casinos up and running. I doubt they even have the staff time to do it."

"It's a question of priorities," said Jethro. "They'd rather rush then engage the public. They'd hate the public to think a small group can bend their ear. So you may be right."

"They could still surprise us and do the right thing," I said. "Either way, we need a plan if they release all or just a part of the documents..." I laughed. "Because even if other reporters don't cover the issue, we *know* Bruce will write a story about it."

It felt powerful to watch the PGCB respond to us and a well-respected reporter agree to risk arrest—completely unlike the dull listlessness I felt on the conference call with statewide activists organized by Diane Berlin.

I kept thinking Jethro would have handled the call better. He would be connecting with the activists decrying the hostile state legislature. He would find common cause and tap their values. He would show patience with their lack of a plan. But to me, it was just frustrating—and boring, because I *did* have a plan.

Diane's earlier remarks, that I did not understand the media and was acting "recklessly," were still under my skin. I had heeded Jethro's first rule of online organizing and called her. But all it got me was her agreement to host this conference call to explain the campaign.

"*Lastly*, on our agenda," said Diane, with a taste of repudiation, "Daniel from Casino-Free Philadelphia is going to present something. It's a little thing they are doing on December 11. We are considering organizing a press conference that day, too. I will tell you all more about that after he talks. Go ahead, Daniel."

For a second, I froze. We had picked that day *because* there were no competitive press events!

I went ahead and pitched Operation Transparency. "This can unite all statewide activists in a common cause, taking on the PGCB where it's vulnerable. Some of us oppose casinos outright, some don't, but this is a big-tent action to move us collectively forward. I hope you all will participate, even if you don't want to be part of the document search." But I felt sure nobody from the state would join. Each region was focused on convincing the PGCB to not license a casino in *their* city.

It wasn't fair, but I held it against Diane. Not only had she rebuked our campaign, declined to share petitions, and refused to forward information about our action—despite sending every clipping about casinos from around the country—she was now organizing a statewide event to directly compete with our action.

After the call, I banged my fingers across the keyboard in an email to her. "Will you send out information about Operation Transparency with *your* press conference announcement?"

"No," she wrote back curtly.

Without thinking my fingers pounded an email back, "That's why I find it hard to trust you. You've blocked telling others about Operation Transparency. Do I need to tell you more how great I think your work is?"

Her two-word response reminded me I had just broken the second rule of online organizing: never send an email in anger. "Insult received." I resisted any temptation to respond. No fights ever get resolved over email. I pounded the table, then called up Jethro.

"I just pissed off an ally," I said, recounting the escalating conflict. "Here we are *doing* something, not just talking and sending emails. To halt or at least delegitimize the PGCB, we need to do more than just register our complaints with the PGCB and tell press we're unhappy! We have to *do* things!"

"Absolutely." His voice was cool.

"Even if she is scared of our actions, doesn't she respect that we're getting in newspapers across the state? She should be coming to *us* for tips on earning media! We're not only getting quotes in the papers, we're *framing* the debate!"

"Yeah," he said.

"We're doing real public education, not just sending out fact sheets that people will never read." I was starting to run out of steam. "It's *showing* not *telling* people that works! We're a model of a smart campaign!"

His stony grunt slowed me down.

"Fine," I said with a sigh. "What should I do now?"

"Well, stop talking to her. Pass off the relationship to someone who works well with her. She respects Rev. Jesse Brown, and I'm sure he can persuade her to postpone the press conference and clean up your mess."

"What did I do to mess it up so much?"

I knew I was asking for it. Jethro hadn't spent a decade as a leader in the Fenway Civic Association without learning to give out direct feedback. "Just about everything you did," he said. "When you knew she was intimidated by us young upstarts, you should have spent time listening to her, building a relationship. Instead, you kept pushing her to do what you wanted her to do."

"But I don't respect her having petitions going to waste or organizing dull press conferences."

"And I love you for that. You want people to be as powerful as possible. I'm not saying you have to agree with her strategy, but you have to respect her years of commitment on this issue. You're too impatient."

I let his words sink in.

"But I'm making that same mistake right now," Jethro added. "I've been talking with a South Philly leader, Rene Goodwin. She's chairing an anti-Foxwoods coalition, Riverfront Communities United. She's been great about passing on information about Operation Transparency. But when she learned we were organizing a press action in *her* part of South Philly, she got angry. She sent me a vicious email accusing me of breaking unity and disrespecting her."

"Why?"

"Because she thinks she should have been informed about any action within *her* community. It makes me mad, because I *don't* respect turf that way. No person represents an entire neighborhood. This turf junk is one of the most old-fashioned, backward elements of Philadelphia politics. It's all about gatekeeping—so I'm going to keep pissing off Rene. *But* I shouldn't lose the relationship, because there's a ton I respect about her. So welcome to Pennsylvania politics."

"That's helpful to hear..." I paused a half-second. "Can I help you with your relationship with Rene?"

"I just need to spend face time with her and others in South Philly to build relationship. They just make me so mad with their 'Foxwoods is the worst site' rhetoric. This is a helpful reminder, so thank you for that."

Only after the call was over did I notice how Jethro had expertly, and genuinely, given me direct feedback and advice, transparently worked out his own similar struggles, and then thanked me for it.

Two days before the end of the ultimatum, there was a noticeable uptick in Philadelphia press interest. Maybe it was the timeline, the PGCB's shifting strategy to release some documents, or Bruce's *City Paper* article announcing his intent to do the document search. Jeff Shields from the *Philadelphia Inquirer* was among the first wave to call me. Jeff was serious and hardworking, with furrowed brows and a reporter's gift for sounding like if he hadn't taken a job as a reporter, he'd be my colleague. "I hear the PGCB just released another wave of documents."

"It's true," I said. "Their website now contains abbreviated traffic plans, the casinos' licensing hearing presentations, and heavily abbreviated revenue projections."

"Anything interesting?" His voice was casual and intimate, as if we were confidants.

"Not really," I said cautiously. A pad of paper and a pen was on the other end of the phone line. "It's less than a third of what we asked for, but the PGCB is moving."

"Any employees sneak you information in brown envelopes last week?"

I chuckled, "No, we just did our Thanksgiving-to-whistleblowers action"—just *barely*—"and sent out letters asking PGCB employees to give us information. It'd be too early to hear anything."

That action had been a near flop. It was scaled far back from my grand plan of handing each PGCB staffer magnifying glass-shaped cookies with requests for information. Once again, I persuaded Jethro we needed to follow through on our word and at least send a sprinkling of letters asking staffers to become whistleblowers.

"Even with this latest release, you haven't gotten much from the PGCB. Will you go ahead with the action?"

"We'll see," I said. "It depends on what the PGCB does by our December 1 deadline. Will you be at the ultimatum deadline announcement outside City Hall?"

"I'll be there," he said. "But I don't think my editor will deem a citizen announcement of whether they're doing an event newsworthy."

I wasn't worried. I knew some papers would cover us—if not now, then at least during the eleven days between our announcement and the document search. Unlike secret organizing, our transparency gave time for our action to simmer.

"Let's say the *very* unlikely happens," said Jeff playfully. "The PGCB doesn't give you everything you want, and you attempt your 'document search.' You try to get into their offices and take the documents. What do you think is actually going to happen? Will they arrest you for trespassing, or do you think you'll actually make it to the twelfth floor? Say they let you up, what then?"

This was not a time for analysis; it was a time for theatrics, for teasing the story. "I don't know what they'll do. We're going to have to see how it plays out."

"But you must have some sense. They're not going to let you up, right? They'll arrest you—or do you have another plan?"

Of course I had likely scenarios, but I wanted the story to marinate. Press cover stories with an unknown ending better than those with a known one. Like a good mystery writer, I was not about to burst the arc of the story by prematurely announcing the end. It's why rallies or marches rarely capture press attention—they have already known outcomes. This story, however, promised drama and confrontation. "We'll execute a document search as far as we can go," I teased.

Attention now focused on *our* timeline.

By the time December 1 came, even Philadelphia press showed interest. The morning of our ultimatum, the city's most widely read daily, the pithy *Philadelphia Metro*, reported on my research into written comments to the PGCB from Philadelphia: 98% of the nearly 3,000 comments were opposed to casinos. Sensing the change in the wind, Councilman Frank DiCicco became the first Philadelphia politician to sign on to Operation Transparency, blatantly timing his sign-on to share press coverage.

In a sign that we were using candidates to push our issue into the six-month-away election cycle, Councilman DiCicco's challenger Vern Anastasio stood beside us at our press announcement, along with two other progressive candidates—Rev. Jesse Brown and Marc Stier. They were the only City Council candidates, including incumbents, to take us up on offers to share the stage at the end of the ultimatum. (Even the progressive candidates excused themselves from joining the document search, saying, "My campaign manager tells me I don't have the time," or "It's not politically wise," or—my personal favorite—"I wouldn't want to step on your toes.")

The timeline had done its job. It gave people a deadline to join us, even if only by taking a few steps toward us. We were utilizing politicians, like DiCicco, as long as they were saying and doing the right things—confident we could keep holding their feet to the fire.

On December 1, a half-dozen reporters circled us during our announcement. After a rushed phone call with the PGCB, Jethro and I theatrically looked at our watches. Jethro announced, "It's high noon, and the PGCB has refused to make all the documents public. We've asked for 100% transparency, and we have given them ample time to do it. We will go ahead and do the nation's first-ever document search."

We had only ten days to recruit people and put logistics into place.

Two days later, I answered a call as I stepped inside the train to head homeward. "It's Randy King," he said, "with the Harrisburg police. You gave me a call about some action you're doing?"

My fingers started to sweat. This was not a good place to have this conversation, as the train waved back and forth and a loudspeaker announced final boarding. But with recruitment such a challenge, I wanted things to be smooth, allay people's concerns, model our transparent style. Reaching out to the police made a good talking point.

I mouthed "Yes," still hesitant. His interests and mine weren't exactly aligned.

Randy's civilian liaison division was to be the soft arm of the police. These civil affairs departments were created by cities after waves of police brutality lawsuits from citizens, especially during public expressions of free speech. Civil affairs departments had a goal of reducing physical harm, but of even higher priority were their goals of protecting property, insulating political reputations, halting law-breaking, and preventing disturbances. To them, we threatened all these goals.

They wanted control of situations—and I didn't want to give up our control. I was going to design and carry out a disciplined action that kept them responsive to us, never giving them an excuse to take control.

Years ago, I watched a civil affairs officer promise one protestor, "You can sit-in on the street. Don't worry, we won't arrest you." Soon as the protestor locked arms with her compatriots on the pavement, the officer whispered to nearby cops and returned with handcuffs, arresting everyone—including the wide-eyed, shocked protestor. It was a lesson I learned again and again: the police will do what it takes to do their job.

I took a deep breath. *Don't forget their role. Where his interests and my interests don't conflict—that's the topic of conversation. No more.*

In a husky, fast-paced voice, Randy said, "I read about what you are trying to do. I understand it—I used to be an activist myself." He described his history as a waste management consultant who witnessed the near complete meltdown at Three Mile Island nuclear reactor. Radicalized by that event, he traveled the country organizing against nuclear energy, until finally slowing down in his hometown of Harrisburg to be a cop. "So I know what you are trying to do and why. We just want to make sure everyone is safe and you get your point across."

"Thanks for your work," I said. Having an activist history was a bit unusual, but every civil affairs officer I knew was good at finding common ground. They were trained in communications to get information. Still, no harm in being friendly on areas of information widely known. "My mentor George Lakey was involved in the anti-nuclear movement." I rattled off my own story of how my friendship with Jethro brought me in to the anti-casino movement.

"Well," he launched. "Tell me about your action."

The train rattled loudly. "What?"

"Tell me about your action," he repeated.

I repeated what was written in public. "It's a document search to release documents hidden from the public's eye." *Not* a civil disobedience action—as far as we were concerned, this was a legal activity. I was not going to get set up describing my action as illegal to the police!

The loudspeaker blared the next stop. He asked, "How many people will be doing this so-called 'document search'?"

I didn't want to make promises, as much because we didn't know as because I wasn't sure what he'd do with the information. "Mmm, maybe a dozen or so, more or less." I changed topics quickly. "Who has jurisdiction on the site?"

"Jurisdiction is complex for the site," he admitted, "so I would expect several offices to be present: Capitol Police, Harrisburg Police, a city representative, and of course the office's own Securitas."

I wondered about the Securitas worker. "Who makes arrests on site? And how long does it typically take to process people?" A nearby passenger cocked his eyes wonderingly.

"That would be the Harrisburg police," he said, responding to half of the question.

It was a strange game. Neither of us would show all our cards. We were feeling each other out, gathering snippets of information, guardedly modeling openness.

"What props will you have with you?" he asked.

I calculated. If he told us we could not have something, that could become evidence in court. However, his concern may have been police safety. "We'll have signs and stuff—nothing sharp or dangerous. We make each person sign guidelines against any kind of violence, since our interest is solely in securing documents from the PGCB."

"Got it," he said.

The train screeched to a halt at my stop, and I hopped off. "Do you have a plan for what you will do?" Even as I asked it, I knew it sounded thin. I hoped he'd say something informative.

"If you plan to do anything illegal," he couched his words carefully, "we'll have to arrest you. For the moment, we'll just be on call. And how many people did you say you're expecting?"

Duck and weave. "We're still assessing, but all of our people who are doing the document search will have gone through training and will be recognizable with green armbands."

He grunted in understanding. With only those risking arrest in armbands, it reduced the likelihood of bystanders or media accidentally getting caught up in the confusion of the arrest. Plus, if someone tried to hijack our event or start a physical fight, we could immediately see they weren't one of us and distance ourselves.

"That's all for now," he said. "Thanks, and good luck."

"Be safe," I told him as we hung up and I headed toward the trolley and my house.

I breathed a sigh of relief. He seemed reasonable. If the police would stick to their jobs, we could avoid an escalated police-protestor storyline and, instead, stay focused on our goal: getting documents and exposing the lack of public input on casinos just 200 feet from people's homes.

On my trolley ride home, I began worrying over the less professional, and less well-trained PGCB's onsite rent-a-cops. I arrived home and ran upstairs to find Securitas' number.

A monotoned young man answered.

"Excuse me, I have a couple of questions. Do you have people stationed at the Verizon tower at Strawberry Square?"

"Yes," he said.

"Do people have a right to access that building?"

"No, it's private."

"So your officers can stop people from entering it?"

"Yes."

"Can your officers arrest people?"

"No." I breathed a sigh of relief.

"Do they carry guns?"

"Uh, no," said the man, concern creeping into his voice.

"Are your people trained in crowd-control techniques?"

He paused. "What are you calling about exactly?"

I sketched out our action, repeating what was printed in our public description. I emphasized our nonviolent guidelines, and that their people had no safety worries from us.

As I guessed, the officer then refused to answer any more questions, only demanding answers. He was not a trained negotiator, just an underpaid worker in a corporate bureaucracy. Between him and Randy, I was satisfied we had modeled transparency and gotten something from the exchange, unaware that our action was causing panic in the offices of the PGCB.

Days after my calls with police and security, Jethro and I read a bizarre story of a group of ministers being kicked out of the PGCB offices.

On December 8, ministers from the Pittsburgh Hill District attempted to hand-deliver a letter opposing a casino in their district. The letter was nonthreatening, showing research that African Americans are four times more likely than whites to become problem gamblers and asserting, "As we look around the nation where casinos are located in residential communities, we do not see the positive impact. What we find is an increase in poverty, addiction, crime, drugs, prostitution and other negatives that we do not want or need in our community."

Despite the holiday spirit evoked by their decorated Christmas tree, complete with fake presents, the PGCB was acting more twitchy than loving and giving. They shut down the elevators and escorted the ministers into the December cold. One clergyman who arrived early found his way up to the PGCB's twelfth-floor offices, only to be told that the time for public input was over. With the elevators shut down, he was forced to walk down twelve flights of stairs to meet with his colleagues outside.

Locked outside for hours, the ministers eventually negotiated a compromise. One minister went up alone to hand-deliver the letter.

Afterward, Doug Harbach was tight-lipped but said this was a "unique situation since a large crowd appeared with the media." Veering completely from his previous position that the public "has all opportunities to communicate with the board," he said the public comment period was over and it was "technically illegal" for PGCB board members to read public comments.

Upon reading the news, Jethro and I noted the incompetence of our opponents, excluding the public in such an authoritarian, obvious manner. "Since the PGCB makes up its own rules, Doug is completely lying to say their hands are tied," spat Jethro over email. "And the media are complicit by not calling it out."

On the bright side, this increased recruitment. Two additional people signed up shortly after: an art student named Ken Gregory and a retired teacher, Marjorie Rosenblum, who I had met years earlier through our mutual work in Burma—where I had been leading human rights and pro-democracy trainings.

"We're giving people something meaningful to do," I said with pride. "We're not just waiting for experts in law or political officials to save us—that's a recipe for despair. We are the ones we've been waiting for."

We sent a note of support to the pastors and invited them to Operation Transparency but never stopped to consider that the PGCB's overreaction might be because of us. This is what legendary community organizer Saul Alinsky meant when he said, "The threat is usually more terrifying than the thing itself." Our deadline was getting to the PGCB, making them act stupid.

Four days before the document search, I met Councilman Frank DiCicco for the first time, along with a group of anti-casino activists, at a meeting set up by activist Marc Stier. DiCicco's sparsely adorned office felt like a blast from the '70s. With a chiseled face and a compact, squat stature, Frank was polite, considerate, and completely immovable.

At first, he simply shook his head as council candidate and ally Marc Stier floated a proposal to request that the PGCB place both Philly casinos in the far northeast of the city. Marc believed this would be much further from residential neighborhoods. While

Jethro said he preferred no casinos, he wouldn't object "if local residents support the change."

"This thing is out of my hands," said Frank with a timbre from growing up in South Philly's Italian district. "The PGCB is going to decide where these casinos go. I have no control of what happens."

Marc frowned. He hated that Philly politicians rarely solved problems, instead waiting for a solution to be generated from the grassroots; then, they'd race to take credit. But Frank wouldn't even entertain the idea, much less take credit for Marc's vision.

Councilman DiCicco kept saying no, absolutely refusing to join the document search.

"If you at least come with us, our constituents will see that it's not over," Jethro said. His voice was solid and showed none of the intimidation I felt. I couldn't help stealing glances at the aging walls and plastic phone. This was where realpolitik happened, where Frank would call his mentor, Senator Fumo, author of Act 71. Here, no doubt, deals were made and advice traded about how to handle "casino obstructionists" opposed to the four casino proposals, which *happened* to be in Frank's district.

Frank flashed a clean-shaven politician's smile. "No," he said, "it's your action."

Jethro looked back and forth at his neighbors, Norma Van Dyke and Ed Verral. Norma, a polite, tiny firebrand looked up at Frank. "Can you at least request that the PGCB delay?"

"I got City Council to pass a resolution asking for a delay months ago. I can't get much more public than that."

Jethro waved his hands dismissively, while Brian Abernathy, Frank's legislative aid, suddenly leaned forward. "We've done all we could. I know you think we have some special power over the senator, but his mind is made up."

Jethro fixed his gaze on Frank. "Whether you like it or not, you will have to deal with this. The longer you wait, the harder it will be to act."

Frank shrugged, a gesture of hopelessness.

Norma almost pleaded. "Would you agree to meet with us again?"

"Let's wait until after the licensing and see where things stand. I can't promise anything. You have to be ready to negotiate if the PGCB doesn't delay. And I don't believe they will."

This was a waste. I looked hopefully at the doorway, even as I expected Jethro to explode. Negotiating was the white flag of surrender, picking your terms of defeat. Jethro hated politicians for offering it as their first and last option for his community.

Jethro leaned close to Frank, almost face to face. "Who here has given money out of their own pocket to stop casinos?" Jethro shot up his hand. Slowly, wonderingly, all of us raised our hands. Only Frank and Brian's hands stayed down. Marc's mouth dropped as Frank and Jethro locked eyes for an eternal minute.

"I get the point," Frank hissed. Jethro kept his arm aloft.

Frank whispered to Brian, "We can afford a bus, right?" Brian nodded.

"Fine, I'll pay for one of your buses down to Harrisburg."

I couldn't believe it. It was bold. It was outrageous. It was Jethro being honest—and getting our largest donation to date, a quarter of our $4,000 budget.

But as Brian escorted us from their offices, it felt like a shallow victory.

In the quiet hallways, Jethro turned to Marc. "That didn't really go how you expected it, did it?" It wasn't exactly an apology, but at least an acknowledgement.

Marc waived it off. "You only said what's true. But whether you like him or not, you're going to have to deal with Frank."

Jethro nodded, "But not on his terms."

I grinned. "And way to use shame!"

"Hey, I'm Jewish," said Jethro, laughing. "We learn how to use it."

"Frank won't do this for us," said Norma, still shaking her head. "Count me in for the document search."

Jethro turned to me, clapping his hands, "See, Daniel? The meeting was worthwhile! Maybe we just need everyone to meet with Frank and see his hopelessness. Welcome aboard, Norma!"

It was the night before the document search. We had just finished the training session. Trainer Michael Gagné, who had worked with Philippe during the first nonviolent search and seizure in Ottawa, spent the bulk of the training on logistics, "what if" scenarios, and our codes of behavior.

It was a fine training, peaking when Michael charismatically told his story of attempting to "liberate" documents called the Free Trade Area of the Americas. It was a high-level trade negotiation between all countries in the Americas except Cuba, with NAFTA-like provisions, expanding "free" trade but restricting environmental and labor laws. Even worse, the texts were secret to everyone except heads of state and 500 business representatives. So a few weeks before the trade meetings in Québec, Michael attempted to liberate the texts, going over police barricades dressed as Robin Hood, along with ninety-eight others.

The resulting public pressure coerced the Canadian government to break ranks and make them public. Exposed to public scrutiny, the plans were quickly shredded.

There was no encouragement like a story that showed we could really pull this off.

I followed Jethro and Ed Verral as they departed the training. Walking in rhythm with Ed, Jethro asked, "So what did you think of the training?"

"It was good! You guys have thought of everything!"

"I'm sure we missed some things, but we try," said Jethro. "What did you like?"

"You had answers for everything! Going up to the twelfth floor with TV cameras in case the PGCB tries to set us up by messing up their own offices—I never woulda thought of that. You two are amazing."

"It was a good training, wasn't it." Jethro stopped and turned to face Ed. "So now you've washed windows, data mined at the PGCB's offices, and gone through this training... What do you think about participating in the document search with me?"

Ed's face dropped momentarily. "You know I want to do it... It's just..." Internal tensions surfaced on his face until he reached clarity. "I'm in."

Jethro turned around to catch my eye, smiling. "We're up to fourteen. See you tomorrow."

*   *   *

At seven in the morning, my feet barely touched the ground. I jumped onto our chartered bus, waving to our deeply caffeinated bus driver. He merely grunted.

On time to our internal schedule—fifteen minutes behind the public schedule—our West Philly bus left at eight o'clock and picked up twenty high-school students in Center City. Their teachers wanted them exposed to citizen action. We were glad to have them boost our numbers.

On the other side of town, Jethro's bus left from Fishtown and stopped in South Philly. There Jethro gave a short TV interview—without Rene's territorial approval—before roaring out of Philadelphia for the two-hour trip to the PA Gaming Control Board.

Everything was smooth. Meredith Warner, a founding member of NABR and resident of Fishtown, had taken on large chunks of the planning and was busy working with Jethro to tighten final logistics, while I made last-minute media calls, wooing TV stations by reporting that their competitors had interviewed us already. The other eighty people prepared themselves mentally, including the fourteen risking arrest with the document search—except an absent Ken Gregory. His alarm clock never went off.

The high-school teacher brought me back to talk with her loud, curious students. After I explained what would happen, one concerned student remarked, "You'll get locked up forever." Her face was grave.

"Why do you think that?" I asked lightly.

"Because you can't just... you can't... you can't go in and just *take* documents."

"Why not?" I asked. "In India, for example, you as a citizen have a right to nearly any non-military document. You can just walk to offices and get them. Why don't we have that kind of freedom in the US?"

"That's just how things are," said another student quietly. "You're gonna get arrested and your family will never see you again."

I laughed at the ludicrousness of their fears. We weren't blowing up a building—at worst, merely trespassing. But they had absorbed so much fear of standing up to authority. "I'll guarantee you that's not true. There's no conspiracy or any intent to break laws. We've chosen this target carefully for a simple action of searching for the documents. What laws are we breaking?"

They didn't know.

"We might be charged with trespassing or disorderly conduct. But they are minor charges."

They didn't looked convinced.

"Well, there's nothing like some experiential learning. So I'll come back to your class and show you how everything is fine when the action is over, okay?"

Most nodded, concern still on their faces. "Unless you're still in jail," shouted one student. But this time, she was joking—mostly. I smiled, and we bantered for a while, unaware of Ken Gregory, awake now and speeding down the highway trying to catch up to us.

Once in Harrisburg, thirty-degree cold hit us as we jumped out of our buses with thirteen-foot-tall magnifying-glass puppets. Meredith passed around "No Casino" signs and duck-shaped "Fowl Play" placards donated by social-justice puppet theater Spiral Q. I ignored the churning in my stomach: *What's going to happen? How will police respond? Will the PGCB overreact? Will the action reach new allies?* I flipped on my boombox, blasting *Get Smart* and other spy songs, as we loped two blocks to Capitol Park, next to the stately capitol building.

Jethro handed silver-tongued Matt Ruben the bullhorn, and he spoke with fiery passion to the frozen apprehension in the air. He got the crowd cheering with news that today two Philly politicians had endorsed Operation Transparency—state representatives Mike O'Brien and Babette Josephs—making three political endorsers from Philly. It was far fewer than the dozen elected endorsers across the state.

Matt ramped up energy after short, punctuated speeches by Lori McCole, Marc Stier, and Vern Anastasio, each appropriately brief, given the cold. Then it was time.

Philippe Duhamel had taught me to get people to walk before actions. It relieves stress, so people aren't as pent up and anxious. So Rev. Jesse Brown, a charismatic pastor of a church in Southwest Philly who had been involved in CFP since the beginning, led us in chants three blocks to the PGCB entrance: "Hey-hey! Ho-ho! The public has a right to know!"

Once inside the mall, people stomped their feet. Rev. Brown led us in a short prayer, and I reviewed the action, as much for participants as for the dozen-plus press who had joined us. "In a moment, we will head into the PGCB's vestibule. Those doing the document search will gather two-by-two, step forward, read the citizen's search warrant, and proceed past the glass doors and up to the offices of the PGCB, chaired by Tad Decker. Photographers will want to position themselves right inside the glass doors and follow us up. Okay? Let's go."

With chants, we crowded into the vestibule: "Hey Decker, what's the rush? Why's the gaming board so hush-hush?" Media angled for prime position.

With surprise, I saw only three Securitas security guards and no police. Dwarfed by the group, a tiny security guard behind the desk stood up and shouted, "You can't be here! No, no! You must go!"

It was the same woman I had talked with weeks before. Hoping she'd recognize me, I tried to calm her down. She engaged with me enough so her voice no longer rose above the echoing chamber, but her face remained panic-stricken.

Meredith silenced the crowd and bellowed instructions. Green-armband-wearing document-search practitioners lined up, with a clear path toward the glass doors, as two security officers emerged from behind the doors. Complete silence descended.

Meredith and Jethro stepped forward, dramatically holding aloft magnifying glasses. Rather than rush the doors and create chaos, which the police could use as a pretext to take control, the action was designed to maintain control with internal discipline. Meredith and Jethro read in unison from our citizen's search warrant, "On behalf of citizens across the state, we are here to demand the casino planning documents from the Pennsylvania Gaming Control Board." A KYW radio reporter shoved his microphone in their faces. "We have consistently said transparency rests on two rights: the right for public information and the right to give meaningful input. The Gaming Control Board has denied our right to public information. Without relevant and updated information, the PGCB has therefore denied our right to give meaningful input, too."

Their words echoed in the silence, surging into the finale: "The right to know is fundamental to democracy. We have a right to debate casinos coming into our neighborhoods before it is too late. We know the documents are in this building, here in the Pennsylvania Gaming Control Board's offices. We are asking you, police officers and security officials, to do your duty to join with us and help retrieve the Gaming Control Board's plans for our neighborhoods."

The two security officers shifted uncomfortably but maintained reverential silence. They had no pretense to seize control.

Jethro took a step toward the doors. "My name is Jethro Heiko. I am here to exercise my right as a citizen."

Then Meredith took a step. "My name is Meredith Warner. I am here to exercise my right as a citizen."

Together, they walked forward as they executed the final words of the citizen search warrant. "Please let us through." They took six paces toward the door, as the crowd quietly inhaled. This was it.

Supporters broke into a cacophony of cheers of encouragement, whoops, and a few jeers toward the police. Adrenaline and excitement kicked in as I raised my voice above the others. I wanted people on message. "Let them through! Let them through!" Others joined, until the whole crowd was thundering, their words echoing into every corner and spilling into the lobby.

Behind the glass doors, eight security officers appeared, hurriedly closing the glass doors, and leaving two security guards standing between us and the doors. Jethro and Meredith continued their slow, deliberate gait.

The police shooed wildly at Jethro and Meredith as they approached the doors. They apparently were not going to do their duty.

As Jethro and Meredith came face-to-face with the police, Jethro looked over his shoulders awkwardly at me as if to say, "What do I do now?"

I signaled that Jethro and Meredith should stay right there, and the next two pairs should wait for a few minutes of chanting. We were in no rush. The PGCB was demonstrating they would rather shut down the offices than allow us to liberate documents. They were acting out their commitment to secrecy.

Jethro's neighbor Ed Verral and Bruce Schimmel stepped forward next. They were a mismatched pair. Bruce wore his *City Paper* press badge on a sharply tailored, grey, button-down shirt, with a red tie. To his right, Ed bulged in his biker leather jacket, razor thin sunglasses, and a bandana over his shaved head. Both wore intense, serious faces with eyes set dead on the elevators, past the doors.

Alongside clamorous chants of "Let them through!" the next pair read the search warrant and stepped forward, joining the now *de facto* blockade of the doors. Pair after pair—magnifying glasses held aloft—walked calmly toward the now clogged doorway. I walked alongside Michelle McCandless and Karin DiNardi, both in wheelchairs, bringing up the rear of the seventh and final pair.

Only then did ten Harrisburg police arrive. They engaged in lengthy side conversations until weaving their way through the crowd to the doors. There, they found our searchers ignoring the security guards' demands that we leave, instead re-reading the citizen's search warrant.

It was loud and a little chaotic, but the crowd's energy was pulsating, with a constant demand: "Let them through! Let them through!"

The Harrisburg police lieutenant echoed the security guard's requests to leave. "If you turn around and go back now, this can be easy."

Dressed in a dark suit with his cleric's collar, Rev. Jesse Brown was one of the few in the group experienced in direct action. He spoke on the group's behalf. "Is there a gambling official we can talk with?"

The lieutenant stuttered. "I'm afraid... Right now, I'm just telling you. They don't want to talk with you."

"I would prefer if they would come and tell us, that so we can talk with someone who has the authority to tell us that," he said.

"Well, I have the authority to tell you to leave," she snapped. "Now, you're under arrest, so if you don't go with me, you're resisting arrest."

Silently and slowly, Jesse turned around, looking straight ahead as his wrists were snapped together with plastic bracelets. As my choreography had intended, he was marched back through our cheering and clapping supporters, the front entrances, and outside to the police vans.

One by one, police arrested us. Speed-talking, Bruce introduced himself to a fellow journalist as an officer tied his handcuffs. "I'm Bruce Schimmel. S-C-H-I-M-M-E-L. I'm with the *Philadelphia City Paper*." The journalist raised an eyebrow.

"Now it's your turn," the lieutenant told Marjorie Rosenblum, tugging on her arm. Marjorie seemed not to even take notice as she was handcuffed and escorted to the women's police van.

My own handcuffing felt uneventful, until the police officer walked me through the crowd. I felt blasted with a heat wave of affection, and tears came to my face.

Only Ed Goppelt of Hallwatch.org caught the irony that during these arrests, Kevin Hayes, PGCB's "Right-to-Know officer" was silently maneuvering through the crowd without speaking to a soul.

When it came time to arrest the folks in wheelchairs, Michelle and Karin turned off their half-ton wheelchairs and refused to leave. The police cleared all media from the room. With three or four police officers per chair, they picked up the wheelchairs and hoisted them out of the vestibule.

That was when Ken Gregory breathlessly ran into the mall, catching the tail end of everything. He had raced for two hours trying desperately to be part of his first direct action.

After a squished but quick trip in the police vans, our crew sat waiting to be booked—except for Karin and Michelle. They were *not* getting arrested, booked, or even given a ticket. They were simply ignored, as the police watched the crowd to make sure nobody else returned to try the search again.

Veterans of the direct action group Disabled In Action, Karin and Michelle were outraged at their separate treatment because of being in wheelchairs. Karin, unable to speak because of her cerebral palsy, banged out on her personal computer. Her computer read the words in a harsh mechanical voice—*Discrimination, discrimination*—drowned out by the crackling and chanting of the crowd.

That's when Ken Gregory strolled up. All during his wild trip trying to catch us, he feared he would miss it all. His initial assessment as he entered the lobby was that he might have. He told the lieutenant that he was part of the action.

With gritted teeth she said, "Sorry, this isn't going to be your fifteen minutes of fame."

Undeterred, he approached cop after cop, explaining that "taxpayer dollars paid for impact studies which are being withheld from the public," until he noticed Karin banging on her keyboard. Then he and she went to several cops, explaining that able-bodied persons were being arrested while chair-bound people were not. The captain in charge nodded inattentively—until Karin suggested they might have to sue. Then he paid attention.

Resigned, the captain took both women's identification cards to process them. Ken interjected, "I'm blocking the same exact door," and hopefully handed the captain his driver's license. The captain paused before finally accepting the license.

Onlookers cheered this odd moment, as police wrote up Karin, Michelle, and Ken. After a late start, he proudly got to be part of the action.

In the end, fourteen people were arrested. We were charged with disorderly conduct as a summary offense—like a parking ticket—for "creating a hazard offensive condition which served no legitimate purpose by blocking an entrance causing a fire hazard." The booking process was quick. In thirty minutes, we were let go and marched ourselves the six blocks back to the PGCB's offices.

"Wait, aren't you supposed to be in jail?" shouted one of the high-school students as he saw me sauntering up.

"I told you it wouldn't be long," I grinned back at him. I knew we were lucky that there was no line at booking and that we had not received heavier charges.

The high-school students were too cool to express their shock. But several came up to me and hugged me or touched me—as if to see that it was really me.

For several hours, the PGCB shut down its offices rather than allow us to get access to some documents. Our message was embedded in our action so we didn't need our signs or press releases to explain our action. We were *showing, not telling*.

The PGCB was exposed for violating the widely shared value of transparency, with our action unmarred by needless confrontation with police or sideshows. The PGCB would pay for it in terribly bad press coverage and political fallout.

As we got back on the buses, I felt nothing but love for the radiant faces of my fellow arrestees: Jethro, Norma, Jesse, Bruce, Ken, Michelle, Karin, Ed, Meredith, Morgan, Christine, Marjorie, and Stephanie. These people would never again believe this was a "done deal." They had wielded what Dr. King called "the sword that heals." We had faced our fear and, through our boldness, revealed injustice. Now, as all eyes swiveled back to the PGCB's licensing, we just needed to persuade others of the power of direct action.

CHAPTER 4
Casino Licensing

DECEMBER 12, 2006 — JANUARY 5, 2007

*the right story gets people outside their comfort zone • setting some boundaries •
don't ritualize losing • thinking ahead and preparing counter-responses •
soaking up the political terrain • communal cider and soup combat the taste of defeat*

MY LEGS PEDALED MY BIKE QUICKLY toward an early meeting, one with unforeseen outcomes. I squinted into the sun, now rising above Spring Garden Street. Brisk air rushed past me. It was early, but good to move my body and release the adrenaline from yesterday's action.

Yesterday's document search. It had gone so well. Jethro called me immediately afterwards with congratulations and reported that Ed couldn't stop talking about how powerful it felt getting arrested, how different from his expectation.

I had reported to Jethro of our fantastic press coverage: front pages on a half-dozen non-Philly newspapers; the Associated Press; our first TV coverage, on the local CBS news affiliate; and even some buried articles in the *Inquirer* and *Daily News.* "Most importantly," I said excitedly, "they didn't merely cover the arrests, but reported on the PGCB's lack of transparency and the hidden documents. All the reports clearly covered our goal. Rather than a rally that just *talked* about the PGCB's opaqueness, we *showed* it: our message was embedded in our action."

Even hostile press had trouble missing it. The *Philadelphia Inquirer* — owned by a TrumpStreet casino investor — buried us on B4 behind an exposé on Christmas lights. But they still reported the message echoed in every newspaper: "Fourteen anti-casino protesters were arrested today at the Gaming Control Board offices in Harrisburg when they demanded to see documents about proposed casinos that they say are being withheld from the public." The article went on to explain the documents and the history of denied requests.

It was what it means to design an action to *show, not tell.* In the muddy waters of political theater, we told a simple story where we were the goodies, and the PGCB were the baddies — a story that would help us at our meeting today.

I turned right, toward the boxy Seamen's Church Institute, where I would meet with the International Longshoremen's Association. They were a union of 65,000 dockworkers and ship-loaders.

I still couldn't believe Jethro had talked me into coming—and not just because of the early time. With Operation Transparency over, I had thought my work with CFP would end. But Jethro had made an effective pitch: "You did what you said you would do. There's no pressure for you to stay. But there's a lot I—and all of us—can learn from you. And I can teach you a bunch more about organizing. Would you come to the meeting with the ILA and see what happens? I think they could be ready to learn something about direct action, and you'd be great at helping me with that."

In other words, he *organized* me. It was a textbook ask: clear, succinct, specific, and a next step rooted in my own interest and passion for teaching people direct action.

I hopped off my bike. Like a thunderbolt, a thought occurred to me, and I fumbled for my cell phone. I made a quick call for advice. Then I hurried inside, up the stairway with its drooping flags from around the world, and down a wide hall past rows of ministers and staffers who serve transient seafarers.

Inside a large conference room, I breathlessly tossed my stuff down next to Jethro and Ed. Dozens of tables filled the room, making a horseshoe shape. At the connecting tables, Jethro and Ed rose to give me congratulatory hugs.

"Did you see?" Jethro whipped from his black scheduler a fresh copy of the *Metro*, with a dramatic front-page picture of him getting arrested.

I scanned the splendidly framed story. *We wanted information. The PGCB was secretive. Instead of giving us documents, they arrested us.* The police were neutral: "There were no surprises. They did what they said they were going to do."

"Amazing," I said, marveling at the front page.

Ed laughed. "The PGCB must be mad at themselves for not just giving us the documents."

At eight o'clock, our chatter stopped. Dozens of people filled the tables. A hulking, muscular, African-American man raised himself and bellowed, "Let's start this meeting."

The atmosphere in the room had changed. My own skinned bristled with tension, though I had no idea why. After years of mediating conflicts, I could identify the sensation: *There are some people in this room who really dislike each other.*

The man spoke. "Most of you know me. I'm Boise Butler, president of Local 1291 of the ILA." I had trouble keeping my eyes off of the man's massive body. Jethro wasn't joking when he said that at their first meeting he and Ed filled one side of the booth, Boise filled the other. It was the body of a man who lifted heavy things for a living. "Let's start with introductions."

I pulled out a pencil to keep track as ILA leaders introduced themselves: Jim Paylor, Sonny Howlett...

Next to them sat State Representatives Bill Keller and Mike O'Brien. They introduced themselves as representatives of waterfront neighborhoods—Bill in the South and Mike in the North. Bill's husky body, once that of a longshoreman, was still dwarfed by Boise. Bill admitted voting for Act 71 but said he "didn't believe they'd actually consider Foxwoods." Smaller, with thin glasses and gregarious laughter, Mike was a newer representative of Fishtown, "a friend of longshoreman," and "would not have supported Act 71 in its present form if I had been in office then."

Boise then gestured across the table toward a line of short, stodgy, white men. They all looked unhappy. Compared to the booming voices of the ILA members and friends, their voices were hushed, and I could barely catch their names. Something about the Philadelphia Marine Trade Association. "This may be the only time we're meeting to not bargain or negotiate," said one.

The pieces fell into place. These were the *bosses*. My head swam. Just arrested, we were now at a rare boss-worker meeting.

I glanced over at Jethro, his face indecipherable—only a slight squint in his eye registered his surprise.

"Finally," said Boise, sweeping his thick arms, "we have the community."

With a shock, I noted he was pointing at us. *Community? We're just three people.*

Ed and I deferred to Jethro, who gave our names and held up the front page. "This is what we know how to do."

Introductions finished, the meeting slogged through ILA leaders and port bosses wading through numbers to explain why this issue mattered to them. I couldn't track the detailed, long-winded speeches, but I understood the gist. If a casino opened on the riverfront, it might double the number of cars on already clogged Delaware Avenue. That would be a problem for truck drivers along the port, who required precise timing to load material on or off the ships and onto trucks heading to their final destination. Delaware Avenue was their route when the interstate backed up, which was often. If Delaware Avenue traffic became worse than it already was, the port would become unreliable. That would be less money, fewer jobs—and right at a time of possible port expansion. They looked shaken.

"Is the riverfront planning process addressing any of this?" asked one longshoreman. "Do they know if any of the three northern casino proposals would be as bad?"

"Let's find out," said Boise, whipping out a cell phone. He called the director of PennPraxis. "Come here, please," Boise barked.

PennPraxis was an ambitious riverfront planning process that came to be after NABR pressured the city for a comprehensive plan instead of the haphazard planning that had left the Delaware Riverfront a random assortment of blight, blitz, and big-box buildings. At PennPraxis's first public meeting, Boise met Jethro, who raised provocative questions about the casino's impact on his industry.

Within minutes, the director of the PennPraxis project, breathless and having cut off another meeting, ran into the room and announced meekly, "A northern casino would have a detrimental impact, though probably not as much on traffic at the ports."

Jethro and I looked at each other, wide-eyed at the longshoremen's finger-snapping influence.

Much as I heard political connections, I heard no solutions to win. Long speeches on the dangers failed to advance a plan. Mostly they turned to politicians for advice, who pled powerlessness. "This thing is wired from the top," said State Representative Mike O'Brien. "We can introduce bills to stop a Philly casino, but there's no chance they'll pass. It's too late. I don't see what to do."

The breakneck speed of the PGCB was designed purposely to prevent what was happening here. The rushed December 20 date fueled people's hopelessness of making a difference. The room sagged.

Boise motioned Jethro toward him and whispered loudly. "You have to talk, Jethro. Tell us how to fight this... It's your job as the community."

Jethro showed no hesitation, though I sensed him caught off guard. "I have fought 'done deals' before and won," he said while returning to his seat. "Years ago, I worked as a community organizer with the Fenway community in Boston. We stopped a Fenway Park Stadium Complex that was a done deal—signed by the mayor, the governor, and all of the state representatives. But through community organizing, we were able to win."

He sounded like a friend thinking out loud about what he wanted to eat tonight. His words were slow-paced, tumbling out, like he realized what he was saying only after it came out. He flashed today's *Metro*. "Actions get results. We were just fourteen people with a few supporters. Imagine what a group like you can do that has way more power than us. The community already supports you on this. You need to figure out how to get ahead of this issue, so that others can follow your lead. What can you do?"

I grinned. He had taken Boise's statement that it was up to community to figure out and turned it back around, but with a context to do it: actions. Where other organizers would start giving prescriptions, he was using strategic questions to organize them and elicit their wisdom.

The tension in the room melted a little. People searched in earnest for options. A *lawsuit? A public declaration? Maybe we could get PennPraxis to oppose casinos?*

The planning director quickly waved his hands. "We are going to stay neutral on the issue of casinos."

Jethro muttered angrily, "How can a planning process remain neutral on big-box development that impacts every aspect of it? Casinos break every rule of a civic vision with waterfront access." Looking at Boise, he apologized. "Sorry, it's your meeting. But we don't have to accept the prescription of traditional institutions: the courts, legislative bodies, or formal planning processes. If those mechanisms prove themselves unable to help, you may also consider direct action, like the action we just did. What would that look like for you all?"

Boise shrugged off the apology—"It's fine"—while others responded, "We can't do direct action," getting nods on both sides of the room.

I took a deep breath. My turn. "Of course you can," I said. "Because you already have." For the first time, everyone's faces turned to me. I hoped they couldn't hear my heart pounding. "In the 1970s, the US government was sending arms to Pakistani dictator Yahya Khan. Those weapons violently oppressed the people of East Pakistan, now known as Bangladesh, killing almost 3 million East Pakistanis in an attempted genocide."

I paused, sorting the details from my morning phone call with Richard Taylor. He was a member of a campaign team called A Quaker Action Group and literally wrote the book, *Blockades*, about that campaign. "A group of Quakers wanted to make a difference. And when they found out the shipments were loaded on local Philadelphia ports, they picked a dramatic action to stop the flow of weapons: a naval blockade! For a month, they publicly practiced naval maneuvers in canoes and kayaks in front of TV cameras. Some days had themes—religious leaders, kids, elders—all leading up to the arrival of the Pakistan-bound shipment. You know the size of these: gigantic multistory freighter ships.

"When the first ship arrived, they jumped into the water with their canoes and paddle boats. The coast guard immediately pulled them out, as cameramen angled for the best picture. Over the next weeks, they played a cat-and-mouse game, with the freighters trying to avoid the public spotlight by changing their arrival times or rerouting to Baltimore or NYC. But a group of people was watching the unfolding storyline on TV— the ILA..." I paused. "You guys.

"Quakers first met y'all in bars. ILA members—and, I don't know, maybe it was some of you—were struck by the Quakers' graveness and the sense of a historical moment. The Philadelphia ILA joined, refusing to load armaments headed to Pakistan. It was the beginning of the end.

"Philly ILA leaders encouraged the national ILA to cease loading any shipments heading to East Pakistan. That meant the US couldn't use any port on the East Coast to send shipments. It was classic civil disobedience and made it prohibitively expensive to send weapons. Soon after, the federal government announced it would no longer support the dictator.

"Direct action can win when other options are closed to you," I concluded. "You can sit in at meetings, picket to shut down the PGCB's meeting, or strike until the PGCB negotiates with you." At the last remark, the bosses shifted uncomfortably. Catching myself, I stuttered, "Of course, I'm not proposing strikes. There are lots of options, like our document search, or interrupting the December 20 proceedings. You just cannot afford this meeting going forward without trying to stop it."

I halted, heart racing.

Boise smiled. "I was involved in some of that. It's good for us to think about what the ILA can do."

I sighed with relief. The conversation turned toward a steady flow of ideas. None were as bold as Jethro or I proposed, but that wasn't our goal. Our goal was to encourage people to take *one step* outside their comfort zone. We didn't know how they worked, what they knew, or what they could do. They were their own experts.

A half-hour of brainstorming, and Boise abruptly closed the meeting. If agreements or decisions were made, I had missed them. But the bizarre, joint worker-boss meeting had shifted its tone to one of commitment and energy.

When the meeting closed, the managers fled, leaving Jethro, Ed, and me to chat with ILA leaders and state representatives. Mike O'Brien, who had signed onto Operation Transparency, shook my hand and introduced himself. With a deep, guttural voice, he boomed, "I don't think we can win. But it's worth a shot."

"Uh, yeah," I said, uncertain whether he was trying to pacify me or deliver a frank analysis. "There's still a lot of time before casinos are in the ground. There are lots of options to prevent permits, do research, and build political support against them."

Mike started to speak but was interrupted by colleague Bill Keller. "I've been around the block, Daniel. I have taken on the governor before. Believe me, the governor is 100%

in favor of these—he's wanted casinos for decades. The deals are done. Nothing's going to move."

I stuttered. "You have your ILA allies... You have options..." My words wilted under Bill's fierce stare. I'd never taken on the governor—how could I say he was wrong?

Jethro stepped next to me, facing Bill. His voice carried an edge. "If the deals are done, help us undo them. If you go around telling everyone it's lost, then yes, it will be lost. If you go around telling everyone what's wrong with the deals, the people will get mad and help stop them."

Bill turned to Jethro. "You just can't move anything at the state level—the governor will see to that. City council has the zoning in its hands and needs to decide what to do. It's completely out of our hands."

Jethro's face turned red, a mixture of rage and passion. "Are you happy the governor can stop anything from moving?"

Bill shook his head. "Of course not! I—"

"Then talk about that with your constituents!" Jethro's voice rose. "*They* are the answer to making things move on the state level. You have lots of things you can do. Are you making sure the state doesn't take away local zoning so the city *can* protect itself?"

I felt unsettled, watching Jethro's eyes dart between the two state representatives. It seemed risky to be combative so quickly. But they had escalated the hopelessness, right?

Bill looked nonplussed. "Maybe we can stop legislation, but we can't pass anything. It's up to the city. Mike and I will do our parts." He reached out to shake Jethro's hand and leave.

"Look, Bill." Jethro gripped Bill's hand. "City and state politicians use each other to avoid taking bold and winning steps. You are a state representative. Take steps at the state. *We'll* worry about city leaders."

Bill grimaced. With feeling, he said, "Jethro, you're just going to have to teach us how to win this."

Jethro smiled warmly and released Bill's hand. "By the end of this, we'll have taught you a lot about how you can win the unwinnable."

The proposed Foxwoods casino site in South Philly was 16-acres surrounded by a lonely chain-link fence. For a decade, it lay wasted as an abandoned eyesore, allowed to pop up weeds by investors who hoped one day for such an opportunity as casinos. Now, they envisioned an open casino by November of next year, with a huge parking lot just north of the Walmart and Home Depot shopping complex and across the street from the United Artists movie theater.

I headed into that theater for a press conference hosted by Councilman Frank DiCicco. "I cannot pretend that I can stop gambling from coming. But I don't believe the board has all the information it needs to make an adequate decision. If they make the wrong one, it could ruin the city of Philadelphia," he said, flanked by political allies, including several ILA leaders. He confidently paced back and forth, announcing a new website to ask state legislators for a six-month delay in PGCB licensing.

My face reddened. *A week before licensing, and this is all the councilman is announcing?*

I couldn't believe it. He was passing the buck back to the state. It was all the more disturbing because months earlier, NABR had fought so hard for "city zoning control." NABR had organized a last-minute petition drive to scare off legislators, even Senator Fumo, the coauthor of Act 71, to make sure the city had the right to enact zoning laws. I had suggested to DiCicco just days earlier that he use those to make tight regulations making it hard, or even impossible, for a casino to build in Philadelphia. Instead, Councilman DiCicco was doing the politician's disavowal dance: *Don't ask me, I have no power – go ask someone else.*

As DiCicco spoke, I stared at the movie posters. I couldn't help feeling jealous that a pass-the-buck press conference netted four times the reporters as our document search. This was not about action and plot—it was pure politics. Politicians' default stance is to avoid blame, and the best way to do that is to claim powerlessness when bad things happen. Twisting the knife, DiCicco reiterated that citizens should sit down for negotiations now.

Discouraged and bored by politicians' mouthed words, I headed down the escalator.

When I returned home, I found I'd missed a big chunk of action. The *Inquirer* reported, "Ed Kirlin, a member of the Pennsport Civic Association, handed out a flyer at the news conference headlined 'Too Little Too Late' that called DiCicco 'a casino flunky dressed now in casino-opponent garb.' Later, Kirlin said, DiCicco aide Brian Abernathy came up during the news conference and in the midst of a heated, expletive-filled exchange, Abernathy put his face close to his. Kirlin said that when he 'snapped my teeth like a dog would in warning,' Abernathy slapped him. Kirlin said he would file a complaint with police."

The *Inquirer* suggested that underneath the incident sat hostilities between two longtime, warring South Philly political factions: those of Senator Fumo and John Dougherty. With Senator Fumo were his protégé Councilman DiCicco and DiCicco aide Brian Abernathy. On the other side was electricians' union IBEW Local 98 leader John Dougherty, allied with Ed Kirlin.

I called Jethro to sort through the implications of their little proxy war. "Are any of them with us?"

"In some ways it's funny," said Jethro, "because they're each trying to out-anti-casino us. Kirlin makes copies for Operation Transparency, and DiCicco sets up a website. That can work in our favor. But none of them can be trusted, because they're using this to score political points."

This explained the constant backbiting on civic listserves and email groups, where different factions took every opportunity to take shots at each other. One attacking DiCicco, saying he was "abdicating control," with DiCicco's allies accusing Dougherty of wanting Foxwoods built so he could take a slice of the money.

"We'll just have to stay on our toes to stay out of it, and use it to further our goals," said Jethro. "It can't be worse than my experiences in Boston."

It would take a while for us to learn that it was.

＊　　　＊　　　＊

The following day, I flew to Florida for an early Christmas vacation with my grandmother. At the airport, my parents and sister picked me up with huge hugs. Conversation wound its way to the casino campaign.

I wasn't sure what to tell them. "It's great! Bad. Excited. Crazy! I don't know how much to share." My sister waved me on encouragingly. "I thought things would slow down after Operation Transparency, or maybe I'd be done. But we're the go-to casino opposition. Reporters call us regularly, and my inbox is filled with arguments over tactics and strategy and questions about our next plans. Everyone's terrified their proposed casino will be the one selected. So I need to set a rule, and your help in following it: I can only check my email in the evening. Otherwise, it won't be a vacation for me."

"Of course," exclaimed my mom, as my dad eyed me carefully. A veteran of fights for civil rights, he knew the personal toll of not taking care of oneself.

The remainder of the day refreshed me—eating ice cream, walking slowly in the warm Florida air, playing cards.

When evening came, I rushed to my hotel room and set up my computer. We were all over the news. A scathing anti-PGCB editorial by Pittsburgh's *Patriot News* used Operation Transparency to illustrate the board's anti-democratic way. In the *Post-Gazette*, *Inquirer*, and *Pittsburgh Tribune-Review*, Jethro and I were quoted about the upcoming December 20 licensing hearings. The latter article exposed the PGCB's paying $25 million in perks to its tiny staff, including paying Chairman Tad Decker's state license and bar association fees. And, apparently, tomorrow we'd get our first national press in *USA Today*.

It made me want to figure out what was next. December 20 was key. How could we shut it down? ILA leadership told us they were "up for anything"—but they didn't know my imagination.

Could the ILA set up a picket line outside the PGCB's hearing? I discounted the idea. The PGCB would cross it, possibly looking anti-union, but go ahead and vote. *Maybe people could disturb the meeting by blowing a loud whistle? Or individuals could shout? If they were pulled out of the meeting at a rate of five minutes per person, only fifty people could cost the PGCB an excruciating four hours. Then the PGCB would likely resort to making the decision in secret—only coming out in public to vote, or meeting later—and our image would be seared permanently into public consciousness as screamers and hecklers.*

No, we needed something higher-ground. But it wasn't coming. I dreamt all night of the casino struggle.

The next morning, en route to visit my grandma, I shouted, "Pull over—I see a newspaper stand." The car decelerated and I bounded out. I inserted a few quarters and pulled out a newspaper. I walked back to the car, leafing through *USA Today*.

Inside the car, I held up the front page of the second section for my sister, with its giant picture of a "No Slots" sign held aloft during the Operation Transparency action. "Our first national press," I bellowed, flipping through the article.

"I can't see," my sister said, trying to read over my shoulder. "Read it aloud."

My voice cracked with excitement. "In Philadelphia, founded by Quakers whose religious beliefs prohibit gambling, slots casinos are facing a cold welcome from the neighbors." The reporter's arc echoed her shock when standing outside Jethro's house. Like everyone else, she had been told by SugarHouse that I-95 was a natural buffer between casinos and homes. But, plain as anything, she could see—jaw dropping at SugarHouse's blatant lie—homes on both sides of I-95.

Still, we hadn't persuaded her we could win. Telling the story of Operation Transparency, she concluded there was injustice but little to be done about it. She quoted Mayor John Street: "No one is forcing gaming on us. It's where the world is headed. Adapt or die."

The reporter gave us the final word. "The state's decision to bring gambling to Philadelphia 'was an imposition in every way, shape and form,' says Meredith Warner, an artist who lives in Fishtown and a founder of the new community group. 'It's unprecedented to take a city of this size and plunk down casinos in the middle of neighborhoods.'"

"It's fantastic for our first national coverage," I said, nearly shouting in the car. "Ed, Meredith, and Jethro were all quoted! It makes Mayor Street look like a tool."

My sister looked at me. "But you're not quoted."

"Yes! Other people are getting out there!"

My sister nodded appreciatively. All of us in the family cared deeply about justice, and I felt proud to be part of a family pleased with my trouble-making. Except my grandmother. When we arrived, she merely sniffed, "How about a game of bridge?"

For the rest of the day, we played card games and only sparsely talked about casinos.

As the sun set, I hurried to check email. I had dozens of emails from community members, as press began a frenzy over the December 20 licensing. I tackled it as best I could and left my hotel room to call Jethro.

"We need to figure out what's next," I told him, basking in the warm air of Florida in December. "People are getting terrified, and I've got lots of ideas and scenarios, but nothing that doesn't end up disastrously for us. My brain is fried."

"All my neighbors are asking me what's next," crackled Jethro on the other end of the line. "We need allies to step up. The ILA hasn't called me back, so I don't know if they're even going to put out a statement with strong language on how casinos will cost the city jobs."

"That probably means they're not going to do anything as bold as setting up a picket line. Without the ILA, we could probably organize a few dozen people at most—but not enough to totally shut down the hearing."

"Probably not," said Jethro, an edge to his voice. "If the ILA wants to change the rules of the game, they need to have their fingerprints on something soon. Don't worry, we'll find the right action!" Jethro brightened. "What about a sit-in?"

"For what purpose? To demonstrate we're angry? They know that. No, it needs to make sense to the outside observer and show us as powerful."

"We'll come up with something," he said.

We lapsed into silence. *If we do something poorly, it'll undermine our credibility for leading crisp, sharp, well-crafted actions.* I watched a bird fly by.

"I got it!" I spun on the spot where I stood. "Let's do nothing at all."

"*What?*"

I smiled, excited to have surprised Jethro. "Let's not wave signs and waste energy going to their stupid hearing just so they can ignore us. Let's ignore them. If we can't get the ILA or large numbers of people to do something meaningful, let's not go."

Jethro was silent.

I continued, persuading myself. "December 20 *isn't* the endpoint. It's a beginning. So don't show up *at the point of losing.*" I emphasized each word. "We want to be associated with winning, not bringing people on a two-hour trip to Harrisburg only to watch us lose."

Confident now, I remembered my coaching to well-meaning activists who scheduled their protests at the point of loss: anti-death-penalty activists holding vigils on the day of executions, anti-globalization protestors showing up outside international trade meetings, or gun-control activists marching only when someone got shot. In each case, they marked—even ritualized—the points of their loss.

"As a movement, I want us to mark our victories and minimize our losses. We won't let our opponents tell us when and where we go," I said.

Jethro caught it. "So we stay off their timeline and say, 'This was not the end.' But what do we tell people? They're going to be shocked."

"Give an alternative action," I said, grasping. "We hold a strategy retreat as soon as the licensing is over. They hit us, we have a counter-response—one that helps prepare people for future organizing." I paused, forming my words. "We tell them we're not going, because the PGCB has no credibility. Going to their anti-democratic, anti-transparent theatrics only adds to their credibility."

Jethro was sold. We planned to lay low on the day and instead get people signed up for a strategy retreat. We pulled out calendars. Avoiding the holiday season, we picked a date: January 6.

Satisfied, we got off the phone, and I rushed to send out news to Casino-Free Philadelphia's 112-person email list. I attached all the good news—the USA *Today* and other articles, plus the growing Pittsburgh paper's editorials and political calls to delay the licensing.

But I didn't want to fall into the trap of many activist groups and avoid talking about our losses—like groups who talk about getting thousands of signatures but don't admit those signatures had zero political impact. I wanted to be honest that, as near as I could tell, the PGCB wasn't going to respond and would go ahead and select two Philadelphia casino licenses.

I wrote as if coaching myself. "This moment—waiting and watching the licensing—can be a stressful one. We'll hear rumors, feel frustration, disappointment, so on. You know what stress does to yourself. So here's a word of advice: Take care of yourself. Be with the people you love—and go gentle on yourself."

"This is not the end..." I searched for a metaphor. Something to acknowledge the loss—and the chance to come back. *Boxing.* "It's just round one of a long struggle. But if we get back up again, it's not a knock-out." *If.*

"Whatever happens tomorrow, we'll be ready with a response. So join us on January 6 for our post-licensing strategy meeting to help prepare for round two."

I relaxed my shoulders and breathed in the warm air. That the ILA surprised us by doing something fit perfectly.

The day before the PGCB's licensing, over a hundred burly ILA members clustered around City Hall, sporting ILA jackets and heavy work clothes. They had asked us—the "action experts"—to set up their press conference and write and send their press release. We had done so, but once the action was underway, they had it.

Facing a sizable press audience, ILA's national vice president Jim Paylor spoke. His voice was steady and forceful, sounding like a working-class Captain Picard. "The PGCB licensing is being done without any comprehensive study of the impact on port jobs. I've had the benefit of working on the waterfront. It's not just longshoremen, we're a small part of loading and unloading cargo. There's Teamsters who store it, there are Teamsters who move it from the pier facilities to all those who use it. There are a lot of jobs related to the waterfront that most people don't understand or equate to the longshore industry, even accountants who work at shipping agencies. It's a lot of jobs along the waterfront that are being threatened."

Others from the ILA and management spoke on behalf of the $17-to-$35-per-hour jobs with union benefits. All jeopardized by current casino plans.

It was short. But now, in every major newspaper, the ILA would be on record as standing, in Boise Butler's words, "prepared to take the necessary steps to protect our livelihood"—whatever *necessary steps* meant.

Afterward, bearded Marc Stier came over to Jethro and me, congratulated us, and suggested a group of CFP's informal leaders grab lunch at Reading Terminal Market. We readily agreed and walked the few short blocks.

We plopped down at a wobbly metal table, a tinny piano barely discernible above the rushing customers. I tossed a huge pile of fries in the middle to share.

Marc Stier picked up a fry. A longtime activist, he was the first among a slew of activist progressives to declare his intentions to run for City Council. "The ILA is a good move, but we need to figure out how to win something."

Anne Dicker stopped, her fork halfway to her mouth. She let the salad drop back to the plate. "We're not big enough to directly take on Fumo or the governor—or anyone at the state level right now."

"The city is the lever we can move," said CFP co-founder Matt Ruben. Like Marc, Matt hoped to become a councilmember. "Council is playing dead, but we won local zoning so that the city can influence how these things are built. The mayor and DiCicco need to use it."

Hearing his councilmember's name, Ed Verral slammed his fist. "Yeah! He's just being a stuffed suit and sayin' he can't do anything!"

Marc slipped into professorial mode. "The city is used to playing dead, especially against the state. A few years ago, there was a movement to regulate predatory lending backed by Councilwoman Marian Tasco. However, when the state legislature usurped that power, the city couldn't enact it. But instead of fighting for their right, the city sat on their hands and claimed powerlessness." After a moment's pause, Marc added his campaign's tagline. "Just another example of our broken politics."

I soaked up the history.

Matt nodded fervently. "It's tough when so much of the state opposes Philadelphia in principle. The rest of Pennsylvania holds a huge grudge against the city—seeing it as a place that their taxes go to waste funding a broken school system or supporting a struggling mass transit system."

"The real problem," Marc's passion overtook him, "is actually our own politicians. When Philadelphia's public schools were partially taken out of city control and run from Harrisburg, only the efforts of Philadelphia Student Union and local teachers stopped it from being even worse. It was Mayor Street who tried to privatize it and give it away. Or on gun control, it was Senator Fumo and other Democratic representatives from Philadelphia that neutered the city. But they're never held responsible—and councilmembers just let them do it, quietly and without a fight."

I continued munching on my soy-turkey sandwich, realizing many of the assembled NABR and CFP leadership were transplants to the city—Jethro, Anne, and myself. It seemed longtime Philadelphians had to fight deeply internalized hopelessness to believe they could change the city.

"We should attach spines to Philly's elected officials," mused Jethro.

"Yeah," Marc chuckled.

Jethro and I locked eyes and smiled, as if in on an inside joke. We were serious, playing it out in our heads, the image of running around trying to attach cardboard spines to councilmembers.

"The only hope is with council," Matt said. "The mayor is completely against us. But council operates with tails between their legs, avoiding any touchy issues. Look at the issues they took up. Months debating bills opposing the Iraq war or endorsing a statewide bill for same-sex couples—spending time not on council business but taking positions on state or federal legislation."

Ed perked up. "What about getting Sylvester Stallone, a native Philadelphian, to support us? You know, Rocky fighting to help the little guy."

There was a momentary pause. "Do you have any relationship to him?" I asked. Ed shook his head. "Celebrities are hard to get to, and unless we have some reason to believe they'd be on our side, I find it tends not to be worth our time."

Ed started, "Of course Sylvester would be on our side—"

I tried not to show my impatience. "Every movement I ever worked with at some moment wonders if they can quickly get some celebrity to their side. Sure, *some* movements do. But unless people have some connection, it's a huge amount of time *not* developing people power but searching for some shortcut that's rarely worth our time."

Ed continued disagreeing, but Jethro cut him off. "We need to build a movement based on who we are. *We* need a different relationship to our politicians, not someone else to be our savior. That's the old way of working. The new way is *we* have a truly participatory democracy where our voices matter."

Ed nodded, letting the idea go. I marveled at Jethro's clarity of speech.

Picking up from where we had been, Anne said, "I asked some contacts in City Council about introducing a bill restricting the casino zoning to make it harder for a casino to get built. Nobody would introduce anything or even touch it. Even Frank DiCicco refused."

"They'll only introduce it if they are certain they can pass it," said Marc. "And at this point, nothing can get passed."

Looking around the table, I asked, "So what do you suggest?"

Nobody moved to answer.

Jethro sharpened the question. "How can we force City Council to do something against its will, especially when we know that the two councilmembers, Frank and Darrell, whose district may have two casinos, are publicly telling people to strike a deal and not fight?"

Another long pause.

Marc Stier's face lit up. "There is a rarely used provision in City Council where citizens can place a bill before council if they have some large number of signatures in support of it. It forces a change to the city charter. I can't recall it ever being used, but I remember reading it in the city's home rule charter." Of course Marc would have read the 300-page home rule charter. He struggled to remember details. "I think it puts a ballot question before the voters."

Our conversation grew animated. *"It'd be like a petition." "But with people signing for a purpose." "And we can frame the ballot question to be something positive." "Like restricting the casino zoning legislation." "Or maybe we could eliminate it altogether." "It's already positively framed: We were denied input, so we offer people a vote. What could be more democratic than that?"*

As we cleared our table, Marc and Anne agreed to do more research on how many signatures we'd need and exactly what the law was. But it was relieving to at least have some options and a goal that would force City Council to take up a vote on casinos. It could build energy and new volunteers. But to win, it would have to be much larger than our six-member lunch crew.

The morning of the PGCB's licensing, I flew to my computer. We would soon know if the PGCB would go ahead and, if so, which two Philly casinos they would pick. *Inquirer* reporter Jeff Shields live-blogged from the hearing. "10 A.M.: Mayor John Street is holding forth, less than 15 minutes before post time. He is definitely excited about the prospect of the casinos in his city, the nation's fifth largest. 'This is going to be good for us,' said the mayor. 'The whole world is going to be watching the Philadelphia experiment in gaming,' Street said."

I tried to concentrate on my other—paid—work, but couldn't. *Will the PGCB go ahead and select two sites? Will they be along the riverfront? Or will they target the mostly African American community of Nicetown?*

"10:09 A.M.: No meeting yet. Word is this is going to go pretty quickly. My prediction—decisions by 11:30."

Unable to work, I stood up to take a walk. Then leaned down and hit "Reload"... just in case.

"10:25 A.M.: Board members have yet to show, and folks are getting a little antsy. Antsy enough that people are starting to spread rumors. The hottest one so far: that Donald Trump had pulled up in a limo outside the Forum and was giving interviews. This is not the case."

I pulled myself outside into the crisp December air and chatted on my cell phone.

By the time I came back from my walk, the board had gathered, and Decker had announced he was recusing himself from the SugarHouse vote because "he is the prior chairman of the Philadelphia law firm of Cozen O'Connor, which did work for SugarHouse after he left the firm."

I waited and reloaded the page once more.

"And the first winner is..."

I held my breath. The PGCB was not going to delay.

The first blow came. "SugarHouse Casino: a $550 million project on North Delaware Ave. Project would include 3,000 slot machines."

My heart broke for Jethro. The SugarHouse site was a few hundred feet from his doorstep.

Two eternal minutes later: "And the other winner is... Foxwoods Casino Philadelphia, a $560 million project in South Philadelphia."

Ouch. South Philly neighbors kept insisting it was the worst site and assuming their traffic experts would dissuade the PGCB. They must be devastated.

Both were on the waterfront. Both near working-class, predominantly white, residential neighborhoods.

Minutes later, the reporter added, "Gaming Control Board chairman Tad Decker would not give any insight into why the board chose the applicants they did. He said the board—which fashions itself kind of like a court of judges—will be issuing a written opinion within a couple of weeks. He did say members deliberated for four hours yesterday before making up their mind—which some critics pointed out was record time for what should be a weighty matter."

I gathered myself and called Jethro. "I'm sorry, Jet." My voice was a whisper.

His response was crisp and sharp. "It's not gonna happen."

"Well, I'm sorry SugarHouse got picked."

"It's not gonna happen."

"You may be right. But I'm still sorry you have to fight it in your own neighborhood."

Jethro raised his voice. "I would fight it in anyone's backyard, wherever they placed these things. They picked the wrong places for these things, and they should not have tried to put them in my neighborhood. They're just not gonna happen."

I waited to see if Jethro would say more.

"That's all I got to say," he said. "I have to go talk with my neighbors." Click.

I was glad we didn't travel to watch the result in the cramped Harrisburg auditorium. The two-hour return trip would have been downright depressing.

Rather than go to Harrisburg, Meredith Warner had urged NABR to plan memorial services for the two sites, regardless of where they were. NABR's plan was to start at whichever site was the more northerly site and march down to the southward site—what we now knew would be a march from SugarHouse to Foxwoods.

I biked across town to the memorial service, where nearly a hundred people were holding a muted vigil. A few lonely, hand-painted signs—"Bad Choice" and "Wrong Sites"—were laid aimlessly. People quietly mingled on the sidewalk, frowning as if at a wake.

I felt right at home.

Behind a large table with bowls and spoons, Meredith whispered, "Cider? Soup?"

Words were hushed. Hands were warmed by the cider. Soup was sipped.

TV camera crews circled the mourners, occasionally grabbing someone who looked like they could express their combination of disappointment, rage, despair, and resignation in short talking points. I nudged Bob Sola toward a reporter.

Ed Goppelt from Hallwatch asked Bob, "What was your first thought when you learned today that SugarHouse received a license?"

Bob had bought a duplex six blocks away, attracted to the pancakes at Sulimay's and the grilled pork and indie bands at Johnny Brenda's. A hulking six-foot-three, he hesitated and looked into the camera before stammering, "I was... I was shocked. I didn't think SugarHouse would be the one. I only heard the news while driving home from my girlfriend, Maureen Duffy. She lives only six blocks from Foxwoods, in a house she bought from her grandmother."

Bob shuffled his feet, looking down. "My initial reaction was melancholy. A lot of things changed. I feel like there's no reason for me to stay here anymore. I want to go where the people who elected you look after you." He looked up. "When you're betrayed, you want to cut ties. I feel like my city betrayed me. What I was here for isn't there anymore."

I passed out the flyer for the January 6 strategy retreat. I could tell it meant something to people that someone was already thinking ahead.

In the center of it all was a grim-faced Jethro, moving quickly, connecting with almost everyone. A half-hour into the memorial, he grabbed a bullhorn. "This is outrageous," he shouted, shattering the hushed tone. Everyone turned to him. "This is not where I wanted to be tonight. But I couldn't be anywhere else!" Like a convex mirror, he reflected our feelings writ large. "Our elected officials should be here standing beside us in the cold. They believe this is over, that it's a done deal. It is not. This is not a time of mourning, it is a time for commitment to a greater struggle."

Jethro was projecting confidence into our fear and anxiety. It was the skill Stokely Carmichael most admired about Dr. King: not his oratory or strategy, but his fearlessness, and his ability to draw it out from others.

Refilling our cider, we half-chanted, half-meandered the dozen blocks to the proposed Foxwoods site for the continued mourning. It was the same gloom, with a dozen new people to share it with.

Despite Jethro's urging, I could also taste defeat. For that night, it was darkness. The deal was made: SugarHouse would build 5,000 slots parlors, and Foxwoods the same in South Philadelphia. It would all be completed by the end of next year. We had already lost.

CHAPTER 5
Strategy Retreat

JANUARY 6, 2007 – JANUARY 11, 2007

groups need safety to make tough decisions • empty chairs drain energy •
standing in solidarity makes a good introduction •
acknowledging small wins halts self-defeating strategies •
use small groups to build a container • organizers understand others' self-interest •
goals, targets, tactics • group "storming" to develop mission and ownership

THE MORNING OF OUR ALL-DAY STRATEGY RETREAT on January 6, Jethro and I took the elevator down from the Friends Center lobby, turned left, and slipped into the darkened Rufus Jones Room's expansive, triangular space. With the *South Philly Review* myopically trumpeting Foxwoods's "done deal" and the *Inquirer* saying we were "tilting at windmills," it felt like a race to get ahead of people's despair that the fight was over. Foxwoods was telling everyone it would start breaking ground by February, and SugarHouse was promising an equally swift start to building, meaning this seven-hour strategy retreat was perhaps our last chance to get anybody on board with us. As Jethro went to find the light switches, I paused, struck by ghosts of past meetings reminding me of the many ways our retreat could crash.

In this space four years before, I had attended a meeting to stop President Bush's plan to invade Iraq. It was right after February 15, 2003, the day I led chants from the back of a truck during a 10,000-person march through the streets of Philadelphia, joining with millions in the world's largest protest. Unfortunately for our motley group, the facilitators possessed no skills for working-group dynamics.

The facilitators started the meeting twenty minutes late, giving plenty of time for awkward social cliquishness and for those surrounded by empty seats to feel fully lonesome. The facilitators opened with a little politically isolating rhetoric and a sixty-person introduction, in which each said their name, organization, and whatever else they wanted to add. By the end of forty excruciating minutes, even I was bored with listening to the wide range of community, activist, and union protestors.

From there, it became barely managed chaos. After asking the group to brainstorm a list of possible actions, a facilitator steered the conversation toward a march and away from anything nontraditional. She cut off anyone who offered out-of-the-box ideas and blown past last-ditch amendments to add music or festive energy to the march.

To shore up support, she took a straw vote. That infuriated labor delegates who represented hundreds or thousands of workers but were being given the same voting power as unaffiliated individuals off the streets. In the heat of debate, a participant's *Simpsons* wristwatch alarm went off and spoken my feelings: "D'oh!" it had repeated, over and over. That was the high point.

The group rapidly split into arguing over process and content simultaneously. "We need a real structure," the process-frustrated labor delegates asserted. Others argued, "We need a more creative action." Brushing off all criticism, the facilitators retreated into bombastic unity language — "We can't attack each other, George Bush is the problem" — and forced a vote.

That was when I left. There was absolutely no hope. Instead of *facilitating*, the meeting leadership was going to browbeat people into a decision. No creativity could have emerged from the facilitators' complete ineptness in building group cohesion. Without safety to be creative and refine each other's ideas, the group had been left with an unoriginal, common-denominator action: a vanilla march, an unsurprising tenth the size as before.

At the group's next meeting, it had found itself a quarter that size, and so on, until the group had shrunk to nothingness and irrelevance. Weeks later, the bombing started in Iraq.

Jethro switched on the lights.

As I opened the full-length curtains, I knew we faced similar challenges: a relatively structureless organization, a diverse group, and potential social cliquishness. But that was not all. Our goal was not a mere single action, but an entire campaign, which would require greater buy-in and identification with the issue and the organization. Further, our political range included Democrats, Republicans, independents, and even political rivals and factions. And though people cared about the war, people directly impacted by casinos abutting their homes feared for their kids' safety and felt helpless. There was abundant raw emotion.

Ken Gregory joined us as we hung newsprint in the front, placed thirty chairs in a circle, and set up a table for snacks, registration, and donations in the back. I took a moment to sit in the front chair and anxiously review my notes, surprised that after years of facilitating strategy retreats, I was still nervous. Glancing around the room, I asked Ken to take a few chairs away.

"But we have RSVPs for twenty-five people," Ken said.

Fiddling with the coffee, Jethro looked up. "Daniel's worried few people will come, since it's a beautiful, seventy-five-degree day and we're competing with the Mummers Parade." A rain-delay had moved the peculiarly Philadelphia institution to today. While we met, South Philly would be overflowing with clubhouses performing in elaborate, outlandish costumes down Broad Street. "But I'm pretty sure we'll get twenty people."

"Even still, we should have fewer chairs then people," I said. "It's an organizer's trick. Empty chairs drain energy and make the group feel small. But if we *add* chairs during the meeting, it creates a feeling of momentum!"

Ken rearranged for fifteen chairs, as I sat in the front to chat with early comers. Eagerly sitting in the front row was Mike Seidenberg, who had traveled with me to the empty offices of the PGCB. And Philippe Duhamel, who had come down just for moral support. But most were people I didn't know and who didn't know each other—a random group of individuals drawn together only by a common opponent.

As ten o'clock neared, we were overwhelmed. We were validated in our choice to not send people to the licensing but to prepare for a counter-punch. Delighted and surprised, we added over *sixty* chairs.

A familiar wave of nervousness tugged at my stomach as the clock turned ten. "Welcome," I said slowly as chatter died down. "Welcome to this strategy retreat!"

I watched as every face turned toward me, each with their own worries and hopes. *Will this workshop really help? Is it worth taking off a whole day? Who else is here? What's the retreat going to be like?* The facilitator's seat can feel lonely, with a burden of responsibility like that of an organizer.

But even as I carried my own nervousness, my job was to project calm and confidence. After years of leading groups through tough meetings, it's something I did well, sitting upright and smiling warmly.

"Welcome, everyone!" I grinned and waited for a few hellos and welcomes from group. I sat even more upright. "This is a great group, with so many dedicated people, to be here at ten on a Saturday!" A couple of people entered the back, causing Ken to clamor to add more chairs. "See? Already we're a growing movement," I joked with a grin.

Moments earlier, I had ditched the idea of introductions. The group was too large— such a go-around would be deadly. Yet I wanted to address people's need to know who was in the room. Every group starts with that preoccupation, and I wanted to address it in a way that built safety in the room.

I quickly jumped into the activity. "Stand up if you are not a morning person." I stood, encouraging others who were the same to stand up, many with coffee cup in hand. "Okay, now we sit back down and someone else goes, saying something true about themselves."

Cautiously, people picked up the theme: "Stand up if you *are* a morning person." The other half of the group stood. "Stand up if you kinda want to be outside in the sun." With the first sprinkles of laughter, most of the group stood up, including myself.

I was not surprised that the group soon turned to the common issue at hand. "Stand up if you have lived in your home for more than twenty years." More than a quarter of the room stood. An elderly woman got up next: "Stand up if your family has lived in your home for more than two generations." A dozen people stood. A middle-aged man stood next: "Stand up if you have been terrified all through the holiday season about this." With resounding exhales, most people stood. For the next several minutes, people stood in literal solidarity with each other over a range of emotional states: fear, defeat, hopefulness, nervousness, excitement, and anger.

As they sat down, one person joked, "So I'm not alone!" As the group laughed, I saw tense shoulders relax. We were building some safety, some group cohesion in which people could take small risks of vulnerability and find they were not alone. There was more group safety to build, but we needed to begin diving into content—and that task was tricky.

One day earlier, I had refined the agenda with Training for Change colleague Nico Amador.

Sitting on a couch in my house, I handed Nico a copy of the agenda and whipped out a pencil. I was fretting over how to transition after introductions.

"First," I said, "there's no basis for trust or history. People are pissed about casinos, but there's no group container, no safety in the group. The group needs to build a container to hold the range of disagreements and viewpoints. Lacking that, I worry people will devolve into attacks on each other, instead of trying to find a common position. Second, few people know anything about activism. Most I've talked with are expressing a ton of despair, caught in the 'done deal' mentality. If people don't believe they can win, they'll create a strategy to match that self-fulfilling prophecy, tear down others' strategies—or worse, retract into the fully delusional belief that if we simply march in large enough numbers or organize a giant action, the entire political establishment will change its mind."

Nico allowed a thoughtful pause. His voice was quiet, as usual, with each word carefully chosen. "Have them share what brought them to the strategy session. That way they can acknowledge differences, but rooted in their shared goals. Make sure they're in small groups when they do this. People get intimidated in a whole group and they can't really meet a whole group. They meet individuals in it. So both the task and the process help strengthen the container."

"Yeah." I chewed my pencil. "But what about the despair?"

"I'm not sure. Maybe next you have Les Bernal talk about how they beat the casino industry?"

I gritted my teeth. "If I introduce him too early, people will generate a whole list of how Les's success in Massachusetts *can't* happen here—you know, our governor would never let that happen, or we're way more corrupt, or whatever."

Nico sat with me, holding the silence as we thought.

"I got it!" I leaned forward to scribble notes. "I get them brainstorming resources and successes they have already. No movement or person comes empty-handed. Let's name what we have to start with."

"Like people acknowledging the win to get local city zoning control?"

"Sure. But I mean the whole gamut of skills, resources, experiences—some people may have access to money, or relationships, or just plain stubbornness. Whatever resources people have, they name it. Focusing on resources you have counters hopelessness."

We reviewed the order: Get people in small groups to build new relationships, tasked with talking about what brought them to the retreat. Then, in new groups again, have people share successes and resources they are bringing to the room. Each step getting people to meet new people, building group confidence.

Nico nodded encouragingly. "Then they'll be in shape to learn strategy from Les."

"Exactly," I said.

*　　　*　　　*

The small groups' loud chatter still hung in the room at the strategy retreat when I introduced Les. People turned their seats back toward the center, some even showing reluctance to turn away from their cozy small groups.

Despite his stiff suit and tie and almost robotic walk up to the center, Les grabbed the group from the start. "The casino industry and your governor designed this to be sneaky. They used slight-of-hand tricks to pull the wool over people's eyes. They didn't say "Let's put casinos at these locations," they spoke generally—two in Philly, one in Pittsburgh, two somewhere roving in the state. They knew people would oppose it in specific places. That's why, by the way, they call themselves the PA "*Gaming*" Control Board. They know that slots parlors and gambling sound like vice and deception, so they call it 'gaming,' to make you think it's like a sporting event or games of skill. It's not. It's about taking money from people, many who can ill afford it."

He was intense and serious, making eye contact with each person. For a decade, Les Bernal had worked as chief of staff for a Massachusetts state senator. But when his state began exploring gambling, he became horrified by the casino industry's anti-democratic tricks—and the predatory industry itself.

"You are part of a national movement. What's happening in Philadelphia is not unique. It's happening in Ohio, Maine, Massachusetts—I'd say probably 75% of the states are battling this thing. This issue burns in my soul." He punctuated each sentence with a finger in the air. "It's not about putting casinos in rich communities. It's about putting them in poor communities, to get people hooked on the most addictive machines in the world."

Les danced through the list of allies they had assembled to halt the advance of casinos in Massachusetts. "First, you need to understand the restaurant industry is going to get hammered, especially those close to the casinos. If I can eat at a casino for five dollars less, I'm going to go to the casino—even if it means I might end up spending that five or even ten at the slots. We needed to get restaurants involved to win. But they aren't the only business. We got the Massachusetts Convenience Store Association, because they sell lottery tickets. If you sell lottery tickets, you'll get hit."

As a progressive Democrat, Les found himself in the unexpected position of allying with the conservative *Boston Business Journal*. They weren't against the industry preying on people, but instead viewed casinos as a mammoth competitor that would threaten local businesses, and not just entertainment facilities like movie theaters. They worried that, as was happening elsewhere, money lost to the casino would decrease the bottom line of everything from auto companies to furniture sales.

"Conservative anti-tax groups opposed it as a tax. Leftist groups opposed it because it's so regressive. Political leaders joined because no state had ever solved its budget problems with gambling."

I furiously tried to keep a list of notes as he continued: Children's rights groups, the religious community, and others opposed the increased divorce rates and suffering from the expected doubling of problem gambling. Homelessness groups came on board right out of the gate, because one of the biggest causes of homelessness is gambling addiction leading to bankruptcy. "In fact, it's one of the leading reasons people go bankrupt," he said. "Even the non-political Good Samaritans, a suicide prevention group, came on board as they came to see there's no question the likelihood of suicide increases with problem gambling."

His organizing chops were impressive. "Don't just target the people who work at these places, but the people who volunteer and donate to them."

"None of your casinos are on tribal land, unlike in Massachusetts. In our case, unrecognized tribes opposed casino expansion," he said.

The issue of Native Americans building casinos was a complex one. Gambling was a rare opportunity to bring money to reservations suffering from historical and ongoing theft by US policy. But casinos came at the expense of other poor people and often inflamed internal strife within Native communities, who fought bitterly over proceeds and management. It created wide wealth gaps between Native nations who brought casinos and those who did not. In our case, neither were on Native land, and only Foxwoods had any Native American ownership, a 30% investment from the Mashantucket Pequot Tribe, who owned the Foxwoods name.

"Because of their political weight and power, casinos practically—and in some cases, literally write their own zoning restrictions, bypassing any kind of environmental regulations and short-shrifting any environmental permitting processes. So that brought on environmentalist groups like the Sierra Club and Audubon Society."

My fingers could no longer keep up with the list. I had no idea casinos had such wide-ranging impacts.

"All of these people got involved because they understood their self-interest and the negative impact of casinos," said Les. "To organize, you must understand what motivates other people and help them understand how they'll be touched by this issue. In some cases, we have hard studies, but the casino industry funds a ton of research where they inevitably emerge by saying, 'There may be some problem, but it's inconclusive, we need more research.' Then they get funded some more."

Finishing his whirlwind tour de force, Les returned to the industry itself. "You need to understand, these are twenty-first century slot machines programmed by some of the best computer programmers in the world. They don't have real reels inside them—it's all virtual. But they've customized these machines to addict your brain with something called the near miss. Say you need three cherries to win. They'll show you two, making you feel like you almost won. What it does to the brain is release endorphins that make you feel excited and want to try again. In fact, some people are so addicted to the near-miss that they say when they win, they're actually disappointed. They even eliminated the pull lever because it takes too long. Slots machines are all about speed. That's why your governor wanted to start with slot machines. It's about getting people to give up money as quickly as possible—to take every last dollar, or what the industry calls 'playing to extinction.'"

As if wanting to cram his passion into the last minute of his speech, he tossed out statistics rapidly: "They've got 90% of the cash coming off of 10% of the players. Crime such as embezzlement, stealing, assaults, and domestic violence increases 10% right after a casino is built—and continues to increase over years." He headed toward his seat, stopping to add, "These are worth fighting, and I'll do whatever I can provide to help you fight and win."

The next activity presented challenges. "I want people to see different strategies for how winning is possible," I had told Nico during our prep session, curled up on my couch. "Most people coming have no experience with activism and seem to think writing letters to politicians, getting a famous person to endorse us, or doing a rally is a strategy. But they're just tactics, and none of them alone will win. I worry people will just come up with tactic after tactic, with no sensible, overarching strategy. But how do I help people with no experience strategize?"

"What about using the Midwest Academy Strategy Chart?"

A standard in the field of organizing, the Midwest Academy Strategy Chart has five columns, with elements building on each other. The classic chart contains the "Goals" column, ranging from long-term goals down to finite, short-term objectives. "Organizational Considerations" includes all your group's weaknesses and resources, such as people or money, and areas desired for organizational growth. The third column, "Constituents, Allies, and Opponents" is the range of players, interests, and power they have for or against you. Then "Targets," who are the specific decision-makers who can get you your goals. "Tactics" apply pressure on the target.

"Maybe." I glanced up in thought. "But it's complex. Using it requires a high learning curve—people need to understand the terms. How have you found using it in groups?"

Nico pulled at his chin. "It's good at laying out different elements of a campaign. For people new to activism, it's really helpful to get clear that you can't target every politician but need to pick a specific one to win over."

I glanced downwards, toward Nico. "But?"

"But the concepts are hard to get. People often think of *target* generically, like 'the casino industry' or 'politicians.' They don't understand that *target* means a specific person who can give you what you want, someone with a name, phone number, and address. I wish there was a more interactive way to introduce it."

I nodded and gazed back up at the ceiling. Most times, I saw people present the concepts and announce, "Now, go do it." That often left people arguing over definitions instead of strategy.

To teach targeting, I'd often tell the story of *Pineros y Campesinos Unidos del Noroeste*, a Northwest farmworkers union. They chose as their target Kraemer Farms, hoping to force them to be the first growers in the area to accept collective bargaining. But a year of organizing made no dent in Kraemer. So they escalated, with a secondary target of NORPAC, which purchased vegetables from Kraemer Farms. They got student groups to organize boycotts against NORPAC. But after seven years, the boycott hadn't won over NORPAC. So they decided to maneuver again, this time picking Gardenburger, which buys from NORPAC, which buys from Kraemer Farms. It's a *tertiary* target—several times removed. But with an explicitly socially conscious customer base, Gardenburger cracked within just a few months and agreed to discontinue using NORPAC unless Kraemer allowed collective bargaining rights. The activists had found the right target. NORPAC wanted Gardenburger's business and soon after accepted bargaining on *all* of NORPAC's member farms. A major win, fueled by finding the right target.

Nico added, "Maybe you just walk people through the chart. Even if they don't use it strictly, coupled with a few stories it could be good skill-building."

"Yes!" I snapped upright and unfurled my lanky arms, my eyes steady with Nico's. "But we use an abridged version with only three columns: Goals, Targets, and Tactics. That way I only introduce three concepts: a specific and achievable goal, which requires a specific target who can make that happen, and then they list tactics to win their target over." My words tumbled out. "To structure it further, we have people self-select into different groups based broadly on different ways to win: direct action, city politics, legal, etc. This way, people stay on the same page, in groups small enough to have needed discussion. And, brilliantly, we avoid fights between lawyers telling direct actionists they can't do that, and vice versa. Now we just need to figure out what small groups to have..."

Behind me, back at the strategy retreat, hung a list of lessons drawn from Les's presentation, next to other lists from earlier. The crowd had settled into a groove, happily moving between small-group and large-group work. Chairs at odd angles faced the front of the room, and some of the more proper people continued to sit in them formally while others lounged or straddled chairs. People were showing up as themselves in the room.

I unfurled newsprint with the names of each group—Legal Strategy, City Politics, State Politics, etc—introducing them one at a time. "Then there's the Direct Action group," I said, flipping the name so everyone could see it. "It will look at grassroots options, say, from full-scale blockades to small-scale tactics. I'll being bottom-lining that group—"

I started to unfurl the last group—which I considered the most controversial—when Ursula Reed interrupted. "What about federal politics, with senators and congressmen?"

"We can get to adding other groups just as soon as I finish the list," I said.

"Can I add something?" blurted Diane Berlin. I was still a little surprised—a *lot* surprised—that she had come. Her commitment to the movement was deeper than our poor relationship.

She went ahead and dived in. "The casino industry has studied the tobacco industry, so I think we need to challenge them at the federal level." She explained that the tobacco industry had spent billions in federal political support. For decades, it was able to scrub research on the negative effects of smoking. But it had taken a massive hit, with a major lawsuit and resulting regulation from the federal government.

The casino industry had taken that lesson to heart. It eschewed federal regulation and pitched casinos as a statewide issue. In fact, it framed each state as competing with the other. In Pennsylvania, industry leaders said the state was losing its money to New Jersey's Atlantic City and therefore should establish gambling—the same argument put forward in New York concerning Massachusetts, Massachusetts concerning Connecticut, and Delaware concerning Pennsylvania. On the rare occasion that a state outlawed or severely restricted casinos, the casinos simply moved to another state, continued to survive, and bided their time. "So we need a committee like Ursula says, to take on the federal level."

Some part of me wanted to challenge her that our tiny band—at this stage—had no chance to take on federal policy. But my job was to facilitate the group, separating my internal state from my role.

"Do you want to lead a National Strategy group?"

"Sure," she said.

"Okay, looks like national goes up!" I wasn't sold on the idea, but showing flexibility embodied good group dynamics. "Unlike our government, we are responsive to the people," I joked as I wrote it up. "And, finally, the last group is Negotiation with the Casinos."

I paused, expecting a noticeable inhale from the group. I was not disappointed.

"I want to acknowledge there can be trepidation around negotiation, because it gets us into a tough dance," I explained. "On the one hand, it can be the sell-out dance, but on the other hand, it can be the dance of success. Jethro will be bottom-lining that group."

Paul Boni raised his hand. He was a civic lawyer who had been shocked when Foxwoods was selected despite his community's meticulous research on the traffic congestion that would be caused by a casino. He had played roles in many community-developer negotiations and worried, like many, this would merely lead to compromise, not deterrence. Speaking before I could call on him, he called out, "How can negotiation be a dance of success?"

Jethro fielded the answer. "Unfortunately in Philadelphia, to this point negotiation is seen as a fallback position. If we aren't successful, the negotiation will be there just in case. In Boston, we saved Fenway Park by using negotiation as a powerful tool to bring up important issues that aren't currently included. By including root-cause issues, you can create an environment where negotiation fuels opposition."

Irv Ackelsberg, who had overseen CFP's first legal challenge to the gambling law's constitutionality, explained that his Nicetown civic group had negotiated with TrumpStreet casino, while still opposing it. "The deal-breaker was our demand for the casino to issue quarterly monthly statements—saying how much each customer spent in the four zip codes around the casinos. In writing, they agreed. But TrumpStreet got so much crap from the industry that they reneged on that agreement. That issue helped us explain the danger of their product. *Why oppose monthly statements?* It helped fuel opposition."

I turned back to Paul. "Does that answer your question?"

Paul nodded slowly, with much consideration.

I started to move to the next piece, when Norma Van Dyke spoke up. "I was wondering if we should add media to the list."

As a facilitator, I wanted to be responsive, but I also wanted to uphold rigor. "No, because media is a tool. Each of these small groups are for different strategies to win, with different targets. Any of the small groups may use media as a tool to influence our targets. But, on its own, winning over media doesn't give us what we want."

With that, people moved to join the various groups: Legal Strategy went with Irv Ackelsberg in the far corner, City Politics with Anne. Jesse Brown headed up State Politics, Jethro Negotiation with the Casinos, and I the Direct Action group. Diane headed up the two-person National Strategy group.

Groups worked furiously into lunchtime, when we broke to eat locally donated pizza Ken had ordered. During lunch, for the the second time, an elderly man approached, urging Jethro and me to let him speak...

During lunch, a good quarter of the room went out to experience the sunshine. I was worried we might lose many of them, but as we regathered from lunch, even more people came into the room. They returned to a large-screen viewing of Ed Goppelt's video of the Operation Transparency arrests and an ovation for the "Philly Phourteen," who would face trial in a month.

"Keep cheering!" I shouted to the crowd. Anything to keep energy up after the notorious post-lunch lull. With ease, they did.

Flipping a pen in his hand, Jethro stood to introduce the next speaker. "What worked about Operation Transparency was we were delegitimizing the process, and groups called for a delay. It's still illegitimate, and the licenses are meaningless if we believe we live in a democracy. Hopefully, the next speaker will help encourage us to believe we can win."

In truth, Jethro had no idea what the man, carefully lowering his frail frame into a chair in the front, would say. But Jethro trusted his instincts—and the recommendation of allies living in Society Hill, who called him an elder who commanded respect.

Despite being hunched over, the man's tall frame and forceful voice made him towering. "My name is Stanhope Brown, and I've also fought and won a 'done deal,'" he began. With this promising start, he launched into his story.

Like the casino issue, when the 1965 design of Center City was unveiled to the public, it was considered final. Powerful allies approved the plan, including revered planner Ed Bacon and the trucking, car, highway construction, and cement lobbies—even though it drove interstate 95 like a wedge through neighborhoods, splitting neighbors and historic Independence Hall from the river, except by narrow tunnels.

"It was a done deal," Stanhope twinkled, with an old-school red-dotted tie, suit, and flood-water pants. "That's what everyone thought."

Unhappy with the plan, lawyers, architects, young professionals, and civic groups came up with an alternative: putting I-95 underground and covering it, so traffic could flow across it unimpeded. The group massed a huge public-relations fight, even enlisting the help of the publisher of the *Philadelphia Inquirer*. More than ninety respected local groups signed a list endorsing the campaign, including historical societies, preservation groups, and nearby civic associations—plus sixty-five national groups from twenty-three states.

"This impressive organizational and individual constituency was our strongest weapon," Stanhope said, "apart from the rightness of the cause. It quickly gave us respectability and, as it grew, political muscle. The result was the 'done deal' was struck down." The city, state, and federal governments agreed to depress and cover the highway for three and one-half blocks.

With a sharp pain, I realized *that* deal left neighborhoods like Jethro's to be divided by I-95, allowing the more wealthy and historic neighborhoods of Society Hill to remain unblemished.

Stanhope re-emphasized his major theme, suggesting we circulate a list of impressive organizations and individuals opposed to the Foxwoods and SugarHouse plans. "A list is the way to win," he insisted.

As he stepped down, I doubted few prominent leaders like the pro-casino *Inquirer* publisher would come out in our favor. We had an engaged, well-financed, and politically connected adversary. But I easily joined the generous applause he received. His story was the gift of hope for fighting a 'done deal'—and for months we'd hear of how his testimony, later written up, helped move people to believe our fight *really* was winnable.

Report-backs from the City, State, Federal, Legal, Negotiation and Direct Action groups took up the next hour. It was potentially mind-numbing, so I tried my best to keep energy focused and high: standing while facilitating, speaking loudly, getting the group to roar with applause after each report, and encouraging befitting brevity.

Irv briskly jumped up to go first, boiling the legal strategy down to fighting "zoning issues, challenging their licenses directly, challenging the PGCB's entire process, or trying to get Act 71 overturned." He explained, "While we believe our lawsuits should hold up in an honest court, all legal challenges have been fast-tracked directly to the Pennsylvania Supreme Court. This deal is wired, so while we remain hopeful, we caution that in the end, the legal strategy may merely delay but not prevent."

In contrast, Meredith Warner's report on behalf of the direct action committee reflected a wandering direction, unable to focus clearly on any single target. She dutifully reported the range of tactics: site occupations, setting up "police stations" outside the proposed casino sites to model increased crime, kicking City Council out for their passivity, and using street blockades to mimic what adding 60,000 cars daily to a neighborhood would do.

Even the direct action group, however, was sharper than both the state group— blandly generating plans to "repeal Act 71 or get the PGCB to not issue permanent permits"—and the national group, with its untamed brainstorm of ideas tossed liberally throughout every column, including recruiting the Department of Homeland Security to intervene, stretching the Clean Water Act to somehow obstruct waterfront development, and twisting obscure consumer-protection laws to limit casino development.

"Keep your eyes out for ideas that excite you," I said encouragingly, "since soon we'll create working groups to bring them to life." Whatever my feelings about each proposal, my job was to float above and be an encourager and motivator whenever people were bringing their best thinking.

The report from the negotiation committee woke up the group. Silver-tongued Matt Ruben contrasted dramatically with Matt Pappajohn's matter-of-fact style, as together they laid out a confused chart but a clear goal: bringing those North and South on the riverfront into a unified negotiation force. Like Jethro, they urged leveraging the power of active negotiation as an offensive tool—or at least not getting caught without a strategy while others negotiated behind everyone else's back.

Even to them, the task seemed daunting. Those in the North already felt the sting of South Philly's arrogance—calling Foxwoods "the worst site"—while many in the South, like Queen Village, scrambled to create an anti-casino committee to respond to Foxwoods's unexpected selection. It made for fractured, untrusting communities—but the negotiation committee felt it had to be tried.

As if waiting to be the culmination, Anne Dicker taped up two pages of newsprint filled with ideas from her city group. Staring at the ideas, she admitted most were far-fetched, from giving the city the backbone they needed to deny building permits, creating restrictive zoning ordinances like those Irv suggested, and pressuring the city's waterfront planning process PennPraxis to create a "no-casino" plan of development. Casting aside the other ideas, she dawdled on her favorite: forcing casinos out of neighborhoods with a change to the city's charter, as discussed in the Reading Terminal meeting. "If we get some number of signatures, we can force a bill onto City Council's desks. If it's worded right, they'll have to say yes, and we get a ballot question on the next election to change the way the city zones casinos—to stop or slow down the casinos. I already have a lawyer working on some possible language."

I no longer needed to get people to cheer. They did so with enthusiasm, and some jumped in with questions. As I had hoped, the group was forming a culture of spirited exchanges and was growing less reliant on me. I didn't need to call hands as much or elicit people to speak. The group was pitching in.

Still, since we had been in a large group for the past hour, I knew some people needed to exhale in small groups. Too much small groups, no group cohesion. Too much large groups, group exhaustion!

I put them into small groups to identify what approaches attracted them and to suggest working groups to explore that. "For example, Anne clearly wants a Charter Change working group," I said. "What shall be other working groups?"

The groups buzzed and hummed, but they looked... off... something about their energy wasn't right.

After a few minutes I gathered them back, marker in hand to make a list of working groups. No suggestions came. I prodded, getting four working groups listed before the group moved back into cold silence.

I waited. "What else is out there?"

Silence.

"I went to a Quaker college." I smiled widely. "I'm okay with silence and can hold it for a lot longer than you."

That took a hair-splitting moment to land, before the group released a cacophony of questions. One gentleman threw his voice above the fray: "We could work on these working groups, but what are we working for?" It was an accusation as much as a question. "Who are we?" shouted one woman. From another direction: "Are we Casino-Free Philadelphia?"

Something had snapped. Questions were thrown out too fast to answer. "Are we just a group of people?" "Do we all have to agree to be on a working group?"

Only my fingers clenching showed my tension, as I consciously told my body posture to stay open, beaming whatever confidence I felt.

Slowly, I reiterated my opening comments: "There are a lot of different organizations with different emphases, visions, and hopes. Our goal at this moment is not to make agreements between these organizations. We're not making agreements for any groups. But this is a Casino-Free Philadelphia event, and if you want to be part of us, then you can be. Working groups can help lay out strategy for our organization, and anybody can be a member."

The panic remained: "Does that mean if I join a working group I am automatically a member of Casino-Free Philadelphia?" "Am I a member already?" "Do I have to be anti-casino to join?"

People exchanged anxious looks. Jethro leaned forward, saying, "If you want to be Casino-Free Philadelphia, then you are. We empower you. This is a movement organization, and if you want to be part of it, then you are."

"What does that mean, to be casino-free? No casinos in neighborhoods?"

"No," shouted someone from the other side of the room, "it means a Philadelphia that's got no casinos."

A gritty voice replied, "But I came here to just stop Foxwoods!"

"I like casinos," shouted another.

Jethro tried again to explain the concept of movement membership. But even as he tried, I could tell it wouldn't stick. This wasn't mere institutional confusion. It was deeper.

The cross-talking and anxious faces continued.

I took a breath and asked myself a question one teacher suggested to me for tough moments: "What's *right* in this moment?" Suddenly I found myself falling away from the conflict and relaxed into my body. My fingers unclenched and I smiled widely. I whispered to Jethro, "Just be quiet. Let this be. This is healthy." He went quiet, but stared at me like I may have lost my mind.

I stopped weighing in as the group escalated, only encouraging people to speak directly to each other. It seemed an eternal couple of minutes as the group battled back and forth, mostly over *no casinos* versus *not Foxwoods* versus *no casinos in neighborhoods*, with only occasional forays back into *Are we Casino-Free Philadelphia or just a group of people, should we be a new organization...*

The group hadn't yet made a leap forward, and I noticed a few faces beginning to look worried, perhaps wondering what this hands-off facilitator was doing. I refused to weigh in on the content, only framing the process. "Right now, the group is raising the questions: *What's our goal?* and *Who are we?* These are important questions." The safety would help the group to find its own answers. Or so I hoped and prayed.

More frustrated, unhinged voices tried to sort through the questions and problems. Then Chuck Valentine stood up.

Little did I know that Chuck was an old-school Fishtown community organizer. But his presence was deafening. His voice matched. "All y'all are angry that they're forcing a casino in your neighborhood without your consent, right?"

He looked around as people gave cautious murmurs of assent.

"So you'd be against casinos in our neighborhoods, right?" The group hushed as heads nodded.

Chuck whirled around to face the group. "You wouldn't want to do what Rendell and Fumo did to us and force a casino down someone else's throat, right? Then we can't support casinos in any neighborhoods!"

The crowd was with him, following both his logic and his voice filled with conviction.

"And Philadelphia is a city of neighborhoods. There isn't anywhere in this city that isn't a neighborhood. So unless they make a bigger Philadelphia, we have to be against casinos anywhere in Philadelphia." He met people's eyes. "Right?"

"Right!" The crowd exploded into applause. "Yes!"

The applause broke the tension, and it seemed the storm was over. I looked around the room and the suddenly bright, relaxed faces. "Is there something else to say on this point?"

"He said it all," someone shouted. I waited a few more heartbeats.

Slowly, cautiously, I stood up and framed what had just happened. "It seems as though this group has made a meaningful decision. Casino-Free Philadelphia will stand behind the mission of no casinos in neighborhoods, ultimately seeing that means no casinos anywhere in this city. That is our goal. That is our mission. Is that right?"

Nods from all over the room.

We had just made it through a storm with its characteristics of thunder, lightning, rain, and the quiet and calm after—what those in group development call moving through a stage of chaos. I thought about explaining the concept, of how groups occasionally throw themselves into questions of mission and goals to develop more closeness. In that stage, wise facilitators let the group work itself out, beaming love and support but not weighing in on the content of the fight. But I decided there was no point.

The conflicts had always been present: *Am I signing up to help stop SugarHouse, too, or just Foxwoods? Do I have to believe that casinos are evil, or can I just oppose them in neighborhoods?* With enough safety, the group could have an honest conflict, finding that one could even be pro-casino in this organization, if you were willing to back the shared mission.

"*No casinos in neighborhoods, none in Philly.* Is that right?" I echoed again, teasing them to repeat it back.

"That's right!" they shouted back.

We were past the storm, and suddenly, with great ease, the group sailed into the last chunk of the day.

I breathed deep and let my shoulders sag as people quickly scattered around the room into working groups. I was exhausted from the day's facilitation, and it felt good to just watch people closely huddle in intensive strategy conversations.

In one corner, the legal working group discussed possible lawsuits. It was a surprise to Paul Boni and some of the other lawyers, who were more schooled in lawyer's veneration of secrecy than transparent movement culture.

Many people were being inducted into that culture. Huu Ngo found himself surprised that other members were happy to support him leading their research and education working group, clustered over in the darkest corner. He was young and new to activism, breathtakingly raising every possible angle and question: *Who are these investors, and why did they get involved? How is the financing structured? How do they connect to the political players? Has any community ever opposed these casinos in the past? Anyone ever won?*

They set out to gather endorsement letters, à la Stanhope's suggestion, and assemble fact sheets, detailing the implications of gambling and bankruptcy, crime, political corruption, senior citizens, suicide, poverty, tourism, education, regulation, local businesses, and families. Even as I knew it was too much to take on at once, they were stepping into the empowerment of movement organizations—or as I later told Huu, "A good movement organization is one in which it's easy to step into leadership, and harder to get out."

South Philly resident Shirley Cook joined the massive charter-change working group, thinking she could help with the part she knew: logistics. A recent project manager, Shirley was more comfortable with charts and lines of authority then activist culture. Like many, she was moved by Anne's passion and confidence to seek a way forward that gave people a democratic vote on casinos.

And then, awkwardly sitting around the stairs, I watched Chris Meck take notes for the negotiations committee. Filled with longtime civic leaders, it sanitized its name to "political engagement" working group, and members boosted each other to carry out an ambitious goal. To neutralize groups who would sell out from fear, they hatched a plan that was a Philly first: promote a *non*-negotiation policy as a way to build power and unity. Up and down the riverfront, they would gather civics under a banner for an "immediate and absolute moratorium on negotiations with casinos" to give them time to unify and hold back the city from making political deals. It was a formidable task, and little did we know how influential they would become.

Even veterans like Meredith Warner were moved. She was sensitive to the tension of organizers determining strategy versus facilitating it. She had cautioned Jethro and me of not again "importing" strategies like Operation Transparency into an unprepared group, instead of skilling up members with self-education. The latter was, she felt, a step toward bottom-up strategizing.

Gathering people back from report-backs felt like soaring off a cliff. There was little to do but enjoy the scenery as people offered brilliant strategizing, stepped into leadership, and supported each other to move powerfully.

Far from that anti-war meeting where we only emerged with a rally, we had options— but more importantly, we had a more committed base, with trust and longer-term commitment. I closed with a few final words and released people on time to the warm weather. In a hopeful sign, a large contingent stayed for more than an hour to continue socializing and planning.

When I finally shut off the lights, I couldn't wait to tell Nico how well it had gone.

CHAPTER 6

No Way Without Our Say

JANUARY 12, 2007—FEBRUARY 16, 2007

*spotting leadership potential in a lawyer • worthy goals entail risk •
the action is the message • when campaign mistakes happen •
an organizer makes certain everything is in place • listening to find out people's values •
pacing/leading • working backwards to set goals • petitioning as art form •
using blank awards to honor each other*

I PUT MY FORK DOWN and stared across the table at Anne in her dignified black suit. "*How* many signatures?"

If she noticed my surprise, she ignored it. "First, we need signatures on a formal petition. That forces City Council to vote on the bill. When they do, that puts a ballot question on the May 15 election that would be a binding change to the city charter. In our case, the wording would be something to keep casinos out of neighborhoods. We think that takes 88,000 signatures."

"*In a month?*"

"Yeah. We can totally do this! My lawyer is working on details."

My words came slowly. "We need that many signatures by February 14?"

"At the latest. Council needs time to vote and maybe override a mayor's veto. But I doubt he'll veto, cause if we get that many signatures—"

"But... how will we get that many?"

Anne smiled. She always smiled. In the face of overwhelming odds, she poured out positivity in unmovable, hypnotizing, bold pronouncements. It's how she became the youngest executive in the history of Spencer's Gifts, before leaving it to fight for her progressive values in one long-shot campaign after another. It's how she *nearly* won a total upset for state representative despite being vastly outspent. Her boldness caught people's fancy, building a vast army of volunteer door-knockers.

She put her fork down. "The Recall Rizzo campaign was successful in getting over 200,000 signatures to try to stop Mayor Rizzo's second term. If we get enough people, we can do it. It's really doable. When I gathered signatures with Philly for Change for the

Howard Dean campaign, a handful of us gathered over 4,000 signatures in one day, just by standing in Rittenhouse Square. It's *completely* doable!"

I respected her vision. But she wasn't helping me see how it would be done. I backed up. "It's great you're taking on leadership, and you've got more petition-gathering experience than any of us, and I know Jethro totally trusts you. I'm just trying to figure out the plan."

"We've got it covered. We're meeting with civic groups to get access to their legions of block captains. We're talking to press. I think *Philadelphia Weekly* is gonna do a cover story on us. And mayoral candidate Tom Knox is gonna donate $2,500 to us. People are fired up!"

"I love the energy, I really do... I guess..." I paused. The result from the strategy retreat's working groups had been uneven. The research group was spinning with questions, the direct action group meandering from idea to idea, and the political engagement working group was turning itself into a real North-South alliance. "Your efforts are the most direct, ready-to-roll strategy to stand in the way of casino development, but to plug people in I need to know the plan."

"We're getting it all together right now, don't worry. Our last meeting was great! Cold, but thankfully Ikea's coffeeshop has decent, cheap coffee."

After a search, Anne had found politically neutral turf, a challenge in strained South Philly politics. And from everything I heard, her meetings had been inspiring. And Jethro's completely hands-off treatment convinced me of his trust in the effort. "I can't make it to the next one," I said. "But let me know what happens."

"Sure. And Mike Seidenberg found the name for our campaign to give voters a say," she flashed a smile. "*No Way Without Our Say.*"

Because I was unable to attend the meetings, Shirley kept me informed on No Way Without Our Say's growth. Her emails were long and detailed, with crisp updates on outreach, methodical tracking on google documents of groups volunteers have contacted, and concerns about the lack of final language to the proposed bill.

Paul Boni was among the lawyers drafting the language. Frustrated by cross-talk and fragmented conversation, he herded folks—minus Jethro—onto a 3:10 P.M. conference call.

"I hope it's okay I pushed us to have this phone call—I didn't know if it's my place," he said. "But we have a draft piece of legislation that needs some work. I guess, Anne, you lead this call?"

"Sure," Anne said. "We've got great news. Apparently we only need 20,000 signatures!"

"Thank goodness!" I blurted.

"But we're still gonna set our goal at 40,000, for safe measure," she said.

"Can't we just say 20,000 and minimize expectations, just in case?" I asked.

"It'll be inspiring!" she shouted, then softened. "What should we talk about first?"

Paul burst, dripping with energy. "I know my comments are last-minute, so feel free to use or not. But we should have the petition say the city is prohibited from giving zoning to Foxwoods or SugarHouse sites. Then add a stipulation that any *other* location must have five hearings in the affected community and provide the community group with $500,000 to do studies on traffic and environment."

"You mean... we put up roadblocks," I said.

"Yeah!" Paul sounded like a kid in a candy store.

"It's a good idea," I said slowly, not wanting to deflate his energy, "and maybe later we can use it. But we can't get sidetracked. Right now, we've got a draft excluding casinos within 1,000 feet of people's homes. It's simple and straightforward."

"I think you're misunderstanding him," said Mike. "Paul's proposing an addition. You see, what's he saying is—"

Irv interrupted. "Paul's proposal could be legally feasible, if tweaked. We cannot target SugarHouse or Foxwoods directly. That's 'spot zoning' and will certainly be struck down by the courts. The trick is, we have to target the casinos on principle, not site. Nor can we exclude them from the city entirely. That'd be trumped by state law, which requires the city accept casinos. The current draft is strong, and will get legal entanglements on its own without adding more complexity. I agree with Daniel that it's not wise to do too much with one charter change."

I braced myself. From my experience with lawyers, this was when a long, drawn out argument would ensue. Trained to argue and compete, lawyers rarely back down. In the last campaign I had run, lawyers had spent an hour trying to micromanage my organizing of a rally with word-smithing signs and a speakers list, until I all but ordered them to butt out. I loved Paul's style of throwing the kitchen sink at the casinos but feared we'd spend hours bogged down, arguing over each idea.

"Too complex—got it," said Paul. "I withdraw the motion."

A brief, relieved silence ensued.

"I have a few more ideas," Paul said. I grinned. "We should include language that voids any previous laws, in case the city sneaks through a contrary law before ours is passed."

"Absolutely," Irv said, as the lawyers drifted through word-selection minutiae.

I allowed myself to zone out. Amazingly, they were keeping to their field of law, not trying to control messaging, implementation, or organizing. I knew Irv was that rare breed of lawyers willing to defer to grassroots organizers. Paul might be that, too.

As the call continued, I jotted a quick email to Paul, wondering if he could fit our gaping hole left by Irv's imminent departure to run for City Council. "You've got a great organizing spirit. Jet and I would love to sit down with you and just talk more about what that would mean. Interested? When can we do that?"

For the next half-hour, the lawyers ripped out extraneous language and argued technicalities. *Does the buffer apply to Institutional Development Districts—or just residentially zoned districts?*

By the end, the language was tightened to everyone's satisfaction. The charter change would place a ballot question on the May 15 election. Voters could create a buffer zone to exclude casinos within 1,000 feet of homes, places of worship, parks, schools, or playgrounds. It would stop Foxwoods and SugarHouse but leave places in the city for a casino, away from neighborhoods.

Still, far before it would get onto a ballot, we needed signatures. A lot of them.

*　　　*　　　*

Twelve days after the strategy retreat, Shirley emailed me. "The charter change working group is ready to launch the campaign. You should get a final PDF in a few minutes, as soon as I figure out how to save a PDF on my computer." Her email was filled with logistical details: "Each signature needs registered Philadelphia voters signing their name, address, occupation; each page must be double-sided in black ink; make sure to get it notarized!" But it was devoid of the bigger question weighing on my mind.

I called Jethro. "40,000 signatures? Are we seriously going to do this? That's over 1,000 signatures a day—for a group that only pulled out eighty people for Operation Transparency!"

"Are folks ready to launch this publicly?" Jethro asked.

"I thought you knew..." I halted. "Haven't you been talking to folks about making this happen?"

Jethro didn't respond.

"Marc is right that it's a huge problem that nobody has been told about this," I said. "We need to get the word out."

Jethro stayed silent.

"Look, Jethro. You're not being clear at all. First you say you need to spend more time supporting Casino-Free Philadelphia, then you go silent to help out at NABR. Maybe it's true you've been telling allies you think the No Way Without Our Say campaign isn't the best idea. Are you behind it or not?"

"I'm just not sure if it's a good idea." Jethro sighed loudly. "Maybe we bit off more than we can chew, between our trial on Monday for Operation Transparency, a Fishtown neighborhood meeting tonight, and a CFP meeting later this week. We need to take a deep breath and get the decision-making structure and leadership in place. I never was certain if this were the right strategy, but you seemed so certain."

"*Wait. What?*" I almost spat the words. "You were the one giving Anne the green light to go ahead."

"*Me?*" His voice soured. "I thought you were in touch with Anne. You seemed to know what's going on!"

"I only know because Shirley is talking to me. You and Anne founded CFP together, and I figured she was giving you the details."

"Anne's a strong, visionary leader," he said. "But she hasn't pulled me in to take on leadership. CFP has no clear structure..." He drifted off. "It's not fair to ask you or me to staff up something without a better structure and some funds to support us. Let's not be martyrs."

"Then build that team. Let's create an executive team of CFP leadership. But I need to know if you really support the charter change, because..." A thousand ways to complete the sentence fought for attention—*because you got me wrapped up in this mess, so you can't abandon me; because we are the faces of Casino-Free Philly, for better or worse; because I respect your opinion on if this is feasible.* "Because if we do this, we have to clear our plates and focus. But we haven't committed to it yet. We can still say no."

Jethro didn't say anything, deliberative gears clicking into place.

Part of me hoped Jethro would say it was impossible. The numbers and timeline were astounding. While the framing of the campaign was sharp, our public failure to reach that many signatures would absolutely confirm the "done deal" storyline and permanently cement our ineffectiveness. It might be impossible to bounce back after that.

Yet, any good campaign carries risk. Fear often holds people back from setting goals that require growth and increased capacity. Or they never set goals, and just organize another one-time event, refusing to step into the boldness of campaigning. We needed boldness to win, because unless we grew, we *would* be swept away by the tide of political inevitability.

I reached my own conclusion as Jethro's voice clicked into reassuring certainty. "Let's do it." His voice was solid. "I'll talk with Anne to help us get on the same page. If we do this and win, we make it very hard to build at those locations. Once the casino locations are up in the air, the 'done deal' mentality is over. Then we have time to set up a citizens' committee to elicit people's opinions about if and where casinos should be built."

I almost told him he was getting ahead of himself, but that was Jethro. "Let's do it!"

I got off the phone and waited for the PDF from Shirley.

The day after Jethro and I agreed, Bruce Schimmel sent us a preview of his article to be published that Thursday. Anne was ahead of the curve, getting Bruce to beat every other reporter in announcing our campaign—even beating us!

> *What have people from Pawtucket, Rhode Island, done that Philadelphians can't? Hint: It's a simple civil right that's also been permitted to voters in Alabama, Arizona, California, Illinois, Kansas, Louisiana, Maine, Michigan, Mississippi, New Jersey, North Dakota, Ohio, Oklahoma and Wisconsin. These states, and others, have let their citizens have their say on gaming. Through a formal, often binding referendum, ordinary people in all of these places got a chance tell their government directly what they want—and don't want.*
>
> *Wow, imagine a public referendum on casinos in Philadelphia. Such the revolutionary idea.*
>
> *Of course, I shouldn't despair over Philly's dearth of democracy. After all, we've got all kinds of nifty rights for all kinds of folks—such as pay to play, zoning by extortion and the ever-popular voting from the grave.*
>
> *But if I might dial down the cynicism for a moment, let me ask you to imagine the pleasure of walking into a voting booth, pulling a lever and having your say on casinos. Even having your way. It can happen, and I think it will.*

He encouraged "media, unions, civic associations, MoveOn, ACT UP and any group dedicated to democracy" to give their mailing lists to the cause. "Because," he wrote in his final line, "the citizens of Philadelphia deserve at least as much as the people of Pawtucket."

The No Way Without Our Say petition drive was officially launched. We sent out an email to get ahead of the article's printing in the *City Paper*.

*   *   *

Days later, the trip to Harrisburg for the Philly Phourteen's trial for our document search felt like a complete distraction. My mind drifted to the reports in my email inbox: Ken Gregory leaving petitions at seventy bars on South Street, Shirley challenging herself to join Kathy DeAngelis to gather signatures at the mall, Anne activating Queen Village Neighbors Association's recently formed casino committee, and stalwart Mary Stumpf collecting the first 100 signatures by hitting the pavement every day.

Operation Transparency felt an eternity ago, even though its pressure resulted in the PGCB releasing 95% of the documents we wanted. Even reporters found the documents laughable: one-paragraph statements saying casinos would have zero impact on crime, *reduce* traffic jams, and have a positive social impact with no downsides.

I wanted to be in Philly recruiting, not arriving at the unassuming brick courthouse in Harrisburg. But since I was here, I tried to make the most of it. I recruited a handful of reporters from Pittsburgh and Harrisburg newspapers who had covered Operation Transparency. Whatever the outcome, I prepared to connect the judge's decision to our petition drive.

We poured into the tiny, cramped courtroom—except Bruce, who had gotten an excused absence to teach ethics to journalists. Karin and Michelle performed hairpin turns to squeeze their wheelchairs into the narrow aisles. I contorted my body into a chair next to Marj Rosenblum, my long legs banging against the seat in front of me.

When the bailiff announced the judge, all whispers in the courtroom stopped. My heart leapt into my throat. Our randomly selected judge, District Judge Joseph Solomon, dispensed with pleasantries and encouraged the prosecution to begin.

A colleague had warned me the judge was especially hostile to protestors. Not a good start.

A frowning, plain-faced PGCB supervisor testified we had created a loud disturbance. "Two young white males were reading statements, yelling," he said, referring wrongly to Jethro and Meredith—a fairly obvious woman. "Building occupants were having trouble entering and leaving."

I bit my tongue. I wanted to stand up and show him the tape of people walking past us. But courtrooms aren't about getting to truth. They're oppositional, with the goal of beating down the other side with a more coherent story. The question wasn't what was true, it was what would convince the stony-faced judge.

The prosecution reasserted that we had needlessly blocked the entrance, creating a fire hazard. They asked the judge for the full penalty for our deliberate, planned action. Next to me, Marj bristled.

It was our lawyer's turn. *Pro bono* attorney Sam Stretton called Rev. Jesse Brown to the stand. Wearing his collar, Jesse recounted how he requested to speak with PGCB officials and the heart of our story: the desire to get documents released. He never once called us protestors. We were citizens looking for documents.

After an hour of testimony, both sides rested, and the judge banged his gavel. Marj sat on the edge of her chair, white knuckles gripping the seat in front of her. Noticing I was in the same position, I told my body to relax.

The worst that happens is we get a fine, I tried to calm myself. My paranoid mind went further: *No, the worst that happens is we get ripped apart by the judge and demonized in the press, SugarHouse and Foxwoods lawyers use this as an opening to charge us all with criminal conspiracy, and we get put away for years.*

Chill.

The judge monotonously recapped the case, hiding his leanings. His pace suddenly quickened. "One of the most basic precepts this country has is the right to redress grievances. A legitimate request was made for information from a government agency, the people's government. With the exception of several agencies on the federal level, everything else either is or should be wide open to any member of the public."

I heard exhales behind me. The judge was apparently making a political point. I cringed, certain he was going to start his next sentence with "But..."

He faced the prosecution's desk. "I can't imagine what documents your agency has up there that require a ~~prior~~ appointment, approval, and an escort to get to that information. The only conclusion I can come to is that you're not working for the citizens of the Commonwealth of Pennsylvania."

I exhaled and grabbed Marj's hands. Tears flowed from her face.

The judge continued, "I would agree with anybody who says there's something wrong here. You should not have these things in a free and open society. Had residents' request for information been honored, there probably wouldn't have been any reason for any of the individuals to travel to Harrisburg on the day in question and act in the manner they did. If your agency continues to operate in this fashion, we're going to have a lot more of these." It was all but an invitation for us to return. He stared down the PGCB officials present, picking up his gavel. "Not guilty." *Bang.*

Filing out, we released emotions in an explosion of hugs and cheers. Embracing me, Marj—the woman I knew from training Burmese activists—whispered in my ear, "This is what American democracy should be about."

Jethro grabbed me. "Being found not guilty, that alone was the right decision. But the judge went a lot further to put the gaming control board and the way they conduct its business on trial."

Several heads nodded. I couldn't resist exploiting the teachable moment for others watching, too. "Jethro, *this* is what happens when we design actions based on doing what's right. You don't have to explain it to others or need signs or visuals—people can see for themselves the injustice. That's the power of direct action when you design it so the action is the message."

Heads down, the prosecution team silently barreled through the foyer and out the front doors. Meanwhile, we reveled in surprised ecstasy and collective shock over the judge's harsh statements. Ed Goppelt, the only Philly press who bothered to attend, was surprised to find the judge open to being interviewed. The judge's stinging words were later quoted in Philadelphia via the Associated Press report, KYW, WHYY, and of course Hallwatch.

We headed back into our buses for a triumphant return trip. The tone for our email communication and spin for reporters would be easy. *We were right about the PGCB's secrecy. We are right about the need to give people a vote. Sign our petitions.*

Which made Anne's bad news even more crushing.

❖   ❖   ❖

"Our legal team informed me of a problem with the petition. We need to change 1,000 to 1,500 feet ASAP. We are right that Foxwoods and SugarHouse would violate the 1,000 foot buffer. Except Foxwoods could subdivide its land out of the 1,000 foot zone."

Anne's email explained that Foxwoods could carve the front part of the building to hold a lawn or restaurants. Then, safely outside the buffer, they could house slots. Apparently Foxwoods's lawyers had used this type of subdividing to dodge zoning restrictions to place a 200-foot building near Independence Square.

Anne closed, "But they will be in the Delaware River if they do that at 1,500 feet."

In my mind, I wanted to send a curt email to her and the rest of the newly formed—if not still informal—executive team. *I thought it was covered. Now we've wasted our volunteers' time. Poor Mary Stumpf standing in the cold.* But I didn't. I didn't want to deflate everyone by passing my anger and frustration onto others. I took a deep breath and typed more slowly. "This feels huge, but it's not a dagger in our heart. 40,000 is a big enough number. It's good we had a good practice round."

I sent it off, stood up, and reached for my cell phone. "Jet, this is terrible! It's kills our credibility. Maybe we should just give up now. We've wasted almost a thousand signatures!"

Jethro listened to my rant, eventually saying, "Yeah, it's too bad... not much to do now except call our active volunteers and keep their spirits up. We should reach out to folks who are on the fence about the campaign to keep them from falling off."

"I guess. The only way forward is to admit our mistake and start collecting over again. But I needed that rant, friend."

Within two hours, we changed the petition materials and our website. Anne personally called stalwarts like Shirley, Ken, and Mary. I wrote to the rest of our supporters with a brave face. "Breathe deep. Remember, this is not what we wanted, but we need the strongest possible language to make sure we can protect our neighborhoods."

A seed of doubt grew. *If we didn't foresee this basic issue, what else have we missed?*

Moreover, if *others* had not foreseen it, then *I* should have been watching more carefully. No longer assuming Anne or others would cover it, I started to wonder: How will we count the petitions? Who is teaching people how to get signatures? How do we gather new allies and volunteers?

I stopped collecting signatures in the street. To make this work, I had to make sure everything was in place myself.

Paul Boni agreed to meet with me and Jethro at his eleventh-floor office on Chestnut. When I walked into his spacious office, I saw Jethro idly reading our front-page article at a long glass table. The *Philadelphia Weekly* carried beautiful pictures of our signature drive. Press smelled a good story with an arc and a meaningful outcome: *Will they get the signatures, and if they do, will council support them to implement the buffer zone?* We would get articles for thirteen of the remaining nineteen days.

Paul looked up from his computer and gave a quick wave. "I'm just finishing up work, hold on."

"Hey Jethro," I said, hugging him from behind. He smiled.

Paul stood up and gave me a firm handshake. He was shorter than I expected, maybe a decade older than me, with fluffy hair and a playful spirit like a muppet in a stiff, stout lawyer's body. "It's great to meet you," I said.

"Thanks," he said, "though we did meet at the strategy retreat."

"Ah. Sorry," I said.

Behind his eyeglasses, Paul flashed a smile and a wink. "No worries. By the way, you write great emails."

In classic Jethro style, our meeting had no definitive goals. It was a chance to get to know each other, find out each other's interests.

I had the urgency of the petition drive on my mind and our need to get more people obtaining signatures. Hoping to continue learning from Jethro on how to increase someone's commitment, I waited for him to initiate talking about the campaign with Paul.

Jethro started by looking out the window. "It's an amazing view," he said, walking toward the full glass windows in Paul's office.

"Sure is," said Paul as he walked next to Jethro.

"What's that building over there?" asked Jethro.

"That's Carpenters' Hall. Back at the founding of our country, when they were trying to decide where to hold the Continental Congress, they needed a place where they could rabble-rouse—and Independence Hall was filled with the more... uh, timid provincial government."

"Politicians were easily frightened even then," Jethro grinned. "So they met there?"

I sighed and got up. *I guess I'm going to join them looking out the window.*

"Yep, at a trade-union hall," said Paul, casting his gaze fondly over the view below. "Back then, all of this was where people lived, traded, sold goods, and socialized. When our founders wrote the constitution, they were right here with the people bustling outside." Through Paul's descriptions, I could hear horse-drawn carriages creaking and murmured chatter rising up. "The Daughters of the American Revolution fought for the federal government to buy up this land and preserve it as a landmark. They went through a long process to decide which buildings to keep. That small one with four windows, for example, was our first Department of Defense."

All this seemed a bit irrelevant. But genuinely curious Jethro continued listening, barely needing to ask questions to keep Paul talking.

"Over there, they want to put Foxwoods." Paul pointed left, toward the river. "There's the stadium further back, past those three churches. When the churches were first built, they were the only buildings to have those tall towers rising to the heavens."

We continued like this for fifteen more minutes until we'd heard about Paul's love of the riverfront, his background fighting bad developers, his advocacy on behalf of Society Hill Civic Association, his love of history, and his experience as a zoning and environmental lawyer—all through the view out his window.

It was textbook organizing: spending most of the time listening, finding out people's values to understand what people most desired. In Paul's case, he carried a vision of a city driven by citizen input, where government decisions were made at ground level next to where people lived and worked.

Only then did Jethro begin talking. "We're not going to win this by fighting as isolated neighborhoods, but together."

Paul nodded in earnest. "We should get together and ask Councilman DiCicco for money to hire us some lawyers."

"Maybe," said Jethro, tilting back to his point. "Before we seek external help, we need to get ourselves together. Up North, we have problems forming a full coalition. Specifically, one politically connected board member of the NKCDC—a northern neighborhood association—is sharing information and strategy with SugarHouse and the governor. The problem isn't really the man, Rich Levins. It's that civic associations aren't set up democratically. Therefore, nobody in Kensington is in a position to tell their civic association or Rich to stop. There's no process for NKCDC to be representative of the neighborhood's positions. So nobody challenges his version of the truth."

"I've seen those kinds of problems before," said Paul.

"This petition can bind us together because it unites all neighborhoods—mine with yours, which is just as close to SugarHouse up North as Foxwoods." Paul looked out his South-facing window in surprise. "If civics can step outside of their NIMBY attitude, it'll make for a dramatic change in our city."

"I'll try to get full support from Society Hill," said Paul.

Jethro nodded. "It'll be fun working with you." He smiled over at me. He sensed Paul would soon agree to be part of Casino-Free Philadelphia's team—moving quickly from in-house volunteer legal counsel to a full-blown member of the executive team.

As Jethro left, he gazed back out the window. "Man, you really have a great view." He meant it.

Though a handful of folks like Mary Stumpf had been hitting the streets already, only by the end of January did we organize our first public presentation. I walked through the doors of Old Pine Street Presbyterian, with its oversized pillars dating back to when the US was still a British protectorate.

Nervous, familiar chills sent adrenaline through my body, as my mind repeated its well-worn list of concerns: *Will anybody show up? Will they trust us it's doable? In this formal space that Paul found, will I do something embarrassing? Can we handle people's questions?* I replayed each worry—my own way of readying for our presentation.

Kathy Dilonardo and her husband sat in the third row from the front. Kathy was curious whether this was a meaningful effort to join or just a waste of time. She had been urged on by her friend and fellow recent retiree from the National Park Service, Mary Reinhart. A now retired park ranger, Mary worried about losing her 1860s home to Foxwoods's anticipated new ramp off I-95. Kathy was surrounded by 130 others from Society Hill and other historical Old City neighborhoods.

Jethro started in a mellow, cool, and almost standoffishly formal way. "A few months ago, when my civic Fishtown Neighbors Association found out about the casinos, Councilman DiCicco came and told us to start negotiations. He told us he can't stop the tide of casinos. When we asked him to oppose it publicly and challenge his mentor Senator Fumo, we stopped hearing from him."

I watched the crowd's reception, wondering if people would rush to defend the councilman or senator. But, no—Jethro had read the crowd. The fact that Senator Fumo had just been publicly hit with the results of a federal probe charging him with 137 counts of fraud, obstruction of justice, and corruption couldn't hurt. But more so, Jethro was energetically matching their low-key, formal style, even while giving them background story on himself.

"A few months later, DiCicco's back telling us that he's been fighting with us all the way, opposing the casinos. Well, I didn't believe DiCicco that we should start negotiations. But—" Jethro leaned into his words. "But I *do* believe DiCicco that he can't stop the tide." He let the words hang threateningly.

"I believe he can't—won't—do anything until we take action ourselves. When we asked, he wouldn't introduce a ballot question to stop casinos being placed in neighborhoods—wouldn't even touch it. So we'll have to get our friends, neighbors and fellow citizens to collect enough signatures to place a ballot question before council, so that the people can vote. Because... Were you offered a say on if a casino comes to your neighborhood?" He paused to allow a few muted "no's" from the crowd.

"Would you oppose them if you had the chance?"

"Yes," muttered a slightly louder, if rhythmically challenged, crowd. This was not the black church of my youth, but a crowd easily stereotyped by pearls and brown dinner jackets. Having paced with them, Jethro was pulling their energy up.

"Already, after just a few newspaper articles, DiCicco is changing his tune. He's trotted out a raft of legislation to slow down the casinos, even while telling his fellow councilmembers that he doesn't think they should pass. That's not leadership."

The crowd bobbed along as Jethro paced back and forth.

"So there's a leadership vacuum." He smiled warmly. "And nature abhors a vacuum, so we must fill it... We are the leaders. That's what we're here to talk about tonight."

He sat down, to rousing applause, just as I jumped onstage to continue and extend the energy of Jethro's call-and-response. In minutes, Jethro had modeled classic pacing/leading. He had warmly paced with the crowd, only then leading them to the energy he wanted them to embody. Raucous crowd? Start there, with big body gestures. But for this reserved crowd, Jethro started small and expanded to the expressive boldness we desired.

The remainder of the presentation blurred with flipping newsprints, describing the rapid timeline, pounding away at the anti-democratic PGCB, and my now-fluid retelling of Operation Transparency. Having gained practice from our one-on-ones, like with Paul, I smoothly handled everyone's questions: "Yes, the deadline concerns us, too. It's one reason we're glad the longshoremen, AFSCME local DC47, and two civic associations have already signed on. But we need more support, which is why we're asking you tonight to join the campaign.

"I agree that our city politicians are not prepared to pass the ballot question. However, if we can gather 40,000 signatures, I have no doubt they'll change their tune. Remember, we're not asking them to be anti-casino, just supportive of giving voters a say on casinos! There are sign-up sheets moving through the audience to get involved, or you can sign up at the back."

As I finished, one woman shouted out, "Don't you need money to make this happen?" I blushed. Jethro rushed back onto the stage, crying, "Yes!"

"I'll pledge $150," she said.

"Uh, fantastic," said Jethro. "We have nonprofit status through a fiscal sponsor. We promise to stretch every dollar."

From another part of the crowd: "I'll give $250!" Dozens of other voices yelled their pledges into the air, like a fiscal-based version of the testifying I grew up with in my church. The crowd sent ripples of excitement to the walls and ceilings.

Kathy nudged her husband, who nodded approvingly. "$100," she shouted, to the annoyance and surprise of the woman sitting next to her.

"You don't even *know* these people," the woman said.

Kathy shrugged, immune to the condescending gaze of her Queen Village neighbor. "It's just $100. Sometimes you have to take a chance. They're showing leadership—we have to support it."

Like others, Kathy would soon be out door-knocking and gathering signatures at malls, streets, and schools.

For the next week, "No Way Without Our Say" became a rallying cry in newspaper letters to the editor and blogs urging citizens to get involved in this massive undertaking. Fox TV devoted a whole segment to Ken Gregory's "pub crawl"—where he and others started in Northern Liberties bars and headed toward Center City pubs, getting beers and signatures. Shirley and I swapped reports of volunteers on trains, outside public libraries, in grocery stores, and doing door-to-door meetings. Anne Dicker even walked out of one symposium with a petition signed by state representatives Mike O'Brien, Bill Keller, and John Taylor, plus political rivals IBEW president John Dougherty and Councilman Frank DiCicco. "Casino-Free Philadelphia gets local politicians on the same page," our next press release lauded.

During the next weeks I juggled many balls: recruiting more civic support, convincing the ILA to send the petition to their membership, swapping stories with dozens of volunteers. Kathy Dilonardo and Mary Reinhart found success with parents outside schools waiting in the twenty-degree cold for their kids. A befriended crossing guard even kept an eye out for any parent who hadn't signed. "With different release times for schools," Kathy advised, "we can get two schools in an afternoon and collect up to seventy-five signatures in one hour."

Some parts were comical, like it turning so cold we had to order special gel pens resistant to the increasingly freezing temperatures. Some parts were annoying, like putting out a fire after a circulator threw a tantrum over the "preposterous waste of everybody's time" when he was asked to sign a second petition against Act 71. "Find some other sucker," he wrote nastily to dozens of supporters, forcing me to respond, urging everyone to just focus on the charter change.

Focus, people, focus, I thought. *With only three weeks to go, we only have 1,006 signatures.*

Fear gnawed at me. When I turned to Jethro with concerns that we did not have enough infrastructure, I only got vague sympathy. "I'm focused on the North/South alliance's wrestling with the PennPraxis riverfront planning project. It reminds me of the Fenway fight against the new Red Sox stadium, when we launched a ten-day design charette. The community guided architects, urban designers, and engineers to design an alternative. It got us away from just being against the city's plan, and creating our own. PennPraxis needs to do something like that. They need to stop assuming casinos are a fait accompli and so refusing to weigh against them. Unless they change, we're going to organize people to bolt from the process en masse." My heart went out to him, but my head wasn't there.

Likewise, Anne gave me her unbridled, broad optimism.

Eventually, I confided my concerns with Shirley Cook. Her role had grown from note-taker to filling her home office with stacks of petitions. *"Don't touch any of them,"* she said sternly when I entered her overtaken house. After seeing if each petition had been properly notarized, she numbered them, combed through to cross off Mickey Mouse names like George Washington or I. C. Weiner, tallied the number of valid signatures, then copied and finally put the originals into a fireproof safe in her basement. It was a masterful job, requiring someone obsessively detailed and content playing an important but unglamorous role.

When I asked her why she did it, she shared her opposition to a casino blocks from her house. She added, "I sometimes would walk through Independence Hall and wonder, if the time came, if I'd step up to the plate. This feels like my chance to stand up for myself and others."

But when I asked her whether she thought we'd make it to 20,000, she responded, "I'm doing my part, but *I* don't know how to do this. You and Anne are the experts. You have to figure it out. We trust you."

It made me feel worse, as if we had conned people. We were making it up as we went along.

Under supportive questioning from a friend, the fear finally tumbled out. I curled up on my couch as if admitting a giant secret. "This is a *nearly* impossible task!"

"I'm not part of the campaign," she said. "You can safely tell me how much you think it's impossible."

Tears welled up. "It's... It's pushing a boulder uphill. But we'll press forward!"

"I know you'll keep going," she said thoughtfully. "But you can also tell me how much you fear it will all fail."

Teardrops rolled down my face in relief. "We have no organization. Barely a dime to our name. We're not even a real group, just some random people. And... Anne's wrong to think we can do this. She got 4,000 signatures in a day because Howard Dean had a national presence—and it was warm weather! All odds seem against us. It's supposed to be getting even colder!"

For several minutes she let me release my fears, schooled in her therapeutic belief that people get smarter when they release emotional blocks holding them back. She listened as I poured out concerns.

After my voice slowed, she turned to me. "Okay, so what if you took the perspective that you have already done it? Work backwards from the day you got 40,000 signatures."

"20,000," I said with fervor. "I've told Anne to stop saying 40,000. We have to reduce expectations, just in case..." Surprised at the new perspective, I grabbed a pen and scribbled on a nearby whiteboard. "If the ILA comes up with 2,000 signatures... civic associations pull out 3,000 signatures... NABR gets 1,000... street efforts get us 14,000, minimum. That's 20,000. That means we need 3,000 by next week, six the week after, then somehow 10,000 signatures in the last half-week."

I stared at the whiteboard. "This helps," I said. "Even if the numbers are wild, we have some goals that... well... maybe... and now I know what we need next."

My friend Brian Kelly looked at me, lounging comfortably on my couch, pulling mindlessly at his beard. "So what would be my job exactly?"

Brian breathed contradictions: a long-haired anti-sweatshop activist who graduated from Wharton Business School, a man attached to systems and details who had all the freedom of an unstructured work life.

"We need someone to structure our outreach and help us stay on track for our number goals. Anne, Jethro, and I are too busy already. There are people in our network who we've only emailed, never even called. We need you to have one-on-one conversations with them... I knew you could step into the breach right away, so Jethro and I agreed to hire you short-term for this campaign."

When Brian said nothing, I added, "For example, we have a list of 200 civic groups, nonprofits, and unions that we think might be supportive. We should just call through that list."

Brian looked at me, as if wondering if I were pulling him into a disaster. He leaned in intimately. "I know you can be... uhm, persuasive, you know, a big visionary. And I know you can do amazing things. But, do you *actually* have any chance of getting the required signatures?"

"Do *we*..." I corrected. "You're us now. Do *we*." He kept staring, but half-smiled.

I leaned back. "Absolutely." My own certainty surprised me. It was partially the strength of having a plan. But it was also the certainty of projected confidence. "The local ILA council agreed to do a massive mailing of 20,000 petitions to their members, so even with a 5% return rate they'd be halfway to the goals I have down for them. Civic groups have really stepped up—Queen Village, Society Hill, Pennsport—they're getting way more than I expected. And I'm sure there are many more who haven't told us."

He slowly nodded, his lips curling into a reluctant smile. "Okay."

Under the circumstances, this was as approving as I could expect. "Part of your job is to coach people where to use their time. Mary Stumpf is like a petition-wielding ninja when she's in the field, using two or three clipboards at a time to get as many signatures as possible. From being out every day, she's learned all the techniques—like setting up a sign to slow down people listening to their iPods. You need to pass her lessons on to others. But she's now cold-calling churches from the phone book, starting with the letter A. That's *not* a good use of her time."

Brian nodded. "It's near impossible to organize people without any relationship, especially churches."

"Others are trying to get Bill Cosby or Kevin Bacon on board," I said. "Not doable in a little over two weeks."

Brian looked up sharply, his face a mix of horror and shock. He mouthed delicately, "Two weeks?"

"Well, fifteen days." I showed none of the concern creeping around the shadows of my mind.

Brian continued to stare. "So... I report to you?"

At this, I looked up sharply. In many ways, visionary Anne Dicker was running the show. But she wasn't controlling and appreciated when Shirley and I stepped into more leadership. Volunteers like Ken, Mary, Kathy, and Paul would recruit others, but it was all decentralized, haphazard, and mostly held together by Shirley's insistence that everyone drop off signatures to her. In short, nobody was taking charge of the big picture—and I knew that meant I needed to fill the void.

Brian saw it all in my hesitation. He smirked. "I see... I'm just gonna report to you."

I nodded appreciatively. "Here's your lists," I said, giving him lists of potential allies and our contact list. "And I suggest you add minutes to your phone plan for the month of February..."

Brian jumped with two feet into the fray. He quickly became a node, passing around information in a flurry of updates: "Ken Gregory is having success asking people while waiting for the underground subway or literally while riding up and down the El. The regional rails are out—too few Philadelphia voters. Susan DeWyngeart just got kicked out of The Gallery—but Mary and Kathy are doing okay there—go figure. Tie strings to the pens, to make sure we don't lose them."

Petitioning became art form. The location needed to match the individual's psyche, style, culture, and approach. For example, Mary was happy to stand outside—gloveless in the snow and belt a quick line at rushing passersby: "Help us stop the casinos from being built near schools, parks, and playgrounds." Once she had someone, she'd match the person's rhythm of speech, find out if they were registered Philadelphians, hand them a clipboard, and then turn to grab another person. Yet she had none of the success on the trains that Ken and Jethro did. She noted right away the split along gender. Men did well at transportation spots, whereas women had more success at grocery stores and schools.

We didn't go deep into analyzing the cause, just shared results and passed them along to others as quickly as possible, all the while continuing to recruit more organizations and civics.

The next two weeks continued like that, a buzz of constant, rapid communication. Each morning, I woke up and rushed to my computer to get the latest whirlwind reports. Union activist Jerry Silberman reported, "Some nerdy SEPTA mandarin at 13th Street Station said I might cause someone to lose attention and fall off the platform. So they called the cops on me and escorted me out."

I had no time to check if this was a breach of our First Amendment rights. I switched gears to report: "Poor Susan DeWyngaert just got kicked out of several facilities: Trader

Joe's, Pathmark, and even Reading Terminal Market. But people should keep going, because Shirley went to those places with no problems."

Mary Stumpf quipped back, "Walmart and Target are being particularly rude. Don't go there anymore."

Jethro wrote, "I just had a SEPTA official threaten to arrest me if I didn't get off the train. So I told him to *please* arrest me—we'd get so much good media off him stomping on my rights. He backed down."

Brian and I gauged which avenues were working: civic associations, block captains, volunteers hitting the streets, neighborhood-based groups. And what avenues were not. Like, aside from organizers with Project H.O.M.E. getting a thousand-plus signatures, most nonprofits were too flat-footed to make it worth our time reaching out to them. And we adjusted our strategy accordingly, devoting Brian's time to hitting the streets and training others to gather petitions. "Too many people think petitioning is scary," he said. "But once they go out and do it, they see how easy it is. I'll help them get started, give them tips, and show them it's easier than they think."

I wondered if I needed approval from someone else in CFP. But we had no face-to-face meetings, no CFP-leadership calls, not even a clear sense of who was on our steering committee. Each of us did our thing. Anne, Jesse Brown, and Paul were off recruiting volunteers and who-knows-what. Jethro was jumping back in, challenging people to join the "500 Club"—his made-up name to encourage people to set personal goals for number of signatures. Shirley was wading through stacks and spreadsheets.

Press coverage added to our excitement and anticipation. Fox and ABC Action News made us a regular TV news story, joined by radio stations like KYW and WHYY. Only the two dailies almost completely ignored our efforts, except in a *Daily News* editorial saying our efforts had "a snowball's chance in hell" to win.

I giddily passed it around, telling allies, "But notice they call our actions 'laudatory' for spurring public debate. That's one more step toward us. Keep up the pressure, and they'll come around."

In its initial coverage of the petition drive, the conservative-leaning *Evening Bulletin* used as its starting point a talk organized by civic associations, loosely quoting the guest speaker, author Jeff Benedict, who'd helped stop the expansion of Foxwoods in Connecticut:

> Restaurant owners and retail shops would be at risk of losing business because casino complexes will offer it all at a lot less, he said. Loads of disposable income is already circulating throughout the city, he said. But casinos would suck dining, drinking, and entertainment spending from local businesses and would funnel it right into the casino. Wealthy casino owners would get richer, while small business owners and individuals lose money.

It was the first reporting on the economic downsides of casinos, closing with Jethro's bizarrely optimistic estimate that we had "a little over 10,000" signatures already. Anne counted 6,952. Restrained as ever, Shirley confirmed only 3,689 signatures in hand. Eight days to go.

Concern finally got the best of me, and I called up Brian in a panic. "What happens if we can't get these petitions?"

"Pull it together. I don't have time for your despair," Brian said. "Remind people to make sure they get their petitions notarized. Anne says Citizens Bank will do it for free."

I relented.

Four days later, a load of petitions was dumped underneath Shirley's doors. The count was up to 6,419. "We know firmly about 8,600," I tried to reassure one Whitman civic supporter, "and I can guess about 14,000 are out there." But time was running short.

Mary Stumpf had helped brainstorm a last-ditch effort based on what we knew was working. Our petition-day blitz had to work.

I called Saturday's final push our "D-Day Operation." Zoë Artz gathered folks at Port Richmond's Thriftway on Aramingo Avenue to circulate in Northeast Philly. Anne Dicker oversaw operations starting on busy South Street, right outside Whole Foods. West Philly, North Philly, Nicetown, and Mount Airy were covered respectively by Harmony Thompson, Diane Mayer, Wayne Jacobs, and Marc Stier. ILA vice president Jim Paylor coordinated dozens of longshoremen outside a Superfresh on Delaware Avenue, a strip mall off 20th Street and Oregon Avenue, and Chickie's & Pete's at Packer Avenue. Only Mary Stumpf didn't have a location. She was best as a solo free-floater.

As Center City coordinator, I stood with Karin DiNardi outside the towering statues of the Free Library on that windy, thirty-two degree day, the bright sun doing nothing to keep me warm. It still was the warmest day of what had been the coldest weeks of winter.

I had initially been worried that Karin's speech impediment would slow us down. I hustled to get people to stop in the cold to speak with me. Karin simply drove her wheelchair in front of their path as her computer intoned, "Read it, read it" while she gestured at the petition instructions. Most stopped and read.

It was the easiest petition-gathering I'd ever done.

"I want a casino in the city," one man told me.

"That's fine," I said. "Many who signed this petition do, too. This simply puts a referendum on the ballot about whether casinos should be within 1,500 feet of schools and people's homes. Do you think people should get a chance to vote on that?"

His resistance melted. "I can support that." He reached for my pen and signed.

Hours went by as my hands froze inside my gloves. Nearly everyone who stopped signed the petition.

At 5 P.M., I headed over to Jake's Pizza, which was run by an Ethiopian who joked that they'd learned pizza-making from Italian occupiers, perfecting it when they kicked them out. Many of the 104 volunteers joined, stomping their frozen feet and grabbing pizza.

Huddled at a table, with icy fingers, Shirley accepted their pages and whipped through them with a practiced eye.

Chuck Valentine's face glowed. He was fresh off organizing the first Fishtown protests against SugarHouse. "I *loved* getting to talk about casinos and politics at our grocery store with our neighbors. We should do this every weekend!"

Jethro nodded excitedly, halfway munching on a cheese slice. "We are politicizing public spaces with talks about casinos, democracy, and citizen input, aren't we?"

Talk inevitably turned to the total number of signatures gathered. Shirley's voice carried above the fray. "At least 6,000 signatures today!"

Tense shoulders released. I looked over at Anne, who grinned widely.

I returned home to reports from other sources: the ILA had 832 more signatures, Wayne Jacobs was getting us 2,000, Pennsport Civic had 1,400, and Diane Mayer alone had networked almost 1,500. On the back of an envelope, I added up the totals. I exhaled fully for the first time in a month. We were going to break 20,000. I closed my laptop and gave myself the best celebration I could imagine: I slept hard and long.

Red and yellow streamers hung around tables overflowing with snacks and hot drinks. In the same room as our strategy retreat—exactly forty days ago—voices of fifty celebrating volunteers filled the room. The impending Valentine's Day blizzard hadn't scared our people off from spending the last hours outside. People warmed their chapped ears and frozen feet with excited chatter.

"Make sure to get your petitions notarized over there in the corner—thank you, Jill," I shouted, hushing the crowd. "But before announcing the final tally, let's start with awards!" I handed certificates to the 500 Club: Jethro, Anne, Mary Reinhart, Kathy Dilonardo...

"Awards go to Ken Gregory for reaching 1,000 signatures and Mary Stumpf for getting, at last count, over 2,000 signatures!"

Ken bounded up, as frozen Mary wobbled to take her certificates. Everyone felt the taste of being part of a monumental accomplishment.

I handed out more awards, including to Shirley for her detailed counting. "But we don't know all the stories and successes here," I said. "Hundreds more people have been involved, including you. So take a blank award. Fill in your name. Add an amazing accomplishment *you* did during this effort. To make it official, you have to get a signature from someone else on behalf of Casino-Free Philadelphia—so that means a signature from anyone in this room." People laughed and took their awards.

I had taken the idea from Serbian movement organization Otpor. When dictator Milosevic gave himself a public award, Otpor made fun of him by handing out blank certificates, encouraging people to give themselves their own awards.

For us, it was a fun way to honor the multitude of stories: The over 400 volunteers who had participated, the eleven civics and four unions that signed onto the campaign. In all, 3,000 petition pages had been distributed at community meetings, talks, church services, five-year-old's birthday parties, and even a funeral for a neighborhood activist. Babies in strollers had the petition strapped to them; a ninety-three-year-old grandmother won the award for the oldest participant. All the signatures strewn out, Ken noted, would stretch 3.6 miles long.

It had taken lots of energy and less than $5,000 total, leaving under $300 in our bank account.

At the end of the night, just as reporters were switching to the storyline that "Activists Still Face Steep Climb" with council, I shouted, "Finally, the news you've been waiting for! By our current estimate, we have achieved 26,943 signatures! Sleep well—we deliver tomorrow!"

None of us were thinking about the plans being hatched by our opponents, who had stood quietly as we gathered signatures. For that night, we were drunk with our own triumph and accomplishment.

That night, people continued to drop off petitions at Shirley's house. Shirley, Kathy DeAngelis, and Brian—his last day of work with us—pulled an all-nighter counting and copying petitions. Overloaded, they left Shirley's slow copier and headed to Kinko's, just as a massive ice storm struck.

The next morning, Shirley met everyone at City Hall, bleary-eyed, with five transparent file boxes filled with signatures. "Transparent," she half-grinned, "because we have nothing to hide."

We stacked them up high as a podium, as a dozen TV and radio stations placed their microphones on top. I couldn't believe we were really here, standing inside City Hall doing this. Even Foxwoods's hometown reporters were now calling us. I didn't know how to communicate to press the hundreds of volunteer hours. It didn't matter anyway. After we announced we had ultimately reached 27,254 signatures, they were on to the next story. "Will any of this matter? The state trumps the city, right?" asked KYW's Mike Dunn.

I stuttered through recounting the fight for local city zoning. "Just as the city has the right to say you can't have a bar right next to a church, the city has a right to say you can't have a casino right next to a neighborhood."

Media had their own storyline, swapping in a new set of political impossibilities.

As Huu and Anne handed the city clerk our petitions, pride overwhelmed me. Our movement had come so far from four months ago. Not only were we fighting against casinos, but we were now networking with other movements and alerting our members to similar abuse of zoning laws by corporations in North Philly to support gentrification. Ken had even testified against media conglomeration at a Federal Communications Commission hearing, having seen up close the dangers of a consolidated media market.

"Happy Valentine's Day, everyone," Anne shouted with a brazen smile. "We've actually done it!"

CHAPTER 7

We Are Not Scared of Stunts

FEBRUARY 17, 2007 — MARCH 15, 2007

*knowing what convinces politicians • being in your opponents' shoes •
getting politicians to touch your issue • not being subservient petitioners •
rebounding attacks onto the opponent • power flows upward •
turning our backs to stop testimony • bracing for opposition research •
checking off agenda items • making media sensationalism work for you •
designing two actions ahead of time • move toward the fear • play the underdog*

I CAST MY EYES AROUND THE OFFICE hoping to find something familiar. Fox's offices were filled with dense cubicles, each with low-level staffers staring at screens. No matter where I looked, televisions blasted the live-cast *Good Morning Philadelphia* program. In a few minutes, I'd be on that. I tried not to think about its 50,000 viewers.

I turned back to the baby-faced Fox News political director. *This is just another interview. At five in the morning. In front of a live audience...*

As if reading my nervousness, he coached, "Look directly above the camera. Avoid licking your lips or scratching your face. Instead of seeing the interviewers, you'll look at a gray screen and hear the questions through this earpiece. If you look up slightly, you can see the live feed."

I nodded mindlessly, wondering why I was doing this alone. *I need to get better at giving away work to others,* I thought. *But this was last-minute. And high stakes. Still...*

"You'll do fine," he smiled encouragingly. "I just wanted to ask one thing." He leaned in conspiratorially, darting his eyes as if a great secret were about to be shared. I knew the look, had seen it a hundred times. "I think it's great you're doing this," he whispered. "But how do you expect to win? You know it's completely hopeless."

It was too early for this. Wherever Jethro and I went, we found most people disliked casinos, or at least had grievous reservations. Yet when we invited people to stop them, they held onto the deeper, more cherished Philadelphia value: defeatism. Our battle often felt like it was more about giving people hope than about casinos.

I yawned and gave my rote answer for reporters. "If this goes on the ballot, it will be a real chance to stop the casinos from coming to the city." It was the short version, but I didn't have the energy to dive deep into his despair.

His mop of hair flopped back and forth as he nodded with seriousness. "There's an election coming up?"

My head snapped up, eyes focusing on him sharply. "You know, the May 15 election."

"Really? There's an election happening?"

I looked for any trace of humor on his face. "There's..." I suppressed a sneer. This is the *political director* for Fox News? "There's an upcoming primary election where we vote on our new mayor and councilmembers. Since our city is Democratic, it's these primaries that are most important."

"Oh right," he said. "The mayor's race. I just didn't realize we voted for council."

"Well, we do."

We gazed awkwardly at each other for a few seconds, before he glanced upward at the digital clock. "Time to start."

My stomach muscles clenched as he put on my headset and I stared at the gray wall.

On came the interviewer, as SugarHouse's spokesperson and I laid out our basic talking points: "Gambling has never been done in a large-scale city so close to dense neighborhoods like this before" versus "SugarHouse will bring jobs that have benefits. That's what SugarHouse is excited about."

The anchor read a written statement from Foxwoods, which refused to have a representative interviewed on air: "Our project will create jobs with strong wages, benefits, approximately $200 million annually for local charities, revenues to fund tax relief, and other basic services for local residents and small businesses."

The anchor turned to me. "Pro and con list—do the pro's outweigh the con's?"

"Well, we have to make the con list, and the casino industry won't do that," I said. "Local restaurants aren't going to be able to compete with a casino, so that means lost jobs..." I was nervous and fumbled slightly to find the words I wanted but managed to stay on point. I'd answered all these questions before.

Then my earpiece fell out.

Inside I panicked. Outside, I kept a steady flow of words. "These casinos threaten port jobs." I couldn't discretely slip the earpiece back in and so missed the anchor trying to interrupt me. Instead, I kept going. "These jobs are already in Philadelphia and are high-quality, well-paying jobs..."

When I finally stopped, there were only a few seconds for SugarHouse to respond. Then the anchor thanked us both and it was all over. The whole debate took less than three minutes.

I swept out of the offices and into the brisk, cool morning air. Relief. Just another interview in front of a few more people. Except this wasn't just another debate in public.

There should have been huge political ramifications that we had gotten 27,000 signatures. The casinos must have been shocked, preparing to hit us hard. Yet on TV nothing had changed—they hadn't even acknowledged our petitions. *Did they know something we didn't?*

I arrived home and tossed piles of unused petitions in the recycling bin. Our strategy had to refocus on winning over our anemic City Council—first, getting a positive vote in committee, and then support in full council. In our focus on gathering petitions, we had spent little time thinking of how to do this—and it would be hard.

Council had no appetite to fight the governor and Senator Fumo. Many of them owed political debts to these men. And worse, councilmembers had built reputations as winners in dog-eat-dog Philadelphia politics—they didn't want to be targeted as obstructionists on the losing side of any issue. They had learned to gauge the political winds and materialize at the front—*if* the issue would win.

Threatening them with our members voting against them would help. Already, many of their council challengers smelled this as a wedge issue. Council-at-large candidate Marc Stier released a TV spot contrasting Jethro's neighbors on Allen Street facing "the front of a casino" with suburban casino investors who "don't live here, don't work here, and never asked us." Meanwhile, Frank DiCicco's challenger in the council race, Vern Anastasio, launched ferocious attacks on DiCicco's "personal and professional relationship" with SugarHouse investor Richard Sprague, "a well-known attorney currently defending DiCicco's political patron, indicted State Senator Vincent Fumo."

But none of that would be enough. Councilmembers often pass unpopular bills when most voters—or even a powerful, organized voting bloc—disapprove, because they fear more than just losing re-elections. Politicians can bounce back from a lost election if they carry the currency most valued in politics: their political reputation. Reputations help politicians make deals, raise money, and mobilize their sycophants.

On reputation, we could hit councilmembers where it hurts: threatening to tarnish them as acting to disempower the city of Philadelphia. That was the bind we were placing them in by hitching our wagon to the widely shared value of voting. Either they opposed democracy and opposed giving people their say on casinos, or they stood with the people and therefore sided with us.

To make it stick, we had to show we could damage their political capital, without actually doing it before they voted against us. We had to be a credible threat, which meant avoiding appearing like a small, irrelevant margin. Whatever we did, it had to appear larger than life—or at least larger than our few hundred active supporters.

All this flashed though my mind in moments. I reached back into my jeans to grab my cell phone, just as it rang. It was exactly the person I wanted. Jethro's cheery voice nearly shouted into the phone. "Hunter!"

"Yo, Jet!"

"I'm pumped," yelled Jethro. "You killed on the Fox TV interview. You had more energy, more passion. All the stories on yesterday's petition delivery were on point. The casinos' spin that they're doing this because they have our best interests at heart is starting to be exposed. Great work. Now the hard part comes!"

"I know, I know," I said, suddenly finding myself short of breath. "We need to get an email to members to start calling councilmembers right away."

"You know," said Jethro, "I've been chatting with my neighbors on Allen Street, and they're feeling more hopeful than they have for a long time. We have a track record now. You should be really pleased."

"Sure. I am pleased." I felt an urgency to plan. "Council gets hundreds of e-petitions with the same letter all the time. But if letters are hand-written, or at least personally written online, it means more. So I was thinking we give out phone numbers and email for councilmembers. Folks are so fired up, they'll do it—it'll look better and larger!"

"Great idea." Jethro kept his slow, meandering pace. "We need to take the time to teach people that lobbying isn't just about letters or meetings. It's speaking our minds when we see politicians at hearings, walking on the street, in the grocery store, when we see their husbands and wives, their legislative aids, anywhere."

"Anne's confident we can win. But I'm not sure. We only have DiCicco promising to vote with us. We all know he's playing both sides."

"Council would be crazy to risk the wrath of your sophisticated press work." Jethro giggled to himself. "But people need to know who to pressure. Maybe we should put on our website faces of every councilmember, where they stand, and info for people to contact them."

"I'm on it." I grabbed a piece of paper and scribbled down the note. "So why did you call, Jet?"

"Just to congratulate you after all your great work."

"Thanks," I said shyly. He was genuinely interested in my well-being. Jethro exuded genuineness. Weakly, I tried to join him. "You did great these past weeks, too."

His voice softened. "So how do you feel?"

"I'm..." My gnawing worries clawed to the surface. Like a surfer on the edge of a wave, to stay afloat, we had to keep moving forward. "We have to figure out the casinos' response to all this. What's in their heads? If I were the casinos... No, corporations don't think. If I were Foxwoods' management team, why wouldn't I send someone to debate us on Fox this morning?"

"People in South Philly say they're passing around DVDs, trying to pick off civic associations. But, as nervous as people are in South Philly, we're getting twice the dose from SugarHouse up North."

I continued pacing, waving my hands to help me think. "So why is Foxwoods playing more hands-off? Do they know something we don't know? Maybe a deep back-door deal?"

"Maybe they're going to let SugarHouse battle in public to keep their own hands clean. It makes it easier for them to negotiate deals with politicians and civic groups."

"I hadn't thought of that," I said.

"Ooh, that's high praise," said Jethro. "Okay, so how about SugarHouse? If you were Richard Sprague, what would you do?"

Richard Sprague was a legendary lawyer, credited with pulling together the SugarHouse collaboration. In well-known political lore, he bitterly sued the *Inquirer* and won a $34 million verdict, opening a host of libel and defamation charges against the media. The *Inquirer* eventually settled out of court, paying what was rumored to be tens of millions of dollars.

"First thing, he'll move the fight to his turf: law," I said. "He's vindictive. He won't want to win, he'll want to grind us into the ground. That means personal, below-the-belt attacks."

"I agree," said Jethro. "But his media consultants are going to hold him back. They'll want distance from anything really nasty, because SugarHouse needs the support of the city, even if they won't admit it. Imagine if the mayor or DiCicco refused to show up to their red-ribbon cutting? It'd be a signal to all city departments to slow down or deny them all their permits. If the mayor had any backbone, he could effectively stop them."

My mind flooded with possibilities. *Could they start rumors about us without their fingerprints on it? Sue us constantly? Physical attacks?* Even as I thought of each idea, I coolly played it out, calculating responses for each scenario. It wasn't the scenarios that scared me, it was not seeing them coming.

"Whatever they do, it'll be with a lot of ferocity," I said flatly. "They've hired nearly every media consultant in the city, and almost every law firm is now connected to them."

Jethro laughed out loud. "And yet, are we scared? Another movement would be intimidated about being outspent by millions. But not us! Just another day in the park."

"Because we believe we win if people refuse to go away... but it means we have to look big enough that they believe we can protect ourselves."

"Most people don't see the attacks coming," said Jethro. "I think Kathy and Paul sometimes think we're close to winning."

"I know, Kathy has been hounding me about what's next." Before her retirement and being recruited to the executive team by Jethro, Kathy Dilonardo had worked her way up in the National Park Service, becoming a high-ranking woman as the chief of visitor services for the northeast region. "Her recent emails have been direct, almost harsh. 'We need to tell people exactly how to help. Now. We can't wait.' Maybe she learned email culture when she was working for the government, but it's more than that. She's tough as nails. But none of her emails have helped me move forward. I know the problems—I need the time to find out the solutions."

"Her hounding means she wants to take on leadership. We just need to find the right position for her."

Of course. Jethro was the consummate organizer. Whereas I saw a reminder of work for me to do, he saw leadership potential. "So, what shall we do next?"

"We have to prepare people for whatever is coming our way, to tell them to expect the casinos to use rumors and threats as they feel desperate. This is just the start of a long, drawn-out struggle. Five years or more."

"I'll mention all that in our next email blast. Got it, thanks. Anything else?" I asked, ready to hang up the phone.

"Good work today," Jethro said.

Four days later, my formal black shoes echoed off the marble walls of City Hall's stairwell as I ran to our first City Council showdown. Though today's agenda did not include our ballot referendum, it would be our first chance to see council's mettle on a slate of bills introduced by DiCicco, ranging from a flat ban on casinos to minor zoning reforms.

I reached the fourth floor and the large open gates to council, placing my keys on the metal detector. For days, rumors had flown that casinos were threatening supporters, orchestrating a vast door-knocking operation, and strolling into council's offices with paper bags filled with cash. But they were just rumors, some easily disproved or discounted. After all, the casinos weren't so dumb as to walk into offices with cash—there are abundant legal ways to funnel money.

I picked up my keys and cell phone and headed past the hallway. The rumors meant people were scared, disoriented, uncertain. When we directed their energy to calling councilmembers, they all gave the same story: staffers would take their name and address, admit all calls they received were opposed to casinos, and then refuse to disclose how the councilmember would vote.

I veered left into council chambers, where large mahogany doors opened into a spacious room, rebuilt in the late 1890s to accommodate the opulent wishes of City Council. Stiff wooden chairs faced an ornate podium, outfitted with the chairwoman's hand-carved chair, onyx panels, and ornamentation of inlaid marble and pearl.

Arising from the thirty anti-casino early-comers, Kathy Dilonardo greeted me with a quick hug. "We *need* to win this today."

"Not really," I said softly. "We'll learn where council is based on how they vote on this. It's like a test run."

Kathy shook her head and gave me a fierce stare. "No, you need to understand that we *have* to win it. If not, the press will repeat all over again that's it over for us."

I wondered how Jethro would turn this into a chance to bring Kathy closer to CFP. When nothing came, I said what came naturally. "Press don't determine or even reflect reality. We can't rely on them for our analysis. If we don't go away, then it's not over. There are lawsuits, the referendum, and other options to fight. The press can't tell us if we're going to go away or not, even if they think they can." She nodded slowly, methodically. "Spread that to others in CFP," I added, hoping Jethro might be proud of that intervention.

"Not everyone sees things the way you do," Kathy said. "You need to understand that any victory helps us."

"*Of course*," I said. "But if council votes against us, people can't lose their heads."

I wasn't sure what it meant that Kathy shrugged her shoulders and took a seat. She sighed heavily. "Council needs to hear from us because it's high time they got educated to the facts."

I dismissed my inclination to argue with her. This was the wrong moment to point out that politicians don't need education, they need pressure. We'd get there. Instead, I surprised Kathy and myself with my sudden loudness. "*That's right!* This *is* the first time the public speaks before elected officials on casinos—it's already a win!"

She nodded in earnest but said nothing.

Is she always this serious? Am I not living up to her expectations of a leader? Maybe it's just anxiety, since her house is so close to Foxwoods. Maybe she's just naturally prickly. Yet, I find her directness refreshing, too.

I left Kathy for conversations with the hundred-plus other supporters. Six months ago, we would have had trouble filling the first long row. But now we filled all six rows and the side rows—even the mezzanine was overflowing with supporters. *Everything* we did was going to be writ large.

It wasn't just our 600-email announcement listserve, or successful outreach to civics, or follow-up calls to key supporters and networks. It was that after frostbitten hands, people were *clamoring* to testify before council. After people fight for things, they often learn they deserve it.

The council president gaveled the committee meeting to order. Briefcase-wielding lawyers for the casinos spoke first. With a suppressed yawn I looked at Kathy, who grimaced, grabbing tightly to her chair and shaking her head fiercely. They repeated their claims of creating jobs and revenues—no response to our petition drive, just like in the Fox debate. "Our site remains our first choice among all the sites in the city."

I wanted action, engagement—not just to watch. I wanted to shout in disagreement at their lies that I-95 was a buffer between them and homes, or that the casinos would bring jobs into the city, or their smooth, smiling assurance the casinos would pay for any road upgrades to handle the 80,000 extra cars on the street—only it was 15,000, they claimed.

But hearings were a one-way dialogue, with panels of three speaking at an oversized table eye-level with councilmembers. It was the opposite of the interactive, experiential method of teaching I used in training mediators and then for a decade with Training for Change. Boring as watching paint dry, the carefully vetted public relations spin continued. Even our message became tiresome to me as forty-plus residents, religious leaders, longshoremen, and business leaders trooped up to deliver our talking points: *Not in our neighborhoods, we don't want them, they were never invited.* Glazed councilmembers walked out. Absent from the hearings were the passion, conflict, emotion, or political subtext that make debates interesting. It was all political theater at its climax of dullness.

In other words, it was a classic council hearing.

Only two events stood out from the doldrum. One was civic leaders announcing the emergence of the newly formed Delaware Riverfront Neighborhood Alliance. With roots in the negotiations committee from our strategy retreat, the DRNA was a wholly unique amalgam of politically conflicted civic leaders, many who had fought each other in neighborhood turf fights. With gentle prodding, Jethro and I had coached several of their leaders; I even sent out their first press release at the request of their de facto facilitator, Chris Meck. Now it was a full coalition of a dozen civic associations, claiming to represent over 200,000 Philadelphia residents.

The second was the testimony of Jeff Benedict. Having testified many times on the dangers of casino expansion, he easily recited how, after originally embracing casino gambling with promises of $400 million a year, his state of Connecticut halted the expansion of Foxwoods, even though Foxwoods promised upwards of $800 million a year. "The promise of new tax revenues had turned out to be a mirage. The infrastructure needed to support the casinos put unforeseen strains and costs on the state and its municipalities, costs ultimately passed on to the taxpayers. And social costs generated by a new wave of gambling addicts brought bankruptcies, property foreclosures, crime, divorce, and suicides, all of which had hidden price tags for the state."

These were many of the same statements we'd heard repeated again and again: casinos would compete with local restaurants and have a vast array of hidden costs, and the promises would turn out to be mythical. But it was when he veered off his script that was most telling. "I did however hear two things today that surprised me. One was the casinos would generate 'spin-off jobs,' and the other one was the quote, 'The arrival of new businesses and thousands of jobs.' I've heard that statement lots of times—that's not new. What surprised me was who made it. The 'spin-off' comment came from the city's lawyer. The 'arrival of new businesses' came from the city planner. I have never heard a city official, attorney, or planner make that argument. It's always been made by the lobbyists and the lawyers for the casinos." He openly wondered what was happening that our officials had bought arguments that were "proven to be not true in almost every location casinos have gone in—except for Las Vegas. To argue that you're going to see spin-off jobs is mythical, unless these two casinos are able to do something that no other casino has done."

The hearings continued for *seven* excruciating hours. By the last panel, the room felt bare and depleted. The shine on the decorative gold around the room turned lackluster as the sun set. The casinos' lawyers had left long ago. Our holdouts—mostly retirees—filled the first six rows, listening as the chair announced a five-minute break before the vote on the raft of DiCicco's bills.

Groggy from testimony, I stretched my arms and stood up to feel my legs again. At the front bench, previously absent councilmembers arrived as if summoned and joined DiCicco in a large huddle. We were spectators once again.

I greeted supporters, many of whom had spoken for the first time before council. My eyes kept glancing helplessly toward the front, frustrated that nobody seemed angry enough to—I dunno—rush the stage and take over the hearing.

Councilmembers took their seats for only a moment. "This will conclude our public hearing today," said the chairwoman, before banging her gavel. "Tomorrow the 1,500-foot buffer-zone referendum question will be introduced, and we'll set a hearing for two weeks from then." The crowd was silent.

"Did we just lose?" Kathy's stage whisper echoed through the crowd.

"Not exactly," I said. "Council's refusing to take a side. Maybe they're... I dunno, maybe our presence made a difference."

"They're chicken," shouted Andrea, joining a crowd around me. "They won't vote for DiCicco's bills." Her face looked crushed.

"I agree they don't *want* to touch this." I rose from my seat. "But they did. Today they didn't vote against us, and that's something. Plus, they've felt our crowd's staying power. Whether or not they want to admit it, today they touched the issue of casinos for the first time."

"That's fine," said Kathy with urgency. "But we *have* to get council to take our side. And we have no plan for that yet."

I couldn't completely disagree with her. We needed a plan quickly.

Jethro insisted we not lobby traditionally. "I cut my teeth as a community organizer in the Fenway Civic Association. They taught me that we're not subservient petitioners to politicians—they're *our* representatives. I once watched the Boston mayor literally beg on his knees for support. They've earned that kind of respect by carrying an attitude of ultimatums and demands instead of kowtowing and requesting. So we're not going to ask for meetings with them, which they may deign to accept—or deny."

Anne and I quickly agreed to Jethro's lobbying strategy: Show up at offices. Meet whomever is there. Make our presence known. "If we're not powerful enough that people want to meet with us," Jethro said, "then we're not powerful enough to influence the meeting's outcome."

So the week after DiCicco's unsuccessful attempt to pass his bills, I joined a handful of CFP supporters stalking the hallways of City Hall. En route to various offices, we waved cheerily to members of the Delaware Riverfront Neighborhood Alliance and exchanged awkward stares with sharply dressed casino executives and lawyers, who frowned disapprovingly at our ragtag attire.

Each meeting had a similar tenor. Jethro, myself, and three other Casino-Free supporters would walk into a councilmember's bright offices. "Good morning. Is the councilwoman here?"

The receptionist looked tired but friendly. "Who may I say is asking?"

"We're with Casino-Free Philadelphia." The receptionist snapped her head up to look at us, as if suddenly seeing us, shuffled some papers while on the phone, and magically, a legislative aide sidled up to the table from nowhere.

"The councilwoman is in a really important meeting right now," the aide would say. "But please, let's sit down and talk."

We would, building up relationships with legislative aides. Each aide repeated similar sentiments from their bosses. Councilman Kenney's told us, "He's sick and tired of being the only entity to solve this problem. This was created by the state, and now certain council candidates are trying to twist this into our problem." And Councilman Greenlee's: "I'm not ready to predict what will happen, or how he will vote. But we're sensitive to the fact that many people signed this petition."

With that, most leaned in closely, intimately. "We agree nobody has really explained how this will impact small businesses, or mental illnesses, or crime, or traffic, or schools. But what do you expect to accomplish? You know it's hopeless."

"Get your councilmember to vote with us," we'd entreat.

Our officials' mantra, "There's nothing we can do," wore on me. They were like limp noodles, needing us to prop them up. But that took time away from building supporters. Hours felt squandered in those meetings.

As Jethro and I finally headed out of City Hall, we ran into Councilman DiCicco. He saw us first and began waving his hands against our expected barrage of complaints. "Look, guys," he said defensively. "I was just speaking my mind."

Downcast by being unable to move his bills, DiCicco had told the press the referendum had "a slim chance of getting passed." Referring to the votes required, "I think it's going to be tough to get the nine."

"Then speak it," said Jethro. "But you know what needs to be done strategically. Share with us. Give us names of who is with us, who is against us. You've got the inside track with Vince Fumo. Fill us in with details."

"I'm doing everything that I can," said DiCicco. "Vince is spitting mad at me and I have to hang up on him because he won't let it go."

DiCicco had gotten council to hire a lawyer to challenge the PGCB—and after weeks of looking for lawyers who were not connected to a casino, finally found a firm. Then they were hired by SugarHouse. So he found another one. Maybe he really *was* challenging his mentor, or maybe it was just a game of political survival.

"People are looking to you," said Jethro, his face impassive. "It's disempowering if you just tell us it's hopeless. It's empowering if you show us how this can be won. Who are the councilmembers that need extra pressure? Where are they vulnerable? You know this stuff and aren't sharing it. You can lead on this issue, or others will."

DiCicco stepped back, as if struck.

"We've never taken sides in electoral races," I said to DiCicco. His opponent Vern Anastasio was embracing us, but that wasn't what Jethro meant. Jethro wasn't making a threat, just explaining that if DiCicco didn't politically lead, our grassroots movement would.

"I have a constituency to think about," said DiCicco, turning to leave. "I've been straight with everybody that I think this is a long shot. Councilman Kenney is with us, and maybe Verna. But I don't want to get anybody's hopes up." DiCicco brushed past us.

"Sure," said Jethro, lifting his voice as we watched DiCicco's back. "It *would* be the worst thing if Philadelphians got a little hope and learned a little strategy."

Anne called me days later, just as I was finishing work and entering an elevator to go home. Her normally upbeat voice was shaking. That could only mean bad news. "I just got a call from Chris Brennan! SugarHouse is accusing us of massive fraud! They're challenging our petitions in court, saying we didn't get enough."

My heart sank. "What do we know?"

"Not much. They're sneaks, making the attack late in the evening so press don't have time to dig into details. They're saying we didn't get close to 20,000 signatures—leaving only 6,000 valid signatures." Anne's voice cracked. "Can you believe it? *Massive fraud!*"

"Terrible," I said. Core activists' faces flashed before me: Kathy, Shirley, Morgan, Paul, Mary. *They're going to be devastated. Angry. Pissed.* I felt selfish for wanting my evening off. "The challenge makes it sound like we're part of some conspiracy."

"I know," she said. Her voice rose with anger. "Reporters don't even have copies of SugarHouse's official challenge! These guys are trying to take our city. First they give illegal campaign contributions. Now they're trying to squash the little guy!"

"Okay..." My mind felt like molasses. "SugarHouse is being smart. Without copies of their complaint to challenge directly, it's just their facts versus our rhetoric."

"We need lawyers to defend the petition drive!"

"Yeah," I said, "but we need a response now, a way to talk about this."

Anne's voice cooled a bit. "Paul suggested restarting the petition drive. If 27,000 isn't enough for them, how about ten times that by November?"

Not another wild petition drive. "Seems like a lot of work," I said, "maybe too early to promise that." I understated it to lessen the blow of shooting down ideas in a time of crisis.

The elevator opened up and I stalked out, pacing in front of a security desk. I vaguely wondered what the officer thought of my agitated hand gestures. "This can rebound on them," I told Anne. "We need a little political jujitsu, to help people see what this is: a bullying tactic."

"We could ask investors to divest themselves."

"Sure," I clapped, "an open letter."

"Distancing themselves from a company that tries to stop people from voting."

"It's a start. It's high-ground and not from fear but from a sense of power. The point here is to show people the casinos are scared of us. Us, the little guy. That means we have power." I paused. "So what now?"

"We talk to press."

The next morning, I awoke from an uneasy sleep, padded downstairs, and tried to ignore the newspaper on my breakfast table. I wanted a moment away from my fears of a protracted legal battle, losing council support, and attacks claiming we were part of a vast conspiracy.

I munched idly on some toast, but the newspaper, strewn by housemates over the kitchen table, kept beckoning. Curiosity finally burst through, and I scanned the *Inquirer*. "The fight over development of two casinos on the Philadelphia waterfront turned nasty yesterday, as SugarHouse Casino claimed 'widespread and pervasive fraud' in the petition drive to ban slots parlors from Delaware Avenue."

The numbers in black and white felt like jabs to the stomach: 9,147 unregistered signatures, 3,813 illegible, 1,278 signed twice, 1,150 incomplete. Any inconsistency—a scribbled letter, a nickname, a missing initial—and it was scrubbed, leaving SugarHouse to claim we had only 6,615 valid signatures. The casinos had found a new talking point, one they could attack with for months. Our reputation could go down the drain.

The article continued, "Mary Reinhart, a retiree from Pennsport, said she spent more than 30 hours collecting signatures, often in the freezing cold. 'I don't care how aggressively and highly paid they are,' she said. 'I'm going to stand right up and protect my house and protect my neighborhood.'"

I pulled up my laptop to skim the *Daily News*. Unlike its sister, the *Philadelphia Inquirer*, it was a tabloid, always dramatic, with an emphasis on the sensational.

I numbly shook my head at veteran reporter Chris Brennan's article. "The casino bringing the suit alleges that many names appear to be forged. Three US presidents, George Washington, Thomas Jefferson and George W. Bush, are listed on the petitions but are scratched out. Bush's signature lists his White House address and his occupation as 'dumbass.'"

It took close reading to notice the names were those that Shirley had eye-numbingly scratched out. *Doesn't that disprove the point?*

No, Chris is going to print any accusations, give us a quote, and act like that means fair reporting.

Calm down. Take a breath. Everything needs to be seen from multiple views. He's just making an interesting, dramatic story. It's not bias against us, it's his journal's bias toward sensationalism, for better and worse.

I tiptoed through the rest of his article. Anne said, "Challenging petitions is what Philly does, it's a kind of sport. But being accused of fraud is far over the top." And, "Hunter said it was good that the casino owners can voice their challenge. 'It's great that they have input,' Hunter said. 'That's what we're fighting for.'"

It was at the end that I noticed: None of the casino spokespeople had comments in any newspaper. Their accusations were solely written in the gravitas of hard numbers. It was another sign their message was targeting the public and politicians. *Even if we win the expected weeks-long, drawn-out, signature-by-signature challenge, it's not over. If the accusation sticks even halfway, it provides more than abundant cover for politicians to hide.*

I flipped to the *Metro*, where I'd hit my stride during my last interview of the night.

Casino Foes Smell Fear: Activists claim lawsuit legitimizes their efforts

Casino-Free Philadelphia organizers said the lawsuit illustrates real concern by the casino that the two state-awarded licenses may be revoked.

"Some people have said this [referendum] won't stand up in court or that the state will merely come in and take over," Casino-Free organizer Daniel Hunter said. "The ferocity with which they're attacking us is a sign that this is a real threat to them."

I barely remembered saying those words. But they were classic political jujitsu, using the attacker's force against them. *The harder they hit us with expensive lawyers and aggressive public relations firms, the harder they fall, if we successfully redirect their attacking energy.*

I stared at the words: they were true. *We know their game, and it means they're desperate. But it's not just an existential threat to them. It is to us, too.*

Later that morning, I packed my things and headed to Swarthmore College. I wanted solace in its lush landscape, far from the craziness of anxious supporters and terrified callers. A short train ride took me to George Lakey's cozy second-floor office. There's nothing like an elder who will offer you space to just be.

I dashed in, slinging my backpack onto the table across from him.

He looked up from his computer and stood up to greet me. "I read the *Inquirer* this morning. Massive fraud, huh? Pretty ridiculous."

"It's overkill," I shouted. "It's the pot calling the kettle black. I know projection when I see it." I sat down and folded my legs onto the chair, clutching them.

He carefully perched on his chair, joining me at eye level. "That's gotta get to you, though. Public attacks are the worst, when lies are printed openly. How are you dealing with it?"

In our motion last night, neither Jethro nor Anne—and surely not press—had asked me that yet. My voice surprised itself with its constriction. "It's ludicrous! They're accusing 70-year-old women, who are trying to protect their homes, with fraud... saying they lied, cheated."

George nodded, his eyes large. "Yes. It's hard to believe. And you're defending yourself already. But it still must hurt."

I gazed toward the ground. "Their claims can't and won't stand up. They're just trying to influence the council committee's vote tomorrow. I've met more signatories than they claim signed the petition!"

George's wrinkled face cracked into an affectionate grin. "It's got to have some impact on you. To have an attack so publicly on your efforts." He gazed into our years of friendship.

My eyes watered, "Yeah, George. It does hurt."

An internal struggle took place: I could vent, let out some of the frustration. It was wrong, them dragging our names through the mud... money versus people... the tiredness from last night... the wrongness of a powerful industry spending thousands of dollars to malign Philadelphians just trying to get a say... to malign us—we—me.

But I was already tired. If I slowed down, would I be able to stay in motion? I had an open letter to revise, leaders to call, supporters to inform of the accusation, hundreds of urgent emails to respond to, lawyers to hire for the challenge, and council offices to defend our reputations to. If I slowed now, maybe I'd never be able to keep going...

I pushed the tears back. "We have to win the challenge. There is too much riding on this."

"Of course." George leaned back, his white hair catching rays of sunshine. "Then what's next?"

"We need to weather this immediate hit. We've got an open letter telling investors to withdraw the challenge or pull out from a firm actively undermining the democratic process."

He smiled at me. "You always have a response."

"We're just getting warmed up."

I pulled out my computer as George turned toward his, transitioning to the warm, comfortable style of working next to each other. Years ago, we had spent hours co-writing training materials for Training for Change, from articles on activist pedagogy to a whole book on training for nonviolent intervention. The familiarity helped me slow down and take time to think about how to communicate with our supporters.

I started writing: "Urgent action alert: casinos challenge petition drive..."

I hit "delete." We needed to move people *out* of urgency. Hype emails can get people to sign a petition or show up to a single rally, but they will burn people out in the long-term. Reacting from fear would never build a flexible, resilient movement. We needed a high-ground place.

"Yesterday, casinos admitted we're a threat to their undemocratic ways..."

Delete. It read well in the *Metro*, acknowledging our power and all. But it was too rhetorical, almost naïve. Too positive in the face of the urgent calls from supporters.

I leaned back in my chair, gazing out at the bright, sunny March weather. The leaves were just returning, a few buds beginning to open.

Like a flash, a quote from Mohandas Gandhi struck me. I typed it out quickly: "First they ignore you, then they laugh at you, then they attack you, then you win."

"We've now fully entered step three in Gandhi's campaigning," I wrote. The rest of the email flowed quickly. Upbeat. Positive. Acknowledging the danger, but without pleading, desperation, or frothy urgency. "So with that, please join us tomorrow for City Council hearings as the referendum is introduced."

I pressed "send" and sat back, pleased. We were refusing to allow their attack to be a weapon of fear or desperation for us. We were going to build a grounded movement, where people could take a hit and keep standing, without shrieking in desperation or miring ourselves in defeatism. We were going to model integrity, high-ground framing...

An email from Jethro interrupted me: "Don't you mean 'we win'? Oh, wonderful typos. Thanks for getting this out."

I cursed my despairing Freudian slip. I had written, "First they ignore you, then they laugh at you, then they attack you, then *they* win."

I rushed to cancel the send, resending a correction.

Thankfully, few of those who saw the first email missed the point. *"Of course you mean we win! I'm in! I'm stoked!"* We were bouncing back from this.

I worked late in the evening for my paid work with Training for Change, to wake up the next morning facing two CFP challenges: defending our signatures, and council's introduction of the 1,500-foot buffer zone.

Mary Reinhart rose from the front row of council chambers to greet me. Sitting to her right and left were Andrea Preis and Kathy DeAngelis, part of the crew of die-hard retirees. At first glance, they looked as intimidating as gray-haired kittens, holding their "CasiNO" placards. But at second glance, one couldn't miss their faces: stern, sharp as claws. It was their neighborhoods at stake.

"How are you doing?" I asked Mary as I gave her a hug.

"Angry! The casinos are shameless, calling us liars."

"Your quote in the paper was perfect," I said. "That kind of high-ground framing makes it hard for council to believe their claims. We're showing what's true: the casinos are bullying the city and its citizens."

"It's not valid," said Mary with a steely gaze. "I was out there."

I nodded. "Otherwise, you doing okay?"

Even without a smile on her face, her animated gestures were filled with life and grace. "I'm very nervous. All my neighborhood is scared. The papers keep saying we don't have much chance to win council's vote. Do we?"

With the mayor threatening to veto, our prospects of getting our bill out of the committee were unclear. Councilmembers gave us no promises, and DiCicco gave us suggestive scraps, but no firm information. From our lobbying visits, only Councilmember Kenney was a certain yes vote. The rest were being lobbied hard against us by the casino industry, the mayor, chamber of commerce, building trades unions, the governor...

Mary and the other retirees looked at me expectantly. I would give her all the information I had, but first I wanted her to hear it without an edge of fear. "Were the papers right about our chances of getting 20,000 signatures?"

She shook her head.

"No, because they underestimate us. They keep thinking in traditional terms of power. They see power as flowing downwards, from the governor to the mayor to council. Many civics see it that way, too, that they should take orders from DiCicco and council, and then tell their people what to do, and so on, downwards. But I don't believe that's true. We're building a movement on a belief that, on their own, powerholders can do nothing—they need our cooperation, our submission. They wanted us to be quiet as they screwed us from having any meaningful say in the PGCB. Now they want us to be silent and believe in their invincibility. And the media and pundits play right into that." My voice rose. "If we lose today, they'll say it proves our efforts were a waste of time and energy. They'll retell the story of the casinos' invincibility. But if we win today, I'll guarantee you this..."

I paused, allowing everyone to lean in closely. I whispered, "... they'll tell the story that it was a fluke, a mistake, or internal political machinations that have nothing to do with us. They'll never give us the credit we deserve, because they don't believe in people power. But whether we win or lose today, we will *still* have power, whether we use it or not."

Mary exhaled slightly.

"As for today," I continued, "we still don't know how council views the accusation of fraud. The council chair has deep roots with the building trades. While on the campaign trail, he's sometimes saying he's anti-casino, sometimes pro-casino—but who knows if the money has bought his vote? His hypocrisy means he respects us enough to cater to us. A social-change philosopher once wrote, 'Wherever there is hypocrisy, there is hope.'" Mary nodded, as anti-casino supporters filled the last of the floor seats. "The bigger concern is whether the accusation of fraud has stuck in their minds—or if we've done enough to avoid that. Whatever happens," I said, "we will fight on."

As at the last council session, anti-casino supporters flooded council, spilling into the upstairs balcony.

First up in the council committee hearing: Bob Sheldon, president of SugarHouse. His tall, lanky body strode to the microphone. "We're anxious to begin operations," he told councilmembers, "that will mean thousands of new jobs and new career opportunities and millions of dollars in new tax revenues." He went on to say that the state would receive 43% of the casino's revenues, which statewide would go to property "tax relief"—except in Philadelphia, where it would reduce Philadelphia's wage tax.

Boos cried out from the floor, as the chairman banged his gavel, encouraging the speaker to continue. The hisses only increased, echoing through the high ceiling of the chambers. The chairman yelled at the crowd to settle down, ineffectually banging his gavel.

This could get ugly. We had a powder keg: a chair unskilled in crowd control and a hostile target whose company had just called us liars in public. The crowd was menacing, frustrated, angry. All we needed was a spark, and I worried someone might do something to cement in council's mind that we're not the underdog, but the bully.

One row away from me, a bulky longshoreman stood up. I whipped around in my chair, readying myself to intervene—not knowing what I'd do.

Security ran toward the standing man, who cupped his hands and loudly booed. Slowly, as if aware of all the eyes on him, he turned until his large back was all that faced Bob Sheldon.

I relaxed. *This won't physically escalate. In fact, it is brilliant.*

Security reached him and beckoned him to sit. But others had caught on. The 100-plus crowd rose to its feet with backs turned. Security wheeled around in retreat as the chair continued to bang his gavel.

The SugarHouse president tried to continue, but, perhaps signaled by one of his media consultants, cut it short. "This bill and this ballot initiative will deny all of these benefits, and we hope you'll oppose it." He stormed off and beelined to the exit. Boos echoed from every corner of the chambers.

I sat back in my chair to see Councilman Kenney's contorted face. Holding his hand over the microphone, he pulled the other councilmembers close and whispered.

The seconds dragged on to minutes. *Do they think we crossed a line? Will they vote against us to make a point? Can they kick us out?*

"What I'd like to do now," said Kenney, "is vote this resolution and bill out of committee, then come back and listen to the rest of the testimony." He added weakly, "if that's okay."

Shocked, we watched the committee move, second, and pass the buffer zone unanimously.

I sat dumbstruck. It was so quick. I eventually heard the cheers around me and joined in. We had won this round. Now the bill went to full council.

The chairman half-stood up, preparing to leave. "Does anyone wish to testify?"

A blur, Paul raced to the testifying desk, motioning toward me.

"Nobody?" The councilman lifted his gavel, as Paul grabbed Chuck Valentine and yelled, "We do, we do!" We rushed to the microphones as the chair reluctantly released the gavel.

Our testimony didn't focus on why we opposed casinos. It was defending our reputation, framing the turning our backs. I told the councilmembers, "That outrage is the result of disrespect. Heckling is nothing compared to preventing a democratic vote."

Paul slammed the pro-casino city solicitor's one-sided treatment of the casinos. "He's violating his ethical responsibility as a lawyer to be candid." Chuck told the story of his freezing fingers outside of his local grocery store gathering signatures, only to conclude in his street-savvy style through clenched teeth, "I'm angry that so many Philadelphians had to work so hard just to have the right to participate in the process. What a disgrace for the birthplace of our country's great democracy."

Council listened passively as up trooped another dozen testifiers, despite the chairman's pleas to shorten our testimony. We wouldn't let them tell us what to do. Instead, *everything* we did was going to be writ large—even in our success. ILA's president Jim Paylor spoke, then Karin DiNardi in her wheelchair, and on and on...

I sat with a big smile on my face. For the first time that week, I believed we might really vote on the buffer zone.

SugarHouse's media teams invested overtime in maximizing exposure of our "massive fraud" in reams of newspapers and TV articles. To slow the hemorrhage of bad news stories, Paul suggested it might be the right timing for filing our lawsuit against the courts. He was more hopeful than I that it would change the narrative. But we needed something—anything—to make a dent against the casinos' constant refrain of calling us frauds.

So the next day, we returned to the industrial-white walls of City Hall, where Paul delivered a stack of papers formally challenging the PGCB's lack of environmental consideration, a widely ignored Pennsylvanian constitutional requirement. This was the sixth Philadelphia lawsuit against the PGCB, including an appeal from a losing casino applicant, a lawsuit by civic associations against Foxwoods, City Council's appeal, and a previous Casino-Free Philadelphia lawsuit challenging the process of selection. Our first lawsuit from four months ago, challenging the constitutionality of Act 71, was gathering dust in the Supreme Court.

A half-dozen reporters swarmed as Paul exited—not because they believed the courts would provide relief, but because they were now focused on every twist in our dramatic storyline of casinos versus citizen's group—or fraudulent front organization. It was something else to report.

"Even if there is corruption and the courts don't take this seriously," Paul told to reporters, rocking on his feet as if to make up for his short stature, "it still behooves us to do the right thing."

I watched from afar, sliding down a wall, happy to have Paul handling the press. The petition challenge weighed on my mind. Suspiciously, the courts had recruited an out-of-city judge to oversee the case. The judge had rushed the court date for the petition challenge—less than a week. We needed lawyers immediately to defend our signatures.

I called the number Anne had given me. A rapid-fire voice greeted my introduction.

"You want to hire me or not?" Lawyer Larry Otter's voice was sharp as a needle.

"How much do you cost?"

"For you? I could go as low as $100 per hour."

I cursed silently. A few hours of his time would deplete our funds, leaving Jethro and me once again without a paycheck. *Why do lawyers get paid when top-quality organizers don't?* Larry's impatient breathing hurried me along. "Look," I said. "I can't make promises about money. But do you know who we're up against? You're up for the challenge?"

"Of course," he said with a trace of impatience. "Richard Sprague is a legend. You're up against one of the most famed lawyers in the country. But I am ready. I've successfully argued hundreds of these petition-signature cases. It'll be a long slog going through thousands. So, you want to do this?"

Of his background, I had no doubt. He had a lengthy record of winning petition challenges locally, statewide, and nationally. But even if we could get Larry's price down a little more, we'd be scrambling for funds. "I'll run this by the executive team—and quickly. We know the challenge starts in days," I said. "Money is our biggest concern, but we know you bring the credentials."

"Let me know when you figure it out." He hung up.

He was brusque, badgering, almost prickish. But that's what we needed, someone to argue each 'dotted i' and 'crossed t' in a signature-by-signature challenge.

I relaxed my shoulders as Jethro came over and silently sat next to me. We said nothing until Paul finished his interviews and we headed together down the elevator and toward the DRNA's second full gathering.

Once at Paul's car, I jumped into the front passenger seat. "I'm taking long-leg privilege," I shouted. Jethro squeezed into the back. The car revved its engine and we pulled out.

On the road, Jethro blurted, "Hey, Paul. What's the worst thing the casinos might learn about you?"

Paul clenched the wheel. "*What?*"

I nodded at Jethro. "The casinos are scrambling," said Jethro. "These aren't their last attacks. They're going to do opposition research on us. The rumors of private investigators against us are probably true. They're going to take the worst things they can find about us and make them public."

"It's about discrediting the movement," I said. "They're going to attack us leaders. We can only defend each other if we are ready ahead of time."

Paul shifted uncomfortably, braking for a stop sign. "I'm not a leader."

Jethro leaned forward. "You are now. We're asking everyone in the executive team."

"Model it for him," I told Jethro.

"They're going to say that I'm a professional organizer," said Jethro. "That's supposed to be a bad thing. But it comes from overpaid public-relations hacks. It's funny—when you're sick, you pay for a doctor. When you need public relations, you pay a PR firm—"

"—and when you need a casino stopped, you pay for organizers," I said.

"Right... To vilify me," said Jethro, "they're saying I moved into Fishtown to be part of this fight."

Paul looked incredulous. "Who would believe that? People don't move somewhere just to fight."

"It's not about truth," replied Jethro. "John Miller and Dan Fee from SugarHouse are already spreading these rumors. I moved to Fishtown in 2003 way before SugarHouse was announced. But I bought my house where I live now three years later, after SugarHouse had a proposal. I didn't know any more about it than any of my neighbors. But they're saying I came to make trouble."

"That's why we have to be ready to defend each other," I said.

"Exactly," said Jethro. "It's all part of a large campaign. SugarHouse has been buying advertisements for months in the Fishtown newspapers. Just last week, they got a big article with pictures of their executives going door-to-door. They have millions at stake and are going to lie, cheat, and buy support to get it. But I can protect my own reputation. The more they pile on, the better most of my friends and allies will think of me. But if they sued me and got my house..." He paused. "That would be hard for me and my wife."

Paul half-turned to me. "What about you, Daniel?"

"My political views are most vulnerable—and that I'm an activist. I believe capitalism is allowing rich people to live in excess wealth while poor people suffer. So they could charge me with being a democratic socialist and I'd happily agree. But I don't drink, I don't do drugs, I don't have a criminal record, except with civil disobedience. It's the activist stuff they'd try to spin on me. But there's not much."

Stopping at a red light, Paul eyed us wordlessly. But I knew that like all the members of the executive team, he would open up and share. We were getting ready for more attacks—and just in time.

Anne called me up early Monday morning. "We have to get reporters to jump on this! SugarHouse is hiring private investigators—it's a news story!"

"Anne..." My voice surprised itself with its almost pleading compared to her steely, determined voice. "We can't overreact..."

"This is intimidation! We have to take advantage of this now!"

Part of me wanted to smother her certainty. She was *certain* we'd get 27,000. Then *certain* we'd win City Council. Now *certain* there were thugs on people's doorsteps. But when it came to the heavy lifting, that fell to others.

"We need you to focus on the petition challenge," I said. "We can't pass around rumors."

"We're hearing it from Pennsport, Queen Village, all over! We know it's true."

I tried to clear my head. *This isn't fair. Anne's a politician, an ex-business executive. To make it in those chauvinistic worlds, she must have built up a strong shell.* She had learned to give orders, bark optimism in the face of overwhelming odds. Even if she wasn't certain, she had learned that strategy to move things forward. And she had never been wrong.

My voice matched her certainty. "Without confirmation, we can't make it public, in case it isn't true. Maybe they're merely doing opposition research, not something nefarious."

Anne paused with deliberation. "I'll get confirmation," she snapped.

A few hours later, she emailed Jethro and me that she had a confirmed story, unearthed by Rene Goodwin. "Lose your caution, we need to get a reporter right away!" Then, seconds later, a second email. "Stop! Chris Brennan just called—he's on the story!"

I wouldn't know how right she was until the next morning.

That night, chaos filled Shirley's house. Drywall lay against the walls in the back room, an obstacle course of buckets and sawdust in the front. With a smile, she told us not to try to go upstairs.

It matched our scattered, nervous energy. Anne raged about "hired thugs" to Kathy Dilonardo, whose eyes grew large at the telling, as Paul and Jethro leaned close, sharing frustrations about getting civics to move more quickly. Even Jethro looked tense.

I slid into the high-back wood chairs at her dining room table. With its extra leaf placed in the center, the table filled the room, pushing us and our expanded circle to the edges of the walls. I brought copies of past meetings' newsprints, my own way to avoid writing lengthy minutes but keep the momentum from meeting to meeting. I wrote out an agenda for this meeting as others gathered and picked their tea.

I had accepted the role of facilitator mostly by default. My early attempts at rotating leadership had gone flat, with most everyone turning me down, either saying they didn't want to do it or that I was "too good—it's a waste to not use your talents."

"What kind of tea do you want?" asked Shirley. Despite the chaos, she looked as bright and cheery as ever. Her years of Buddhist spiritual practice made a difference.

I grabbed the last mint tea bag from her Tupperware container.

We descended into the agenda: *tomorrow's petition challenge.*

"We're as prepared as we can be," said Anne. "But we haven't gotten copies of SugarHouse's complaint against us."

It took a moment for Kathy to register this. "What? Why not?"

"Technically," said Anne, "SugarHouse is challenging the *city's acceptance* of the 27,000 signatures—not us. That means we aren't defendants and not technically in the case. And SugarHouse is playing hardball and refusing to give us the challenge."

Paul looked shocked. "We should have gotten a copy! The city solicitor? Someone? You have to tell the lawyers we have a right to it."

"They're pissed about it, too," said Anne, managing to sound both optimistic and aggrieved. "Everyone denied our request to see the complaints."

"But..." Paul stumbled to find his words, his face turning beet red. "That violates the basic civil decency of every lawyer. I've never heard of anyone doing that. It's just... it's wrong... wrong."

"You're right. It's sleazy," Anne said. "They want to make us fight blind."

"We need to get a copy of the challenge," said Kathy.

"You know what we should do," said Shirley. "We should write a press release. This is an outrage."

"Our lawyers are on it," I quickly interjected. "It's not press-worthy on its own, but everyone will see the injustice tomorrow. We can't let our nervousness cause us to micromanage each other's work." I stood up to transition the energy of the room. "Thanks, Anne."

I made a big checkmark on our agenda and elicited a cheer from our group. Years of meeting facilitation had taught me that the key to a good meeting was creating a sense of momentum. The physical check, cheer, and the look of relief on our faces as we moved through the agenda was just that.

Report from last strategy retreat.

"Our second retreat was shorter," I reported. "And hard for us to not talk about all the immediate issues. But we did make one big decision at that retreat."

I unveiled a newsprint with colored circles representing active committees: Lobbying, Legal, Media, Outreach, Admin, Fundraising, and Research. Each had a chair, represented at the table, who together made up the executive team.

"Some, of course, are more active than others right now. But we're going to work on it," I said.

Kathy raised her hand, then blurted, "But who makes decisions when we don't agree?"

"Hopefully we'll make all the important decisions together," I said, as Kathy and Shirley exchanged glances. "But there's a core of decision-makers—Anne Dicker, Jethro Heiko, and myself."

We hadn't been appointed, but by the amount of experience and energy we gave to the movement, we were easily identified leaders. Jethro and I had grudgingly accepted the role, more comfortable in a flat structure.

"Can we move on for now? There's a lot to cover."

Kathy nodded, still looking unsatisfied. I gave a checkmark.

Create an action to challenge SugarHouse's door-to-door harassment.

"Whether Chris Brennan covers Anne's story or not," I said, "we need an action to stay on the offensive." I proposed a press-friendly action for Wednesday's lunch-break, during the week-long petition challenge, calling it the "We-Are-Not-Scared-of-Stunts action." It was quickly accepted, even as people were a bit confused how it would work. "Show up on Wednesday and we'll all find out," I laughed.

Check.

Lobbying City Council.

Updates, decisions, check!

Press releases for upcoming actions.

Check.

We ended our meeting only ten minutes over schedule.

The next morning I woke up groggily, pulling my laptop onto my bed. There was nothing further I could do to prepare for today's court challenge. But I had nervousness to burn and so poured my first waking hour on emails—nudging the East Kensington Neighbors Association to join the DRNA, editing press releases, and sending invitations to Wednesday's We-Are-Not-Scared-of-Stunts action. Only when I headed downstairs did I see how right Anne had been.

The *Daily News* front page featured a shadowy green image of *X-Files*-like aliens sinisterly entering a doorway. The headline blared in bold letters, "Intimidating? You Bet!" The subheading: "Private eye grills petition signer. Judge to hear casino challenge today."

I clapped my hands, eager to see Jethro's face and thank Anne. The *Daily News* sensationalism worked for us, painting SugarHouse in the absolute worst light. *Nobody reading this will think we're anything but the victims!*

The article told the story of Cindy Engst and Fred Farlino, a couple on Federal Street in South Philly who had been confronted by a hired lawyer and a private investigator from New Jersey:

> The two men who knocked on Cindy Farlino's door Saturday had a stack of papers and a couple of pointed questions. They showed Farlino a "Casino-Free Philadelphia" petition and asked if she had signed it.
>
> "I looked at it and said, 'Yes, that's my signature,'" Farlino said. "Then they said, 'Do you have a lawyer, because we'll talk to him.' That took me aback, made me feel like I did something wrong."
>
> Farlino asked to see some identification. One man showed her a New Jersey driver's license and said he was an attorney from "the other side," meaning from one of the two planned casinos in the city. The other man produced a private investigator's identification.
>
> Then they asked if Farlino was a registered voter and how she found out about the petition. Farlino said she wasn't answering any more questions. Still, the men stayed in front of her South Philly home, flipping through copies of the petitions.
>
> They finally took off when she went outside with a digital camera. One of them popped the trunk of their hatch-back car so she couldn't get a shot of the license plate as they pulled away.

Even John Miller's assertion that this was "a normal and ordinary part of a challenge to petitions" somehow just made them sound more out of touch, deceitful, and thuggish.

The trolley ride to City Hall for the courtroom showdown seemed short.

I slipped into the spacious courtroom and was blasted with a wave of tension worthy of a game-seven final match. Dusty pictures of dead men hung from the walls, asserting the formality of the space. Near the front was a large, imposing bench for the judge and, lower, three facing tables for SugarHouse, the chief clerk—the technical defendant—and us. We still had not received SugarHouse's formal challenge.

I moved through the tense crowd. The first person I saw locked eyes with me for a brief moment. Then his brain registered who I was and he hurried off, scoffing. He was on the opposing side.

Finding a natural balance, the two teams slowly established their sides: the ragtag anti-casino folks to the left of the room, pro-casino suits on the right, and a mash of reporters huddled in the back, ferrying to each side for interviews.

I found a seat next to Anne. Her normal confidence notwithstanding, I sensed her nervousness as I gave her a quick hug.

"Good work on the article today! You were right—I was wrong," I said.

She flashed a smile. "It's not about that. It's just important that we win today."

"The article will go a long way to combat people's fear. It's exactly political jujitsu—and I bet SugarHouse will think twice about pulling something like that on us again."

"Yeah..." She tugged at her power-suit. With that and her pearl earrings, she looked more like she belonged on the other side than among our group's casual attire. "Look over there." She pointed. "They brought Richard Sprague to handle this case personally. We're big-time."

He looked old, sharp, and crotchety. Like the kind of man who had given up on earning respect and chose instead to be feared.

At that moment, the judge marched in and dispensed with pleasantries. Anne and I watched as our lawyer argued for us to be in the case.

"Your Honor, I have no objection, but I would like to make a statement," Sprague barged in.

"You'll get your opportunity," the judge said politely. He looked awestruck to be in Sprague's presence.

Sprague ignored the judge and spoke anyway. I didn't understand each word of his legalese; still, I caught the sentiment: *We won't challenge the city's legal standing, but we will challenge Casino-Free Philadelphia's lawyers—we don't want them in the case.*

"Our client created the petition—" cried Larry.

"Your Honor, may I respond?" interrupted Sprague.

"Have I ever cut you off?" smiled the judge.

The judge waded through "Section 1310A statutes" and "indispensable parties aren't part of the litigation" and "amicus brief asking you to dismiss the case" and "law shall not allow their intervention" and, finally—"petition to intervene is granted." We were in the case.

It was a shallow victory, quickly followed by the judge denying the city clerk's and Larry's requests for time to prepare because "we have never been served a copy of the complaint in the exhibit."

With that, Sprague began his arguments. After a lengthy review of the petition drive, filings, and challenges, Sprague brought up witnesses to show our fraud.

Sprague pointed at our petition, asking a witness, "Can you identify your signature there?"

"Yes, sir, right here."

"On there you have what other information?"

"My address, my current residence, my occupation, and the date of signing."

"By the way, where were you living at the time?"

"At the time, I lived with my girlfriend there, but I'm not registered to vote in Philadelphia. I'm registered in Montgomery County."

"The person that brought this and asked you to sign the petition—did they in any way ask you, 'Are you a registered voter in Philadelphia?'"

"Not at that time, no."

"When you say, 'Not at that time,' did they ever come back to you?"

"No."

Next, Amy Michael, a die-hard CFP supporter. Sprague leaned in. "So you signed that as a circulator?"

"Absolutely, yes."

"Now, in addition, you are a notary public, are you not?"

"Correct."

"You notarized a great number of these petitions, correct?"

"I believe 28 pages."

Sprague pulled out the 28 pages with 445 signatures she notarized. "The position is that a notary cannot be an interested party. There's a case by the Supreme Court that when a notary is an interested party—"

"And the circulator is an interested party," said the judge, nodding.

"—and a signer of the petition is an interested party, all names that that notary has notarized are invalid." Sprague smiled with snakelike confidence. He then turned serious. "Your Honor, the next witness, who's blind, will be up here in one or two minutes. Can we wait for two minutes?"

"Anything you request, up to three minutes," said the judge... and so on...

Glancing at my watch, I felt torn. I had to go to work but wanted to stay and be prepared for what would be a late, long night, going through the evidence line by line. Hesitantly, I left the courtroom and entered the cool hallway. Out of the boiling tension, I breathed deep.

A few blocks away, I worked, as Sprague continued a parade of witnesses, culminating with a witness's explanation that only a few thousand signatures were valid, far short of the 20,000 required. Anything wrong with a signature and it was scrubbed: no notary, notary was an interested party, address did not match a registered voter, wrong address, incomplete address, no listed occupation, unable to read the writing.

Infuriated, Anne Dicker called me a few hours later with details of what had happened in the courtroom.

By lunchtime, Sprague had finished his attack and was content to spend the afternoon defending against the only document we had seen: *their* signatures challenging us.

To file its complaint against us, SugarHouse legally had to submit 100 signatures. Apparently, it had had a hard time finding people, because it only had 134 signatures. And two of those signatories told me in strict confidence they had been threatened by their bosses to sign.

If we could prove SugarHouse did not get 100 signatures, its entire complaint would be rejected. So our lawyers quickly put Mary Stumpf on the stand, who had found over forty invalid signatures—many for the same reasons as Sprague's dismissal of ours.

Sprague moved to verify that Mary had used the state database and had methodically searched each person. "Are you telling this court that some of the names on that counter-petition are not registered voters?"

"Yes, I am," said Mary Stumpf.

Sprague studied the pages carefully. He moved to introduce her notes as evidence and called up a systems consultant, with access to the city database, confident that he could disprove her.

"Colleen O'Neal, 3820 Patrician Drive, P-A-T-R-I-C-I-A-N, Drive."

"No, sir," the consultant responded. "I don't see that." Sprague looked surprised.

"The next is Alison Tepper, T E P P-E-R, A-L-I-S-O-N, 2016 Brandywine Street."

The consultant shook his head.

"You do not have Alison?"

"I will double-check. No, sir, I don't."

"Kyle, K-Y-L-E, Wirshbu, W-I-R-S-H-B-U."

"No."

After a dozen signatures were discounted by this method, Sprague's veneer of confidence began to sag. His own witness was proving our claim: Sprague didn't have enough signatures.

"Phillip Griffen, G-R-I-F-F-E-N."

"I don't see it with an EN."

Sprague stopped short. "That can be a problem, Your Honor. We were presented that these papers were the names from our petition. Now I'm hearing that the name that's here that I'm reading from is not the name in our petition. The name is Phillip Griffin, G-R-I-F-F-I-N."

"Your Honor," said Larry, "we're off by one letter. I think we can continue with this exercise until you exhaust the possibilities."

The judge halted Larry to get his bearings. He turned to Sprague, "Hold it. You're saying the exhibits do not accurately reflect the people on your petition?"

Sprague nodded.

The judge said, "It's apparent. You originally offered the exhibits?"

"Yes, I did."

The judge coached, "You want to withdraw that?"

"I sure do."

"Granted."

Larry tried to cross-examine the witness. "Not unless you call him up," the judge snapped, then refused to let Larry call him up. "It's a question of credibility for me."

Larry tried to hide his disgust. "The easiest way to resolve this is to bring in the records—"

"No," the judge cut him off. "I've been resolving credibility for 22 years, counselor. I already decided when Mary Stumpf was testifying and didn't think she was credible," the judge snapped. "Now sit down."

"All I'm asking is that we go through the list of forty, and if we come up with forty bad ones, we can all go home. If we come up with less than that, maybe we have to stay a little longer."

"I heard you say that a few minutes ago, and I'm not impressed," said the judge.

Larry turned red-faced. The judge had just led Sprague out of the wilderness of his own making. "Your Honor," said Larry with urgency, "that's a jurisdictional requirement. They have to have 100 registered voters. They submitted—"

"You think I just walked in here off the farm," the judge barked. "I know what the law is." The judge paused. "Both sides rest?"

Stunned, Larry tried some final maneuvers to call up other witnesses or resubmit evidence that Sprague hadn't reached the 100. The judge denied them all. Desperate, Larry asked for copies of the original complaint.

"We will give him copies now," said Sprague, dripping with sarcastic graciousness.

The judge banged his gavel, siding with Richard Sprague on all points—except Sprague's demand that we pay for their costs. We had lost hours before dinnertime. The challenge did not even take a day.

Anne was indignant, raving, and insisting we appeal immediately. I could hardly breathe. I headed home to tell Casino-Free Philadelphia supporters what happened, even as I needed to purge myself. The words tumbled onto the screen:

> Dear friends,
> Let me start with the bad news: SugarHouse investor Richard Sprague and team successfully convinced the judge today that we did not get the 20,000 signatures.
>
> My own immediate response was anger and frustration. We know we were not involved in "massive fraud"—political folks who watched our discipline were impressed at our dedication, consistency, and ability to follow the rules of signature law.
>
> And that was added to by the injustice of the court themselves. While the court showed the utmost respect to lawyers, they were dismissive of brave—but non-lawyer—citizens like Mary Stumpf who testified about her experiences. We never even got copies of their evidence accusing us, not from the city solicitor's office or opposing office. Further, as we were challenging their 100 required signatures (we believe they did not receive enough), the judge cut off the testimony and instead decided to rule against us.
>
> A signature challenge of a few thousand signatures in other cases typically takes weeks. **The challenge of 27,000 signatures took under one day.**
>
> So I got mad, even felt a little depressed about the whole thing.
>
> And then I also went to my strategic mindset. We know SugarHouse and Richard Sprague are comfortable in the court of law. But they are not comfortable in the court of public opinion. **Because the people do want a say.**
>
> City Council is still going to move forward on the referendum. This Thursday it will be introduced to full City Council, as per the unanimous support of the Committee on Rules and Government, for a first reading of the referendum. The next week on March 15 it will

be voted on. We will have the support of those who support the right of citizens to be heard, no matter what the judge's decision.

We who gathered signatures know that the vast majority of people support our cause.

So I went back to our core message: democracy means people have a vote, and have a say. Bringing in the casino industry to Philly will only further make a broken politics more broken. After all, who is left saying voters should not have a say? SugarHouse investors, Foxwoods investors and an out-of-county imported judge.

That helped me ground back into my own hopefulness. They may have shown that not every signature was perfect, but we know that every signature was a person who took the time to sign. ***We believe City Council members will understand this, which is why we call for a unanimous decision to support our referendum.***

So I want to thank all of you for your weeks and months of work on this issue. We are not defeated, merely engaged in a long protracted battle. They have shown their teeth and their desire to engage on a witch hunt.

Now we will continue the struggle, grounded in our own strengths, sense of previous accomplishment, and commitment to the defense of our neighborhoods.

But we will continue the struggle. Why? Because we still have not had our say. For our kids and grandkids who deserve better than casinos on the riverfront backed by the money and greed that put them there.

Yours for a greater democracy, Daniel

The next morning, I sat across from my friend Nancy Brigham at my kitchen table.

"You need to go," she said. "It'll be good for you to be with others."

I looked at Nancy, her thin, barely graying hair and tiny frame. Evening after evening, she had listened to my complaints. Now she was giving me advice. I glanced outside, snow whipping in the wind.

"I slept terribly all night... the casinos just creamed us in the courts! I want to curl up and drink hot cocoa."

"You don't *have* to go," she said. "But won't you feel better to be with others who are mad, too?"

"I'm just so tired. I don't want to go." I didn't care that I sounded whiny.

"Isn't the event already planned? People will be showing up."

"I know, I know." Today's We-Are-Not-Scared-of-Stunts action was scheduled for this exact reason: to keep momentum going. It was a key lesson from Operation Transparency: design at least *two* actions ahead of time to keep on the offense. When the first action is over—e.g., the petition challenge—you have something else to carry you forward, even if your emotional state isn't ready.

"Then don't do it for you," she said. "Do it for those leaning on you. For today, be their fearless leader."

I melted. *Responsibility* was my parents' mantra. It had coalesced in me as an inner voice. *Finish what you started. The world needs people like you. No matter what, follow through on your word.* I couldn't rise for me. But I would for others.

I grabbed my thick leather coat. "You coming, Nancy?"

She shook her head and smiled. "It's way too cold to be outside."

We laughed at that.

My phone interrupted us. "Excuse me," I said to Nancy.

"Hey, I need your help," said Anne breathlessly. "Sprague just texted me. He wrote, 'May I suggest that for the health and comfort of your supporters you pick a day when the weather is better.' Help me come up with some sugary response. You're good at that sort of thing."

"Well, the decent thing for him to do is welcome us to his warm offices."

"Got it."

Anne got off the phone and texted him right back: "Dear Mr. Sprague: Thanks for your advice. Since the weather is so cold, and the emails and phone calls are already out, I hope you'll be very gracious in receiving us when we arrive at your office."

I thanked Nancy for her advice, heading into the cold and onto a trolley bound for Rittenhouse Square.

Through the short trip, I reflected on the appropriateness of today's We-Are-Not-Scared-of-Stunts action. Originally, we had thought the signature challenge would be still going. Jethro and I had considered harassing SugarHouse's people (too vengeful!), holding a rally (too boring!), gathering 100 signatures protesting *their* signatures (too unclear!). But this was the right one.

It was a take-off on a moment in the Montgomery bus boycott, a story my mother—a historian—told me as a kid. After Rosa Parks' famous refusal, the movement led a bus boycott for months, facing down physical hostilities, numerous legal challenges, and a deeply ingrained sense that change was out of reach. To crush the movement, the segregationist mayor dusted off anti-boycott laws and announced public warrants to arrest the leaders of the bus boycott.

As predicted, that move demoralized leaders who were frightened to be labeled as criminals. Leaders shied away from public meetings, several even fleeing and going into hiding. The fragile morale of the movement was threatened.

A fierce direct action activist, Bayard Rustin, suggested to Dr. King's advisors to move toward the fear—go to the police station and *demand* they arrest you. Turn the fear into a strength. Unable to reach Dr. King or convince those closest to them, Bayard was able to convince E.D. Nixon, who, with a small entourage, filed into the police station. There he announced, "Are you looking for me? Well, here I am." He was fingerprinted, photographed, and released on bond.

Word spread in the black community, and within hours, dozens of leaders emerged from the woodwork to follow suit, demanding that they too be arrested. A supportive crowd swelled outside the police station, cheering the "criminals," who held up their citations proudly. A few disappointed leaders not on the list argued with police that they *were* important leaders and they should have the honor of being arrested, too. The fear had melted.

In our action, we hoped for something of that rebounding and melting of fear.

My rainbow scarf dangled awkwardly to one side as I hopped off the trolley and ran to the park. I met up with four dozen warmly dressed members, underneath frozen trees and a downpour of flurries. Anne shouted chants into a bullhorn: "We are not going to be silenced! We are not scared!"

Supporter Dorothy pulled me aside. "I couldn't believe all of this. But now that it's happening, we can't give up! I grabbed a bunch of folks from my office and told them to grab their coats. We need to be here and show everyone that we're not scared of Sprague's money."

Dorothy's husband, Jay, patted me on the back. "Get up and speak, we need you." He gave me a gentle shove.

I was still out of breath as Anne handed me the bullhorn.

"I have some questions for you. Are you a real person? *(Laughing, the crowd shouted yes.)* Do you care about this city? *(Yes!)* Do you want your say, even if the casino industry doesn't believe you matter? *(Yes!)* Then let's go tell 'em!"

I whipped out my driver's license and lifted it high in the air. Others followed suit, pulling their ID from their wallets and back pockets, as we turned to head to Sprague's offices.

One supporter came over and shyly asked, "I couldn't find my driver's license. This is a student ID card—will it count?"

I laughed. "That'll work fine."

TV camera crews raced to get to the front of the march. I slowed the crowd to a shuffle. After watching marches for years, I noted that crowds walk more slowly than individuals, and a stretched-out crowd leaves empty spaces—bad for the visual message of strength and unity. And today's message was targeted to the public—especially via TV stations that only occasionally covered us.

We shuffled three blocks to large, glass doors with Sprague and Sprague's names lettered in gold. A large security guard closed the doors. "I cannot let you in."

TV cameras angled to see if a physical drama would ensue. But we had no intention of physically pressing the point. "We have documents for Mr. Sprague, a poll we are releasing showing 79% of Philadelphians support the 1,500-foot buffer." The security guard looked on with empathy. I added, "He said he was worried that we would be in the cold."

The security guard called upstairs, while outside we huddled with ID cards held high in the air. Mary Stumpf shouted, "Come down and face us, *Dick* Sprague!" Others joined the cat-calls. Laughing, one person yelled, "Sprague, come here and check my ID!" Another added, "I'm not sure if I'm real until you lawyers tell me!" Communal anger dissolved into laughter.

The guard returned and cracked the door carefully. "I can let one of you in, but not all of you."

"Tell him all of us," I snapped loudly. "We are one body." A meeting with one person across from Sprague and his cronies, on his turf, would be neither fun nor productive. "All of us or none of us."

"None it is," came the reply.

With that, we wound up the action, closing with announcements, encouragements, and some more laughter.

But as I headed back home, I realized the true positive spin for us. Warm and unwelcoming inside his gilded offices, Sprague was by all accounts more powerful than us. Yet the bigger Sprague looked, the smaller we looked in comparison, and the more his smashing us looked excessive. Dr. Martin Luther King said unearned suffering is redemptive. Defying political wisdom, I was ready to embrace getting squashed by the big guy. This could be a good loss, a chance to highlight injustice. It's not losing that's the worst thing that can happen. It's giving up. And we had no intention of doing that.

In the following days, SugarHouse's media machinery tried to swing press back toward our "fraudulent" petition drive. But we had built a bigger frame. Without ever casting a disparaging word against Sprague and his cronies, we had exposed their efforts as bullying.

TV stations replayed our snowy We-Are-Not-Scared-of-Stunts action, contrasting with SugarHouse's opulent claims of victimization. Blogs like *Philadelphia Will Do* joked amply about the *Daily News* front page, "Casino Sends Aliens To Harvest Organs Of Anti-Casino Folks."

The *Inquirer* noted the shifting political winds. They quoted an optimistic DiCicco, who noted the "emphatic court decision may turn my colleagues against the measure." Our very public loss had turned sympathy toward us. The art of direct action isn't based on never losing a fight, it's about always staying on the high-ground—and we had done that.

Richard Sprague responded with open anger at the notion council might vote in our favor. "These council people, they don't stand up. They see 27,000 names and what do they do? They run for the hills." He was off-message, furthering our storyline that a vote against us was a vote for bully Richard Sprague.

We wanted to keep the momentum going, to feed the story of us as—because we were—the righteous underdog. So we told reporters to show up for a press announcement on whether we would appeal the court's throwing out of our signatures. As we expected, a dozen press crowded us to find out.

We took our time. Standing before TV cameras and reporters' notebooks, Larry Otter blasted the judge's precedent of ruling without looking at a single page of the petitions (something the Green Party later clarified they had faced before, too). Jethro noted movement at the state level, with Philadelphia state representatives attending the first state public hearing organized by anti-casino stalwart State Representative Paul Clymer. Anne Dicker announced two new councilmembers in our favor. And I gave press copies of our professional polling data showing a majority of Philadelphians in all neighborhoods supported the referendum: 79%!

Press mostly treated all that news as fluff. Few believed the state apparatus would lift a finger to help us. None would cover our poll results because, they flimsily claimed, they came from "an interested party." And *if* council voted with us, they pivoted to the new contrary narrative, the referendum would be shot down by the Supreme Court. They shrugged off Paul countering that he'd read hundreds of cases on this and, "I have no doubt the court will side with us." Whether we liked it or not, press had a focus, a driving narrative.

We had our own priorities. Off to the side, I updated Jethro with news that Foxwoods had threatened us with a lawsuit. We had been selling T-shirts on CafePress, mocking their logo. "We could win a court case as a social parody, no question," I said. "But we took it down—we can't afford to have too many irons in the fire. It does raise the question of why SugarHouse is attacking us in public while Foxwoods attacks in private. Maybe

Foxwoods really believes this deal is completely wired, that they can wait us out." I also told him of a long conversation with the guy who had picked our out-of-county judge. "We need to tell people he's not a target. He went out of the city hoping for a less connected judge—any Philly judge would have been even *closer* tied-in with Sprague. It's icky, but true."

To close up the all-over-the-place press conference, I smiled at the crowd of reporters. "So, on the question of whether we're going to appeal the court's decision..." Pens stopped, and reporters leaned in close.

I wondered how the news would go down. In a fit, I had asked Jethro earlier if he thought reporters would think it all a manipulative ploy to get them to cover us. "Maybe," he said, "but press do plenty of things *we* don't like. Besides, they need to be updated on the many moving parts."

They had been. And now I delivered the anti-climactic news concerning our intent to appeal. "We'd love to, but we just don't have the money." Reporters rolled their eyes, asked a few final questions, and hurried back to write stories on their short deadlines.

At every moment, we were building a frame based on who we truly were: tenacious, powerful, and vastly under-resourced underdogs.

After a week of trying to stay strong, we returned to City Council chambers. Just before eleven in the morning, Council President Anna Verna stood at the lectern and announced, "At this time, I would ask the chief clerk to please call the roll." The murmur of the 300-plus crowd dropped to stone-cold silence. Twelve "Yes" votes would pass the referendum. Any fewer, and our strategy would be torn to shreds.

All our letters and continued unannounced lobby visits with councilmembers had either done their job—or not. We had done our best to update their ignorant staff members on the financial and social costs of casinos. Like others, Councilman Greenlee's aide insisted they were empathetic with our sentiments, "but there's nothing we can do." Even after his jaw dropped when we recited the varied reasons casinos in neighborhoods is a bad idea, he closed, "I'll present this to the councilmember, but it's a political calculation for him. You understand. I just can't say how he'll vote."

The good news was that no councilmember believed we were part of fraud. Most councilmembers had faced petition challenges. They all believed we were merely beaten in the courts by a powerful, well-connected lawyer.

Our internal council tally had six yeses, three undecideds, and the remainder without *any* indication. Nobody would admit if they were voting against us, because they knew we would turn pressure up on them. We didn't even trust all the yeses.

The chief clerk started to call the roll. There was nothing to do now. But I needed to do *something*. I whipped out my notebook to scribble the vote results as they came.

"Councilwoman Blackwell. (*Aye.*) Councilman Clarke. (*Aye.*) Councilman DiCicco. (*Aye.*)"

No surprises. DiCicco was trying to stay ahead of his community's wrath. Blackwell's late husband was a longshoreman and closely tied with the ILA. And Clarke, though privately hostile, was held in check by his vocal Fishtown constituency.

All the others were the question marks, especially because in addition to passing casino lobbyists in council's hallways, we now saw the powerful building trades union lobby. The building and construction trades were fulfilling their reputation of selfishly advocating for any short-term building jobs, regardless of the building's function or danger. Like councilmembers, they staked their reputation on winning. That meant they didn't do anything partway. It was full-court pressure, as they hung over each councilmember the threat of withholding their massive street presence or financial support in this election year.

To defy their rumored plan to pack city hall, our people arrived extra early to grab floor seats. That relegated the balcony to a fiery cocktail of our members, burly anti-casino ILA members, and rowdy pro-casino building trades unionists. On the floor, union leader Pat Gillespie urgently beckoned councilmembers, who nodded and bowed their heads, as he whispered insistently into their ears.

"Councilman Goode. *(Aye.)* Councilman Greenlee. *(Aye.)* Councilman Kelly. *(Aye.)* Councilman Kenney. *(Aye.)*"

Seven votes. My heart fluttered with hope.

Unexpectedly that morning, the *Inquirer* had penned its first editorial in our favor: "Let the people vote!" The editors carefully delineated their disagreement with the process but neutrality on casinos themselves. Their architecture critic Inga Saffron went further, blasting the poorly designed "slots boxes" and the legal challenges from the "status-quo powers."

"Councilwoman Krajewski. *(Aye.)* Councilwoman Miller. *(Aye.)*"

Krajewski whispered to her aide the same message that DRNA delivered at its council lobby visits, "Ya know, if those casinos were in our district and our people didn't want them in their neighborhood, I'd want Frankie to vote with me." That message was the DRNA's carrot. Casino-Free Philadelphia was the stick.

Casino-Free Philadelphia's reputation had been growing for weeks. Just two weeks ago, 300 longshoremen union members had shown up at a PennPraxis planning meeting. When the lead planner insisted PennPraxis assume the arrival of riverfront casinos, the ILA hijacked the entire process, shouting down the leader with "This is a sham!" They threatened mass walk-outs if PennPraxis didn't create a plan *without* casinos. Grapevine rumors credited our direct action coaching—and while our role may have been slightly overblown, it was true that we were urging all our allies to use their power.

"Councilman O'Neil. *(Aye.)* Councilman Ramos. *(Aye.)*"

Like a ball flying toward a player in the end-zone, the eleven votes hung in midair, needing just one more to complete the game-winning touchdown. ILA members with "Foxwoods Worst Site" or "Pay to Play?" signs rose from their seats, as if it get a better view.

"Councilwoman Reynolds-Brown."

As the councilwoman said *"Aye,"* we rocketed to our feet in loud exultation. Like churchgoers, we whooped and hollered. Mary Stumpf, who had stood in the cold and faced down Richard Sprague in a courtroom, burst into tears. Shirley flourished her sign: "Thank you." ("We'll Remember You At the Polls" was on the other side—just in case.)

I was too emotional to stand. I wiped tears away, notebook in lap, exhaling. *It's going to happen.*

We cheered and hollered victoriously. It was a seventeen-to-zero unanimous message of support from council.

I jumped up and immediately started passing out flyers. "We're meeting on the south side of City Hall for our celebration," I announced. Worried about potential bullying and violence from the notoriously combative building trades union, I rushed people outside.

I couldn't help but stop to listen as SugarHouse spokesperson Dan Fee spit bullets. He was a bald, thick-skinned man who treated politics like a contact sport. At home leading smear campaigns with Mayor Street and Governor Rendell, he argued to reporters, "There were days of public input. There were community meetings run by both of the major newspapers. Today, they asked the equivalent of, 'Do you favor puppy dogs and rainbows?'"

I shook my head, disgusted. Only the *Daily News* had held a public forum, where they told anti-casino activists, "We are here to talk only about design and architecture" and ordered anti-casino signs to be put in the hallways. But the fast-paced medium of press doesn't trade in truth-telling as much as spin. The next day, Dan Fee's spin would be the lead headline of the *Daily News*: "Council Unanimous on 'Puppy Dogs & Rainbows' Slots Bill" and the *Inquirer's* headline: "Referendum Still in Doubt." The mayor might veto. City Council might still cave. Even if they didn't, they'd lose in the courts. Or the state would pass new laws to trump them.

None of it mattered to me as I skipped away. We had done one more impossible thing. I danced down the steps and joined the celebration outside of City Hall.

Jethro ran to me, with a stunned face and open arms. *"We did it!"* For the next hour, we celebrated, clasped, thanked, and encouraged each other.

I ducked into a quiet corner to write supporters. They deserved to know as soon as possible—and from us. The positive tone was not hard to find, as I described the "raucous and intense City Council session packed with concerned citizens." It was going to happen. On May 15, with a unanimous City Council vote, the referendum would be placed on the ballot—"a landmark day."

The tone that was hardest was acknowledging the massive challenges ahead of us:

Tad Decker of the PA Gaming Control Board has already promised to sue the city to try to stop this referendum from moving forward; and the mayor might also try such tactics. On Monday we'll be sending out an email about next steps. For now we want you to do two things:
1) Celebrate the success—tell others the story of people power trumping insider politics and backdoor "done deals";
2) Please donate to Casino-Free Philadelphia—we will be facing either a major legal or a major media campaign against us. Now more than ever we need your financial contribution to continue this work.
   Thanks for all your help and work in making today's victory! *They have the money. But we have the people.*
   Warmly,
   - Daniel, Jethro, Anne

CHAPTER 8
Vote Yes on #1

MARCH 16, 2007—APRIL 12, 2007

*spectrum of allies • a reporter's trap • learning word choices from feedback •
defend against false narratives • protecting the precious high ground •
having an opponent strengthens you • inoculating yourself from rumors •
the three-touch rule • building structure with limited resources •
not getting caught in transition • playing the "newspaper-framing game" •
get hit—hit back quickly*

AFTER USING ALL OUR RESOURCES to pull off 27,000 signatures and then defend them in the court of public opinion, we had won a spot on the ballot for the 1,500-foot buffer zone. Now we had to remake ourselves to into a citywide ballot referendum turnout operation. While CFP activists chomped at the bit to get moving, the executive team huddled, debating and designing the best structure.

Lacking a strategy and structure, we gathered supporters to build leadership and political analysis.

"We can't rest on our laurels just because 79% of voters agree with us," I said, standing in front of thirty or forty core volunteers. "You know we can't afford advertisements, TV, radio, print, or paid operations."

Heads of now-seasoned petition gatherers nodded grimly. It was obvious, like reminding a mouse that's being chased that it didn't have sharp teeth or fierce claws.

I poured on the obviousness. "We don't have money—our bank account is, as always, nearly empty. We don't have an extensive citywide network. We don't have political leaders fighting in our corner."

Some part of me wondered how often I would have to keep saying those lines. *Won't we have any of these things, ever?*

But whether because I wasn't daunted by the challenge or because of experiences—like Mary's—of facing down powerful opponents, none of the faces before me looked overwhelmed.

"So what do we have?" I asked the group.

Without a pause, Mary shouted, "The people!" Others echoed that, adding: "Democracy!" "Truth!" "Our neighborhoods!"

My heart smiled—it was just like us to talk in values.

I moved to the blank newsprint and drew a horizontal line across along the bottom. "Yes, we have the people. But not everyone. And not to the same degree. Tonight we're going to get nuanced about thinking about our allies and opponents. On the issue of actively supporting the referendum, we have some people who completely agree with us." I pointed toward the left side of the line. "Who are those people?"

Mary Reinhart rattled off a list of civic associations that had supported the petition drive. Of those, only Society Hill had taken a stance against *both* casinos—most were sometimes crassly articulating only opposition to the casino in *their* neighborhood.

"That's most of the civics in the DRNA," said Chris Meck. "The DRNA should be up there."

"CFP!" said Ken Gregory.

"Don't forget the longshoremen," shouted Terry Paylor.

I wrote up the names of those groups on the left side of the line. "Okay, and then there are people who completely disagree with us. Who are those?"

"Senator Fumo," spat Andrea Preis, as if suppressing other choice words.

"Chairman Tad Decker and the Pennsylvania Gaming Control Board," said Paul.

"The casinos," said Mary Stumpf.

Those I wrote on the right side of the line.

Some laughter in the back of the room attracted the group's attention. "What's up?" I asked.

Shyly, someone said, "We think DiCicco goes on that side, too."

Some people laughed. Others looked offended. DiCicco was a polarizing character.

I smiled. "This is perfect. I'm glad someone raised this. Because most people are neither completely with us nor completely against us. There's a spectrum—hence this tool, the spectrum of allies."

I drew a half-circle over the line, like a half-pie with five evenly divided slices. "Some people are completely with us on the leftmost slice, or totally against us—on the right. But most people are somewhere in between. There are people in the middle slice who are totally on the fence, or who don't know anything about this issue. Or people lean slightly in a direction, but are not active on the issue. Passive allies are on the left—they're not activated on the issue or doing anything, but may agree with us. And on the other side of the fence are the passive opponents—people who disagree with us but aren't trying to stop us. Thinking in this way, where is DiCicco?"

Nobody moved, eyeing each other as if looking for reassurance that it was okay to wade into these contentious waters.

"Frank has always been hostile to the community. He's a Fumo man through and through. He said he wants casinos!"

Someone I recognized as a longtime South Philly native responded. "People love bashing Frank. But he's there when we need him. He knows that, which is why he's helping us."

"Then why does he support casinos?"

"Not these casinos! He believes in protecting neighborhoods!"

"This raises an important distinction," I interrupted, trying to steer away from rhetoric. "It's not about *beliefs*. We know DiCicco supports casino development but says he doesn't want casinos at these two locations, at least certainly Foxwoods. But this spectrum isn't about what people say—it's about behavior, their actions. Based on behavior, where is he on this issue of getting the referendum on the ballot? What slice would you put him in?"

The flood of comments stuttered as people took a moment to regroup.

"Active opponent. Why won't he use council's ability to call for hearings and put some of these liars under oath? After the election, we'll see his true colors as he rejoins Fumo in pushing these down our throats."

"You can't say that! Frank's getting angry calls from Fumo over this issue—he's had to hang up on Fumo because it's so tense. He introduced the freaking legislation that's now on the ballot. Active ally."

"Ally? The weaselly politician who wrote the zoning legislation that the casinos need? The same man who keeps telling us that there's nothing he can do, so sit down at the negotiation table? No way, he's an active opponent."

The group tacked back and forth on the issue. I found myself wavering back and forth. He could truly be seen in nearly every slice. He was untrustworthy, because his behavior was not consistent. Yet, a loose consensus emerged to place him in the passive ally category. There was clear recognition he wasn't doing many things we wanted him to do, but he *was* acting like a passive ally in helping us get votes on council.

"The point of this tool isn't agreement," I said. "You can see, this tool can elicit useful debate and help clarify where people stand. It's useful because we make different requests to different slices. For example, with DiCicco as a passive ally, our ask is for him to be more active. That means we need to give him specific asks that make him more daring and invested. That's different from, say, a neutral group. Who is one of those?"

"The public," someone said.

"The public is too broad. Activists make the mistake of talking about educating 'the public.' We don't do that. We educate specific groups, or specific readers of newspapers, or specific networks. Who are some groups that are neutral that might move one slice over to become passive allies? Think specific."

"Project H.O.M.E.," offered Kathy, referring to the homeless advocacy agency. "Some people inside the organization helped with the petition drive, but as an institution they haven't put any weight into the issue."

"Okay, and what could we ask them to do?"

"They could write a letter saying they oppose casinos, since so many people will become bankrupt and then homeless."

"Perfect," I said. "And the request isn't too big—it's measured toward who they are, but that step would help bring them from being neutral on the issue to moderately in our corner. That's different from, say, a passive opponent. We want those people to stop what they're doing. Who is an example of that?"

"PennPraxis! If they could just stop insisting on a riverfront proposal with casinos, we'd be set."

"Or almost any of the mayoral candidates—they keep saying it's a done deal."

The group continued listing groups and talking about them. I interrupted only enough to make use of teachable moments: "Note how this thinking helps us move away from obsession with our opponents. In fact, social movements rarely win over those active opponents. It's a mistake to spend all your attention on people who won't move." I thought about folks who kept advising me that we should write letters to Rendell or make personal appeals to the PGCB. Common sense and persuasiveness would not move people so entrenched. "Instead of pounding away expecting to move Rendell or the casinos, we try to move people one step over. In fact, I should share with you the good news: social movements don't win by moving everyone all the way to the left. Most win by moving each group one step toward them. If we get Project H.O.M.E. to be a passive ally, PennPraxis to be neutral, mayoral candidates one step closer to us, and so forth, we will win this referendum and this struggle."

The crowd's determination was as set as ever. Soon, people were in small groups fleshing out the chart and identifying which groups they had relationships with and wanted to reach out to, to woo and move a step closer to us.

Chris Brennan's voice sounded irritated. "Got a minute?" He always sounded irritated, or at least rushed. Like most city reporters, with staff cuts at his office, he was asked to cover more and more topics, including all local politics for the *Daily News*. That would turn most people sour.

I sighed and leaned back in my chair, moving my cell phone to its usual position tucked in by my neck. "Sure, Chris. What's up?"

"You all must be very proud of what you've done. Getting the referendum on the ballot sure surprised a lot of folks. But now, I assume you all expect to be outspent for the referendum."

That was an understatement. At last night's executive team meeting, Huu had presented chilling data about casino money in referendums. In Louisiana, the gambling industry outspent its opposition by $200 for each dollar spent by citizen's groups. In Ohio, the industry twice failed at persuading the populace to bring in 31,500 slots parlors, even after pouring in $27 million, compared to the anti-casinos' meager $1 million. But the industry could afford to throw good money after bad—it was already organizing another campaign in Ohio.

Our team's response was almost formulaic. Anne soared with confidence at our 79% polling, while Paul countered that a paid media blitz could evaporate that support unless we worked hard. Jethro emphasized that we build citywide relationships, nonchalantly noting that without deep, grassroots support we'd lose, especially if the casinos bought off Philly's bribable ward leaders, whose sample ballots carried undue influence in elections. Shirley and Kathy harped on getting our organizational life together, with Shirley asking to be replaced as freewheeling office manager and Kathy urging us to get an office to manage. Listening to it all, I facilitated the group to stay on the same page with a big picture of the tasks needed: recruitment, writing outreach materials, contacting citywide grassroots groups, and tightening our organizational structure. Our meeting had ended with bold goals: 500 organizational endorsements, 1,000 volunteers, and growing from an email listserve of 800 to 15,000 people.

Chris's question pulled me back to the moment: "So do you plan to run ad buys, or just run a ground game?"

"We've got barely $2,000 in our bank account, so it's a fair bet we'll be focused on door-knocking and person-to-person outreach. Today we announced a series of trainings on outreach. A dozen people have already signed up, and you know us, we're just getting started."

Chris pivoted. "You think the mayor will veto the referendum?"

"He shouldn't. He has a reputation that'll be undermined by going against the will of the people—"

"Fine, fine. But do you think he is going to veto?"

"We're hearing from his office that he will," I admitted. "But council will override his veto."

"Yes, your *unanimous* support. Impressive. Will council abandon you, or do you think it's all an election-year stunt to relieve pressure from the reformer challengers vying for their offices?"

Chris seemed in no rush to get to his point, content with swapping tips and information—the journalist's version of small talk. "Neither, Chris. I think the real question is what's best for the city, embracing an industry whose sole goal is to take money from Philadelphians and move it to their own pockets, or siding with the people. Councilmembers might be doing what's right for a lot of reasons."

"Like 27,000 signatures... even if they were thrown out as fraud."

"You know—" I cut myself short, remembering Chris's pen standing at the ready.

After his front-page article slamming SugarHouse's goons, I had thought Chris was our guy. But after our council win, it was his article that gave SugarHouse's Dan Fee free reign, calling our referendum the equivalent of asking, "Do you favor puppy dogs and rainbows?" Jethro still was angling to find an action with rainbows and dogs—teasing with the idea of leaving dog poop on Sprague's front steps. "With rainbow sprinkles?" I joked.

But I wasn't going to raise objections to Chris's sensationalist articles. That was his job. Instead, I tried to turn him on to better stories. "Have you asked mayoral candidates how they're going to vote on the referendum?"

"Not at this point."

"You know, it's important for your readers to know where the candidates stand on this issue," I said.

"I'll be sure to ask them in time. But right now, I'm working on a different story. I'm trying to get a big picture on you as an organization and how you, Jethro, and Anne have been so effective. You're leaders in the reform movement and part of an important fight. To start, tell me about what you were doing before working at Casino-Free Philadelphia."

I sighed. A human-interest story about the founders of CFP was a puff piece barely worth our time. *Fine, get this over with.* "Even during this campaign, I work for Training for Change. It's a small, nonprofit organization that trains groups like CFP in organizing and leadership skills—mostly focused on developing their own training infrastructure. I've been there for almost a decade. We work all over the world."

"So you're used to nonprofits. How much do you get paid to organize with Casino-Free Philly?"

I paused. *Does it make sense to have this public? Does it make us look too small? What is there to lose?* "$400 a week."

"A week?"

"Yeah, on the weeks I get paid."

I heard his pen scribble. "I had some questions for Anne that she didn't have the details. For example, where do you get the funding to pay you?"

I laughed. "From supporters."

"Who are your supporters?"

"Individuals, some groups, some unions."

"Can I see the list?"

"Um, sure. I mean, I'd have to ask... What's this all about?"

"Just trying to get a big picture on your organization." Chris shifted gears. "Anne said you opened up a bank account earlier this year. Do you remember exactly when that was?"

"February, maybe mid-January. I'm not sure. Why would you need to know that?"

"There have been questions asked about how you support yourselves."

I furrowed my brow. "I've never heard any questions... *Who's* asking that?"

"It's just a question out there from people who wonder if there's a hidden agenda."

"A hidden agenda? We are who we say we are! We get support from local residents trying to stop casinos," I said with indignation. "What are these rumors?"

"If you are funded totally by residents, then you have nothing to hide. So I can see a list of supporters to confirm?"

I stopped, sensing a trap. "*What* are the rumors, from *who?*"

Chris's voice was sharp, quick. "Can I get just a straightforward list of your donors?"

"I'll... uh... have to talk to others here," I said, scrambling. "I'll get back to you on the bank account. Any other questions?"

"Not now. But I can call you later, right?"

I steadied my voice. "Sure." But as I hung up, I knew it was only going to get worse.

In a large jury-selection room packed with hundreds of people, I winced as I balanced my computer on my lap and opened my email. Building a referendum campaign wasn't going to be easy, and the executive team was rapidly trading emails to create materials for our training sessions. My inbox was deluged with comments from supporters—critiques, suggestions, encouragement, rumors.

I typed hurried responses: "Thanks for the encouragement! Let's get together soon."

Then: "There's no evidence the PennPraxis riverfront planning process is funded by casino money. Please stop passing on that rumor without evidence."

Then: "CBS 3 made a mistake in being the only TV station to not cover us. They'll regret it, because we were way more important than what they covered. But there's no need go to slashing at them. Action News previously made the mistake of not coming to our press events, and they're now hounding me to make sure I send them every press release. Don't worry, we'll win them over by turning ourselves into an irresistible force with creative, fun actions."

Then: "We don't know the extent to which the city can change the language of the charter change or what ballot position we'll get. Hold off on telling people a 'No Casino' vote is a 'Yes' vote until we know if that's true."

And so on.

A bailiff called my name, and I spent several frustrated hours waiting and pacing with other jury candidates, while outside of City Hall work piled up—Jeremy's first-draft of doorknob hangers, Huu sending along outreach materials, and people responding to my email request for graphic designers for new window signs.

Inside the courtroom, it was all routine until the judge asked about my previous arrests. When I mentioned Operation Transparency, he stopped the proceedings to encouragingly ask me to update him on the current status of the casino struggle. The whole courtroom listened intently until I finished—and the prosecution promptly asked that I be removed from the case.

I walked out of City Hall with a call from CFP supporter and respected Society Hill civic leader Susan DeWyngaert. "Your email made me wonder exactly what you mean by 'If they're not with us, we'll go after them.'"

My head swam, trying to remember what I had written.

Susan continued, "I hope you mean that if they are not covering stories important to the citizens of this city, we will hold them accountable—not that we will pursue anyone who disagrees with CFP. I think keeping the focus on good process and accountability will have the greatest level of engagement and therefore power."

"Yes, I believe in that," I said defensively, slowly remembering what this was about.

Supporter Jamie Paylor had been frustrated that CBS 3 editors ignored the council vote and personally told her it was "unworthy news." She urged CFP to organize a boycott.

In response, I tried to talk her down, coaching activists to stay focused instead of picking up battles that would lead nowhere. But I had used the language Susan quoted.

I tried to choose my words carefully, feeling defensive. "It's true that my activist style includes lots of words of fighting, struggling, and going after people. But I mean no harm."

"Maybe you just have a stronger activist style," she said. "But I wanted to let you know how it read to me."

"Thanks for coming to me directly about this," I said, relaxing a little. I was so used to being challenged, it was hard to see it all as feedback. "Paul and I talk a lot about our different emphases and styles. He once caught an email I wrote talking six times about 'fighting.' *We'll fight this, we'll fight that, we'll go after this.* It's true that I talk in a more aggressive activist style sometimes. I'm a huge believer in keeping the high ground—that's why we're compelling. We've never lied, never gone to dirty politics, and never will. It's just not my style."

"I think we're in complete agreement then," she said.

"And I appreciate the feedback about my word choices," I said, "because I want to get better at consistently saying what I mean and projecting myself in a way that's consistent with what I believe."

I didn't vow to remove the language from my writing, but instead not to use it casually, littering it in my emails. When I wrote stronger language, I would mean it, honing it to make it sharp.

Given our history, I knew there would always be a new crisis on our horizon—and more chances to practice.

The next day, I sat in Clark Park near my West Philadelphia home, hanging out with a friend. My phone rang, and I immediately answered it.

Paul's voice was quick, rapid-fire. "I was right! The *Inquirer* article was just the beginning. Now the Associated Press is repeating the same myth! We have to get in front of this!" He paused. "I'm sorry I'm calling you on your day off."

"It's fine," I said. "I've been answering calls all day." I reluctantly stepped from the chess set and headed toward an unoccupied picnic table. I waved apologetically to my friend.

One more urgent crisis. Paul always seemed to have them for me. But I couldn't blame him for my poor boundaries. After weeks of reacting to emergencies, it felt like par for the course. Besides, there was something nice about feeling needed. And it was just a phone call.

"As your legal counsel, I need your advice about how to proceed."

Without thinking, I blurted, "Our legal counsel? Paul, you're way more than that. You're a press spokesperson, a bridge-builder, a strategist—"

"No, no. I am a member of Society Hill and DRNA. I can't be too associated. Just call me outside legal counsel."

"Fine," I snapped. "But it's not healthy that you and Shirley and Kathy do all this work but want to stay off being listed on the emails. Being associated with a high-ground, direct action, grassroots movement is not a blemish." Then I added, "We'll talk more about this later."

"Okay," said Paul, letting the issue drop. "For now, the point is the city solicitor released his own memo taking the casinos' side, saying the referendum is illegal, and the Associated Press is reprinting that argument."

The AP article was the fourth bad article for us this week—and it was only Wednesday. A *New York Times* article only quoted casino proponents, lamenting "casino delays." Before that came the *Daily News'* "puppies and rainbows" article and a terrible *Inquirer* article that quoted "legal experts" who all claimed the referendum would be ruled illegal.

The AP article affirmed Paul's fear of a coordinated media offensive. In the article, the city solicitor explained the supreme court could not stop people from voting on the ballot question. But once they did and the city made the buffer zone law, then—so he said—it would be found illegal. The AP article backed him up, with Duquesne University law professor Bruce Ledewitz asserting that the state trumps City Council. Drawing parallels to past city-versus-state fights, the article read, "Constitutional law professors point to the state supreme court's 1996 decision on Philadelphia's assault weapons ban. The justices voted 4-1 to uphold a 1995 state law that sought to overturn gun ordinances in Philadelphia and Pittsburgh. The court said the state legislature, which overrode a veto by then-Gov. Robert P. Casey, was able to preempt those ordinances, because the constitutional right to bear arms made gun laws a statewide issue." *State trumps city. It's that simple.*

Reviewing the article made Paul all the more furious. He barked, "The newspapers are getting it wrong! You know my legal opinion is that the referendum is perfectly legal. The city has the clear legal authority to legislate zoning laws. In fact, I like the odds of winning this. Their 'legal experts' have not done their homework—probably never even read casino law—and the PGCB and city solicitor are just BS'ing."

I grinned. This was bulldog Paul. And his teeth had clamped down onto this.

"Glad you're not going to let this go," I bellowed. "So... you figure the casino owners are going to keep telling everyone it's illegal, until the public begins to accept it as truth?"

"Bingo," shouted Paul. "They're printing it as if it is a fait accompli. The current public view that we are going to lose makes it easier for the court to rule against us. It's real bad."

"And... it could be worse," I said. "Look at it this way. Reporters assume the question will go on the ballot, despite the mayor's claims of being able to 'work something out' with council. They're asking SugarHouse and Foxwoods if they're going to run a campaign against us. *And* everyone assumes, without explicitly admitting it, that people will approve the referendum."

Paul sniffed derisively. "The point is they're just making stuff up to delegitimize the referendum in the courts of public opinion. You have to look at the *law*."

Law is always political, I almost said. No, this was not the right teachable moment. I returned to the politics of the here-and-now. "So what's your question about all of this?"

"You're the best at public relations. Are newspapers going to be writing this story in the next couple of weeks? Or is it better to go into court as the underdog in the public's eye, thus making our victory more dramatic?" He quickly added, "I'm not inclined to go this route."

I giggled at Paul's dramatic flair. "Nor me." I paced around the green space to help me think. "Newspapers have invested ink in this story, they needed follow-ups. But there's really nothing worthy to report. 'Ballot Question Still on Ballot'? 'Anti-Casino Folks Still Anti-Casino'? And since reporters refuse to do their own polling or report ours... and since they don't have time to dig into allegations of corruption... yes, that means they're going to generate their own pundit-based narrative. They're going to latch onto the question of legality. It could linger for months." My voice carried my certainty. "It's a hot story now. We need to combat this."

"What should we do?" asked Paul.

"I don't know. I don't really have any energy for this. Maybe..." I paused, hoping an idea would emerge from my head. I looked back at the chess board and moved a piece. *"Your move,"* I whispered to my chess partner. "Reporters could be the public executioners of the legality. My instinct is creative actions would do little to convince them. They respect 'expert' opinions. I'm not sure." I glanced around at the trees.

"What about calling up Bruce Ledewitz and other lawyers reporters respect?" suggested Paul. "I'm sure if they see more information and the facts of the case, they'll change their minds."

"If you think lawyers might openly change their minds... yeah, that'd be great!"

"I'll write something up first, to educate reporters and show my colleagues," said Paul.

"Make it understandable. Reporters aren't lawyers. Pretend as if *I* have to understand it."

"No problem, the issues here of preemption law are pretty easy to understand."

"You lawyers are crazy," I laughed. "Just make sure that after reading it press can ask tough questions to the mayor."

"I'll have it done by tomorrow," said Paul. "Then I'll go through my rolodex and start calling lawyers. I'll start with Bruce."

Bulldog that he was, I knew it would be solid. Perfectionist that he was, it'd be done in three days or more. I put down my phone and continued to play chess under the chestnut trees of my neighborhood park... until Chris Brennan called, asking the same line of questions as before. He called the day after that, and the day after that.

At Friday's executive team meeting, Paul passed out neatly stapled copies of his five-page technical briefing trashing the casino's arguments of the illegality of the referendum. It cut through the dense legal terrain: "The supreme court struck the exact prohibition that would have negated the referendum"—section 1506 that preempted the city's zoning rights. "Rather than enact a new preemption provision, the legislature rejected new preemption language and chose to fill the gap by inserting a provision requiring expedited judicial review of local zoning and land use decisions. In so doing the legislature expressly acknowledged the right of the local municipality to make decisions about the 'location' of a casino." In other words, the referendum was perfectly legal.

"Daniel and I sent it to lawyers, press, councilmembers, staffers, candidates, and anyone we thought might need it," he said. "But we're still not certain if we can retake the framing."

I halted questions. "We're bleeding on the legal argument," I said, looking around Shirley's table. "But we have to talk about Chris Brennan—"

Several people interrupted at once. Anne blurted, "He's called me every day this week!" Jethro pounded his fist. "It's time to take the gloves off with Chris!" And Paul shouted, "It's a hit job!"

"Wait, what's happening?" asked Kathy.

I recounted to Kathy my interactions, how each day Chris had asked more questions seemingly designed to diminish our reputation: "How can you afford all that you do? How can you accept nonprofit funds if you're not a registered nonprofit? What day did you sign a contract with your fiscal sponsor?"

I had tried to answer honestly. "Both Jethro and I come from small, grassroots groups that know how to stretch a dollar. We accept nonprofit funds through our fiscal sponsor, the Gandhian Foundation. It's a common practice for very small groups without the money to set up their own nonprofit structure. People write checks to them, and they legally hand over the money to us."

Chris responded with requests for copies of our agreement with the Gandhian Foundation. I reluctantly found them, worried how he might misuse them but committed to modeling good-faith transparency.

Then he called again. "How much money through the fiscal sponsor? How much money did you raise each month? Who are the major contributors? How come you pay off your fiscal sponsor 2% of all donations?"

I grew resentful. "The Gandhian Foundation is a Quaker organization. If you want to know so much about us, you might as well just join us—you're asking for more details than our bookkeeper! Ask around and you'll find out that 2% is a really low rate to pay a fiscal sponsor. It's not a pay off."

His questions climaxed: "Has anyone from Atlantic City ever contacted you? Wouldn't you agree they stand a lot to gain by keeping their competitors away from the Philadelphia market? Do you take money from casino operators?"

"Absolutely not," I responded angrily. "Chris! We've only received $25,000 since we started. Atlantic City casinos wouldn't even know how to write a check that small."

But Chris kept up the interrogation. "How can you prove it to me?"

All of us had been receiving similar calls.

"I told Chris it sounds as if the headline of the story would be 'Grassroots Organization Acts Like Grassroots Organization,'" said Paul. "So I asked him what this was all about. He admitted SugarHouse's Dan Fee has been pestering him with, 'How do you know CFP is not funded by Atlantic City?' Chris is just forwarding those questions."

"That explains it," I said. "Dan Fee must have harangued Chris's 'one-sided' reporting of SugarHouse's private investigators. Fee's smart enough to avoid direct statements, which would be slander. So he's asking leading questions to convince Chris that a puny grassroots group can't win what we've won. We must have some 'real' muscle behind us—like Atlantic City."

"Chris is just wasting our time. We shouldn't be this stressed out," said Jethro. He stretched his back, then added angrily, "Next time Chris calls, tell him to give up being a reporter and let Dan Fee just write all his questions for him."

"We have nothing to hide," Kathy said. "We should release the list. Not doing so makes us look like we *do* have something to hide."

Anne shrieked, "Absolutely not! Dan Fee just made this up because he wants access to our list of donors to harass them."

"Or to pierce our corporate veil," said Paul.

"We can't let this rumor stick," I replied. "We've spent months building up a high-class reputation."

"That's why they're attacking it," said Anne. "It's a low blow. Dan Fee's a nasty man who likes throwing mud."

Shirley looked back and forth at us. "How serious is this? I mean, has Chris uncovered anything bad?"

Anne and I exchanged awkward glances. "Well... not exactly... But he knows we switched to the Gandhian Foundation after we learned our first fiscal sponsor may not have had all their paperwork together. Anne?"

"We haven't done anything wrong... unless we needed to file a nonprofit charitable solicitation form with the state." She looked around at blank faces. "Do you know, Paul?"

"I'm not a nonprofit attorney. I don't know."

Shirley eyed me sharply. "This is why we need all our organizational pieces in place! This is unacceptable! Chris is going to dredge up whatever we've done wrong unless we're perfect."

My lips felt stuck, unable to mount any defense. We didn't have the resources to hire lawyers to tighten every part of our organization.

Anne interrupted my thoughts. "The point is SugarHouse went after people for signing a petition. Who knows what they will do if they get ahold of our donor list. We will comply with every aspect of the law. But let's stop giving Chris Brennan info. This just gives SugarHouse ammo."

Kathy tentatively asked, "Aren't we the transparency people?"

"Question time is over." Paul shook his head. "If Chris wants to print that we refused to say when we opened our bank account, then print it. If he wants to print scurrilous allegations that we are taking AC money, well, we think he is a better reporter than that."

I was torn. "But we're gonna get creamed on transparency. We asked for it. We should model it."

Jethro leaned forward fiercely, "Does that mean any question Dan Fee can convince a reporter to ask deserves an answer? Where does that end?"

The executive team fell into a rare silence.

Shirley spoke slowly. "I believe transparency is important. But our first priority is protecting our members. Chris isn't playing straight with us. Let's get our house in order."

Jethro's teeth clenched tightly. "It's *over* for Chris. This is just a fishing expedition. Ignore all his questions and repeat our basic message: "We are a grassroots organization that has spent very little while the casinos have spent millions to destroy our riverfront and city.""

I looked around as everyone nodded. My own hesitancy wasn't just about values. It was fear that our underdog status and precious high ground would be undermined. This hit job could take us under. "Fine." I took a breath. "I'll play my role as media spokesperson. Nobody accept calls from Chris until this article blows over. I'll tell him we've given him all he's going to get."

We spent the next hour on our "real" work: preparing a referendum campaign.

That night, I dusted off my journal and poured my fear and worry onto each page. Chris's hit job. Dan Fee's unrelenting nastiness. All just the beginning. Shirley had spent hours meticulously backtracking every deposit and expense down to the penny, setting up a solid bookkeeping system to go forward. But we were vulnerable. We didn't even have director's insurance to cover us if we did get sued.

Look at this differently. Find another angle.

Suddenly I stood up, causing my journal to fall to the floor. I raced to my computer and typed to the executive team.

> *I want to give a positive framing for the Chris calls. While he's been causing us to freak out, he's also raising questions that are causing us to dig a little deeper into answering legal questions. We've been legal and now we're going to be a little bit more legal as a result of his line of questioning. That only strengthens our position—and, ironically, we have Dan Fee and Chris Brennan to thank for that.*
>
> *Mohandas Gandhi always said that the advantage of having an opponent is that they strengthen you. He believed his people were not ready to be free until they insisted on their own freedom—freedom handed to you isn't truly yours. One must earn it.*
>
> *What's happening between the city and the state is similar. We have a weak City Council and a weak city government and therefore the state is bowling us over on crime, education, transit, and more. Our movement comes from our opponents at the state level offering us a lesson on how to stand up for ourselves. If we take it and win, we can graciously thank our opponents for being the dickwads they were to teach us that valuable lesson.*

Shirley quickly jotted a note back. "And to quote Daniel quoting Gandhi: as we strengthen, we need a professional bookkeeper ASAP!"

As I lay down to sleep, I started to feel a little sorry for Chris. He must have guessed Dan Fee might be pitching a real story. He must have convinced his editor to free him up for a week of digging. Now all he had were shreds of a story about a struggling, small nonprofit. He got nothing, and it was too late to cut his losses.

But the next morning, Chris called me again and tried to wring a few remaining details, insisting, "How can you prove that you are not getting money from Atlantic City?" And a few hours later. And one last time.

"Look, Chris, we're done. You've asked your questions for a week. You got your answers," I said, uncomfortable at holding such a tight boundary. I hung up on my cell phone, gasping for air. It was done. *Nothing else to do now—just wait to see what Chris writes.*

At 2 A.M., I awoke with a start. Groggy as I was, I knew I *should* go back to sleep. It'd be the same article in the morning. And I'll be better rested, relaxed after a good sleep.

But I found myself in front of my computer reading his article, then reading it again while wiping my eyes. *Did he really include details like when we registered with the Pennsylvania Department of State and our major expenses—but nothing on the casinos' expenses?*

I read it a third time. It was not a hit job. But I sat wreathed in anger at his far-fetched connections. Noting the Gandhian Foundation's international work, he had written, "a small portion of the donations may be heading to surprising places like Sri Lanka and Indonesia." It was like arguing buying a local newspaper supported China, if the paper bought Chinese ink. Even the most wishy-washy supporters should see through that.

After saying we "declined to release a list of donors," Chris Brennan's article continued:

> *Noting a judge's ruling that Casino-Free Philadelphia had committed fraud in circulating its petitions for the referendum, Dan Fee, a SugarHouse spokesman, yesterday suggested the group could be at it again.*
>
> *"Why am I not surprised that a group that submitted fraudulent petitions would want to hide the source of their money?" Fee asked in a written statement. "Is it money from another casino that wants to stop gaming here? If not, why are they hiding it?"*
>
> *Fee provided no proof of his theory that Casino-Free Philadelphia might be taking money from another casino.*

It's just one article. Let it go. Go back to sleep.

But my google alerts found another casino-related article from the *Inquirer's* Jeff Shields: "Minds Change on Challenge to Slots Sites."

"Now, some of those experts who previously believed the referendum would be illegal, after reading arguments by anti-casino activists and revisiting the 2004 law legalizing slot parlors, say that it is not an open-and-shut case and that the law may allow the city to dictate where casinos are built. 'They've convinced me that local government has zoning power with regard to casinos—and I had thought not,' said Bruce Ledewitz, professor of constitutional law at Duquesne University." State Representative Mark Cohen and University of Pennsylvania professor Wendell Pritchett sustained our arguments, with the regular pro-casino forces—mayor, Senator Fumo, and PGCB—all siding against us.

My fingers pranced over the keyboard for a quick email to the CFP executive team. "Hats should go off to Paul Boni for fighting tooth and nail for this article. It's a change in the legal winds. And then Chris Brennan's article definitely isn't a hit job on us and makes us look pretty much like exactly what we are. It's not killer for the casino industry, but their paranoia is clear; it's not aggressively anti-casino, but I bet he won't play that role for Dan Fee again. We've weathered this tough week well."

But Dan Fee wasn't done.

Anne called me the next morning. "It's not worth panicking about, but Josh Cornfield from the *Metro* just called asking questions about where our money comes from and if there's any connection to Atlantic City."

I cursed loudly. "What did you tell him?"

"I told him to read Chris's article. The questions are dead-ends. Then Josh kinda just gave up, like he didn't really stand behind the questions."

"Good. As long as it's just Josh."

But later that night, a call from Jim McCaffrey at the *Evening Bulletin* pulled me out of a tense meeting of the DRNA. The reporter's heavy, full-throttled voice asked, "Do you have any relationship with Atlantic City? There are rumors—"

I cut him off and pounced. "I know what you're going to ask. It's outrageous that we are being scrutinized over our $25,000 expenses, a drop in the bucket for SugarHouse. We're exactly what we are: a grassroots group. Chris Brennan did this line of questioning for over a week, and his pathetic article was the best he could come up with. You want to waste a week on a dead end like Chris? Your job is not to shill for Dan Fee. If he has questions, he can ask us directly. If he has accusations, make him go on record saying them."

I halted, reviewing my words to make sure I had made each statement quotable, in case he quoted my moment of passion. Adding what I hoped was a bit of a flair, I sighed dramatically and said, "Let's get this out of the way. Ask me every question—you know we have nothing to hide."

Jim shyly admitted that Dan Fee had brought him these questions. He parroted a few of them before giving up.

When I got home, Anne and I agreed we should inoculate other reporters. I started with Jeff Shields. "Dan Fee was pitching a story to Chris Brennan about how Casino-Free might be accepting money from AC casinos—we're not—or inappropriately accepting contributions—we're not—or getting rich off this—we're *definitely* not. So if he pitches it to you next, don't be surprised. But do be offended that he didn't think of you first."

Jeff didn't respond as I expected, instead asking confirmation of some facts in the *Daily News* article.

Instead of immediately answering, I paused. I had learned from Chris. *We are not in debt to reporters, as if they're doing us a favor. We are doing a favor for them, giving them stories that are meaningful and important. They ought not mistreat us. If we don't want to answer their questions, nothing says we have to do so.* As Jethro had said, "Grassroots groups especially get abused by acting as though media can just walk all over them. Set some boundaries and stick with them. If they don't respect integrity, well, tough for them."

But Jeff's questions were fair, and I answered them, adding, "It makes sense that folks are interested in us, but really we want to stay on the issues. Anyways, we appreciated your article today. I've passed it around, because it's untangling a couple of the finer points in law which don't necessarily make for sexy reading material."

Jeff's response was thoughtful. "Of course you want to focus on the issues, but your organization will also be vetted in the process—that's only fair. You and Jet are part of the story, because it is your savvy strategizing that has focused, coordinated, and developed the support that you have. But Dan Fee can throw out as much garbage as he wants— maybe he didn't run that junk by me because he knew it wouldn't get in the paper without anything substantial behind it. When you get rich off of this, I'll be happy to take you down!" He added, "And *all* my articles are sexy."

Our inoculation mostly worked. Fee's rumors never made it into the *Metro*, the *Evening Bulletin*, or the *Inquirer*. They were relegated to minor blogs and anonymous online commentators. Now we could focus on winning a referendum. Somehow, during the week, our team had gotten ready for our first outreach training session.

St. Peter's Church wafted with the sights and sounds of Old Philadelphia. Its creaking, original pew benches carried markings from the days when they were owned by wealthy Philadelphians, including some of the nation's founding fathers. St. Peter's kept its doors open since 1761, in part with money raised on lottery—before Puritans considered it gambling.

I brought my sagging body into the church, glad that I wasn't leading any of today's sessions. Too many sleepless nights and a crushing inbox, filling up faster than I could respond.

Volunteers frantically spread out. Mary Stumpf dropped off 10,000 freshly printed postcards encouraging people to vote in the referendum. The ink on Jeremy Beaudry's designed postcards was barely dry, without either a ballot number or whether the vote was a "Yes" or a "No"—a sign of how much we did not know. Kathy breathlessly ran in, arms filled with extensively edited get-out-the-vote materials designed by volunteer Linda Johansson, still warm from photocopying. She glared at me, still angry that I had sent her the wrong version last night, causing her to rush this morning.

"I'm sorry," I muttered as she rushed past without saying anything. But I understood. Her number-one priority: get the job done. We'd say whatever needed to be said at our next face-to-face encounter. Kathy headed to help Anne set up a map with every division in the city.

Glancing at the elevated, two-story-high pulpit, I talked to nobody in particular. "Maybe we should speak up there!" Kathy gave me a withering glance.

Shirley grabbed my arm and thrust some markers into my hand. "Why don't you help Anne write up the goals?" I wrote on large newsprint: "Pass the referendum on May 15 with 1,000 trained volunteers. Start tomorrow in your neighborhood."

A trickle, then a stream of over 100 volunteers arrived. Kathy took each aside. "Where in the city do you live?" With Ed Goppelt's assistance, she and Anne found out people's electoral ward and division. "Ward twenty-nine? Okay, go over to that pew."

Each pew represented an electoral ward. Riverfront wards were quickly filled up. Surprisingly, pews from other parts of the city were crammed, too.

I watched Jethro interact with people in each pew, laughing and clasping hands warmly. He never had trouble talking to anybody.

Kathy tapped her watch at Anne, who nodded in response.

"Welcome to the first Get Out the Referendum training!" shouted Anne. "Our goal is to win the referendum to give us a chance to protect ourselves from casinos. We can totally win this. We just have to identify people across the city who support us and make sure they vote in large numbers.

"Because you talk to someone who says they will vote with us, that's not enough. In electoral campaigns, we talk about the three-touch rule of organizing. First touch: knock on your neighbor's door or meet them on the street. Get them to put up a window sign and sign the pledge. It's super important you get their contact information, so you can have the second touch: call them a few days before the election to remind them to vote. Finally, the third touch on the day of the elections: make certain they voted. Offer a ride if necessary."

I slipped off to a quiet corner and watched people's faces from the side. After No Way Without Our Say, there wasn't a trace of nervousness in the room about approaching strangers. People took notes and listened attentively.

Anne continued, "Electoral campaigns live and die by this basic concept. Winning electoral campaigns is *not* about having more people agree with you. It's about organizing them to turn out and vote. Many politicians have been elected merely because they have a better turnout operation than their opponents.

"As you meet people, stay on the same basic message you used when gathering signatures—just adapted: 'Please vote May 15 to keep casinos away from schools, homes, places of worship, parks and playgrounds.' Be polite. Be friendly. Be positive. And *don't* waste your time arguing with people who disagree, just move on to the next person."

For a split second, Anne looked uncertain, then put on a big smile and waived Jethro over.

Jethro rocked on his heels. "Today we'll set up a structure to handle pledges you receive. Each ward will pick a ward captain, who will collect the pledges and feed that information to us. Since our hands our full, that pushes down leadership. It's a model I used years ago in an action called Turn Your Back on Bush. Originally, we just thought it'd be a few of us and our friends at George Bush's inauguration, literally turning our backs on his motorcade. Then it turned out to be 5,000 friends. We needed a structure that allowed us to coordinate everything, but without us answering every single question and email. So we created state captains, who played a similar role to ward captains in this get-out-the-vote operation.

"Ward captains build close-knit relationships, collect information, and alert us to problems as they arise. This way, I get to do what I'm good at—building up people's confidence and supporting people to set boundaries about what they do and don't do."

I stopped paying attention to Jethro and noticed Shirley and Kathy huddled together a few feet from me, holding a muted, animated conversation. Kathy waved her hands at Shirley, who held up her hands in protest. Anne explained how each ward would select a captain, while Kathy continued hounding Shirley. Withering under Kathy's stare, Shirley turned and bolted toward me, looking around to make sure nobody could hear us.

"You have to stop abdicating your responsibilities!"

Oh-kay. Here it goes.

Shirley's hands shook. "This is serious. We are up against major, well-financed opponents. We can't afford to have things like our financials in the hands of someone like me. We *need* a professional bookkeeper."

My voice was controlled. "I agree. It's been hard to find a volunteer—"

"No, it's not okay!" Shirley wagged her finger at me, leaning close. "We can't just wing it. We need to be 100% legal, with every *i* dotted and *t* crossed! We can't have some loose structure where people do whatever they want. Anne has to be up there telling people *exactly* what we need them to do. We have people in their fifties, sixties, seventies, eighties... Many of us grew up with hierarchy."

"I absolutely agree we need to be legal. But it's not fair to assume we therefore need a strict top-down structure—"

"I know *you* believe that!" Shirley stepped toward me, causing my back to hit against the pew. "You have experience in consensus egalitarian structures—we don't. Our people need structure. 'Do this.' 'Volunteer for that.' We need to make every volunteer's time count. They have families and jobs. If we don't use them well, they won't stay with us."

"I *agree*," I said, frustrated. "Our way of operating is different, but it's not like we don't know how to use people."

Shirley's voice only rose more. "It's not working for me! It's not working for Kathy! And we're just the tip of the iceberg!" Surprised at her loud exclamation, she looked around. Nobody was paying attention.

"Then give concrete suggestions!" I shouted back, my voice and hands matching her emotion.

Shirley lowered her hands. "We need a *real* listserve—not just your hard drive—and a nonprofit lawyer to assure us our organization is perfect. We can't have any holes."

"Okay, okay, okay," I relaxed my shoulders. "I appreciate that you and Kathy are our bridge to older and professional folks. I don't think that's in contradiction with more decentralized leadership, but we agree on the need to get these things."

Shirley took a breath, still glaring at me. "You hear me?"

"I do, and I'll do my best. But," I broke into a grin, "I want you to yell at me again if I'm not doing what you think is best."

"I will," she smiled. "I do it because I want what's best for us. You and Jethro built this organization out of nothing. I trust you, which is why I'm so honest. I just want to bring what I know from years of business consulting, which is building a solid structure."

"I know," I said. "Thanks."

Shirley turned and gave Kathy a thumbs-up. Leaning on the pew together, Shirley and I watched the rest of the get-out-the-vote training in silence. It had been only nine days since council's vote for the referendum.

In the middle of the next week, Shirley and I met at her house, still filled with construction materials. The referendum was gaining steam, with hundreds of people hitting the streets and recruiting others. But energy was sagging amongst our leadership. Across from me, Shirley's eyes still sagged with late nights for the petition drive.

As I learned from Jethro, I tried starting our meeting emphasizing postive news. "Tomorrow you'll be seeing big news in all the press. Katie Recker just told me about a potentially game-changing law. It outlaws any 'adult entertainment facilities' in that part of Fishtown—right where the SugarHouse site is. And... well... SugarHouse is definitely adult entertainment."

Shirley's eyes sparked open. "That's stupendous! Game over, right?"

"Well... it's a big deal," I said. "But we have to keep our heads clear. Katie thinks the mayor could interpret the provision in such a way to ignore it. Or City Council could change the law. The point is nothing is over until it's over."

"How did nobody know anything about it? What's the law?"

I quickly explained that in the late '90s, Fishtown and Northern Liberties were plagued by Delaware Avenue nightclubs. Fishtowners suffered pee on doorsteps and drunken behavior. After some serious shootings, in 2002 they pushed Councilman DiCicco to create the zoning prohibition. Why nobody had remembered the law was mysterious. "Today Katie told me and the councilmember about it, which meant I knew we'd have to pounce before DiCicco. I'm certain he's going to send out a press release with all his defeatism and caution. But... who knows, *maybe* it's our silver bullet! If the law was followed, it certainly would kill SugarHouse."

Shirley wanted to talk more about the implication that—for once—those in the North opposing SugarHouse seemed to have the upper hand. "It could be a real shift in relations in the DRNA," she said.

But I returned to our meeting topic. "Let's maximize our time focused on the organizational questions," I said, grinning. Shirley laughed.

With under $1,000 in the bank, she reluctantly agreed we weren't in a position to hire a nonprofit lawyer or rent a downtown office.

I assured her, "It's the reality of small nonprofits, especially doing edgy work, to not have money."

"That's at least helpful to hear," she said, plopping down tea in front of me. "You have to remember, Kathy and I come from the business world. This is a new industry to us."

"Well, I've got more bad news for you. The latest accountant just emailed me back. He declined, too."

"Was this after you showed him Brennan's article?"

"Yep." A smile crept over my face. "You're getting a taste of life as an activist. You're now so radical you can't even hire an accountant—that's the third to turn us down!"

"I'm not an activist," she recoiled. "Just a citizen... We'll just have to keep looking."

I laughed to myself, wondering if she knew how silly she sounded to me. *Not an activist. Ha!* I kept on smiling. "There is one area where I think we can immediately take a next step: a database." I rolled out options to replace our email lists, housed on my personal computer.

After weighing different features, she selected Democracy in Action, a Swiss army knife of online organizing with the capacity for volunteer tracking, fundraising, email blasting, and online donations. It was my preference, but I choked at spending $250 a month—almost as much as a new part-time staffer.

Shirley leaned back in her chair, her voice cool. "It'll make it easier for you and Jethro to coordinate captains, create petitions, help us collect information—and fundraise. All that saves us a precious commodity: your time. And it's easy enough that old fuddy-duddies like me can use it. So, yes, it's absolutely worth the cost! Get it now! Stop dawdling!"

I sucked it up and rushed home to start our database subscription, beginning the transition of our mere 859 supporters' emails onto the DIA database. As I did, my heart wrenched—we had never added the 27,000 petition names into a database. I still couldn't believe it. It was like I'd failed at Organizing 101. Lists are an organizer's lifeblood. Jethro kept saying our power wasn't in lists but in our relationships with people. But not writing up that list was just stupid.

We had just been constantly reacting to new crises, unable to mount the hundreds of volunteer hours to type up the pages. I shot a few emails to volunteers, only half-hoping someone would have the energy to coordinate data entry. We wouldn't.

I returned to integrating our website with our database.

*   *   *

Late Wednesday night Frank DiCicco emailed a blind cc'd list, "The mayor *will* veto the bill tomorrow. He believes he has the necessary votes to sustain his veto! Possible defectors: councilmembers Krajewski, Savage, Campbell, Blackwell, Rizzo, Kelly and O'Neil. I repeat. Possible supporters of the veto!"

Anne and I believed those councilmembers were solid and would override his veto tomorrow. It smelled of a DiCicco-manufactured crisis, to play the dramatic hero—and pull energy from the streets to City Hall.

Kathy disagreed. "We can't sit on our hands! We'll lose nothing by showing up in force. But if it is something and we're not there, we disappoint everyone."

"DiCicco shouldn't determine where we direct our energy," I urged her over the phone. "Tomorrow I have packed meetings. I don't want to be wasting my time at a hearing!"

Kathy hung up, dissatisfied. But over the next half-hour, my inbox flooded with panicked emails: "What do we do? Should we write letters?" "We need to fill council chambers!" "We're going to lose!"

I called Kathy back. "Our people are being too reactive—you, too. It's fabrication for political point-scoring. Notice how immediately after DiCicco's email, all his backers added, 'There's nothing we can do.' Jeff Rush wrote, 'If it holds, it'll show what good leadership can do, so thanks, Frank.' DiCicco is trying to get re-elected, and this is an election strategy." Persuaded by members' fear, however, I agreed to encourage our membership to show up to Thursday's council vote—but *without* passing on DiCicco's rumor.

The next morning, I confidently headed into City Hall—after a successful meeting in which Chris Meck and I recruited Project H.O.M.E. as the first social-service agency to take a stand against casinos, departing from its previous position of merely negotiating with the casinos to get money.

I arrived forty minutes past council's official 10 o'clock start, hoping to miss council's frivolous orchestration. I still heard as council passed a resolution honoring a swim team, gave rote speeches, honored local jazz musicians, and praised Northern Ireland's recent power-sharing deal. It was wasted volunteer time, to see councilmembers parading in front us—watching power instead of building it.

Unknown to me, Dan Fee was boasting to reporter Bruce Schimmel, "we've got the six to sustain an override." But I did see building trades leader Pat Gillespie whispering in councilmembers' ears and Councilwoman Carol Ann Campbell very conspicuously negotiating on her phone through the whole hearing. It appeared something *was* up.

Fear ran up and down my spine. We had *no* plan if we lost this vote. Even if SugarHouse could overturn the ballot after the election, we would have hundreds of thousands of Philadelphians feeling the sting of the courts overturning their will. It'd then be easy to organize people. We *had* to win today.

The pomp and circumstances ended. Council promptly voted.

All *aye*'s. Unanimous. The referendum was definitely going on the ballot, and there was nothing our opposition could do about it. The crowd cheered loudly.

"Visitors," said the chairwoman, banging her gavel, "please leave quietly so that we can continue to conduct our business." I stood up and joined members outside of chambers with a creeping smile on my face. We were done with council politics and could finally devote all attention to winning the referendum.

In the hallway, reporters swarmed like bees, buzzing between clumps of disappointed building trades union supporters and CFP's more numerous, upbeat supporters. Unlike last time, there was no plan in place for us to gather outside.

"When I looked inside City Hall today," an *Inquirer* reporter began, "I have never seen so many of the powerful political players in one room: building trades, powerful lawyers, business executives, chamber of commerce. *Every* single one of them was against you. So how did you win?"

"Their story is that casinos will bring jobs and revenue. But we appealed to a bigger value: democracy. Philadelphians have seen broken promises before and are rightly cynical about being told they'll get jobs and that some industry will save them. Everything we have done shows our belief is in Philadelphians having their own say about a reasonable standard that makes immediate sense to people—a 1,500-foot buffer between casinos and our homes, our schools, our places of worship. Every step the industry makes to stop that vote, they are showing their true colors. They don't care about Philadelphians. They want unfettered power and access in government, which is why they prefer a backdoor process."

Out of the corner of my eye, I saw Ed Verral heckling Pat Gillespie. I moved toward Ed, as he glared and shouted, "You wouldn't want one in your neighborhood!"

A reporter put a videocamera in my face and I took another interview, as Ed shouted at Pat, "You would build anything—you're just a snake-oil salesman!"

A building trades supporter described later by the *City Paper* as a "younger guy with serious forearm muscles, slick black hair, and a building trades union shirt" towered above Ed and bumped his bulging belly into Ed, pushing Ed backwards. "Show some respect!"

Ed quieted down, long enough for my interview to end. "Let it drop," I urged Ed.

"He and Dan Fee are just lyin' the same way they been lyin'," Ed spat, "tellin' everybody council's just saving their jobs and that there was plenty of time for input."

"We'll get him in the press, but people have a right to share their side of the story, *however wrong*," I said, loud enough to elicit heckles. "Just let it go and meet up with the rest of our crew." I yanked Ed and hurried him toward the stairs.

But I was also curious.

I wheeled around on Pat and looked down at his bulging figure. "Mr. Gillespie, do you really believe that it's wrong for citizens to have a vote on whether casinos are close to neighborhoods or not?"

He looked me up and down. The vibrations in the hallway almost crackled with lightning. Someone tugged on his arm, but he ignored it. "Stop wasting your time tilting at windmills. Focus on neighborhood issues—something you can do something about."

"But why do you care if the casinos are built in one location or another?" I asked.

"We will build them where they are. They aren't moving."

"But why does location matter? What do you care if they move to the airport, or the Navy Yard?" The DRNA had been regularly encouraging these options instead of casinos in neighborhoods.

He took a heavy breath, as if talking to an idiot. "The sooner these casinos get started, the sooner the convention center gets under way." He walked off, a few of his lackeys shoving me aside.

It took only a little research to confirm their angle. The $1 billion to expand the Pennsylvania Convention Center was legislatively tied to the so-called "casino" funds. It was written so that until casinos were up and running, building trades workers would be left waiting to build the large, and dubiously cost-effective, expansion project.

Gillespie was used to getting his way and was infuriated that council bucked his union. As revenge, the union vowed to withhold resources from *all* council members. In turn, reporters and council found some backbone to openly challenge them. Council soon initiated hearings on the gender and racial makeup of the building and construction trades unions, known for a century as a segregationist, patriarchal club. And WHYY's Susan Phillips reporting on their possible loss of influence angered their public-relations operative, Frank Keel—also hired by SugarHouse.

"What you're witnessing," he wrote on WHYY's blog, "is not an erosion of the strength of the building trades, but rather the neutering and spaying effect an election year can have on members of City Council, even the handful of smart, honorable ones. The 'tensions' in the hallway scrum were caused by one or two ignorant anti-casino activists. Dipshits like the shrieker of 'Snake Oil Salesman' were too busy preening for the TV cameras. If I'm wrong and the casinos get killed or moved, I'll be the first to apologize and admit I was wrong. But I don't think I'm wrong."

The building trades would never forgive us for beating them so badly in public. In other words, we had made permanent enemies.

The next Monday, Jethro groggily answered his phone. "What time is it?" He coughed.

"It's noon."

Jethro's voice was unusually faint. "I've been sleeping all day... I'm still sick."

"That sucks. Everybody's sick... Shirley, Kathy. Even Mary Stumpf isn't feeling well."

"That makes it an emergency!" He blew his nose. "We need some time off... You really need a vacation..."

"I know, we all need a break," I said. "I was calling to propose we call off everything this week."

"What was on the..." He trailed off.

"... on the calendar," I finished helpfully. "The Bowl-A-Thon fundraiser is this Friday, which is Good Friday and should be moved anyways. We've got an executive team meeting and two get-out-the-vote trainings, on Wednesday and Saturday. I think we should just cancel everything."

Jethro sniffed loudly. "Yeah."

"I'll do it and let you go. You go back to sleep, Jet," I said.

He promptly hung up.

I returned to my computer to write an email on our new database to tell supporters we were canceling this week's events, reminding people of the long road still ahead of us. "As a movement we are learning that we do not win by going along with the political landscape, but using social pressure and the power of people to *shift* the political landscape. Today candidates are forced to confront the issue. It's a far cry from a few months ago where nobody wanted to touch this. So let's pace ourselves, because this is a bigger issue than just casinos. We're in this mess because of larger politics—the insider politics and corrosive power of money on government. These are larger issues we are challenging, too. We not only have a chance to protect our neighborhoods, we're doing so with a lot of style and in a way that's teaching people in this city about what it means to be engaged citizens. We are all modeling positive leadership for the city, and that's something to be very, very proud of."

I hit "send."

The rest of the afternoon I puttered around the house, doing laundry, cleaning out stray emails, and thinking. Canceling meetings felt like a huge weight off. We had a crisis every week and a major crisis every month that required totally reworking our strategy.

Now that the referendum was officially a "go," it was ours to lose. My mind leisurely played out scenarios of what was ahead of us.

I plopped down at my computer, munched an apple, and wrote to the executive team:

> We need to think ahead. A very strategic opponent, and we may finally have a worthy opponent, does not fight you when you're on the high ground—classic Sun Tzu Art of War. Our high ground is public opinion. Theirs is the courts.
>
> I suspect they're going to accept losing the referendum, not wasting resources on a doomed ballot fight. Instead they will pour resources into a court battle. That doesn't mean we shouldn't organize to win the referendum—we have to win it. It still seems likely the casinos might mount a Vote "No" campaign.
>
> Running this campaign expands our structure, increases momentum for anti-casino candidates, and keeps pressure on the state to not trump city zoning.
>
> But the referendum is one line of attack. As a chess player, I've often made the mistake of opening one line of vigorous attack only to suddenly see my defenses are left wide open, and I'm unable to switch gears. We can't afford to get caught in transition.
>
> If the May 15 election happens and we win, they will immediately take us to the courts. If we win in the court, let's just celebrate for a long time!
>
> But if we lose in the courts a series of articles will come out to trash us again. 'Waste of time, thoughtless but idealistic activists, Mayor Street was right, etc.' Internally some people will be pissed. Another set of people will be resentful that we've brought them so far along only to lose at the last moment. We will likely get accused of not thinking ahead (an accusation we've weathered before).
>
> We need to prepare a game plan for after May 15. Legal and political avenues need to be pursued. In terms of direct action, if the courts deny people's votes, we have a chance to get people on the high ground. We need a response. I propose:
>
> June 1—We have four days of a "practice occupation" outside of the SugarHouse and Foxwoods sites; it is legal and on the sidewalk, we train people in how to do an occupation and let them know we are "coming" for them. It is media-friendly.
>
> June 15—We begin a three-month site occupation, literally taking over the two SugarHouse and Foxwoods sites. We use the election results as saying we're simply implementing the only standard that has been set. Having walked the sites, I believe if momentum were sustained we could legitimately do that, implementing the will of the people.

I happily spent the next week catching up on sleep.

✳   ✳   ✳

"If you look back, you can kind of make out the old sugar refinery, where SugarHouse wants to build."

I squinted as Jethro pointed at the edge of the Delaware River, standing in the middle of overgrown weeds. Jethro insisted we walk north from his house, passing numerous empty buildings and stepping over broken-down fences. It was the ruins of old Fishtown, reaching back to when it was the center of a vibrant shad-fishing industry, and later, industrial work.

"There's so much history here," Jethro said, walking through a half-fallen building held up by concrete columns marked by red and green dots from paintball guns. "Back at Penn Treaty Park underneath an oak tree, William Penn signed his treaty with the local Lenni Lenape—the only treaty respected by whites while Penn lived. Local historians are suggesting that maybe the actual location wasn't in the park, but nearer to the SugarHouse site."

"The proposed SugarHouse site," I corrected. The wind howled loudly as we reached the river.

"Right. Just back that way is buried Batchelor's Hall, the first botanical garden used for growing medicine. Apparently it was a big social spot for Ben Franklin and other men. Further up this way is where the British built outposts, while trying to retake Philadelphia. It might be under our feet now."

"You're like a walking Fishtown history book," I said.

"It's important to know where you live. When I talk to the old-timers on my block, they love telling the story of Fishtown and all its transitions and changes. It's been a neglected part of the city, which is no doubt why they decided to put SugarHouse on it."

I sat on a concrete dock, my feet dangling over the river. Jethro sat next to me, chewing a piece of grass. "I wanted to bring you out here..." He smiled. "You're doing a great job, especially with the press. I'm learning so much from you about how to frame even bad news and keep the high ground. Press are tough. And you've even gotten them to start nailing down mayoral candidates. We're moving a lot of people who didn't want to touch this."

"Last night's Society Hill town hall had all the mayoral candidates say yes to everything we wanted. They all said they'd vote for the referendum and include literature supporting it in their campaigns."

"It's a great example of how smart and effective organizing leads to winning new allies, without *us* having to do all the work," he said.

I grinned. "Well, shall we start practicing?"

Jethro nodded. I pulled out a copy of the *Philadelphia Inquirer* and handed it to him.

Jethro scanned it. "Here's an article on the increase in gun violence. Go!"

I smiled. "That's easy. The reason there are so many guns on the street killing people is the city cannot pass decent gun-control legislation. New Jersey has half the number of homicides as us, largely by passing basic handgun laws outlawing buying more than one handgun a month. But Philly keeps suffering because the state trumps the city, bypassing all city hopes for gun control. If someone wants to pass that legislation, they need to strengthen the city—and one clear way to do that is to join Casino-Free Philadelphia in our fight against the state. We'd love them to work with us."

"Your turn," I said, taking the paper from him. "Here's an article about the batch of new political reformers running for council. Make the pitch."

Jethro smiled. "If they want good government, they cannot afford to have a powerful industry who controls the city's and state's purse strings, who *even before* they are in power, are already controlling and buying off politicians. The casino industry has their own interests at stake—and they have the money and muscle to get their way. Any good government person should join our campaign."

Jethro took the newspaper back. "Let me find something challenging... How about this one. It's an editorial challenging Detroit automakers for not using fuel efficiency. How would you speak to environmentalists fighting for fuel efficiency?"

"No problem," I laughed. "They've got to be interested in reducing reliance on car travel. Casinos result in huge car tie-ups and 80,000 additional cars on the streets, and these things are completely designed without any consideration about public transportation. Someone who wants fuel efficiency would surely want to join a campaign to stop an environmental nightmare. There's much friendlier, local development that encourages walking and public spaces—not another big-box development."

We played our newspaper-framing game for almost an hour, connecting our campaign to every news article. It was great practice for us to talk with anyone in the city about every major issue.

It was late by the time we walked back across the history-laden land of Fishtown.

Paul called me on April Fools' Day. His voice was cold, calm, and relaxed. "The PGCB did it."

I knew immediately. The PGCB was going back to the courts, suing the state over the referendum. Paul explained the PGCB's varied, sometimes strangled arguments: that council had improperly passed the bill, that council couldn't change zoning laws via a referendum, that the 1,500-foot buffer would leave no places in the city, and, ultimately, that the state had sole authority in placing casinos.

"Well, what's done is done," Paul said.

"Just watch, SugarHouse and Foxwoods are now going to throw their hat into the ring and join the suit. We'll get a string of public attacks. We've got to reframe this away from legality and into rightness and wrongness. Jethro and I have been noticing that *corruption* is a theme across a range of current city issues. And on that, the PGCB is still highly vulnerable."

"I assume you've got a plan?"

My media support team—Bill Kosman, Jay Grossman, and Kathy DeAngelis—had suggested it was time to turn the attention back to the PGCB's chairman, Tad Decker, and his connections back to SugarHouse. "It's the perfect time to ask for Decker's removal. With his insistence that the vote was a 'waste of time and taxpayer dollars,' he is a clear target. His dirty dealings with the casinos need investigation. Without anybody yelling 'Fire!' nobody is sufficiently motivated to dig deep into the story. So we send out the letter today."

"I need to review it some more," said Paul.

"You've had the draft in your mailbox for over a week."

"I know, but there's a lot on my plate."

"Then let me take something off your plate so you can edit the letter today."

Paul stammered. "We have to tighten up the letter considerably. Decker's a lawyer, he'll look for a chance to sue. We need to be more than precise—we must be flawless."

"Just hurry on those edits, okay? Bill Clinton used to say that in politics, when you get hit, you have to hit back quickly."

"Aren't you a pacifist, Daniel?"

"Yes. It just means when we get hit, we have to speak some truth to power. It only looks like hitting because it stings."

Days later, I walked into a public meeting of the city's election commissioners. It was a tiny, overheated room, more like a stuffy broom closet than a place where lawyers and election experts decided meticulous details of elections, including confirming the wording and placement of our ballot.

I spotted Ed Goppelt and awkwardly tried to sit as close to him as possible. It felt so weird, surrounded by stuffy realpolitik and political intrigue. A large, sharply dressed woman asked for her garage to become her district's new location for a polling site. "The current place isn't considered neutral," she said. "But the ward leader is a close friend of mine and knows my place would be much better." She handed the commissioners a letter of recommendation. After a cursory review, they agreed to move the voting location.

It seemed like the worst of Philly: key decisions made away from the public's eyes.

At first, the commissioners made a few snarky comments about the "excessive" ballot—with ninety candidates for over twenty-five offices, plus nine ballot questions.

"Let's get to the ballot questions," said one election commissioner. My ears perked up.

"I propose we move the buffer-zone question to the first slot. My neighbors are passionate about the buffer-zone question," said one commissioner with emotion. Catching himself, he turned solemn. "That way, people will be able to find the question more easily. We'll have long lines if people are merely searching for this question that there's such... eagerness about."

The deputy commissioner looked worried. "Why should the first question now be second? Why should the third question now be the fourth?" He suggested that moving it might cause the casinos to sue them.

I laughed to myself. That was the kind of self-centered, conservative thinking that kept people from being bold. They were acting from fear, not empathy, when it was clear that the casino industry would gain nothing by attacking election commissioners.

After further debate, the argument to move the ballot won. "The count, in terms of what the public says, will be fairer if it's in a prominent position, listed as number one." And I got confirmation that we'd be asking the public for a "Yes" vote for certain.

I hurried out, a KYW reporter trailing me. He thrust a microphone in my face. "What do you think of being question number one?"

I didn't have an opinion going into the meeting. But I felt haunted by another decision made without public input. "I think it's reckless to change... I mean, to move the ballot question. It invites precedent, makes no sense. It's..." I looked for a word Paul might use. "Capricious."

The reporter eyed me doubtfully, and—thankfully—promptly ignored my comments.

As soon as he left, my head cooled. This was way better for us. More people would vote, and the commissioners were giving us a badge of honor. We now had a new, positive slogan that could finally be posted on our materials: "Vote Yes on #1."

That evening, Jeremy Beaudry designed Vote Yes on #1 materials urging people to support the 1,500-foot buffer between casinos and homes. The next day, Scott Seiber ordered tens of thousands of flyers and window signs from our favorite union shop. By the end of the week, our website reflected the new campaign, backed by our sophisticated database. With the new site, anytime someone signed a petition, they could click to be added to our database. It made Jethro proud to have what he called a "sticky" organization—one that made it easy to become part of it and get connected to the movement. Between that and our fieldwork, our database tripled to 2,534 in that last month and gathered a whopping $2,000 in online donations.

As expected, SugarHouse and Foxwoods signed on to the lawsuit. SugarHouse spokesman Dan Fee argued, "Changing our charter is an important and serious matter, and there is a reason there are strict procedures and mandates. Unfortunately, this process has not followed those rules and the referendum should not go forward."

The chamber of commerce piled on, adding their names to the challenges, saying, "When you look at the law, it gives one entity the right to site the casinos." The PGCB. Now we must accept it.

Unexpectedly, DiCicco defended the referendum, arguing that the casinos "must be worried. Why else would you do it? You just create more anger and frustration. The more you try to tell people that they don't count, I think the more resistance you get."

Six days later—far later than I wanted—Paul hand-delivered our seven-page letter to Governor Rendell, asking for Decker's removal due to "unfitness for office" and his refusal to "disqualify himself from any proceeding in which the member's objectivity, impartiality, integrity or independence of judgment may be reasonably questioned."

Press ate up the story of Decker's perceived conflicted interests. His former law firm, Cozen O'Connor, seemed to be on both sides: hired by SugarHouse and, through him, involved in the PGCB's selection of SugarHouse. And rumor held that Decker would return to Cozen O'Connor at a cushy job. It reeked of corruption.

I was even more pleased that it signaled to supporters we would defend ourselves. As people knocked on doors, passed out flyers, and recruited new signatories for our campaign, CFP leadership showed our organizational mettle. Every time the PGCB and the casinos knocked us down, we brushed ourselves off and came up with another response.

It was an important lesson, as seismic changes were afoot to alter everything we had been doing, resulting in the most uncertain, anxious week we had ever faced.

CHAPTER 9

A Failed Pledge for Democracy

APRIL 13, 2007—APRIL 17, 2007

anything to move out of paralysis • radicalizing from a loss •
where there's anger, there's hope • halting sweet, misdirected revenge •
"if this, then that" • the Movement Action Plan • collective action as a healing balm •
history tightens an action design • picking vision, selecting a name

I HAD NEVER MET ANY of the judges on the Pennsylvania Supreme Court, and they didn't know me—or any of us. They didn't know of our failed meetings with legislators or our finger-numbing petition-gathering. They never investigated the details of our petition or allowed our lawyers to argue our side of the case. That, however, did not stop them from clobbering us on Friday the 13th. In the afternoon—the media low-ebb when weekday reporters are closing shop and weekend reporters are not yet in the office—they quietly released their ruling.

I have no memory of where I was when I heard the bad news. It didn't matter—once Paul or some reporter alerted me, I couldn't concentrate on anything. I was swallowed by shock, numbly tapping my computer to forward the supreme court's fifteen-line ruling to reporters without comment.

"Even the city solicitor said the referendum couldn't be stripped off the ballot," I yelled at no one in particular. "No explanation. No reasoning." *This can't be happening.*

It was as if the supreme court had written a personal letter to all Philadelphia residents telling them they had no right to control city development—or have a say about it. Democracy was a joke, controlled by more powerful interests that knew better. They would not let us even *vote* on the buffer zone.

I instinctively reached out to call Jethro, but he was working in Maryland over the weekend. Instead, my cell phone rang. It was *Daily News* reporter Chris Brennan.

"So the supreme court ordered an injunction against your referendum. What do you think of this decision?" he asked.

"The feeling is just outrage." I bit my tongue, pushing down my rage, reaching for words. "Stripping the referendum off the ballot is a cowardly way to avoid public opinion."

"It's a preliminary injunction," he said without emotion, "which means they may end up allowing the referendum to go forward in the end. But I'm guessing your lawyers would agree it seems unlikely. What will you do now?"

The question stabbed me. We had just been ambushed, with a body blow from the supreme court. Now I was expected to have a well-thought-out response? My mind went blank. "We will continue our struggle. We are not deterred." I felt like I was betraying my own despair and hopelessness.

Chris pushed for specifics, but unless he wanted to hear me vent, I had nothing to give. We had not seen this coming and had no back-up plan.

As I hung up the phone, another reporter called. And another. And another. Each asking, "What are you going to do now?"

"We will keep fighting," I told them gamely. My despair whispered silently: *Or maybe this is the end.* "We will not let this stand." The internal ugly voice persisted: *though we cannot prevent it.*

Unable to reach Jethro, I was inundated with calls from reporters and allies. My mouth dried out. I felt light-headed, forgetting to eat or drink, as my cell phone rang over and over again. For two hours, I felt like I was emotionally lying to the press.

Near dinnertime, reporters reached their deadlines and my phone stopped ringing. I wanted to curl into a ball with some hot cocoa, but I thought of all the CFP supporters who, when they heard the news, would suffer the same traumatic reaction as me.

I faced the organizer's monumental task of changing consciousness through sheer force of will. I shook my head fiercely, trying to loosen my tight, scowling glare, then settled down to start a draft to CFP supporters. They would be in better shape if they heard the bad news from me, rather than from the glee of our opponents printed in black ink tomorrow.

Through the early evening, I traded drafts of a letter with Jay Grossman. Realizing that we needed to offer *some* action step, we hastily assembled a condemnatory response petition. Like me, Jay was uncertain whether it should be sent to the PGCB, the supreme court, state legislators, or Governor Rendell.

"It doesn't matter," I told him. "Folks just need to do something to move out of paralysis." We settled on the PGCB.

Despite the late hour, Jay's voice stayed cool. "We also need to express anger at the courts that did this to us."

"Let's do something at the supreme court on Monday, during people's lunch breaks," I said. What we would do was unclear. But I knew we needed to express our collective outrage.

As Jay and I finished final touches, the executive team began weighing in on the news. Kathy Dilonardo had heard it as a rumor and suggested a late emergency meeting that night. Shirley agreed, maintaining her characteristic equanimity, "I take off two hours for a fundraising meeting—and look what happens in the meantime!"

But I couldn't match her calmness. "I worked an intense couple of hours and am in no shape to meet," I wrote them back. I didn't know what I wanted—to go to sleep, run around, be silent, break things, or sob. *Just finish the letter.*

I willed myself to do it and sent the letter Jay and I had written.

Glad for a distraction, I arrived very late to a small gathering of friends. At the table, I couldn't help but rail, "A body of individuals sworn to uphold the Constitution and tenets of democracy is threatening a most basic right: the right to vote."

"What's the status? Is it definitely off?" asked one friend amiably.

The uncertainty made it hard to grieve. "I really don't want to talk about it," I told them, then minutes later abruptly interrupted the conversation with "Can you *believe* what they did? Outrageous!" My friends smiled and nodded, graciously accepting my shattered state, with its alternation between clenched reluctance and sudden explosions.

My cell phone interrupted me for the last call of the evening. *Inquirer* reporter Jeff Shields was still working on the story. He read aloud to me the rambling quote I had given earlier.

Curled up in my friend's stairwell, I listened on the edge of tears as Jeff asked if I wanted to clarify. I breathed deeply, stuffed the tears down, and told him "the PGCB should hang their head in shame for stomping on democracy in order to get their way." Tentative about lashing out at the body that still held our referendum in its hands, I moderated the attack against the supreme court: "We're hopeful that they'll lift the injunction, though we're dismayed that they're threatening our right to vote."

"Thanks, keep your head up," said Jeff, and he got off the phone.

I cried only a little more before returning to dinner.

The next morning, I did not want to wake up. My head felt heavy, and my fingers barely lifted up my laptop so I could read the news.

For once, "done deal" was not snuck into the subtext. The *Philadelphia Inquirer* printed, "The fight to stop casinos is likely to continue irrespective of what happens to the referendum."

Though it was better than I had feared, I felt no joy. Neither did I feel despair as our opponents crowed with triumph. Nor did I feel anger as Paul cursed the decision and jotted, "I am going to the law library today." Nor did I feel encouraged as Kathy wrote, "What they have done has made me very angry at their arrogance and misuse of power— as well as interpreting the law with no real explanation—so I am ready to take the next steps. Some of our members took this really hard. We need to help pick them up and get back to the issues. Let's meet on Sunday night."

I felt like running away and joining Jethro in Maryland—or going anywhere away from Philadelphia. I tapped a reply. "I did not sleep well last night and am feeling beaten up. I'm outraged and pissed and likewise ready to act." I agreed to a Sunday night meeting, but only if I could do it from the safe confines of my home on conference call.

I pulled myself out of reactive mode enough to scrawl a few ideas for Monday's actions. If we framed it right, maybe the corruption of the court system could bring in some new allies.

It was hard to mourn without the clean death of the referendum. We had to ditch today's plans to do outreach on the Vote Yes on #1 campaign and instead used volunteers to make calls for Monday's as-of-yet unplanned supreme court protest.

Shirley sensed my wavering. "Take a deep breath. We're merely at a course correction point. We've been moving ahead steadily with conviction, resolution and credibility. This is one of those three-steps-forward and one-step-backward moments. But Daniel, this meeting is important. We have to get together and think this through. You have to come—I'll pay for a cab ride if necessary."

I could not serve the group by staying victimized by shock. I needed to rise, with everyone else, to the occasion. I could not pick myself up for my own sake, but I could do it for others.

I knew she was right, but I didn't like it. After agreeing to a Sunday meeting, I headed downstairs for some breakfast.

All afternoon, I recovered slowly. Reflecting on all the hits we had taken, I realized that what made this one so hard was its unexpectedness.

As a kid, I learned to protect myself from other kids' bullying by watching and observing. I learned what things would set them off and what words would shut them back up. After one harrowing encounter with a racist bully, my dad took me aside and broke down for me what was going on for everyone: the bully, the bully's racist parents, the neglectful teacher, and even my own self. The lesson was clear: knowledge and an understanding of others can protect you.

But my ability to guess what was coming next had failed. Despite learning to be constantly on guard, I never saw this coming—and deep inside, I vowed to never let that happen again.

Nobody knew if the supreme court was going to ultimately rule against us, and the uncertainty made it worse. The more we learned, the worse our chances looked: a SugarHouse investor was an ex-member of the supreme court, and both Foxwoods investor Peter DePaul and SugarHouse investor Richard Sprague had been part of the Court of Judicial Discipline of the Commonwealth of Pennsylvania, which has jurisdiction over the supreme court on—of all things—misconduct and ethics violations. The whiff of finality was even acknowledged by Justice Saylor, one of the two dissenters in the 5-2 decision, who argued their preliminary ruling would likely be permanent.

Since the supreme court asked for an expedited review process, our lawyers saw a slim glimmer of hope. But if the court didn't quickly rule in our favor, they saw no path to challenge the decision in the federal courts. The Pennsylvania Supreme Court was an ultimate authority.

As I scrolled through emails from supporters, I saw the impact sink into our organization like a damp cloud. People were overwhelmingly critical of the court and tempted by naysayers and politicians to give up.

But our people had developed stiff backbones. Beneath expressions of hopelessness, they were searching and flailing about what to do next.

DRNA delegate and Society Hill leader Rosanne Loesch's email grabbed me as a bellwether of our movement. She seemed freshly cynical about the court's political nature. "My fear is that the court will wait to the last minute to let the vote go forward. Meanwhile, during this period when the vote is in limbo, the wind is taken out of our sails, which makes it more difficult to mobilize people. Then the court can say, 'We let you vote.' But the voting results might suffer because of this long period of temporary injunction."

Uncertain what to make of her analysis, I uncharacteristically distrusted my own thinking. *I didn't see this coming—how can I know how far the supreme court will go to screw us?*

But Rosanne wasn't stuck in cynicism and despair. She suggested seeking some legal response—unsurprising, given that her husband was a successful lawyer. What did surprise me was that both she and her husband vowed to go against legal tradition's deference to the supreme court and join our Monday protest again them.

People had seething pessimism but offered bold options—from "voting out the judges" to "lockdowns at the voting booths where everyone says they will not vote at all for anyone unless this referendum is put back" to even withholding taxes by putting "state tax money into escrow as a protest." The latter idea came from a banker. People were radicalizing.

Seeing people struggle for a meaningful response snapped me out of feeling sorry for us to focus on what move to make next. To do that, I knew I needed grounding and advice.

Hundreds of miles away in his Québec home, Philippe offered as much energy as when he first coached Jethro and me on Operation Transparency. "Make their repression," he urged over the phone, "rebound on them. You've earned credibility, so don't feel deflated. Just make them pay."

"But Philippe, this is months of work down the toilet."

"You always knew it'd be hard," said Philippe briskly. "So the supreme court ruled against you. Don't let them tell you what you can and can't do."

I sighed, trying to convince myself that Philippe simply did not understand. We could not implement the 1,500-foot buffer because of the supreme court ruling. We could not even vote about it.

Philippe filled the silence. "Step back for a second. If the supreme court orders stickers over the ballots, why don't you remove the stickers?"

"We can't do that. That's tampering and probably a major offense."

"Oh-kay," said Philippe, pausing audibly to leave that option on the table. "What about putting stickers over the other ballots that day in protest?"

"That's a waste of energy. It's not high ground."

"Do you have write-in ballot questions?"

"No," I said curtly.

"Can you pull the lever on the question anyway?"

"I doubt it. Even if we did, a few thousand votes would get thrown away and it wouldn't matter."

"Are there other mechanisms to write your voting preferences?"

"There's no way."

I felt a kind of power shooting down each of Philippe's ideas, a kind of sweet misdirected revenge. He refused to collude with the despair and kept offering ideas until he finally closed, "Where there's anger, there's hope. You have to help people tap it."

I snapped my phone shut. Part of me gripped tightly to my grinding despair. Philippe's optimism was infectious and therefore unsteadying to me.

A few deep breaths later and I found an email from George Lakey, responding to my request for advice:

> You could get small and stay in a defensive stance. Or you can come back with an escalated strategy. I think that's what you need to do: stay on the offensive. Argue the state's outrageously high-handed anti-democratic moves force a resort to more bold people power.
>
> My thinking borrows from Rubén Berríos' strategy. He was the president of the Puerto Rican Independence Party, the lead organization in a coalition that kicked the US Navy off the island of Culebra. I had challenged his emphasis on Puerto Rican independence in the campaign we did together, which was primarily about the more modest goal of stopping the US from using the island as a bombing range. I asked him, "Why put a radical theme in there along with the portrayal of the plight of the residents of Culebra?"
>
> Rubén told me, "Because powerholders don't like radicalization. They are managers, and if a movement is growing they want to take away the issue while it is still perceived by most people in a moderate way. They don't want the movement to grow and, through being frustrated, move toward a more radical stance."
>
> Rubén argued that one way to accelerate a concession on the part of the powerholders is to send the signal that the more frustrated the movement gets, the more it will turn to more radical views, expand its analysis, make its vision for change more fundamental, and increase its militancy.
>
> I was skeptical, and was proved wrong. The US government watched more Puerto Ricans turning to the view that if the Navy can't even stop doing target practice on Culebrans, then maybe Rubén is right and what we really need is to get rid of the US altogether! Washington decided to give in and withdraw the Navy.
>
> You have to see this outside of just a defeat for anti-casino forces. Make bigger connections. If I were Rendell, I would take a managerial perspective and not want something that should have been smoothly handled get more and more out of control. From his perspective, the increased linking of issues to each other: not good. Increased militancy of tactics: not good. Increased linking of these issues to capitalist greed: not good. Increased connection between bad old Philadelphia and the suburbs: not good. Increased linking to the reformers around the state: not good.

Feeling lighter, I replied to George with a swift thank you. Not that any brilliant solution had emerged. But I felt like I had the seed of an idea.

Three days of watering and it would be ready to break ground.

Sunday morning, I sat at the table half-reading the newspaper, pleased to have a few minutes with my housemates and not thinking about casinos. I held tight to my tea, trying to ignore the haunting images of gavels and robes from my previous nights' dreams.

Suddenly the table vibrated. I looked at my cell phone. It was Jeff Shields from the *Philadelphia Inquirer*.

Again? I thought to myself as I answered it.

"I'm doing a follow-up story about what's next. I talked with some folks over at DRNA and they seemed pretty downcast. DiCicco was surprisingly angry but didn't have any real strategy. Now, I know you don't have everything figured out, but what do you have at this point? What can you do now that this has happened?"

"We have an action protesting the supreme court decision on Monday. We are going full strength for the Vote Yes on #1 campaign, since the court may still allow it," I said. My voice dropped, betraying my gloom.

"That's not a long-term strategy," he said dismissively. "Say this referendum is knocked off the ballot, what will you do? Is there any way for you to win?"

To buy time, I sipped some tea. Then, out of the depth of my churning came answers. "The referendum is not the only way to stop casinos from being built on these sites. There are lots of ways to stop the casinos. Legally, they may be found in violation of our constitution. Politically, they can be stopped by a City Council vote for the buffer or other zoning legislation—or if the state decided to act right, too." My voice rose and strengthened. "And if the courts and politicians won't act right, we will engage in nonviolent protest, training people to lie in front of bulldozers, if necessary."

I had found my emotional stride. I felt grounded as I got off the phone, only dimly aware of the impact I would make.

Later that night, Jeff's editor helped permanently shape our image by giving the article the banner headline: "Activists Say They Will Even Lie in Front of Bulldozers If the Courts Reject an Anti-Casino Referendum." It was one approach of a myriad of strategies. But the timing was key: right at the moment of exposing the failure of current institutions at protecting us, we were proposing a radical solution to protect ourselves without them.

Over the next several days, our threat to "lie in front of bulldozers" echoed on Fox 29 News, 6 ABC Action News, and elsewhere. SugarHouse spokesman Dan Fee publicly mocked us for it and even stoked it among press, assuming further attention would marginalize us as a crazy fringe group. But we knew deep anger and resentment on this issue was now mainstream, and we encouraged allies to embrace the image.

Some supporters later admitted they thought the threat was purely tongue-in-cheek, but others knew we were serious. A month later, one donor told me, "I was stunned when in a debate over casinos one woman in a fur coat ended the argument by declaring, 'If they try to build Foxwoods casino, I'll be right there with CFP in the dirt!'" He smiled and added, "I assume without the fur coat."

Because virtually none of the people in CFP had a history of activism—and, moreover, many held a lot of trust in institutional politics and law—radicalizing was a long journey. But I saw at once that Jeff's article had prepared people for the possibility of escalated direct action—talking about it, feeling about it—all without actually having to do it.

New ideas were in motion.

That afternoon, just after getting off the call with Jeff, I took my time with chores, catching up on cleaning the house and grocery shopping. My mind continued to chew. *What do we do next?*

When I was in school and my mind got stuck on problems, like math equations, I would often miss the answer if I kept thinking about it. But if I distracted my mind, my creative subconscious would kick up the answer. Cleaning the house did that for me.

I didn't have the answer. But I knew how to get it.

"Jethro, you've got to get on the phone with me and Philippe."

He was finally back and, though also in recovery mode, he readily agreed to join the call.

I dialed. "Philippe, are you there?"

"Yeah, I'm here."

I patched us into a three-way. "There's a germ of an idea here, and we need to tease it out. We need to find a way to give people the opportunity the courts took away."

Without hesitation, we began throwing out ideas.

Jethro suggested, "What if we pushed the button over question #1's sticker?"

"It may not get counted," Philippe said.

"Plus," I said, "we'd only have our people voting in favor. It wouldn't be fair. Maybe we could pass out some kind of voting cards for people to take into the polling places?"

Our pace increased as we sensed ourselves on the edge of a breakthrough.

"What would people do with the voting card?"

"Hand them to the polling workers?"

"Poll workers wouldn't know what to do."

We sped up.

"Slip them into the machines?"

"No. That's tampering."

"Could they slip them into the physical provisional ballots?"

"They'd probably get destroyed."

"What about getting them in absentee ballots?"

"Too late."

"Take it outside and drop the cards into a hat?"

"And count them ourselves."

"Set up polls outside of each polling place."

"That's it."

A moment of silence descended. We slipped back into first gear to flesh out the concept: setting up a station outside of each polling place where people could mark their preference on the ballot question.

"I guess this might take a couple hundred people," Jethro calculated. "Anyone know how many polling places there are in Philly?" None of us did.

Philippe saw the chance to gain powerful new allies. "There have got to be other groups you can bring on board, even if they don't agree with you on casinos. ACLU, good government, and even conservative watchdog groups should be up in arms!"

"True, and it can help motivate our people either way," I said. "We get them to sign a pledge saying *if* the supreme court does take the vote away, *then* they'll volunteer to sponsor a polling place. It's the perfect 'if this, then that' design." I thought of the Pledge of Resistance, when 42,000 people signed a pledge vowing *if* the US government invaded Nicaragua *then* they would engage in civil disobedience. That future focus got people's commitment for an action before they took it, allowing them to commit to bolder actions than they otherwise might have.

"Right. And while recruiting volunteers for that, it allows us to keep organizing for the referendum as if it may still happen," said Jethro.

"And send a signal to the supreme court," added Philippe.

Jethro and I hurried to get off the phone. I felt fully energized to pitch this idea to the crew. I wouldn't even need a cab—I was excited to bike to the meeting.

Jethro and I showed up at the meeting nearly bursting. I sat down between Kathy and Shirley around our table with snacks, waiting for Paul and Anne to arrive.

I bounced slightly up and down in my chair, racing to get past the check-ins and review of all the many people we had talked with over the past couple of days. They were a blur. I wanted to hurry up to get to the idea. This was big.

When our time on the agenda came, Jethro explained, "It'd be a massive operation, called Pledge for Democracy, where people get to register their preference for or opposition to the buffer zone. We'd stand outside of each polling place for people to cast their opinion."

"When the government does not fill its role, citizens have to do it," I said. "We would be at each polling place, and the results would show the opinion of voters."

We explained our vision of hundreds of volunteers at polling places. Then sat back bright-eyed.

Kathy was the first to roll out her hesitation, "Soooo, it's like a big poll?"

"No, it's a dramatic action," I said.

"Uhm," started Shirley, "and what would it accomplish exactly?"

I was irritated nobody was getting it. "It would dramatize the injustice," I answered defensively, heading to rhetorical justification.

Shirley took a deep breath and then another stab. "I see that. But people know it's an injustice. We need something that can help us win."

I wanted to yell back: *You're missing the point completely!* "This can work," I said. I looked over at Jethro, who had suddenly gone quiet.

"How many volunteers would it take?" asked Paul.

"We don't know, but we can figure that out. People want to be mobilized," I said.

I looked around at the blank, discouraging faces of my teammates. Nobody seemed excited. I knew the idea was sunk.

"People are raising a lot of good points, the idea just isn't there yet," said Jethro. I glared at him, frustrated at his ever-flexible, changing mind.

"Let's at least think about it further," I said.

Sure, the group offered. But their hearts were not in it.

We meandered through other ideas for the rest of the meeting, talking about lawsuits or strategies to compel City Council to vote directly for the 1,500-foot buffer. I tried to hide my sulking.

We agreed to meet on Tuesday.

Back at home, I slumped at my computer. Kathy's email urged that "people need to hear from us." But what was there to say? The Pledge for Democracy was dead on arrival. Tomorrow we would march to the supreme court, then what? We had no campaign. Other than platitudes, what reassurance could I offer?

As I stared at my computer, my mind spun, grasping for a new perspective. How could we declare progress, even in the midst of defeat? Struck by the need for a bigger perspective, I sat up and reached for my worn copy of Bill Moyer's *Doing Democracy*.

Bill Moyer developed the arc of his Movement Action Plan during a workshop for anti-nuclear activists. Bill had been struck the first evening at participants' consistent sentiment of hopelessness. The movement had an amazing arc: months earlier merely eighteen people arrested blockading the Seabrook Nuclear Power Plant. Then 108 arrests. And just a few days ago over one-thousand people have been arrested—so many the police could not cope and threw them into large National Guard armories.

That it was a growing movement, Bill had no doubt. But instead of plunging into the workshop, the group sat stymied and despairing. "Despite the massive arrests," they declared, "the plans for this power plant are still moving forward! We can't win!"

Bill had seen this let-down after large actions before. As staff to Dr. King, he saw the civil rights movement go through similar ups and downs.

Sitting up late with his co-facilitator, he spent hours sketching those ups and downs into distinct stages of movements—what he would later call the Movement Action Plan.

The growth that led to the mass arrests, Bill knew, was the result of movement groundwork that often gets hidden from view. At first, virtually nobody cared about the problem, even ignoring the terrible near-meltdown at the Fermi nuclear plant in Detroit. "Stage 1: Normal times," he scribbled.

Next, the movement had gone through public hearings and official channels, until it showed that the government had no interest or ability in protecting citizens from the radical dangers of nuclear energy. "Stage 2: Prove failure of official institutions," wrote Bill.

This set up a faster pace, as anti-nuclear activists like Bill ran around the country speaking at houses of worship, union halls, civic associations, house meetings, and news conferences. Quietly, public opinion against nuclear power rose to 30% of the population. "Stage 3: Ripening conditions."

Activists moved from sporadic to frequent direct actions around the country. A crisis atmosphere neared as networks connected across the country and ignited. Eighteen people arrested. Then three weeks later 180 people arrested. And then the trigger event: 1,414 people arrested! "Stage 4: Take-off."

In the take-off stage, the movement captured major media attention and attracted new people. It also brought unrealistic expectations. People worked around the clock with the belief that the policy was on the ropes and a victory was around the corner. Powerholders actively discredited grassroots efforts but made no major changes.

That can lead to discouragement—"Stage 5: Perception of failure"—wrote Bill, thinking of his workshop participants. A natural depression set in because they hadn't won their goals. There would be a further uphill climb, despite the excitement from the lightning energy of the take-off.

Bill wanted people to see that movements never reach a take-off stage without the earlier stages, even though few politicians or historians pay attention until the take-off phase—Rosa Parks in Montgomery, the grape boycott of the United Farm Workers, or the 1999 Seattle anti-globalization protests. Bill saw that few people reacted to the

Detroit meltdown, but he watched national outrage from the later Three Mile Island disaster. The difference wasn't the disaster, it was the movement: those earlier stages built networks and sowed seeds so that take-off stage could happen. But that was not enough.

As Bill presented his model the next morning, he knew their question would be "What do we do at Stage 5?" He delivered his answer with his customary directness. "We give people a big picture, introduce the model, and get them back into long-term organizing for 'Stage 6: Building majority public opinion and winning over policyholders about our preferred solutions.' We win—Stage 7—and then we create watchdogs or enforcements to protect that win from backsliding—Stage 8."

I flipped through Bill's book, trying to figure out where we were. Operation Transparency had proven the failure of established institutions, finishing off any respectability the PGCB had and exposing politicians as too timid to save us (Stage 2). And No Way Without Our Say had shifted public opinion and mobilized us into larger numbers (Stage 3). So maybe we were on our way to Stage 4: Take-off.

Yet my internal state pulled me to Stage 5: Perception of failure. Its name matched my emotion, so I rationalized that the court ruling must have been our take-off event.

I realized later it was a botched analysis, blindly ignoring the reality that there wasn't a massive outcry from *outside* our movement to the court ruling. It wasn't a take-off event, just a bad hit, setting us up for a take-off stage. But precision didn't matter in the moment. It was something to provide assurance that we were on some trajectory.

I nevertheless found some useful advice based on my wrong analysis, writing to supporters, "We need to lay out strategic, achievable, and measurable objectives, and celebrate as we achieve them along the way."

I finished my email to supporters and headed to bed, but still felt unsettled. We needed next steps. Around 2 A.M., I jumped out of bed, wrapped a cover around myself, and pounded out a draft of the Pledge for Democracy. It was the best we had. It could work. I was sure of it. I worked on it until 3 A.M. Then, too nervous to send it to everyone, I shared it with a few members of the executive team.

I returned to bed, resolved to find a way to sell the idea.

Monday was a wet, miserable day. It complemented my emotional state perfectly.

Dripping on the wide, white hallways of City Hall, seventy-five protestors banded together with chants standing outside of the supreme court's stately doors. Most brandished Vote Yes on #1 materials. Stalwart Mary Stumpf wrapped herself in a giant American flag.

"We should just go inside the supreme court and sit down," whispered Paul to Jay and me. We still didn't have an action design. "Our presence will be enough of a message."

"We shouldn't just sit—people need to *do* something," I whispered back. My anger was cooling, even as the referendum was leaking water, appearing less likely day by day. But our folks' anger was rising: hence the large, last-minute turnout during a lunch break.

"The supreme court still holds our referendum in their hands. We can't aggravate them," Paul rebutted.

I stared at him. "The hell we can't! We're not here to stroke their egos."

Jay's bushy eyes watched as Paul and I ping-ponged ideas.

"People could silently walk out and hold our cards up," said Paul.

"We need a message, something pro-active. People could shout and walk out."

"Too confrontational! The courts aren't used to anything like this, Daniel."

I was frustrated. I wanted a free hand to design the action. But I knew if Paul kept pushing, he'd make it better.

"Okay, Paul, how about one person speaks, everyone stands up, turns their backs, and walks out?" It would be a clear message, signaling to the court we were angry.

Jay offered the compromise. "If I hear Paul right, just turning our backs is confrontational. Courts aren't used to this kind of action. We do that and file out?"

"That will work," said Paul.

"Fine, let's do it," I nodded, aware that some people would speak their minds anyway.

We turned back to the crowd, facing the stolid faces of supporters as Rev. Jesse Brown finished leading the group in prayer.

Paul was right that protests against the supreme court were rare—rare enough that the oldest law journal in the US, the *Legal Intelligencer*, placed our action on its front page. Next to a picture of South Philly volunteer Joe Bridy hoisting a "Casinos Take Ports Pay" sign, the reporter described the scene as we "calmly and quietly filed into the courtroom during a lunch break." The reporter ignored Mary balking as the bailiffs seized her flag "for security reasons."

As the supreme court justices returned to call the afternoon session, we stood up, turned our backs en masse, and exited. Through clenched teeth, several firmly told the justices, "Don't take our vote away"—or what the *Intelligencer* called "verbally scolding the justices."

As we walked outside, Jay pulled me aside. "This was important. The justices looked terrified, like they had never seen anything like this. We needed it."

Watching the determined, angry, and confident faces, I felt better. We were going to keep fighting. Collective action was our healing balm.

That afternoon, I sorted the hundreds of emails in my inbox. My email about the Pledge for Democracy only netted a few textual edits from Paul and Jethro, with the reminder that "there's a lack of capacity and no clarity about the action goals or what happens to the results."

I remained convinced this was the right next step, but slowly I accepted Jethro's reflection that the executive team's critiques carried validity. The action *was* unclear and needed to be tightened up. It was too loose—but a real-life example could show the idea's efficacy. So I called my mom, a professor of labor and African-American history.

"Hey mom, has anyone ever done anything like the Pledge for Democracy?"

Her pause was indiscernible. "There's the Mississippi Freedom Democratic Party."

"Give me a quick recap," I asked, surprising myself with my urgent tone.

"After years of trying to organize Mississippi blacks to register to vote, the Student Nonviolent Coordinating Committee realized that wasn't a winning strategy. Whether through the use of poll taxes, dusty grandfather laws, biased quizzes on the Constitution, or outright murder and violence, white election commissioners kept them out.

"So they joined with other groups to create their own party, open to all races, and ran a parallel election to the white Democrats' party establishment. They called it the Mississippi Freedom Democratic Party. Their 'Freedom Vote' election was run like a real election, registering voters, collecting ballots from 93,000 voters, and ultimately trying to seat the elected officials at the 1964 Democratic National Convention."

I remembered the rest: having run a cleaner election than the official exclusive, racist one, they made a bid to be seated as Mississippi's official delegates. At a dramatic and televised hearing before the credentials committee, folks gave testimony, including sharecropper Fannie Lou Hamer passionately sharing her story of being beaten and denied at every turn in her quest to vote. This gained public sympathy while splitting the national party internally, as it roiled over who to seat: delegates of the official election run by white exclusionists, or those of an unaccredited "shadow" election run on open and more democratic values. President Johnson eventually insulted the delegation with a meager offer of two nonvoting seats, insulting the MFDP further by naming the two who would be seated. The whole turmoil became a defining, touchstone moment for the civil rights movement.

The MFDP understood that a vote is only as powerful as the collective makes it. It forced the white establishment to take it seriously, which was what we needed to do. Instead of a dramatic polling operation, we would set up a *real* election and treat the results as real, too.

"This is really helpful, mom."

"Your welcome, I love you. And how are you doing? What's the latest with the campaign?"

I didn't want to repeat the last several days. "I'd like to share," I said quickly, "but I really gotta go. It's been all bad news recently, but I think there's good news on the way... I love you, too."

I had clarity. The idea hadn't been ready for primetime—but redefined and strengthened, it would be soon.

Tuesday night marked our most important meeting yet. Newly inspired, I pitched the Pledge for Democracy with a clearer purpose.

"We are going to make Philadelphia take it seriously," I told the group. My feet were on the floor and I felt clearer. "That means this isn't about just 'giving people a say.' It's a politically relevant referendum. We hold elected officials to recognize the results. It is as real as we make it."

Jethro spelled out the plan. "That means we need to handle registration, voting, counting mechanisms, fraud..."

"Exactly. This isn't just a 'Yes/No' ballot in a hat, but a genuine election." I explained the MFDP and contrasted the original Pledge for Democracy as a mere stunt compared to the fuller, richer action of setting up ballot boxes in a true election.

Kathy asked how we would make sure people didn't think it was just a big poll.

Unlike last time, I wasn't annoyed by people's concerns. I invited, even appreciated, the questions.

"I don't know what's the answer," I said. "But we have to hold it as a legitimate operation. We need a name to show our seriousness."

"But we don't know how to run an election," said Shirley.

"True," said Jethro. "But we can learn. Monday's action showed that people are ready for boldness."

"And that means a lot of people," said Anne.

"You know it. It's going to be tough work," I said.

I looked around the room at the enlivened faces. The idea was tighter, stronger. Perhaps Monday's action helped heal them, too, because this meeting was energetic in every way our previous meeting was not. It was just like the arc from my first downcast call with Philippe to the boisterous second. Whereas last time defeat and despair filled the room, now everyone pulsated with energy.

The team exploded into planning. Anne was in fine form, thinking through the political angles to the campaign. Shirley and Kathy were laboriously detailed and methodical in their thinking, approaching it with the sharp eye of now experienced organizers.

Enthusiastically, if unrealistically, we set a goal to field 3,300 volunteers with ballot boxes at all 1,681 polling locations during the upcoming election in under a month. To help others understand the action, we profiled the MFDP story and coined a punchy phrase to explain that this election would "not be legally binding, but would be politically binding."

We talked far past our scheduled one-hour time.

Abandoning the generic Pledge for Democracy, we stood around the table scribbling new names for the campaign. We wanted something to deliver our action's message, but something short, punchy, and unique. I suggested a subtle criterion: people shouldn't be able to delete words from the name, causing it to lose its ring. I noted that people often shortened No Way Without Our Say into the hardly inspiring No Way campaign.

When the meeting concluded, we walked away with more than just tasks and next steps. We had an inspiring vision—and a name. I buzzed on my bike all the way home, burning to write the next email. I had not dealt with the full emotional impact of the supreme court's blow. But we had moved fast enough to develop a brilliant response to help us rise from the ashes.

I typed to supporters an introduction to our new campaign, describing the Mississippi Freedom Democratic Party and our rationale:

> They expected us to give up when they threatened our vote. Instead, we will implement the most ambitious voting campaign in recent Philadelphia history. If the referendum is taken off the ballot, we will hold our own election. We will set up tables at polling locations on May 15 so that people can vote on ballot question #1.

My fingers blazed. We had a strong response: Philly's Ballot Box.

CHAPTER 10

Philly's Ballot Box

APRIL 18, 2007 — MAY 14, 2007

redesigning on a dime • good organizers know how to learn things • Team Types •
designing a rolled-out media strategy • honest relationships with reporters over easy ones •
walking away from meetings without work • noting our power in opponents' moves •
politicians are like a balloon tied to a rock • ignoring a threat •
jangled nerves but no snafus

"WE'RE GLAD YOU AGREED TO TALK WITH US," I said, offering Karim Olaechea a seat in our new offices. The space felt perfect—large, open, bare rooms with half-assembled metal cabinets, scattered cubicles, and artistic photographs left hanging by its last tenants, lit by oddly angled spotlights dangling from metal joists. It felt like a blank canvass made for us. Even the main room's walls matched the deep red color of Philly's Ballot Box materials. Jethro had done a great job finding this space, thanks to Chris Meck and her husband's generosity.

"Tell us a little about yourself," said Jethro.

Karim Olaechea leaned forward. "My sympathies are already with you," he said. He was young, wearing tight jeans, and his loose shirt pulled up slightly, revealing a dark tattoo on his forearm. "When I came back to Philly from DC—okay, so I'm a nerd—but I got interested and read Senator Vince Fumo's entire 272-page indictment. I took notes in the back and started tracing all the connections. That's when I found out my Philly apartment was *in* the indictment! The floors I lived on were installed with misspent state funding, all orchestrated by Fumo. It made me furious. This guy is one of the biggest villains in this city's history. I want to take him down a notch—and this is my chance."

His voice was smooth and his eyes deep, almost foreboding. Like Jethro and I, he seemed driven, intense, and attracted to the heat, fire, and challenge of the campaign.

Jethro leaned against the high-back vanilla-colored couch, stretching his jeans. In his meandering way, he explained our need to hire someone to free me up and expand our communications work. He admitted it wasn't exactly as though people skilled in communications with political campaign experience were clamoring to work for our rag-tag outfit.

Karim animatedly explained he had a history working in communications in DC and electoral campaigns locally. With a fervent glance, he said, "If you hire me, your opponents will do opposition research. I'll put everything on the table now. I'm Palestinian, and my dad is a freedom fighter... that's what we'd call him... I've written about our struggle publicly but have never advocated violence. But you know your opponents can and will twist words, so you have to assess if that's baggage you can carry."

"Not a problem," I said, as Jethro nodded quickly. "And I appreciate your forthrightness. What do you want to know about us?"

"Well," Karim's eyes darted between us, "how are you going to run this election?"

"We're getting our house in order," Jethro said. "But our plan is to set up boxes at every polling place—"

"Whoah!" Karim choked. "You must be crazy. There must be over a thousand polling places."

"1,681," I said.

Karim eyed us doubtfully. "Break the numbers down. Most volunteers won't commit for the entire day. With three or four rotations covering 1,600 polling places... that's roughly, 5,000 volunteers. Even paid campaign operations can't find that many people."

Jethro's face was relaxed. "We know it's a bold, ambitious goal—"

"On a single day," Karim's voice rose, "what's the largest number of volunteers your organization has pulled out for more than just a one-hour action?"

The words stuck in my throat. "A hundred."

"*Yeah*," he said. "Election day is highly competitive. Every political group and campaign asks people to volunteer. You're setting yourselves up for failure if you insist on 5,000 volunteers. If you are committed to going that direction, I'm out now."

Jethro bit on his pencil. "Oh-kay," said Jethro slowly. "What would you do instead?"

"*Not that*," said Karim, his tangle of black hair fluttering. "You need some other form of representation throughout the city... You never promised press you'd cover every poll, did you?"

"I don't think so," I said, trying to remember the jumble of last week's conversations. "I knew if we launched too early, press would rip apart the idea. So we haven't told them much about it."

"Good, good," Karim nodded. "How much money do you have, if you're willing to share?"

"Rosanne Loesch helped us get our largest donation of $10,000 from Society Hill Civic Association," I said. "And online donations are up to $4,000. That's about it."

Karim shook his head thoughtfully. "Not a lot of money..."

We are crazy, I thought. No Philadelphia electoral campaign would even consider running with so little. Most electoral campaigners like Karim made their reputation by joining the winning teams, not marginalized long-shot campaigns. For me, the difficulty only added to my excitement, like the challenge facing a heavily guarded turnaround jumper. As in basketball, I played better under pressure.

Jethro gazed at the noisy air conditioner. As if thinking about the campaign for the first time, he muttered, "There must be a way to get participation across the city even with only a few hundred people."

I smiled with new-found appreciation for Jethro's flexibility to change on a dime.

Karim's muscular frame sat up suddenly. "Put some ballot boxes around the city, but not everywhere. Then add online voting." He hesitated, selecting his words with care. "Set up a secure way to vote on the internet. Then you can say with a straight face that anyone who wants to can vote in the people's referendum."

I glanced at Jethro. "He's got our flair and language exactly." I looked back at Karim, "For people without the internet or unable to get to our ballot boxes, we can take votes on the phone. We'll point out that the elderly, people confined to their homes, disabled people, and others will actually have greater access to vote with our system."

"Yes," exclaimed Karim, leaning toward me. "I know a guy who can donate computers and phones. Then—"

Jethro interrupted with a soft, almost conspiratorial whisper, *"This* is why we need you, Karim. You have the passion and the skills to make this operation work. Are you in?"

Karim broke into a grin, recognizing effective recruitment. "I assume virtually no pay, and long hours?"

Jethro nodded, "It will be an intense four weeks. But if we do it right, we can forever imprint ourselves on city politics and show what angry people can accomplish, even when denied at every political and legal turn. Plus, Fumo will hate you for it."

"I'm in," Karim said quickly. "What's first?"

We agreed to give ourselves one week to design an election structure. Then we'd launch it publicly, leaving three short weeks for recruitment of an ambitious 500 poll workers. Our new communications director opened his laptop and familiarized himself with our past press releases. Jethro cradled his laptop and opened his cell phone to work on recruitment. And I worked on my priority: designing a foolproof election in just seven days.

I opened my full page datebook on the card table and jotted down what I needed to know to design an election system. It was a short list, but only because I didn't know what I didn't know. Next to questions, I scribbled names of people who might be able to help. Long ago, I had left behind the notion that good organizers know how to *do* things. They know how to *learn* things.

I rang the first person on the list: Sue Severin.

"Yeah, no, uh-huh, I'm awake," said a groggy-sounding voice. In my haste, I had forgotten the West Coast time difference. "It sounds like a neat project... no, really, I'm fine."

Sue had been an election monitor with Peace Brigades International, serving as an unarmed bodyguard to human rights workers in high-risk parts of the world. "To do this, I need to understand different voting mechanisms," I explained, trying to hide my sense of urgency.

"Most countries use some kind of paper ballots," she explained with a yawn. "There is electronic voting, but monitors hate them because they're easy to cheat and have no paper trail to double-check."

"We're pretty wedded to a ballot box—the name Philly's *Ballot Box* certainly suggests it."

"If you're using a ballot box, you need to think about how people mark their preference. Then, how do you gather those votes and assure that each vote correlates to a real voter. Then transportation, tabulation, and how to distribute results."

My fingers rushed, trying to keep up as she added to my growing list. It took a leap of faith to assume that somehow all these questions would get answered. But now I was developing *specific* questions, an important step in getting answers.

I circled one item on the list. "Let's talk about the element of transportation. What's involved in that?"

"It's a long day," Sue said. "You never want to leave the ballot box or ballots unaccompanied. You need a strict chain of custody the whole time to make sure it's always protected from tampering. Last year, the Democratic Republic of Congo held elections with over 20 million potential voters. It was a logistical nightmare with a costly international observing operation. The sheer size of the country plus very remote parts meant it took three weeks to collect and count the votes from over 50,000 polling places. Even then, boxes were not to be left unattended. They sealed the boxes to reduce the likelihood of tampering."

"Sealed? Like with expensive lockboxes?"

"No, you could use cardboard boxes and seal them with special security tape that leaves a readily identifiable mark if it's pealed off," she said.

"Does anybody actually use cardboard boxes?"

"Lots of countries do," said Sue. "I just returned from East Timor where they used them. El Salvador uses them. Mexico. In fact, most places I've gone use them. They're handy. They can be collapsed before and after use, so they don't take up a lot of room."

I filed away the names of the countries, just in case. Cardboard boxes, check. Security tape, check. "Then what stops someone from just filling the box with votes?"

"Well, that gets into how people mark their voting preference. There are a slew of ways to vote: tear-off sheets where people toss in their vote of yay or nay, simple check marks, or you could try punch ballots with chads like in Florida." She paused, as if waiting for an obligatory laugh. I was too focused. When none came, she added, "In many countries, ballot stuffing can be a real problem..."

"Like Philly," I said, trying to lighten up. "We have dead people casting votes."

She chuckled lightly, "You *could* have open, non-secret voting. People can see their vote, to get assurance it's counted."

My pencil scribbled "transparent voting." I circled it several times. I liked the sound of that, even though I misunderstood that open voting means you can double-check if *your* vote is counted—I simply assumed all votes were open.

"What are other ways to stop ballot stuffing?"

"Some countries mark each voter, like dipping your finger in a purple ink. That requires discipline at each polling place. Others mark each vote so it can be correlated to a voter, often with a list of voters."

The Philadelphia voting list. Of course, check.

"But the biggest thing," she continued, "is to make sure the ballot boxes are never alone. If poll workers need to go to the bathroom, or anything, the box can never be alone from the time it's set up to the time it's counted."

That meant two volunteers per box. A reluctant check.

I thanked Sue and breezed through a dozen calls and one-on-one meetings—language agencies to inquire about on-call interpreters, the Advancement Project for expertise on how to counter voter disenfranchisement and intimidation, and the election watchdog group Committee of Seventy to hear its director's bureaucratic reluctance to endorse our non-institutional vote.

Within days, a rough structure was shaping up: two poll workers at cardboard boxes with votes checked against the voters' database. Votes would be tallied like absentee ballots, where someone checks "yes" or "no" and then sticks it in an envelope. They seal the envelope, write their voter registration information on it, and drop it in the ballot box. When tallied, voter information is checked first, leaving the vote discarded if the voter registration information is invalid, thereby eliminating bias at the source of counting.

We wanted to support different languages but could not afford an expensive phone interpretation service. On hearing my concern Karim suggested, "It's our election, right? So let's make the ballots in Spanish and English." Outside of English, the most common language spoken in Philadelphia is that of the 10% Spanish-speaking population, many huddled in the Northeast not too far from the proposed SugarHouse casino. "We'll be the first Philadelphia multilingual election," I said proudly.

So that was added to our plan.

Just four days before our scheduled launch, I found the perfect ballot boxes, causing Jethro and Karim to crowd around my laptop as I showed the website. "Cardboard ballot boxes at four feet tall. Twenty dollars each. But they are self-standing, which eliminates the need for a stand or table. One problem," I said shyly. "Printing takes three weeks—that gives us zero wiggle room."

Karim cursed softly. Jethro scratched his face and encouraged, "Get a sample and see if Jeremy Beaudry can make an initial mock-up. Good work. We'll figure out something."

"We'd better," I said. On a timeline on the wall, I added the new information into winding lines of dependencies and tasks to be accomplished.

In a few days, Jeremy spray-painted a sample box—a stunning, four-foot-deep, scarlet box with "Vote Here" and a white arrow pointing toward the slot. The ballot's text was written on all sides and "Ballot Question #1: Casino Referendum" on the top header.

The supreme court announced it would not expedite our case. Its foot-dragging was tantamount to a de facto ruling, with the city election commissioner responding by placing "Removed by Court Order" stickers over our ballot question.

Two days before our public launch, however, that news was only briefly mentioned at a meeting. Instead, over a food-laden folding table, CFP leaders updated each other about our work on Philly's Ballot Box.

I wanted everyone to share my excitement about inviting international election monitors to give us credence. Anne posted an oversized map of Philadelphia laying out districts and wards, explaining her attempt at talking with progressive campaigns. Paul proudly displayed letters from the ACLU and Committee of Seventy confirming our legal right as nonpartisans to set up ten feet from polling places. Far short of endorsements, they still calmed Paul's concerns over the casinos seeking an injunction against our action. Shirley interrupted to pass out the $55,000 budget and asserted, "Yes, we might really raise that amount."

Excited as we were, I felt the outlines of some larger tension. It wasn't the constant interruptions—those were commonplace in our meetings. Nor was it just the sharpness with which Shirley shot down Karim and my proposal to spread our election over several days to mimic a more open, fair election model ("Keep it simple, stupids"). Even when Jethro announced that his business partner Nick Jehlen had agreed to design our website and would come from Boston to help volunteer, the reception was cool.

"This is all nice and good," said Kathy, "but people can't vote if we don't tell them where to go. Do we have an exact list of where we will be?"

Karim pointed at dots on the map. "I marked a few places we'll cover. We picked the highest-turnout locations in each of the state house districts. Maybe we can be at others, but we're not sure yet."

"We'll let everyone know poll locations when we know them," Jethro said hopefully.

"Right," said Karim, as Jethro, Karim, and I began brainstorming different avenues to give out poll locations. "If we put an ad in the newspaper, we may be able to get a press story from that!"

Kathy cut us off, frowning. "We have to make this stuff *easy* for our people." Shirley nodded. "Look," said Kathy, looking around the room, "how many volunteers do we exactly *have?*"

"I wish I had number commitments, but I don't," said Jethro. "Our calls to civics did not lead to number commitments as I had hoped. I am a good organizer, but only with the people I have strong relationships with. I can't push people I don't know. This is far more challenging than I thought it would be."

"On our website 105 people have signed up so far," I said. "Maybe twenty people committed from different organizations and groups. That's my best guess."

Kathy folded her arms as Jethro, Karim, and I jumped into brainstorming other groups to outreach: "Project H.O.M.E.? They're pretty busy with their own get-out-the-vote operation. Democracy Rising PA? Their board seems unduly fearful of 501c3 violations. Neighborhood Networks? Candidates? Other civics?"

Kathy slammed her notepad on the table. "Look, guys," she said through clenched teeth, "all these lofty ideas about international monitors and getting a website running— they are all great. But volunteers need a real structure. They need to know exactly where they will be placed and how we will get them information." Red-faced, she stared at us.

Jethro spoke quickly. "What about text-mobbing through the day? With Turn Your Back on Bush, we updated volunteers throughout the day with text messages. It's a great way to coordinate people."

"Not everyone *has* a cell phone," said Kathy, angrily muttering about techno-babble.

With fire in her eyes, Shirley spoke. "Kathy has vast logistical and operational experience running large events and working with large teams of volunteers. You need to listen to her."

Jethro started to respond, when Kathy exploded. "Guys, this is not a walk in the park. You can't just expect people to understand whatever wild ideas you come up with!" Kathy folded her arms.

Nobody spoke.

Something in Shirley's words reminded me this wasn't just anxiety or stress. Sure, we were all nervous about this massive operation. But when we get stressed, we act out our personality traits even more. I thought of "Team Types" leadership styles.

Different directions represented different styles: East were visionaries who generated lots of ideas, constantly integrating them in the big picture with large sweeps. Karim, Jethro, and I all trended toward the East, completely opposite from the West's style of crafting a plan through carefully sorted, concrete data. Kathy and Shirley were fulfilling that West role.

Yet Jethro could also be South, focused on the maintenance of relationships, responsive to others' needs—just as I could also play North, the implementers, or sometimes known as the "shoot first, aim later" crowd.

Years earlier, I had introduced this framework to Jethro while he was organizing Turn Your Back on Bush. In his case, he noted they had North, East, and his own South style. But no West. Realizing that gap explained to him why people were asking questions that his team hadn't even considered. Like a table missing its fourth leg, he went out to recruit West analysts, asking his listserve for help in "research and trouble-shooting"— code to get West.

I nudged Jethro, "Be South."

He nodded knowingly. "Kathy," said Jethro quietly, "you're right." He paused to collect his words. "If you are willing, we need you to take over the volunteer logistics and help us answer these questions."

She hesitated. "I'll only do it if I get 100% support from you. You have to finalize things like poll placements right away."

"Will do," said Jethro. "But you have to promise to chill out when you see gaps we haven't figured out yet. You must try not to get mad just because you see holes."

She nodded as a slight smile crept on her face. "You should see me when I *am* mad."

"I'll look forward to that moment when it comes." His face showed me he meant it.

The remainder of the meeting, I joked about our style tensions, with Team Types on my mind. I warned "with all this detail on the ward captain system to trouble-shoot problems, you analysts are bogging us visionaries with meticulous details." Then later joking, "now us visionaries have become all airy fairy," as we agreed to confidentiality in voting only after an expansive conversation about the values of our election representing democracy's core pillars of education, representation, and participation.

The group made decisions more smoothly. But underneath it, I sensed us even more deeply acting out our personal traits from our fear of failure. I closed the meeting with a challenge. "In two days," I said, loud enough to quiet the rowdy meeting, "we are planning to publicly launch the campaign. But we can still back off. We don't have to go through with Philly's Ballot Box." I was speaking heresy. Yet I saw relieved faces, as if speaking the unspeakable gave us more power. "We don't have all the resources yet, there are virtually no volunteer logistics in place, and our strategy requires grabbing massive turnout and media headlines. Do we really, *really* want to go through with it?"

The pause was a mere split second, but it felt like hours of weighing fears on our own internal scales.

Shirley gave a thumbs up. "We don't know what we're doing, but why should that start stopping us now?" Instantly, everyone's thumbs went up.

Three weeks left. Two days to launch.

"You awake?"

Karim muttered indistinctly.

"It's 5:15 A.M.," I said. "I'll meet you downtown!"

"I'll be there... I just need some coffee," Karim's voice drifted off.

I closed the phone and biked down to City Hall, hoping the cool wind would wake me up. Response from press had already told us we were onto something big.

Two days ago, a *Philadelphia Inquirer* reporter caught us in a meeting calming down irritated city election commissioners who worried our election would cause "chaos." Though it got our name wrong, the tucked-away article sparked interest among city politicos, and I was forced to tell reporters to wait until our announcement.

That made Karim suggest a more nuanced strategy than a straightforward, single announcement: roll out the announcement with different messengers for various media.

As soon as he said it, I loved the idea—it reminded me of what my first mentor taught me. After being arrested for a highly controversial civil disobedience action, he was hounded for interviews by national and international press. Instead of accepting them all, he counter-intuitively turned down all the major press and gave exclusives to local, small-time press. Glad for the rare opportunity to break a national story, local reporters dutifully reported his every word. Slowly he took bigger press, each time divulging a new twist or piece of juicy detail. By the time he took the national, high-profile, high-stakes interviews, he had established a public storyline. He got positively framed, dense coverage. "At each stage," he told me later, "we gave reporters something new that hadn't been covered before—but on our timeframe."

Conscious of reporters drooling with anticipation, Karim and I laid out our strategy. Yesterday, we had given the first interview to public radio's Susan Phillips. We killed two birds with one stone, getting good initial coverage and healing a press relationship, since we had accidentally left her off our recent press releases.

Then this morning—our release to TV stations. I locked my bike near towering City Hall and acknowledged Karim with a mere nod. Karim gripped his coffee cup and beelined to the cameramen to advise them on how to get the best shots.

I wondered: *Will the sometimes cynical TV stations call it a big publicity stunt? A joke? Will they ask questions we haven't thought of and rip it apart, poring over far-fetched ways to derail or steal the election?* Still, I was far less nervous than when we launched Operation Transparency. My stomach was fluttering. But more softly, less laced with panic. *We've vetted this idea with dozens of people. For a week... but an intense week.*

For TV stations, we promised them visuals via the first glimpse of our "shining receptacles of liberty"—a Karim phrase if ever there was one. Fox officially took us up on the offer, but Karim recruited additional TV stations by walking up to the van drivers parked outside City Hall and convincing them their editors would want them to cover us. Karim kept teaching me how to reach media.

My interview with the Fox reporter went by quickly. Wearing the most brilliantly orange makeup I had ever seen—a trick to help his pale face on camera—he echoed questions I would hear through the day. "How do you make sure everyone is a real voter? How can you say you're giving everyone a chance to vote?" They were *easy* to answer.

Leaning close at the end of the interview, the reporter smiled. "Good luck—I wish you luck with this election."

The rest of the roll-out strategy flew smoothly. A few hours later, we gave print reporters a formal press conference featuring Rev. Jesse Brown, Rev. Dick Ullman, Chris Meck, and Rich Garella. In the afternoon, we emailed bloggers, talking about our advanced text-mobbing coordination (after Kathy conceded that *ward captains* should have cell phones). Then we re-sent our press release to every statewide reporter—over 1,000 contacts. Then we rewrote our press release for local neighborhood newspapers. In a sad display of media understaffing, many locals take well-written press releases and reprint them in their entirety. In short, we had something special for each medium.

As morning ended, Karim and I rushed back into the office, dropping the ballot box in the center of the room.

"I'll start follow-up calls," I said, settling into my seat. For months, I had gotten lax about follow-up calls. With Karim by my side, it was easier to check back with reporters who hadn't arrived or check up on those who had and maybe double-check facts, which was often a chance to challenge the casinos' counter-spin.

Karim dropped his messenger bag on his desk. "Please edit the google document for local newspapers. Most go to print on Thursday, so we should get it to them by Tuesday at the latest."

I nodded and we began tapping silently on our computers—until Karim shrieked with delight, *"You have to see this!"* He pointed at his laptop. "Come here!"

I hurried to his desk, pushing aside draft ballots. His laptop played this morning's Fox 29 news report.

The anchorman started, "Today PhiladelphiaBallotBox.org will unveil a citizen's ballot to vote on how close the casinos can come to schools, playgrounds, and the like." Karim glanced at me knowingly. It was the wrong web address, so we'd need to buy that domain, too. "Steve Keeley is live with more details, and I guess, Steve, it's more of a symbolic move."

Steve's hideous orange-face looked gently tanned as he answered. "Yes, it's very symbolic, and the symbol is right here with us." The screen zoomed in on our shining ballot boxes backdropped by grand City Hall. It was a worth a thousand words.

The picture turned to me as Steve asked, "Now casinos, of course, will argue they're not in every polling place, who's going to count them, and people can vote more than once—what do you say to that?"

I explained our efforts to use the voter database and do double-blind counting to ensure this would be the cleanest election in Philadelphia history—even inviting the casinos to observe every step of the way. For nearly a half-minute, they showed me talking about the campaign's history, its reasoning, and describing our inspiration from the Mississippi Freedom Democratic Party. Every talking point was made.

They even showed pictures of Philly Ballot Box's website, alerting people they could vote online on May 15. The anchorman wrapped up the segment. "Should the numbers come out as this group expects them to come out—against the casinos on the river—this group for now can use that as added support and extra argument against the casinos, which plan to start building this summer in the face of all this opposition."

"It's everything we could have wanted," said Karim, dazed.

"I can't believe it!" I shook my head, staring off in glee. "It was positive—giving us full space to prove it's a real election. The lines 'inviting international election monitors' and 'citizen's ballot' rang well!"

"That's a nearly perfect piece," said Karim, almost shaking with excitement. "Nearly two minutes long—an eternity for TV!"

We idly wondered why Fox News would—of all TV stations—give us the most reliable coverage. "Maybe," said Karim, "because other stations are too connected to Governor Rendell. Because Fox News is such a conservative news program, it has more flexibility when it comes to attacking the Democratic establishment's corruption."

It felt uncomfortable to have them in our corner. Our issue was *way* bigger than a political dispute; we were challenging the power of corporations to write the rules and buy off politicians, something I was sure Fox and I disagreed on. But for the moment, I shrugged. "Let's watch it again!"

Disappointment came hours later, when Karim fervently pointed at his laptop and angrily bellowed, "Look at this!"

Fox's afternoon program was completely unlike the show in the morning. It was littered with innuendo about Philly's Ballot Box: "It can't handle ballot stuffing... It won't interact with the voters' database... Casino-Free Philadelphia will be counting it in isolation—so we know the result."

Karim pounded the table. "I know what happened! Dan Fee called them up and yelled at them. I'm sure he blustered and intimidated them for not quoting the casinos in the first piece."

"But it's not true," I said with a soft, deflated voice. "They didn't even have the courtesy to call us to double-check their facts."

"No," said Karim with mischievous gleam. "No, they didn't. But I have a plan..."

Karim dialed the Fox News editor's telephone number.

"Hello, this is Karim from Casino-Free Philadelphia," he simmered. "You just ran a story about our election, Philly's Ballot Box, correct?" He paused, waiting for a response.

Karim sprang from his chair, putting the full force of his movement into his yelled words. "How do you suddenly go televising false information about Philly's Ballot Box?" His face turned red, as he yelled without giving the editor a moment, "Your news report said there was no way to handle ballot stuffing—that's not true! If you had watched your *previous* newscast you would have known that was false. Then you told your viewership we don't have any verification with the voter database—completely untrue."

For a minute, I watched thunderstruck as Karim continued on a rampage, tearing apart the falsities from the afternoon's segment, stopping abruptly to ask, "Then why did you put all that bull in there?"

He listened, and then launched again, spitting caustically, "You let Dan Fee and our opponents tell *you* about *our* campaign? That's not reporting, that's spreading accusations for them. It's our campaign. We designed it. *We* know how it runs. You have to run any accusations by us to see if they're true. This is unacceptable!"

I watched, aghast. This went against everything I had been told about building a positive relationship with press: be kind, be courteous.

Karim listened as the editor pleaded her case. Then, as if responding to a question, his voice dropped five notches into a relaxed gear. "What we would like is a chance to come on your show to explain the ballot box. We can clear up any rumors. In the future, if you're going to change your story because of what the casinos say, you have to fact-check with us."

I couldn't hear her response on the phone. But he nodded with a scowl and hung up.

I looked blankly at him. "I have never seen anything like that, Karim. You yelled at a reporter!"

He looked up sharply and smiled, "I sure did, didn't I? We can be pretty certain she won't do another story without checking it out with us again."

"But... what about your relationship with her?"

"It's based on truth," he said. "Everything is a negotiation with reporters. It's like a good friendship. Sometimes you have to have a blow-out with your roommate, and more will come out than if it festered and became a passive-aggressive relationship. My philosophy is building an *honest* relationship is more important than an *easy* one. I was yelling because she had broadcasted *wrong* information."

"Not just to push her around, like Dan Fee," I said.

He nodded.

My gut relaxed. "I've seen you be tough with reporters," I said. "But you never yelled before."

"Well," he tugged at his facial hair. "The way I think about it, reporters are very much like us. They go into journalism with idealistic goals of benefiting society. In a lot of ways, we have a lot in common with them. It's okay to talk to them as your friends and relate to them that way."

I shook my head at him, amazed.

Karim looked thoughtful. "That's probably more true for print journalists. TV producers are a whole different beast, but they must be even more thick-skinned in that business."

"What would you have done if it had all fallen apart?"

At that he grinned. "I figured you're good at playing the nice guy. You'd apologize for my angry temperament, tell her I'd never interact with her again, and take over the relationship." I laughed along with him. "But I was pretty sure it wouldn't come to that."

I sat blankly. "Amazing," I muttered. Remembering what was at stake, I sat up. "So, did you get what you wanted?"

"Absolutely. Future stories will be much better." He paused and then smiled proudly. "And she agreed to get us another morning interview."

The next day, Karim sent out press clippings of the Philly's Ballot Box launch. The launch had exceeded our most dense press to date. In addition to a string of mediocre-to-fair follow-ups on Fox 29 news and echoes on other TV stations, we earned front page on the *Evening Bulletin* and exploded into a whole new raft of mid-sized local media: *Al Dia*'s Spanish-language coverage, the African-American newspaper the *Philadelphia Tribune*, multiple hits in weeklies, conservative radio interviews, and a handful of neighborhood newspapers, including our release being fully reprinted in *University City Review*, among others. Numerous local civics within DRNA were forwarding everything we wrote or writing their own endorsements for Philly's Ballot Box, including front-page articles in the Society Hill Reporter.

Karim noted with anger that only the *Inquirer* and the *Daily News* had given us the cold shoulder. "They're timid when it comes to citizen action," I told him. "They'll come around when they see everyone else writing about it. Don't worry about them."

He didn't. We couldn't afford to sweat what was out of our control.

The energy from the launch immediately translated into a rapid rise in volunteer sign-ups. Unprompted, Brad Aronson offered to coordinate bloggers to drum up support, Mary Reinhart volunteered to help Kathy assign poll workers locations, Caryn Hunt outreached to her extensive network, and dozens jumped into attending hundreds of hearings, civic meetings, and community events to find more volunteers.

All of us were driven to even more intensity by the electricity in the office: the sounds of John Donley's booming voice swapping bawdy jokes with Scott as they rearranged the back room into a call center, Morgan armed with screwdriver and power cables setting up computers that Karim borrowed from friend Laryn Kragt Bakker's nonprofit, and Kathy Dilonardo's sharp voice training poll workers in the front room. It was all thrilling.

Yet, what looked like a tornado of people's magical arrival into the office originated from Jethro's knack. Jethro himself seemed to rarely do work—I noted his constant phone chatter was mostly spent getting people engaged.

"My goal as an organizer," he said, "is to walk away from every meeting without work. All I do is follow up with people to make sure they have support to do their tasks. I guess I'm just lazy." He laughed. "You take too much work for yourself. You're being selfish. Look at all these people who want to do work—and you're hoarding!" He poked me playfully.

He was right. But I wasn't sure what to do about it.

The arrival of Rich Garella exemplified Jethro's knack. Rich was a serious-looking hipster from the Center City neighborhood Washington Square West. Jethro had invited him to our pre-launch executive meeting, coached him to give a few words at our launch, and spent hours talking with him, learning that Rich had more experience in elections than any of us. In 1998, Rich was the press secretary for the unsuccessful Cambodian opposition party. His first day on the job, he was forced to pen a contentious *Wall Street Journal* op-ed threatening to pull out of the election if basic conditions were not met. Despite assurances from the government, the process wound up as an international poster child of how to steal an election.

Still, I was surprised when Jethro interrupted my harried work, insisting I sit down with Rich.

Rich spoke in a slow, measured pace. "I feel strongly that if this is going to be a fair election, it cannot have Casino-Free Philadelphia materials in its offices."

I looked at him in surprise. "Because?"

"In Cambodia, elections were stolen largely by the cozy relationship between the political government and the electoral commissions. It sends the wrong message and makes Philly's Ballot Box appear partial."

Jethro smirked. I wasn't sure if he thought it was funny, or if he was just reacting to my look of strained frustration at something so apparently trivial.

Then again, if we were pushing Fox News and others to be exacting, then we should be that, too. It was the organizer's version of the third law of motion: every action has an equal and opposite reaction. Our push for truth from others meant we'd end up facing that, too.

It's why Gandhi said his third opponent was the British, his second the Indian people, and the first himself. We earned high ground by imbibing it.

But still...

"Fine," I said with a touch of resignation. "We'll move stuff out of the middle room."

"No," said Rich, "I mean all of it, everywhere. We can't have any CFP materials visible while we're doing volunteer training for Philly's Ballot Box."

Karim snuck up on the conversation and inserted himself. "*Every* CFP poster?"

Rich nodded, "Anything with CFP's name on it."

Karim tossed his hands in the air and stalked off, shaking his head.

"It makes sense to me," said Jethro, pacing with Rich's methodical tone. "Rich and I talked for a long time about how we are setting up a real election. If so, we need to be beyond reproach."

"Okay, we'll do it," I said good-naturedly. "We'll toss it all in the cabinets."

Rich walked off to start moving boxes. "Making rules for the election," said Jethro. "Seems like we've got ourselves an election commissioner."

Sunday afternoon, I was in a meeting in the back room with Jethro's business partner Nick Jehlen, Rich Garella, and computer expert Aaron Kreider. The room was circled with long desks and filled with a dozen phone and computer stations and stray bags of chips and juices from Friday's volunteer phone-banking.

Together we were proving our geeky credentials by our thrill at designing our online election system. Though Nick and I had experience building database-backed websites, it was the thin Aaron Kreider that was the expert designer. He studied online election systems—like how last year an "ultra-secure" system meant to be used in US elections had been hacked in mere minutes. To combat hacking, he explained his plan to implement security protocols by randomizing keys, flagging IP spam, and tracking any discrepancies consistent with indirect or brute force attacks. Consistent with our values, it would be open-source, he said, "but after the election, you know... just to be safe."

Suddenly Karim burst in, jumping up and down. "I've tracked down the rumor! It's true: SugarHouse is sending out mailers! Get a look at this!"

I excused myself. Karim and I hurried through the main room's mess of potato chips and scripts for turnout calls and arrived in the front room. Karim stuffed a flyer into my hand, with an idealized middle-class white family walking down a street and the text, "Time we make Philadelphia a safer, stronger city."

"Where'd you find it?" I asked.

"Norma was sent a copy and sent it to me. They seem to be all over in Northern Liberties, Fishtown, Society Hill. It's got to be tens, if not hundreds of thousands of mailers. Plus the thousands of robocalls we've been hearing about."

Holding the flyers felt like a big deal. For days, SugarHouse had denied making robocalls, until a Pulitzer-prize winning *Inquirer* reporter received a call. Even then, they argued with her.

Now we had proof of their flyers, too.

I looked closer. "That can't be a picture of Philadelphia!"

"I know! I've never seen a Philly street like that! Must be some some professional photo image."

Karim handed me a second flyer. This one had a police officer on the front with the headline, "More cops on the street? We're putting our money on it."

"Hypocrites," I spat. "They know the police commissioner just said the rise in crime will require at least 100 additional cops. They've got so much money... they're inoculating themselves, since mayoral elections are becoming all about crime. They're trying to jump on the bandwagon to dismiss the fact that casinos cause crime."

Karim said nothing as I kept reading. "*6,000 jobs?* They're... how did 1,000 jobs turn into 6,000?"

Karim spoke hurriedly. "They generously calculated spin-off jobs and ignored the cannibalization effect. They worded it to sound like they're giving $50 million to schools. It's all being used to gather names for support." He pointed to their signature line: "YES! I want to see Philadelphia move forward and I support building SugarHouse NOW!"

I shook my head and frowned. "Those are deep pockets..."

"But don't you see?" Karim locked eyes with me. "SugarHouse is running against us in our own freaking election!"

I clapped my hands. "You've got the idea, Karim."

It was classic Casino-Free Philadelphia. For months, I had consciously built our culture to emphasize *our* power in everything. Too many movements I had worked with had emphasized their opponents' influence and power. They'd spend hours and reams of articles studying their opponents' strategy, holding it up as a model of effective organizing and never devoting that kind of positive attention to their movement histories. Rather than seeing how power rises up from the people, they'd lean back on the moral self-congratulations of speaking "truth to power." I wanted us to speak truth *and power* to power. That meant showing how the "powerholders" are actually in a constant dance with us.

"I'll write a draft of the press release," I said. "This will definitely make it into the blogs and cement us as one of the most talked-about issues during this election. I'll let our members know our opposition takes this seriously—so they should, too!"

The next morning, Jethro grabbed Karim and me for an early huddle. He wagged his fingers at the mailers. "Those are *just* the tip of the iceberg! SugarHouse has an all-out offensive up North. They already got Councilman Clarke, they're buying ads in all the Fishtown newspapers, they've given $10,000 to Chuck Valentine's church and given money to the Fishtown Athletic League and several soccer programs, steam-cleaned sidewalks, and even put on a swing-band concert. Wherever they give money, they tell everyone the checks will get bigger when they arrive. They're trying to buy Fishtown off—and it may be working."

"You know what this is?" asked Karim rhetorically. "This whole mailing operation is SugarHouse building up an astroturf group."

"That's exactly right," said Jethro. "SugarHouse is pushing around to reporters a new group called Fishtown Action—or FACT." He grinned. "*FACT.* They have no shame, no sense of irony."

"Wait, astroturf?" I asked. "What do you mean?"

"Like rolling out astroturf on a field," said Karim. "Instead of real grassroots, they spend thousands to build the appearance of a grassroots group. It gets full media staff, all the resources of their bank account, but with the appearance of a humbly built operation. I did some digging last night, and it looks like SugarHouse may have hired Saint Consulting, a company that professionally builds astroturfed groups."

"We need to shine a light on how this industry works," said Jethro. "They're dividing the community, exploiting 'old versus new' and class divisions. We need to go on the offensive now. Can we hire some organizers to do outreach up North, or maybe launch a new campaign just focused on Fishtown?"

I looked at Jethro like he was crazy. "You're kidding, right? Focus, Jethro."

Jethro looked at Karim. "*You* know the media are getting baited by FACT. We've got to do something."

Just days ago, I had watched Karim pivot quickly on a reporter. The *Daily News'* Ronnie Polaneczky had called Jethro to talk about pro-casino FACT. When Karim heard Ronnie impugning Jethro with accusations on his character, Atlantic City connections, and asking when he *really* moved into Fishtown, Karim grabbed the phone. Karim rightly sensed it would be a slant piece, painting FACT as "almost subversive" against the "intimidating" anti-casino movement. He refused to answer more questions and threatened to expose her bias to her editor if she printed the piece. Karim correctly predicted, "She'll print the piece, but she'll think twice about doing a second one."

Karim shrugged at Jethro. "Media are suckers for the 'two sides to every issue' attitude. So SugarHouse gets away with spinning this as 'Some people are for casinos and some people are against, it's a split down the middle.'" None of us suggested reminding press of the polling data. We could show them, but facts weren't important to them.

Jethro bobbed anxiously. "These people are my neighbors. We can't demonize people who are feeling beat down. The real problem is Fishtown has been ignored for years by politicians. Now people are begging a casino to be their savior. But right now, it's less than a dozen people who are active. Maybe we should have a public debate with them."

Karim and I snuck looks at each other. "No way," I said. "We shouldn't validate them by giving them more attention. The best strategy for a small organization to grow itself is to pick a fight with a larger organization. That's what they're doing with us. But we're a citywide group—they're local. It's best for us to publicly ignore them."

"We need to do ground work," said Jethro with exasperation. "They picked Fishtown 'cause they know we're vulnerable."

"Everything we do must stay focused on this election," I said. "If it doesn't, I'm afraid we can't support it at this point."

"There are things we can do," said Karim. "We can get people writing letters to the editor. And I'll keep digging into how they're operating."

I sighed. "How about this, Jethro? Philly's election laws require publishing advertisements in newspapers ahead of the election. And we're, of course, following the law." I smiled. "Scott is getting us some good deals in the *Metro, Inquirer,* and *Daily News* to advertise Philly's Ballot Box. I know we can't counter SugarHouse's weekly ad buys in every Fishtown paper, but I'll make sure he buys some ads in Fishtown and Northern Liberties. I guess the *South Philly Review,* too, to keep the South Philly people happy."

Jethro waved exuberantly. "Good start! That'll be a help."

"Last thing," I said. "I found a printer able to print 300 ballot boxes matching Jeremy's design. They can guarantee getting them printed by May 10." I wrung my hands. "The problem is they're far away, and it'll cost a fortune to ship them overnight. They can't be late."

"Where are they?" Jethro asked.

"In Chicago."

Jethro chewed the edge of his pencil. "Order it. We'll figure out something..."

Ten days left.

The days merged into a fast-paced blur: Kathy with ear glued to her cell phone begging neighbors to fill empty time-slots at poll locations; Paul rushing through the office handing out large stacks of the latest articles on Philly's Ballot Box; Shirley directing new volunteers to test phone lines, get training in election law, and write blogs and letters to the editor; and Karim frantically typing a new press release.

Karim's latest press release reported that a new anti-casino political video made by Kevin Nalty was given the sixth highest rating in YouTube's comedy category and watched by over 5,000 people in one day. "CFP is sending 345 press releases a day," exaggerated one blog, noting we were operating like a real campaign.

It was fun. It was exciting.

Arms filled with brochures, Jethro ran in from one meeting to announce that the Young Republicans' angry, anti-establishment Kevin Kelly had donated radio ads to our cause, as I yelled across the room to announce the endorsement of both the Coalition of Labor Union Women and radical labor leader Tom Cronin. Criss-crossing the office to give instructions to volunteers, Jethro and I plopped in front of Republican donor Bob

Guzzardi. As we explained casinos' impact on increasing divorce rates, bankruptcy, and the loss to local community, Bob shook his head. "I never would have believed you liberals understood family values." Without a pause, I grinned. "And I never would have believed you conservatives could understand that businesses can cause searing social and economic damage." It would take us a minute to seal the deal, before Jethro and I rushed off to the next meeting.

Every free moment, I tracked the politics of—as we called it—"the other election." The contested council elections were overshadowed by the charged mayoral election, from death threats against Bob Brady to Presidential nominee Barack Obama unexpectedly endorsing former front-runner Chaka Fattah. Most endorsements were coalescing around new front-runner Michael Nutter, in a tight race against wealthy Tom Knox, who was bombarding the airwaves with hand-over-fist spending topping $12 million—mostly his own personal money.

The mayor's election was staying close, which was good for us. In a tight race, our anti-casino supporters' swing vote could make a difference in choosing the next mayor— who would play a big hand in the future of our campaign... if we could last that long. That required Philly's Ballot Box making an impact on elections.

At first, mayoral candidates waffled. At Society Hill and DRNA's forum, all the mayoral candidates pledged support to the referendum. But days later, in a series of articles, they backslid into feeble mutterings of powerlessness or retreated to the moral high ground of "Let the people vote," side-stepping any personal opinions on the matter.

Without much prodding, people sent dozens of letters to the editors, swarming reporters, elected officials, and candidates, all urging the candidates to take stronger anti-casino stances. The governor felt the heat and, for the first time, wrote a curt response to one letter, saying he had "no authority" over the PGCB or the casino process. Even Senator Fumo requested a meeting with the DRNA.

I encouraged folks to postpone the meeting and not waste too much time writing letters. The organizing work required for Philly's Ballot Box was our lever for more power. By contrast, direct lobbying was an inefficient way to move mayoral candidates and meant less time for organizing.

Instead, we urged reporters to get tough with the candidates, suggesting more direct questions to pin them down. When reporters didn't go far enough, DRNA organized additional town hall meetings and Kathy organized attendance at community and mayoral forums—which all doubled as outreach for Philly's Ballot Box. Mary Ann Leitch drafted a Casino-Free Philadelphia *Voter's Guide*.

At first, reporters pushed back, starting with Chris Satullo, who had penned "That train done gone and left the station" over a year earlier. His own *Great Expectations* public straw polls—sponsored by the *Inquirer*—resulted in 76% of folks supporting the buffer zone. In his public releases he downplayed his data, following his gut that the referendum "would be very, very close," reiterating in interviews that support was about "fifty-fifty."

Scorn was heaped on his blog—"a total tool" with "no respect for democracy." But I urged people to let it drop. "Ignore the media aristocracy and focus on organizing your neighbors and friends," I wrote. "Our goal is that wherever mayoral candidates show their faces, they hear opposition to casinos."

In the face of tougher questions, new articles showed the candidates moving to vaguely anti-casino stances. A slew of progressive council candidates advanced our issue and added fuel to the political fire.

That sparked a backlash from the building trades unions who staged a rally of a thousand pro-casino workers and a handful of FACT members urging, "Build Them Now!" One reporter called it the "saddest rally ever." The single-action rally had no momentum, no storyline, and was a small ripple against the overwhelming tide of organized voices behind Philly's Ballot Box. Several members caught our framing and sent us notes: "*They're* campaigning in our election, too!"

Wherever political candidates turned their heads, especially in the riverfront wards, they had to address casinos.

The shift was major. Within weeks, every mayoral candidate—except Evans and Fattah—sent confirmation to our *Voter's Guide* that they supported the referendum and would advertise Philly's Ballot Box in their campaign literature. Both front-runners, Tom Knox and Michael Nutter, said they would "attempt to keep casinos from being built within Philadelphia."

All this confirmed my view of power. Politicians are like a balloon tied to a rock. If we swat at them, they may sway to the left or the right. But, tied down, they can only go so far. Instead of batting at them, we should move the rock: people's activated social values. When we move the rock, it automatically pulls all the politicians toward us—without having to pressure each one separately.

Candidates now began raising our issue at debates to prove their pro-democracy stripes. While very much secondary to issues of poverty and violence in the city, our issue was now part of the discourse. The mayoral candidates were feeling the heat and moving toward us. They were not alone.

Exactly one week before the election, I reached Brian Abernathy, Councilman Frank DiCicco's right-hand man. Before I could say anything, he cut me off. "I've been hearing about it all day."

I knew he had. We were frustrated that Councilman DiCicco had called Philly's Ballot Box a "gesture" that nobody will "take seriously." To push back, Karim and I quietly stoked the issue by passing his quote in the *Inquirer* to close allies and urging them to angrily call him.

I spoke gently, but with a hard edge. "Let me read our draft email to our members. I don't want to send it, but what Frank said is unacceptable. The draft reads: 'We know Councilman DiCicco is wrong, because volunteers are flooding in. And the casinos are running scared, running their own ads against us—'"

Brian cut me off with fire. "That's a threat! Friends don't *do that* to each other. The councilman's comments were taken out of context. He was asked a direct question if he thought the alternative ballots will influence the supreme court or state lawmakers going forward."

"He's an experienced campaigner," I said flatly. "No context makes those statements acceptable."

Brian breathed heavily, "He's tired. It's been a long campaign against an opponent who will stoop to anything to win."

That would be Brian's view on Vern Anastasio. Vern was running a competitive race, wielding DiCicco's acceptance of thousands of dollars from casino developers, DiCicco's pro-casino stance since the 1990s, and the public view that DiCicco was playing both sides of the casino issue.

"We're all tired," I started. I couldn't wait until Philly's Ballot Box was over and I could get some long, restful nights. "But you know we've stayed out of the race. Don't put us in the cross-fire."

"Yes," he said, calming his tone slightly. "I respect that about you."

"Well, we don't want to send out this letter, but there's no reason for us not to. If the quote was a mistake, then you should make a serious effort to correct the impression." I knew I was pushing him, but having a relationship with DiCicco wasn't a currency worth anything on its own. Too many groups confused access to power with power itself. We needed results.

Brian heaved, as if emphasizing his aggravation. "DiCicco has always been with you—"

"Don't give me that line," I said with passion. "We're full-tilt running an election to give people a say when they were denied the opportunity. Friends don't bash each other's efforts, friends don't *do that* to each other."

"Okay," said Brian. "What should we do?"

"We want Frank to re-introduce the 1,500-foot ordinance into City Council on Thursday. If voters pass it in Philly's Ballot Box, Frank promises to go ahead and push that bill full force. If the referendum does not pass in Philly's Ballot Box, you have my word I'll let it drop. We cannot accept less."

The phone jangled, and I couldn't tell if he was surprised or adjusting his phone. His deflated, exhausted voice echoed over my cell. "He'll introduce it tomorrow."

It took me a moment to respond. "Uh, thank Frank for us." Brian hung up.

I sat dazed for a second, processing the implication. Our election now had a concrete stake. Philly's Ballot Box's outcome was tied to a piece of city legislation.

"Karim, we have a new press release!"

Piles of materials and scraps of paper filled the main room as I sat across the table arguing with Nick Jehlen, Jethro's business partner. I didn't have much time to argue, but all of us needed to be on the same page, so we kept up a range of rotating meetings through the offices.

"It makes no sense to have all these people participate in our election," I said, "to have all this contact information, and not add it to our database."

Nick shook his head fiercely. "It's not right for people to think they're participating in the nonpartisan Philly's Ballot Box and suddenly find themselves on the mailing list of the partisan Casino-Free Philadelphia."

Jethro observed undecidedly from the other side of the room.

I leaned toward Nick. "Look, I'm not saying we keep *what* they voted for—but when someone votes, we should be able to get in contact with them afterwards. This is a massive recruitment opportunity for us, and we shouldn't blow it."

Nick's voice was steely and unyielding as he leaned closer. "If this is a real election, then we wouldn't keep people's contact information for the future." His mother was a Massachusetts state senator and Nick, like Rich Garella, was sensitive to the need for everything to be above-board and internally consistent.

"But this isn't a real election!" I pounded the table. "We're spending tens of thousands of dollars and need to increase the size of our mailing list and have something to show for it."

For days, Nick and I had pulled our hair out at each other's stubborn refusal to see the obvious truth in our positions.

Rich entered and smirked at Karim upon seeing Nick and me arguing again. Rich listened for a while before interrupting, "I think..." Nick and I halted our debate.

"I think Nick's right," Rich said. "We need to act as if it's a real election, so that anybody looking at us is going to say, 'They're running a real election.' We can't put people on a mailing list without their permission."

"It's a missed opportunity! At the very least," pleading entered my voice, "we could send people a follow-up letter to thank them for participating in Philly's Ballot Box and invite them to join the organization that ran it: Casino-Free Philadelphia."

"It's not ethical," said Nick. "That would still be Philly's Ballot Box endorsing Casino-Free Philadelphia." There was no tone of vindication, just an icy unbending.

Rich shrugged, unwilling to take a side on that point. But I could tell it would never happen. Philly's Ballot Box was now emerging into a real election and wouldn't expand our mailing list this way.

Jethro looked back at me. "Look, it's Rich's decision. He's the election commissioner. And I think it's a good one, strengthening the integrity of the election. We're softening up a whole city to our message, and that's more important than a few names."

I frowned unhappily. I could not appreciate that Nick and Rich were making Philly's Ballot Box into a real election with integrity checks. Far from just treating it like a poll, they were making it real. They were doing what I'd often urged others to do, to take a metaphor and genuinely play it out, like not just doing a citizen's arrest as a piece of street theater, but taking it seriously, complete with a citizen's judicial panel, arrest warrants, and full efforts to carry out a citizen's arrest. But at the moment, I wasn't appreciative.

I glared around the room and let it go—we had too much to do. I began heading toward the front room when Jethro stopped me and handed me a set of receipts.

I glanced at them. "Another $200?" He nodded.

"Jethro, we can't keep spending money. We can't walk away from Philly's Ballot Box broke. We may never see money like this again."

The entire operation was going to cost no more than $40,000. But that was thousands more than we might find again.

"We're investing," said Jethro. "We're building name recognition. People will expect nothing but the best from us. That'll make it easier to fundraise in the future."

In Jethro's upper-class upbringing, one spent money to get money; in my mixed working-class and middle-class household, we stored money for a rainy day, assuming our income was relatively fixed.

But I couldn't see our class backgrounds—all I saw was my exasperation. I scrunched my face in disagreement. "But... I don't know, we need to be careful with each dollar."

"Of course we do, we stretch every dollar," Jethro said. "But if we run the best election possible, people will be attracted to us. Every door will be a little easier to get into."

"But if we don't have money to keep on staff, we won't be able to do anything." I glared at him.

"If we grow to cultivate new donors, and they see what we're doing, we'll grow. Trust me, donors will be more willing to give if we do this right."

Reluctantly, I took his receipts.

"Oh," I said, turning to face him, "you figure out how to get the ballot boxes from Chicago yet?"

"I'm working on it..."

It was days before the election. I slammed the door to the back room shut, urging Karim to sit down next to Paul and Jethro. Gazing at each of us, Karim looked fervently around the room. "You mean he threatened Casino-Free?"

I took a seat near the desk and recounted to Karim what had happened.

Just five minutes earlier, I had received a call from Ed Kirlin of John Dougherty's electricians' union IBEW local 98. Ed had been ardently anti-Foxwoods from the start, even while we believed his boss, John Dougherty, was hedging and playing both sides. Ed started his call by asking me again if Casino-Free Philadelphia would sign a letter endorsing Tom Knox for mayor. IBEW had full weight behind Knox's candidacy.

"No," I told him. "It's not our thing."

Ed's voice was choked with urgency and stress from the increasingly hostile and tight mayoral election. "You got to, or you won't stay relevant to the anti-casino movement. If you won't be political at election time, when the hell can you be? All the civics are scared because they're nonprofits."

"I'm not. We're a 501c4—we can be political, and we've done plenty to get out the word with the *Voter's Guide* and pressing reporters and allies to ask candidates tough questions about their casino stance. It's now a major issue in the mayor's race."

"You can't pussyfoot with Nutter. He's leading you on, and everyone is too blind or scared to say the emperor has no clothes," Ed said breathlessly. "Nutter told the civics he can't help them, he thinks it's all a done deal and has no plans!"

"No politicians have shown us plans on what they'll do with casinos—"

"Nutter's just playing you," Ed seethed. "Knox has given money to the cause, he's said he's absolutely against casinos—you can't get Nutter to say that. You have to sign."

"Look Kirlin, we've always said that getting our movement hitched to electoral work causes too much drift, it pulls you in and you start thinking electorally. We don't endorse candidates—they endorse us." I paused to collect my thoughts. "If they want to be anti-casino, they should be anti-casino, and their record, their experience should speak for themselves. We're not in the business of endorsing candidates."

Ed quickly said, "If you don't do it, you can be replaced."

I didn't believe my ears. "*What did you just say?*" My tone caused Jethro and Paul to suddenly stop talking and listen.

Ed screamed into the phone, "You're not the only game in town! You can be replaced."

Signaling for silence and the door shut, I pulled the phone away from my head to press the speaker-phone button.

Kirlin continued his rant. "Nothing's special about Casino-Free—a new one can be built that does have a backbone."

I toggled the button to avoid sounding like I was on speaker phone, responding, "I hope you're not suggesting what I think you are. By not endorsing candidates but pressuring all of them—by changing the political atmosphere—that's how we work. You need to understand, that's how we've had the successes we've had."

"And you need to understand," Ed whispered forcefully, "that in elections, windows get smashed and headquarters get broken into. It happens all the time."

My stomach dropped. IBEW had a long history of intimidation and violence.

"That's... that's not a good way to talk to allies," I said, understatedly. "It's not going to get you what you want."

"Watch your back," he spat.

Finishing the story for Karim, I told him that was when Ed hung up.

Karim looked at us. "IBEW has done plenty of nasty things. They've allegedly tried to run Vince Fumo off the road, broken into campaign offices, and roughed people up."

Jethro sat up. "He just can't do this. He doesn't know who we are."

Paul looked shaken. "I just... I just want to talk to Ed directly. He doesn't know I heard him. Maybe I could call him up to sort things out with him."

"I don't see what there is to sort out," I said. "It's organizational politics, Paul, it's not personal."

"The hell it's personal," snapped Jethro. "He just threatened us and our offices. We need to get this out to people."

Karim nodded thoughtfully, "*Daily News* might love the story... or leaked to a blog..."

"I just need to take in what happened," I said. "I need a minute to breathe."

In the next few minutes, Paul advocated for talking personally with Ed, Jethro wanted to send a public message back to Ed that he couldn't get away with threats, and Karim strategized ways to reach press. I listened uncertainly.

Karim cut off the discussion. "Look, guys, later we'll look at this and think it's somewhat amusing. We're having a hard enough time building a grassroots organization. How is he going to do better?"

I smiled, appreciating Karim's lightness. "Either it's an idle threat or a real one. If it's real, we have to remind him it will backlash. But if it's idle, what do we get by making this public? Kirlin will deny it. Either we'll be called fabricators, or we look like potential victims. Neither help us."

"We have to protect ourselves from him doing it," said Jethro.

"Right," I said, "but now any violence leads back to IBEW. It couldn't have been a calculated threat. Any windows damaged, anyone hurt, anything happens—"

"—and we bring it right to Dougherty's big fat doorstep," said Jethro, puffing out his chest like a general.

"Right, right," I continued. "But it's more important to protect our people from fear. If people are scared by his intimidation, we'll have less numbers to recruit, and we just have too much going on to get into a press war with IBEW now. He's just fear-mongering us to back Knox. That only works if we react in fear." I looked at everyone, catching Paul's eye for an extra minute. "So we ignore it, okay?"

Heads nodded.

"Let's get someone to sleep in the office," said Karim. "You know, just in case."

We left the anger, fear, and whatever other emotions we had and hurried to the next task. It was just one more thing piled onto our increasingly full plates.

Two days before the election, when we needed to have a Philly's Ballot Box meeting, we didn't even have to schedule it. I just walked into the different rooms to grab people for a check-in.

In the front room, I grabbed Kathy as she managed five volunteers making phone calls. Eschewing our computer database to coordinate volunteers, she had plastered our walls with names of volunteers matched with each hour of the day.

"A meeting? We have to fill the rest of these slots," Kathy spurted.

"Just a short check-in," I called out. I headed out to the hallway, where eight members were assembling poll-worker materials. In each donated Whole Foods bag went Philly's Ballot Box T-shirts, name tags, pens, and laminated letters from the watchdog Committee of Seventy and ACLU. Plus water and plastic bags in case it rained. Kathy had thought of everything.

"Two minutes," I said, walking past them toward the living room area to recruit Jethro and the crew of short-term organizing staff doing last-minute recruitment.

"Meeting now," I said. It'd take two minutes for most of them to just get off the phone.

Crossing to the back room, I found Karim and Nick on the phone with Aaron discussing website details. "Meeting to make sure we're ready to roll! It'll be quick!"

I returned to the main room to wait. I cleared off some of the leftover cups and broken pretzels from sessions of training our poll workers and flipped through newspapers left on the table. The *City Paper* editor had turned over half his column to me for an op-ed, in which I urged people to vote in Philly's Ballot Box. The *Metro* had another column about us. Bristling with excitement, I picked up the *Inquirer* to re-read its unexpected announcement in our favor. Without a single meeting with us, the paper's editors had followed the momentum of the times and finally come out in our favor: "Philadelphia anti-casino activists who are being denied a vote could express their anger and frustration with a spirited City Hall rally, and then go home. But on Tuesday, they intend to go the extra mile—many miles, in fact—in a worthwhile effort to make their case to policymakers.... Tuesday's straw vote is their chance to be heard at last."

It felt like a major achievement to see the turn-around in the *Inquirer*. Volunteer George Kelly had seen that it was a big deal and insisted we distribute copies. When I hedged because of money, he offered to pay for them so we could put them in poll-worker bags.

Jethro interrupted my reading, shouting at the top of his lungs, "They're here!"

Members bolted out of the office to find a moving truck slowly passing. Seeing the emerging crowd, the truck stopped under the bridge.

A disheveled Aaron Hughes jumped out of the driver's seat. Jethro, who had met him in their mutual work with Iraq Veterans Against the War, helped Aaron steady himself. Years of driving trucks for the US military in Iraq had prepared him well for his fourteen-hour drive without sleep.

I kicked at the stuck latch on the U-haul, trying to force it open. Volunteers swarmed.

The latch unlocked and the doors swung upwards, as a police car drove by, stopped, and backed up. "You have to move," the officer said. "You're under a bridge and a potential threat." He cast his eyes suspiciously over us.

"Come see what it is for yourself, it's nothing dangerous—just cardboard boxes," said Jethro, clapping. Under the gaze of the officer, our eyes feasted on the just-in-time, drop-dead gorgeous ballot boxes. We returned to the offices for a quick meeting, preparing for the final day.

That final day of preparations was one of jangled nerves and deep silence, gripping the office like a large, sustained inhale.

With all the systems in place, there was uncomfortably little to do. Awkwardly standing behind our Peace Brigades International–trained volunteer George Lakey, who had done election monitoring in South Africa, I took a quick break to watch the ballot-box assembly.

Standing behind a table facing the three lines of chairs in our open space, Election Commissioner Rich Garella announced, "This is ballot box #34." He wrote #34 on the side of the box and handed it to Scott Seiber, who assembled it with security tape.

Waiting for Scott to finish, Rich then held up the box to the small audience. "You can see it is completely empty." He held it up to the web camera, telling our web audience, "There is nothing inside." He sealed the box with security tape and placed it in the webcam's line of sight. He then continued, "This is ballot box #35..."

I left, thinking: *This is eye-pokingly boring.*

Later, Rich would oversee placing envelopes, ballots, and pens into the poll-worker bags and then lock the boxes, to which only he and Nick had keys. He was serious about making everything above-board.

I headed back to the front office to re-read releases for tomorrow, while others tested phone and online voting mechanisms.

It was an eerie experience: supporting a massive operation that had few logistical snafus. Through great effort and many twisted arms, Kathy had managed to have two poll workers signed up through shifts at each site for the entire day. Paul had smoothed our way with all the electoral officials. Karim and I had a full game plan for the media and outreach to supporters that day. Nick had prepared web updates, while Brad Aronson worked with other techies to get citywide bloggers to provide a one-day link to our website at the top of their websites. Scott finalized newspapers' election-day advertisements. Everything appeared to be in place for the massive day of operation.

CHAPTER 11
Election Day

MAY 15, 2007 — MAY 21, 2007

using media's lulls for high visibility • setting the stage, writing politicians' scripts • actions are fun • the downside of integrity • political jujitsu on TV • organizers need to ask, and ask, and ask • not legally binding but politically binding

THE MORNING AIR WAS CRISP on our big day. My stomach twisted, and I pranced up the now-familiar steps of City Hall, the waking sun just barely showing its rays.

With a big smile, Jethro thrust today's *Metro* into my hands. "Front page, baby!"

"Ground Forces Roll In," declared the headline, with two dozen four-feet-tall Philly's Ballot Boxes. Behind them stood Jethro and Scott, backdropped by iconic Love Park.

"I swore that it was going to be our first action without press," I said, trying not to simper.

"You were wrong again. We successfully stole this cover from the mayor's election. It's huge!"

It was initial confirmation of our roll-out strategy. Yesterday we had whetted reporters' appetites with the "march of the ballot boxes." It wasn't my best idea—putting dozens of ballot boxes in Love Park—but it took little effort and organization. We could put it together quickly.

Today would be the real test. We had events timed during the natural lulls of election day: before polls opened when media would have little to talk about; the afternoon quiet periods; and that awkward time when polls have closed but results aren't yet coming in. We would try to avoid direct head-to-head competition over media attention with the "other election."

So there we stood, two hours before the other election's polls opened, having invited all the candidates to get some free press as they cast the first ballots in Philly's Ballot Box, live on television. A crowd of progressive candidates nervously wrung their hands and straightened their suits, as lanky mayoral candidate Tom Knox strode up, literally head and shoulders above his handlers. As Karim had predicted, a half-dozen TV cameras captured the event.

I swept my eyes toward the streets, hoping front-runner Michael Nutter would unexpectedly show up. We had pulled strings to get him—even offering to set up a ballot box outside of his house—but were turned down.

Anne explained the mechanisms and handed Tom Knox the first ballot. The TV cameramen shifted to get into position, flipping on the live feeds as Tom Knox clumsily filled out the form. Cameras zoomed in as Knox dropped the first vote in Philly's Ballot Box.

My heart quickened at the powerful symbol of politicos vying in our election. Instead of voting for politicians, politicians were voting for us. It felt *so* right.

Through the day, my job was to fill in wherever challenges arose and spot check throughout the day. The morning offered no problems. Near Wilson Park at 25th and Jackson, I met up with staunch labor activist Terry Paylor, wearing dangling hoop earrings and the Philly's Ballot Box T-shirt. "I'm hoping to get as many votes as I can," she said, "to take to the supreme court to say, "Yes, we have a voice—and no, they cannot stop it." One hundred thirty-six of her neighbors voted at that box.

Steve Zettler held down a box at tree-filled Starr Garden Playground on the corner of Sixth and Lombard. Like most, he set up outside of the polling station, thankful that it was a warm, sunny day. "I'm here because I resent the fact that Harrisburg took away our rights on this issue: whether you're pro-casino or anti-casino. They're not allowing us to express our opinions." Nearly 300 of his neighbors voted there.

Over at Fourth and Ritter, Lyn Evangelista and her partner set up picnic chairs and a tiny folding table beside their ballot box. Outside Taggart School, 176 folks voted. Lyn explained her presence: "To me it's not really about casinos, it's about democracy. While our sons, daughters are being sent to Iraq and all over the world to fight and die for me—it's not freedom if we have no input on the laws that are being imposed on us."

I was getting a small taste of the fifty-plus polling locations around the city, where young and old volunteers of all stripes were holding down ballot boxes—from members of the Oregon Club Mummers in full regalia to anarchist punks in West Philadelphia who explained, "It's socializing the cost and privatizing the profit for a few. The majority of people will be taxed for this and will get nothing out of it."

By eleven o'clock, the next action for the media lull was about to begin.

Rose Shanahan and I hurried down Fourth Street with ballot box in tow. We walked toward the large black and white lettered signs: "Famous Fourth Street Deli."

"Not famous to me," I chuckled.

Rose, a South Philly gal to the core, merely smiled and continued walking. Famous Fourth Street Deli's election tradition was well-known and oddly Philadelphian. Taking a break from campaigning, politicians would gather over lunch and socialize—even those running against each other.

As we crossed Bainbridge, Rose suddenly froze. "What are those cops doing?" She pointed at two cops heading toward us.

I called to them, "We're just gonna set up a ballot box here," gesturing to the wide sidewalk, left of the entrance.

"No, you can't," the policewoman said, stepping to get in my way.

Her command barely registered, bouncing off my adrenaline-rich excitement and positive energy of the day. "Of course I can," I said. "It's a sidewalk. We're allowed freedom of assembly. We won't block passageway."

"No," she said, raising her voice threateningly, "you're not allowed to block the sidewalk."

I looked at her, as if seeing her anew. The law was clearly on my side: the sidewalk could accommodate us and a whole crowd of people. "Our action is protected free speech. There's plenty of space here. We've already contacted the ACLU about setting up our ballot boxes around the city."

"You cannot be here." She glared and stepped toward me, motioning to grab my arm.

Her colleague stepped forward. "You can go there, or over there," he said, pointing across the intersection. We didn't want to be there. We wanted to be where the politicians would be entering and leaving.

"No," I spoke slowly, cautiously pulling my arm away to be nonthreatening, "we're going to set up right outside the entrance."

"We will arrest you if you do," he said.

"Go for it," I said brightly. They stepped back as if slapped. "If you do, press will have a field day about you stopping our election and preventing our freedom of speech."

They eyed each other. "Look," the policewoman said, "you just have to go." She waved me on hopefully.

I didn't move. They didn't move. We glowered at each other awkwardly.

"I'm calling my lawyer," I announced, walking back across the street. I called Paul and told him to hurry, as the police and I exchanged uneasy glances.

Minutes later, Paul arrived breathlessly, wearing the unofficial garb of lawyers: a dull tie and shined briefcase. It took only a minute of negotiation before he returned. "It's settled. We'll be where we want, and the police will watch from across the street." Catching my eye, "And it would help if you would apologize, they didn't like your tone."

"Didn't like *my*..." I gestured angrily. "Paul, they can't go around intimidating people. I'm not going to go apologize for them bossing me around."

"Well, they felt you were disrespectful to them."

"If they wanted me to grovel in front of them, then yes, they would be disappointed."

"What do you lose by just going over there and doing it?"

I looked at Paul sharply. "Self-respect."

Paul stared, pleading, "Please, just do it for me."

I withered and walked over to the police. "I hope you did not feel I was being disrespectful to you," I said. "I was just trying to assert my rights." They nodded coldly, saying nothing.

Immediately, I wished I had stood my ground with Paul. Even that non-apology was dishonest to my experience: police shouldn't abuse their authority. And nobody should ever apologize to abusive authority for standing their ground.

Suddenly catching wind of what was outside, the owner of Famous Fourth Street Deli came outside and waved the police away, affirming our right to be there. The police frowned and backed off.

Rose, Paul, and I set up our ballot box, soon joined by Maria Walker. Maria lived two blocks from the proposed Foxwoods site and was upset about her three boys living near the congestion, traffic, noise, litter, and crime.

Slowly, politicians started arriving. "That's Senator Fumo's office manager," Maria whispered to me, as she beckoned the stout woman over by name. "And that's the register of wills," she whispered almost conspiratorially, recruiting his vote in the elections.

The first mayoral candidate, Chaka Fattah, walked by, waving off Maria and saying he couldn't vote. Five minutes later, he re-emerged with a ballot in hand.

"Here's the money shot, guys," Maria yelled to the now-assembled TV and print photographer crews. She whispered to Fattah, "You forgot to fill out your name." He ignored her and flashed his stately smile, posing for the camera as he dropped in his vote. With no name, his vote wouldn't count.

Bob Brady soon followed, surrounded on all flanks by large, bulging men. "I am happy to sign," he said, beaming. "It's a yes vote," he assured us in front of the gathered press.

I tried to seer in my mind the image of his big paw hands dropping a vote in our election. We were living out the belief that we don't endorse candidates, they endorse us. Even though I knew it was political calculations for them, it felt like a balm to watch them take part in our creating a new channel, when all the formal ones had failed. Rather than playing a minor role in *their* play, we had set the stage and written the script.

Only a few people refused to vote: Senator Fumo, lawyers from the casino industry, and a wildly confused Sharif Street, the mayor's son. He appeared so perplexed when we asked him to vote on the casino question. He froze like a deer in headlights and then spun around five times, perhaps trying to find a handler to help him out, until finally, he awkwardly walked into the restaurant without a word.

As the deli filled up, Paul Boni had to shout to catch Michael Nutter as he passed by. "Mr. Nutter, would you like to vote on the casino issue?"

"I did at 15th and Market," Nutter said. "I filled it out already."

With sincerity, Paul yelled back, "Thank you very much, Mr. Nutter."

Nutter had begun speaking more eloquently of the dangers of unchecked casino development on the riverfront. His people were even distributing door hangers with an endorsement of our vote. But I wanted to confirm.

I pulled out my polling-sheet data and called up the poll workers at City Hall. Shawn Rairigh answered, "Yes, he did vote. We weren't sure what to do. All we had was a camera phone. But we got some photos. He told us he voted yes."

Hours later, when the crowd of politicos thinned, I headed home to West Philly to grab lunch and check out polls in my neck of the woods.

At West Philadelphia's 58th and Christian, retiree Kathy McGrann stationed a ballot box outside a local corner store. "This referendum should have been on the ballot," she said with a mix of exasperation and pride, "so I'm excited to give people a chance to vote on this."

Next to Kathy, young activist Rebecca Ennan hid her face from the glaring sun with a brown patrol cap. "I'm doing this because I think Philly needs good urban renewal.

Casinos are the worst kind of stopgap—especially the zoning that has not been done around that is bogus." One hundred eighteen people voted at the box.

Escaping the heat of the afternoon, short-term staffer and volunteer Tommy Bendel took his ballot box inside the doors of First Spanish Baptist Church in the Kensington neighborhood, where eighty-four people voted. "Philadelphians have a right to vote about what happens in their neighborhoods."

At Society Hill Towers, a jovial Paula Turner helped 240 of her neighbors vote, explaining, "I actually like casinos, but I don't like them in my neighborhood. It's important that we keep the history and beauty of Philadelphia alive."

Over at Oregon New Years Association, 236 people voted at a station staffed by a team including John Calla, who wore the Philadelphia volunteer ID badge over a green polo shirt. He hissed, "I'm totally against the question being off the ballot. It's the most un-American thing I can think of."

At the busiest polling place of the day, Richard DeWyngaert joined a busy team of volunteers at St. Stanislaus Parish Hall, polling location for three separate divisions. Bouncing with elation, Richard said, "I believe the people have a right to a vote on this critical issue. This day is fabulous and might be a tipping point in Philadelphia politics." Six hundred eleven people voted at that bulging ballot box.

Taking lessons from our petition drive, we had placed some ballot boxes at locations that weren't official polling places, like at 40th and Market and at City Hall. At Rittenhouse Square, underneath the tall trees, Francie Shaw explained, "I'm doing this because I really believe that the citizens of this city should vote on what gets built in their residential neighborhoods." She was joined by Freire Charter High School students, who wanted to witness this second direct action by Casino-Free Philadelphia, having watched us get arrested in the document search. I teased them, "No arrests this time!" They teased back, "Not yet!" Three hundred forty-four people voted at that location.

In the end, we had ballot boxes in every state representative and councilmanic district. We were in every neighborhood, on the phone, and on the web, to truly allow every voter a chance to have their say.

At eight o'clock, polls in both elections closed. Around the city, volunteers sealed the ballot boxes with one-foot-long security tape, adding their signatures to ensure no tampering.

I was among the first to return to the office. "Welcome back," said Kathy. She wore a big, relieved smile. "No problems to report. The phone rang all day and I heard no complaints."

That was Kathy saying, *things went perfectly*.

She made me sign before accepting my ballot box, pointing me toward tables filled with drinks and veggie and meat platters. I glanced back at her, "Is there anything you didn't think of?"

Someone else might have flushed at the compliment. Instead, Kathy quickly turned back to greet other arrivals.

I grabbed a plate and yelled out to those returning, "Hey! How was it out there for you?"

The replies were loud and filled with deep sentiment: "It was great!" "Best election day ever." "We made history!" "Let's do it again tomorrow!" The pride and heads held high were a victory unto themselves.

The crowd swelled, filling the main room. All the clutter from the month had been cleaned, no doubt by Kathy, Mary, and her band of retirees, and replaced with open couches, refreshments, and a party atmosphere.

With only a flicker of regret, I noted that media had not arrived for our party—the last of the roll-out events for the day. It seemed obvious now that we could never compete with other campaign parties around the city.

Jethro tapped my arm, "Give a few words." He pushed me toward the center of the room.

I shouted toward the buzz of arrivals, "Casino-Free—are you here? *(Yeah.)* Are You Here? *(Yes!)* ARE YOU HERE? *(YES!)* First thing—thank you, Kathy, Mary, and everyone for this great food. Thank you to all the volunteers who made this possible. You all are amazing. This whole election is amazing. There are still two hours to vote in Philly's Ballot Box online or via phone. So call your friends and make sure they voted. We'll be sending delegations to election parties, too. For today is a momentous day. Today we have shown that the citizens of Philadelphia can still have a say in their neighborhoods."

Riffing off the crowd's energy, I declared with staccato emphasis, "Philadelphians deserve better than the supreme court. We deserve better than Governor Rendell. Better than our so-called state leaders. Better than casinos in neighborhoods." Escalating to a pitch, "Today we have showed we had a say. All of you are part of something special. It is a movement not of great leaders or powerful interests, but a movement of the grassroots. A movement of people. This is where our power comes from—and today we made it known!"

The crowd cheered, celebrating for hours, far later than most other campaign parties.

After clearing the food and emptying out the office, we held a very late, frosty meeting in the front room.

"We just want *some* results to share," I said, trying to keep open my heavy eyes to glare at Rich. "Something to present to press tomorrow morning."

"We'll emphasize it's just preliminary," said Karim.

"Figure out what you are going to say," said Rich, looking at us blankly, as if unaware of the late hour. "But I'm not releasing the numbers. If we did, they'd assume that's the overall result—and we're not releasing skewed numbers, in any direction."

Jethro and Nick silently nodded in affirmation of Rich's decision. Karim cursed loudly and readjusted his chair, turning away.

"We have the numbers from the phone and online votes," I asked Rich. "Right? *(Right.)* You can see them now, right? *(Right.)* Most elections release preliminary results, right? *(Right.)* But you're not going to release them?"

"Right," said Rich. "Not until we hand-count all of the written ballots, too. That may take until Friday."

His impassivity enraged me. I folded my arm.

Talking vaguely to the air, Karim started, "We'll figure out something..."

I bent forward in my chair, close to Rich's face. "*We* built Philly's Ballot Box. You only came in a few weeks ago. We built it. We need to know it. Give us the numbers."

Rich's face didn't change. "No," he said, as indifferently as before. "Under the rules I set for this election, we only release results when they are completed."

I leaned back in my chair, casting eyes around the room, while Karim stared at the ceiling in frustration. Philly's Ballot Box had real integrity, real boundaries, and I wasn't happy with it.

"Come on." Karim grabbed my arm. "We'll figure out something." We stormed off to a corner to plot how to announce election results tomorrow without numbers.

The next morning, I woke up to my alarm clock blaring at five in the morning. I groggily headed down to the Fox 29 news station in Old City. I continued practicing *the* line Karim and I had written for the morning.

I threw open their entrance door—only to nearly run directly into Michael Nutter.

"Congratulations on your victory," I stuttered, "*Mayor* Nutter." With a politician's smile and handshake, he thanked me and walked out—the first of three times I would follow Nutter in interviews that day.

I meandered upstairs to the second floor, waiting for the interview to begin. I braced myself, knowing that SugarHouse's spokespeople couldn't attack our numerical results, since they didn't have them *either*. They had to destroy our credibility. The camera went live.

"Daniel, I'll start with you. We understand you're still counting votes from yesterday's shadow election. What have you found so far?"

"We are not able to announce preliminary results at this point," I said. "But people were excited. They turned out in high numbers. We were amazed at the response. People showed up at polling locations just to vote on this question—we actually increased voter turnout."

"What is your response to this shadow election?" asked the anchorman, turning to SugarHouse's John Miller, their replacement since Dan Fee's rumor-mongering.

"The notion that this is democracy and the first time we ever had a citizens' election is frankly offensive," John said. "They had ballot boxes at about 3% of polling places. Clearly they cherry-picked places where they thought they would do well. There was about 300,000 votes cast yesterday. If they got more than 10,000, or 20,000, it would be miraculous. Regardless, it is well less than half."

My stomach clenched in cold anger at the dismissive and patronizing tone. *I bet he had a full night's sleep,* I thought idly, remembering to keep a relaxed, beaming face. Miller continued attacking the election, arguing it was time to "put this charade—this little PR stunt—behind us" and move forward with what the voters wanted: gambling.

The anchorman pivoted on Miller. "In all fairness, it did resonate with supporters in some respects, because Tom Knox received quite a few votes, and one of the platforms he ran on was he didn't believe citizens wanted casinos."

"Well, well," John bumbled for a second, "He funded Casino-Free Philadelphia to a large extent. So bully for him. But regardless, they have not won the majority of the votes."

"I can add to that," I jumped in. "Michael Nutter put on his campaign literature 'Vote Yes' on our question—so he was actively campaigning for our issue. Michael Nutter came out and said that he personally doesn't believe casinos should come to Philadelphia, and furthermore, he put forward a proposal without any casino revenue. What we saw was every mayoral candidate—major mayoral candidate—came out and voted in Philly's Ballot Box."

I'd found my stride: upbeat, optimistic, a positive vision for the city. "It was fun, it was exciting—people were very excited to participate, because the casino industry stopped people from voting on this question. The reason they stopped people from voting on the question is because they know the majority of Philadelphians do not believe that casinos should be built right next to residential neighborhoods. That's what every poll says."

John Miller, with an aggressive, almost fatherly tone, struck back. "There is so much misinformation in the anti-casino crowd. This organization has a track record of fraud. They committed mass fraud in their petition drive."

I wanted to jump and correct him, to protect our reputation. But it was more important to win the high ground than to be right. I waited as John continued attacking. "They told everybody who donated to them it was a tax-deductible organization by sending it to an out-of-state nonprofit organization. The fact that we are going to believe more lies is ridiculous."

I had practiced saying the line about a dozen or so times, until Karim and I agreed that I had it down solid. John Miller paused, and I unhurriedly inserted, "John, you really have no credibility on this issue." My tone was sharp, with finality.

As expected, he immediately yelped, defensively, "As opposed to *you?*"

I pivoted back to my positive tone. "We gave Philadelphians an opportunity that you took off the ballot."

John blustered. "Not me!"

I continued, ignoring him. "It's really been an amazing response from Philadelphians. And, you know, if I were in your shoes, I would be wanting to discredit what happened yesterday. It was a phenomenal response from Philadelphians."

For the rest of the interview John squirmed, barely able to contain himself, interrupting me nearly every chance he got. He looked like what he was—a bully.

The Fox interviewer gave me the last word. "We are going to see the results," I said. "It will be a political mandate about whether casinos should be within 1,500 feet of people's homes when they increase crime. That will be the political mandate of the people."

The live feed shut off. I stumbled downstairs, twisting inside with the heated debate still raging within me. All the unsaid statements and defensiveness poured out of me.

But as I walked out into the street, heading east toward the office for another dozen interviews, I allowed myself to feel some pride. We *couldn't* win the argument over numbers, not without any numbers to show. But we could win the argument over which player was more respectful, high-ground, and speaking for Philadelphians.

It was another example of political jujitsu. My playing on those themes, and John's expected childishness in response to being challenged, earned us the high ground once more.

It was the tone for the rest of the week: positive, pro-Philadelphia control over its destiny, and the hopeful day of Philly's Ballot Box.

Rich Garella held up a box amid the room of a half-dozen volunteers. "This is box #57. You can see that no tampering has occurred." He rotated all the sides toward the web camera, which was live-streaming the entire counting process. "I am now opening the box and pouring out the contents."

Rich had a special kind of patience. Unlike the rest of the staff, he plowed right in the day after the election with this counting—no vacation, no day of rest. Two days later, and this was fortieth-odd box doing this ritual, even though we didn't know who was really watching.

Press weren't watching online. Instead, they kept badgering Karim and me about when we'd have *some* preliminary numbers to share. Finally, one reporter unearthed data from a few polling locations where the "Removed by Court Order" sticker was missing. We passed out those results: 70% in favor of a buffer.

"I am now handing out the votes," said Rich. I grabbed a stack of votes, sitting between Andrea Preis and Ramona Johnson. Like Rich, they had been counting each day since the election.

Rich droned on. "Each volunteer has been instructed to correlate the voter's contact information with a voter in the voter database. If it matches and that voter has not voted elsewhere, they open and count the votes. If it does not match, the vote will not count."

I picked up a ballot, questions breaching my mind: *what happens after this? How do we move to the state level? What's next?*

Slowly, my mind to drifted into the repetitive tedium. *Pick up another ballot. Read its address and name. Try to match it with the voting database. If it matches, open up the record inside and record a yes or no vote. If it doesn't, toss it out without opening the inner seal. Repeat.*

For hours without end, dozens of volunteers methodically went through, box by box.

My mind checked out. It was a welcome change of pace to have clear, concrete results.

Hours later, Shirley took me to the front room. It was her serious, I-have-something-to-talk-about face.

"First, I want to thank you for finally hiring a lawyer. Paul and I met with Laura, and she'll be great. She brings exactly the nonprofit law experience we need. And I think we found an accountant, but we *need* a bookkeeper. I hate doing it, and I'm not going to do it for another month."

"You sure you're not about to fall in love with it," I said, poking her.

"No," she frowned. "The sooner you find someone else to do this, the happier *all* of us will be." She glared at me for a half-second, before relaxing into a broad smile.

"I'll do what I can," I said, feeling the rising desperation of being turned down repeatedly.

Shirley nodded. She no longer had any doubts that I was serious about solving our problems. "I just need to be the squeaky wheel. I can't stay in this role much longer."

I nodded and walked into the mostly empty main room. I grabbed a few snacks, wondering about how to find a volunteer bookkeeper. Even with donations growing from Philly's Ballot Box, we didn't have more than a few thousand in the bank. I worried a public ask for volunteers would get a mole from the casinos.

With pretzels in hand, I sat down next to a volunteer. "We've never been formally introduced. I'm Daniel Hunter..."

"I'm Rose Shanahan," she said, offering me a hand.

My mind flashed to Jethro's recent advice to me: "Your biggest problem is you're good at doing a lot of things. You end up carrying everything on your own shoulders, and that's a horrible skill for an organizer. Build relationships by asking people for help."

I turned to Rose. "Rose, can you help me? I'm looking for a bookkeeper who wants to help us."

She nodded quickly, "Sure, I'm a bookkeeper."

"No, seriously," I said. "We're looking for someone open to volunteering with us."

"I am serious."

Rose told me her story of being a professional bookkeeper who had just moved to part-time work and had free time to volunteer with us. Plus, she lived a few blocks from Shirley's house. This must be a cosmic joke.

I made a mental note to tell Jethro he was right: organizers need to ask, and ask, and ask. Though sometimes we get lucky.

I yelled to Shirley in the front room, "I found a bookkeeper for you!"

By Thursday, it was clear we would not finish counting by the weekend. From the couch, I heard Rich's voice, "Here is box #74, you can see no tampering has occurred..."

Across from me sat State Representative Mike O'Brien. He looked more comfortable here than in the stiff settings of government offices. In his husky voice he said, "Can't promise I can pass any legislation. But you tell me what to fight for, and I'll do what I can."

"We want you to stop these two casinos," I said. It meant something that he was the only official to accept our invitation to watch the ongoing counting, but I had learned caution in dealing with politicians.

"I'm not anti-casino. You gotta understand that," he said. "But SugarHouse is bad development and bad use of land. That riverfront could be beautiful, not wasting it with a big box. And I respect my colleague in South Philly about Foxwoods being bad for his community, too. But I'm asking you what you want." He paused to take a drink. "You know how many bills were introduced in the house this year?"

I half-shrugged, hating to come up short on a test.

"Over 3,000. Only a few hundred passed. I can introduce any bill you want," said Mike. "But you've got my word that a straight no-casinos-in-Philadelphia bill won't pass."

My heart wanted to say, *Fight for the no-casino bill.* I wanted the DRNA to be strong enough to carry the 1,500-foot buffer zone, so we could be fully and truly anti-casino. Political impossibilities can change. But even the 1,500-foot buffer would be a stretch.

Even if Republicans came aboard, Rendell, Fumo, and their cronies would fiercely beat it down.

"Fight for the 1,500-foot buffer zone," I said. "Representative Babette Josephs offered to introduce a bill for the buffer zone, so expect to hear from us soon about that. But understand we *are* anti-casino, and you can take that to the bank. We recognize killing casinos outright won't happen at the state level—at least right now. But we do believe that if we can make them move, than all the deals are off and we can open up a real debate about casinos in our city."

It was a bold assumption and a grand strategy that I had eventually persuaded our executive team to adopt. If we could win that the siting was bad and force the casinos to find new spots, whole new neighborhoods would get radicalized and involved—and the casinos would have to jettison all their plans and come up with new ones. That meant new political sweetenings and new backdoor deal-making. All of which we would now have the energy to disturb.

Whether that would work or not, none of us knew. But as Mike shook my hand, I remembered my own quote, now becoming true: Philly's Ballot Box is not legally binding, but we're politically binding.

The next day, I received a fax from Center City's state representative Babette Josephs' office. Babette had joined the tide to protect Philadelphia from casinos, despite voting for Act 71 years earlier. It was the same turn-around we needed from most Philadelphia state politicians.

At first glance, the bill appeared to be everything we wanted. But Paul scrutinized it and noted that the copy of the 1,500-foot buffer for the state wasn't exact. It excluded casinos from nearby places of worship, schools, and playgrounds—but not homes.

Having been schooled in the rough waters of Philadelphia politics, Paul and I immediately wondered if it was a ploy. Maybe she was introducing the bill only to control it and screw us later. Maybe she was being put up to it by Fumo or Rendell to give us false hope.

I called her office.

"It was totally an oversight," said her legislative aide. "Please suggest better language."

My heart skipped. *Babette is an experienced legislator, and I'm an inexperienced citizen who's never interacted with a piece of formal legislation in my life.* I barely had time to recover when the legislative aide added, "The drafting attorney must have just neglected adding homes."

I almost asked if this was how government was actually run. I had surprised myself with some naïve assumption that politicians have the resources to actually look at the bills they draft and write. In my mind, I deleted that assumption.

Paul led a team to draft language with a fine-tooth comb and make sure all the technical ends were tightened up. We sent the draft back to Babette's staff, who made all the changes we requested, after sending it through their own lawyers and—some part of me still hoped—Babette.

With a bill in the house to fight for, we now just needed it to get introduced with dozens of sign-ons from other legislators, miraculously pass the Pennsylvania House of

Representatives, get introduced in the even tougher Senate, and get passed there, too—only to have them all do it again when the governor vetoed.

All the while, Rich continued leading the counting: "Box #33..."

It was Monday. A packed crowd of supporters filled the lines of chairs, flanked by a dozen reporters to their left and a fleet of TV cameras in the back—including our own webcasting the entire event. Never before had so many journalists been in our office.

Giddy with excitement, I bopped between supporters, hugging and thanking them, declining to give them the results quite yet. They would find out very soon.

Rich started the press conference, reviewing the scope of the campaign: "Number of volunteers working on election day: 293. Volunteer hours to verify votes: 288. Number of radio ads publicizing: 66. Number of ads in city and neighborhood newspapers: 13. Miles that an Iraq War vet drove to deliver ballot boxes from Chicago: 761. Ballots included in tally that did not match a registered voter: 0."

I watched as print reporters didn't scribble down a single word.

"Fact sheets will be distributed after I speak," I said. "It includes notes from our election monitor, who found the election fair and witnessed no problems, except long lines of people patiently trying to vote in our election. But you all want the results, right?"

"*Right!*" shouted supporters.

My heart leapt with excitement. "After tallying the 13,319 registered voters, the results of Philly's Ballot Box are in," I said. "Philadelphians do *not* want casinos in neighborhoods—95% to 5%!"

The crowd erupted in cheers from supporters. *Can you believe it? That's incredible!*

I waited for the crowd to settle before continuing. "Nowhere were there less than 84% of voters in our favor. But that's not the biggest news."

After the last hours with Karim crunching numbers, I didn't even need to look at our handouts. "At each precinct, our turnout was 68% of active voters where we had a Philly's Ballot Box. So catch this carefully. Even if *every* person who passed our ballot box but voted in the other election had cast a *no* vote for us, *we still would have won with a strong majority of the vote!*"

Statistically, that was significant. Voting is more reliable statistically than polling. And our election was statistical gold.

I smiled around the room, seeing tears in some supporters' eyes.

Free from any emotional connection, reporters immediately badgered, "So now that this is over, what's next?"

Frustrated, I connected the question back to the issue for the day. "This may not have been legally binding, but it is politically binding. Philadelphia has spoken, and the message is clear. We want a buffer between casinos and neighborhoods. In the attached handouts, you can see we show support in every City Council district, every state representative's and every state senator's district. These results are our mandate, and from here we move to have our voices heard in City Hall and in Harrisburg."

We had weathered a major storm. I finished up and shared hugs and kisses with supporters. *This* was worth celebrating!

CHAPTER 12
Aftershock

MAY 21, 2007—JUNE 23, 2007

*dishonestly dangling a break as a carrot • getting stuck in crisis mode •
creating a culture that doesn't internalize the stress •
dampening rumors is an organizer's job • a good loss can be the best teacher •
declaring victory—nobody else will do it for you •
high-ground culture trumps walking on eggshells*

WHEN EVERYONE LEFT after the Philly's Ballot Box announcement, Karim and I happily closed the front door and relished the silence of our office's humming. We didn't clean up the chairs or scattered papers. He and I didn't even say anything to each other as we spread out in the office. I collapsed into a nearby couch, considering a nap. Instead, I found myself idly surfing the internet.

This was what I had earned: some time for reprieve. Not just these few minutes of quiet, but the satisfaction that having climbed over the mountain of Philly's Ballot Box, nobody thought we were going away anymore. We could take time to regroup and prepare for what was next—finally without being dictated by crisis. And thank goodness for that!

I leisurely read articles on issues unrelated to casino gambling, by reporters who covered our movement. The more I learned how those reporters wrote about, what they noticed, and what they cared about, the better I would be at working with them.

A few hours later, when the first article on Philly's Ballot Box appeared, I was excited. *How will they capture all that energy of the past intense month? How will they show the power we've built?*

It was not what I had hoped for.

The *Inquirer* gave large chunks of its article to our opposition. It reported our numbers, but then quoted SugarHouse calling the results "statistically insignificant" since only 1% of the city's population voted at under 3% of the polling sites. "This isn't a mandate, it's an embarrassment."

Foxwoods piled on. "We've always said that only a vocal minority oppose these casinos. This vote dispels the myth that Philadelphians are opposed to casinos."

I couldn't believe it. I felt nauseated and angry. But as the articles kept coming, most were like that.

For a while I kicked myself, turning my anger inward, forming it as guilt. *I should have pitched the numbers harder. I should have thought ahead how the casinos would discredit us and prepared reporters better.*

I reminded myself that's how media goes some days. It's just a set of second-rate articles, which do nothing to take away the tide of Philly's Ballot Box. We had permanently seared in Philadelphia's consciousness that this fight was the people versus powerful casinos—and that we had a chance to win.

I willed myself to relax and returned to my blissful state, relaxing after nearly two months of nonstop work.

Then independent journalist and supporter Ed Goppelt called me.

His voice betrayed his own anger. "I know this isn't what you want to hear. But the Philadelphia City Planning Commission is taking up SugarHouse's proposal tomorrow. SugarHouse wants their stamp of approval before going to council. We're only getting a twenty-four-hour warning—and near as I can tell, it doesn't even have a location public yet."

I sat up heavily and closed my computer. *Right after Philly's Ballot Box? Can't we get one day off?*

It was then that I half-realized I had created a dangerous belief: that I'd get deep rest and relaxation in the wake of Philly's Ballot Box's tidal waves. I'd used that belief as a crutch to get me waking up each morning day after day—a belief that's mobilized many organizers through tough, exhausting times. But it was a delusion.

When I got off the phone, I yelled out, "Karim! We have to work tomorrow!"

But I wasn't ready to let go of the delusion. I told myself: *It's just one day of work. Then I'll get sleep.*

Two days later, annoyed, I headed into the darkened auditorium of the Free Library's basement, wading through the procedural patters of the Philadelphia City Planning Commission. It was a dull hearing, punctuated only by frustrated CFP members cheering each other's testimony—even while the pit of our stomachs knew the outcome was preordained.

I took some deep breaths, stretched my neck, and noticed my aching tiredness and sore jaw. More than anything, I wanted to avoid the pestering question "What's next?" from reporters and activists—because I just plain didn't know.

I had no doubt SugarHouse was off their game plan. Instead of a slick presentation, it was littered with wrong slides, faulty facts, and an odd Freudian slip from the presenter that "the new casino will be a great place to take a shower." *But maybe it doesn't matter— maybe the suspicious press were right that we only got any support because it's an election year. Maybe it's all over.*

Yet we had every politician touching the issue—and things *felt* ready for a major political breakthrough. Maybe City Council would openly flaunt the supreme court and pass the buffer referendum. Maybe this commission would surprise us. Or maybe the

House of Representatives would pass our buffer zone, recently introduced by State Representative Babette Josephs, out of committee.

I didn't know and felt frustrated to be at this hearing instead of out talking to members. I wanted to return to street-level organization. *But* this hearing had been called last-minute — just one more slight to add to my list of grievances.

The planning commission's recommendation was abrupt. Halting further testimony, a commission member called the SugarHouse project to vote, resulting in jeers from the crowd. The member bristled, "I listened to all your bullshit out there" and had his motion seconded, then passed unanimously.

The Philadelphia City Planning Commission had now endorsed SugarHouse's plan. The finger of responsibility no longer pointed solely at the state — it was now poised at the city, too. I was too stunned to feel anything. It was a slap in the face, just after everything...

I ducked and weaved as reporters tried to pin me down on what was next for us. I didn't know — but I assured them we'd have a response soon enough.

I was gathering my stuff to leave the auditorium when a volunteer came up to me with more bad news: Councilman Juan Ramos had just introduced the zoning bill for SugarHouse, bypassing council's norms for respecting DiCicco's leadership as head of that district.

Armed with the planning commission recommendation, council could cave, and SugarHouse could get all the requirements it needed to start building by the summer.

Okay, we address this crisis. Then I get a summer break.

My delusion was well alive.

I hadn't seen Jethro since his vacation post-Philly's Ballot Box. When I arrived in the office, ahead of our executive team meeting, I was surprised to see Jethro looking haggard, his eyes burning. Not that I felt much better, but he didn't ask me how things were going or even hug me. He just blurted, "DiCicco needs to publicly scold Ramos!"

I shrugged noncommittally and slouched into a couch. It seemed pretty evident that the mayor had struggled to find anyone to introduce the bill and that Ramos wasn't exactly popular for what he had done. The mayor had admitted that "no one else wanted to" introduce the bill, before his spokesman reframed that he had *meant* that Ramos introduced the bill because he lived sort of close to the site.

"Who is this guy? He's some lame-duck councilman that his constituents didn't even like and he doesn't know anything about my neighborhood or what's going on. DiCicco should be up in arms, instead of saying some weak bullshit that the legislation is 'a little bit premature.'"

"I feel you," I said, nodding my head. "But we aren't DiCicco. We have to figure out what *we're* going to do. What do you think *we* should do? I'm tired and we all need to stop being in crisis, reactive mode. It's unhealthy, and it's getting to me. I can't be my creative, brilliant self tactically while I feel wiped out just answering press wondering if it's all downhill."

"You're doing great," he said, mindlessly patting my arm. "But this is terrible! I could have a casino building this summer —" He halted abruptly and leaned on a chair, as if he were going to sit down. Instead, he straightened his back. "You know what you call a group of ducks?"

In response, I just eyed him.

"It's a *paddling*."

I looked at him. "What are you *talking* about?"

"The lame-ducks Mayor Street and Ramos. We should give his paddling of lame ducks the paddle. Or if council caves, there will just be a larger paddling in four years. I even created a blog called *Paddle of Ducks*."

I rolled my eyes. "Come back to us, Jethro! We need to figure out a serious plan to respond!"

Instead, I watched in a mix of horror and amazement as Jethro continued to ramble about his blog. Watching him rapidly move from fist-pounding to wild arm-waving, I touched base with my own internal lurching. The waves of negative emotions had weighed me down. But it hadn't been only bad news since Philly's Ballot Box.

There had been the post-election celebration, generating 105,000 emails to state representatives for the state buffer bill, and the news article days earlier from *Philadelphia* magazine, which still thrilled my heart.

That article had been *the* perfect article. It started by meticulously detailing Governor Rendell and Senator Fumo's journey to create Act 71 by earmarking millions of dollars for representatives' pet projects. It went much further than anything else, detailing how Pennsylvania politicians had received over $6 million in donations from the casino industry, many close friends of Fumo and Rendell. It explained peculiarities in Act 71's law, like a ten-mile buffer zone around horse race tracks, which virtually forced Philadelphia casinos onto the riverfront, where—*surprise!*—Rendell and Fumo had friends with land ready to build casinos. Money from casino investors went to Rendell and Fumo, who created the casino law and hand-picked people for the PGCB, like a lawyer from the Cozen O'Connor firm named Tad Decker—who had given more than $113,000 personally to Rendell.

The article explained, "Decker left the firm when he took the gaming job, but has continued to meet privately with the firm's president and CEO, Pat O'Connor, a longtime friend. SugarHouse hired the firm two weeks before the winning casinos were selected. Richard Sprague, another powerful local attorney, is a SugarHouse investor, and has for years represented—and here we come full circle—Vince Fumo, mastermind of Act 71."

The author then confronted Decker on the "relationships and perceived conflicts of interest"—since Rendell and Fumo refused to be interviewed—and Decker threatened the reporter, saying, "Why don't you say that publicly, put it in your article, and I'll sue your ass off!" The reporter put it in print.

It was another example of the power of Philly's Ballot Box—even without further framing on our part, we were getting phenomenal press, hands down the best yet—and one we happily bought and got on the desk of every councilmember and state representative.

As I sat in my chair, even then I had delusions of grandeur, imagining that *now* this would help us return to the offensive. I knew we needed to be there, and I thought somehow this article would spur indictments, prosecutions, and true exposure.

Just as Jethro was going up and down—and currently stuck in a loop about a paddling of ducks—all of us were getting stuck riding the waves of an emotional tidal wave. Instead of surfing them, though, we were lurching with and ripped apart by them. We were too raw, too exhausted with moving *against* the times, instead of just *moving the times.*

As if trying to take control of my own internal state, I cut off Jethro sharply. "You're losing perspective!"

He looked slapped, but quieted.

"I am, too," I said quickly. "We need to lean on each other. Your blog is fine and good if you're just releasing your anger and getting your creative juices flowing. It's fine as self-expression, but it's a dead-end for building our power. Don't do what other activists do and get those two confused. As for me, I'm lost about where to go. I know politicians will actually respect us more if we *keep* leading and organizing social power, not like those in the DRNA who are urging politicians to take the lead. But... where to go?"

Jethro paused for a second, and I worried he was going to keep talking about the blog. His voice was relaxed. "Okay, let's think it through."

For the next half-hour, we sorted through the divergent forces at play. The mayor was clearly pro-SugarHouse. And Ramos was just a tool, likely trading this favor for a cushy post-government job. But DiCicco's role was as murky as ever and would be tested when council committee voted in a few weeks. If it was unanimous for SugarHouse, then DiCicco had caved and SugarHouse would start building in the summer.

As we said it, a chill went through us. Having come so far with Philly's Ballot Box, it felt horrible that we could lose it all so quickly.

The rest of the executive team arrived in the offices, weary and exhausted. Karim loved intensity but was exceptionally snappy and caustic. When he wasn't doing something, he seemed lost, and he fell right into sync with the fatigued Anne and a nearly silent Paul—even as Paul occasionally looked up to say he was now unwilling to win anything less than complete elimination of casinos in Philadelphia. Kathy and Shirley were uncharacteristically late.

I was preparing to start the meeting when Kathy and Shirley burst into the offices. I tensed up at their beeline straight toward me, bracing for more bad news.

They exchanged glances, as a smile crept over Shirley's office. "Happy Birthday!" they shouted in unison.

I clapped my hands—I had forgotten!

Shirley thrust cookies into my hands. "We couldn't find vegan cake, so here you go." Paul plopped a bright-red party hat on my head.

As the executive team sang, I relaxed. *We're building organizations to fight and love. Our culture isn't going to internalize the external stress. We're still good to each other.* Jethro told me to take a week-long vacation as my birthday gift. The external circumstances needn't taint our relationships.

I took a week-long vacation trip. There, I only thought of casinos while asleep.

*　　　*　　　*

Despite my renewed post-vacation energy, when I returned to Philly I sensed something simmering underneath, buried deep. It was dark and brooding, like a threatening shadow. It showed itself with my constant refrain to Jethro, "We need a new campaign," and my worry that we weren't advancing anything and would get stuck permanently in a defensive posture.

Not that I didn't feel better, because I did.

My empathy for my opponents returned. Instead of being surprised at their actions, they made sense. After the supreme court ruling, pro-casino folks must have thought they were moving into the clear—and then we ran Philly's Ballot Box. Their media team would find it bruising to lose complete and utter control of the media narrative. Their political advisors must have worked hard to convince themselves that politicians were merely playing populist for a few votes. Our joint press announcement with Rep. Babette Josephs on the buffer zone's introduction to the state—supported by a majority of the Philadelphia delegation—would have only caused further concern. Now, their preparing a counter-offensive made total sense—and they had used the time of Philly's Ballot Box to prepare.

And I felt lighter when we heard bad news. Like when our newly hired nonprofit lawyer told us that the state had rejected our application for a minor form to register to solicit charitable donations. She had never seen anything like it in her years of nonprofit work and was surprised enough that even she was suspicious of political motives. But instead of getting angry or caught in the flow, it only made me laugh. "Powerful opponents in the state hate us. Tell us something we don't know. Stay on it, we'll get it filed."

But there was that aching feeling beneath my own self-description as being relaxed after my vacation.

I knew the feeling most as the troubling lack of strategic direction. Philly's Ballot Box had given us all something to do. Now it was easy for the movement to fracture into merely responding to our opponents' moves. When DiCicco agreed to meet with pro-casino group FACT, Jethro's neighbors responded vociferously and built their own counter group: Fishtown Against SugarHouse Takeover, or FAST. FAST attacked DiCicco's meeting and decried his apparent dishonesty when he revealed he met with Foxwoods "three weeks ago" to "look at alternative sites, beyond the boundaries of his district."

Our ally, the Delaware Riverfront Neighborhood Alliance, went another way—several ways, in fact. Without a campaign created by CFP, they wrestled with mission and tried a little of many things: lobby visits in the Harrisburg state house for passage of Babette Josephs' bill, influencing media reporting with editorial visits, recruiting more civic associations, tightening their internal decision-making structure, and accepting high-level meetings with Senator Fumo and others.

But all that chaotic disagreement over strategy escalated geographical and factional differences. The last DRNA meeting I had attended descended into alpha-male rivalry as one leader threw a chair and challenged another leader to a fistfight. Though still miraculously holding civics back from negotiating with the casinos, the group was spiraling toward mistrust and split directions, frustrated by the many possible directions to invest time and energy.

As if looking for targets, some members began attacking CFP for our "subversive anti-casino agenda"—worried that CFP's goal was too radical in the face of their more modest goal to protect their neighborhoods. Gossip leaked out of DRNA meetings and emails, in which CFP was accused of "controlling the media" or lobbying for the state bill merely for our own glory.

I tried to dampen rumors. *No, CFP is not trying to control DRNA—in fact, we're going to stop attending meetings to keep the separation more clear. And No, the DRNA is not controlled by Fumo—or DiCicco—or Dougherty. And DiCicco is allowed to meet with his constituents, it doesn't mean he sold out—but we have to stay on him. And If DRNA wants media, we won't fight them for it, but they can't send a three-day-old press release and expect deadline-tormented reporters to cover it.*

I joked that 75% of my job had become squashing rumors. But all jokes have meaning, and mine certainly did.

The shadows grew, telling me we weren't advancing anything. There was no campaign, no graceful transition to the state level to push the buffer bill there.

That energetic falling off is so common after massive direct actions that I felt I should have seen it coming. But whether I had or not, I didn't have a plan. Unlike our normal way of operating, we hadn't planned two actions ahead. Just this one.

I pressed forward, continuing to dangle taking a longer break like a carrot before my own eyes. *For now, I work to stop SugarHouse from getting permits. Then I'll take a break.*

I was stuck in defense. I didn't like it. But I didn't see how to get out of it.

Returning to council chambers for the vote on the SugarHouse zoning permits felt like a failure of sorts. I didn't want to be there and told as much to the hardcore retirees sitting in the front row, donned in their red *CasiNO!* T-shirts.

"We have to be here to show them we won't go away," said Mary Reinhart. Her face was set, with a stern chin and thin glasses, like a librarian who was unrelenting on late books. "Besides, we heard the building trades unions were coming in force. We needed to get here early to hold onto the front seats."

I held my tongue on saying 7 A.M. was *plenty* early. "It is going to be packed," I admitted. "Everyone is supposed to be here, so thanks for coming early. I even asked for a second room for overflow, because I think this will be the largest turnout yet."

Kathy DeAngelis peeked from behind a sign. She was an ideal volunteer, willing to pitch in wherever and always with a ready hug and laugh, but today even her face looked severe and worn down. "I went with the DRNA lobbying team, and three councilmembers said they'd vote with us. But most wouldn't say anything, and a lot of them were pretty hostile to us. Do we have a chance?"

I wanted to throw up my hands—*How would I know?* Yet my voice was relaxed. "You remember Councilman Greenlee? To help get re-elected, he falsely advertised that he and Councilman Kenney had introduced the buffer zone. Well, now he won't say he's with us. A big reason is the building trades union funded him in the past, and he wants to win back their support. It's like that for a lot of them."

Mary impatiently interrupted me before I could say more. "So it's over? You know I trust you, and if you think there's something we could do, let us know so we can do it."

I continued. "I also think something happened that's big—bigger than our few lobby visits and bigger than the casinos' moves these past weeks. Because council had something stolen from them by the supreme court. They lost *their* rights and authority when the supreme court squashed on them. And nothing can motivate people like a good loss—so I'm actually hopeful. They're pissed!"

I flashed a smile. They knew what I was talking about. We were unhooked from the political "realism" of the media aristocracy and didn't have to write foundation reports requiring us to frame *everything* as a victory. We had shown how a good loss can be the best teacher.

"That doesn't mean I believe we will win today," I said. "I honestly don't know. But we're trying to reframe this argument yet again, bringing in the social costs of casinos."

Kathy asked, "You think the *Wall Street Journal* article was because of us?"

I was taken aback. "I hadn't considered that. It's probably just because of the national growth in the industry. But it is the case that they're making our argument that casinos are a zero-sum game. And it's enabled us to use that with other reporters, because like a lot of industries, reporters actually trust each other more than their sources, activists, or even economists. So that's why the *Inquirer* and the *Daily News* covered it—even when we've been saying this stuff for months."

"Plus, I'm sure we nudged them," said Mary.

"Karim worked hard on that," I said, smiling. "But now we have, on the desk of every councilmember, copies of Philly's Ballot Box in their districts, plus articles concluding that the net cost of a casino is at least ninety-seven dollars per resident per year. CFP is going to live up to its name as an anti-casino campaign."

Yet even as I thought that, like a punch in the gut, I berated myself: *We need a real campaign.*

I headed toward a seat as chambers filled up—even faster than usual, 200 citizens on every side of the issue cramming in. Someone whispered to me that the second overflow room was already filling up.

On my way to my seat, a Foxwoods attorney snatched me aside and nastily said, "I'll wipe the floor with you people." I was surprised at how heated everyone felt—but merely ignored him and walked away.

The testimony began with its regular set of talking points: pro-casino forces lamenting the "costly delay of thousands of jobs and millions of revenue to the city" and our forces challenging the process, the lack of studies, the suffering caused by casinos.

As if to distract us from the dragging testimony, the increasingly red-faced chairwoman banged her gavel ineffectually to quiet the divided and often contentious booing—or cheering—crowd. "We've had enough entertainment for this morning," she pleaded. Unusually flustered when people only booed more, she threatened to shut down the hearing if people weren't silent. Folks shouted back: "Please do!"

Frank DiCicco's late entrance emitted boos from the pro-casino forces. To them, he represented the political roadblock to getting casinos built. Not to be outdone, the much louder and more numerous anti-casino movement gave him a standing ovation. I was surprised to even see Paul joining in the chanting and warm fist-shaking: "Frank! Frank! Frank!"

The positive feelings toward Frank were spurred by his recent unequivocal advocacy for council to pass the 1,500-foot buffer *instead* of Ramos' bill. Maybe DiCicco needed to be the underdog to do his best work, because now that things seemed most dire, he quickly tore into the city planning commission. The commission's director withered under DiCicco's finger-waving questioning and quietly admitted that neither Foxwoods nor SugarHouse were "ideal" sites—an admission that caught the eye of the rarely politically astute TV stations, which replayed her admission for days. Despite her stamp of approval, the city's planning director admitted the casinos were bad sites because of their "proximity to neighborhoods."

Casino-Free Philly's only new contribution to the hearings was the testimony of economist Robert Goodman and local professor Dr. Fred Murphy. Goodman was a plain-spoken academic who had carried out the country's largest casino study not funded by the casino industry. "The number of problem gamblers will increase," he testified. "Every researcher says that—even the gambling industry's researchers say it. But *problem* gamblers don't pay their debts. They tend to embezzle money at work. They tend to write bad checks. Fraud on credit cards. A whole host of other things. So now you have money being lost to other people. And you're picking up the social costs." Goodman explained how he had tried to find any other place in the country where casinos were within 200 feet of a community. "I hadn't seen it. I was curious, so I decided to check it out. I knew they put some in Detroit. So I called up people at Wayne State in Detroit and talked to the city planning department. Where is the closest to a residential community? Half a mile away. Even Detroit wouldn't experiment with casinos close to neighborhoods!"

We were tilting to a truly anti-casino position, aided by Dr. Murphy's research, who used Goodman's data to show that Philadelphia would lose about 4,000 jobs and $26.1 million, money moved from the city's economy to the profits of investors in Chicago, Connecticut, or the Philadelphia suburbs.

Hours later, public testimony finished.

Instead of immediately voting, councilmembers pulled themselves into a huddle with frantic whispers. DiCicco looked angry, as members pulled in aides.

This is American democracy, I thought, *elected officials playing power games while the people watch on.*

With little pomp, the chairwoman announced, "All the bills will be held. No vote today."

Kathy and Mary swiveled around to look at me. Somewhere I heard some of our people making a noise that could be construed as cheering.

Councilman Greenlee muted the crowd. Addressing civic leaders, he said, "Strike a deal with the casinos now. This summer is your last chance."

Councilman Clarke grabbed a microphone to emphasize the point. "I have seen no evidence that there is going to be any changing of the city sites by the state or by either of parties involved."

I immediately worried. *Will Whitman or others split from the coalition? Will the already tenuous Fishtown neighborhood group negotiate with SugarHouse up North? This could doom the DRNA—and rip our movement apart.*

Even then, I could sense what I would later confirm, that DiCicco had the votes to kill Ramos' SugarHouse bill. But DiCicco was out-maneuvered, and council was crumbling. Defeat hung in the air.

But in movement after movement, I'd learned that pundits, politicians, and press will almost never give credit to a social movement for anything. If we don't declare success, nobody will do it for us. They'll only note every movement failing.

I immediately reframed what we *had* just achieved: a whole summer without any casinos—with no chance until October for SugarHouse to get its city permits.

After the council meeting, I wrote an email to our supporters, "Accept this huge success up against a Goliath of an industry! We now have three-and-a-half months to continue our organizing." I abbreviated testimony from ILA's Jim Paylor, Allen Street neighbors Charlie Hocker and Joanne Sherman, and Jeff Rush of DRNA and Queen Village. We had stalled SugarHouse's zoning legislation, miraculously held onto DiCicco, and commenced the battle of the economic argument against casinos.

Our members poured out a torrent of congratulatory emails. As if a dam had broken since Philly's Ballot Box, there was a palpable sense of relief. Chuck Valentine wrote of "eyes welling up with tears of joy... Our tiring work is paying off because it is genuine and the purpose and intent is well rooted in what is right." He was followed closely with congratulations from over two-dozen supporters.

The luxury of time, I told myself, meant we *finally* had the chance to allow ourselves to regroup, refocus, and return on the offensive. We were *now* on the upswing and we'd get both a break and time to build a new campaign.

It was the same belief, wrapped in new clothing.

Inside, I was still deep in crisis mode, frozen in a reactionary posture. It made it hard to get out there and reframe the debate—no press quoted us on our new tilt to the economic argument—and it was unusually challenging for me to generate new tactics or even the beginnings of tactics.

We still had nothing planned—not even a single action coming up.

But at least we'd managed to grow our team a little more.

The following day, I prepared our executive team for our newest executive team member. I had invited Nico Amador because his timing was perfect. He was moving from California right after Philly's Ballot Box, when we needed an energy infusion from outside our movement. And Nico brought a history of direct action, something few others in our movement had. "Nico Amador wanted me just to say a little bit about him," I said. "He's moving here to work with me at Training for Change. He's a young, sharp, mestizo man with experience in organizing anti-war and anti-military recruitment work." I took a deep breath. Nico had told me how he wanted to be introduced, and I loved and trusted our team, but I was still nervous about how his identity would be received. "And he's transgender."

"What's that?" asked Shirley.

"It means that he was originally born in a woman's body but identifies as a guy."

The group looked around awkwardly. "Uhm, so he's a woman?" asked Paul.

"No. He grew up raised as a woman. But he identifies as a guy. So when talking about him, we just call him a guy, like me or Jethro."

Slowly, quietly, Shirley replied, "You mean like me?"

I choked. Kathy gasped. Paul's eyes grew wide.

Shirley, looking at the puzzled faces, went on. "I mean, I was a guy who identifies as a woman."

The silence descended into confusion.

"Like you, Paul," Shirley said, a small grin on her face.

"Yeah, like me," nodded Paul. "I was a woman who identifies as a guy."

My head swiveled to look at Paul. *Have I been making wrong assumptions this whole time? What's happening?*

Jethro broke into a smirk. "Yeah, me too. I still identify as a woman."

I looked around the room, baffled. Shirley prodded. "Like you, Daniel!"

"Ah... yes... like me."

The group began laughing. Kathy was the last to finally catch on. By the time she did, we were all uproariously laughing about our own if only temporarily—shifted identities. None of us were really transgender, but the laughter at no one's expense lightened us up. Without tip-toeing through political correctness or gratingly polite uptightness, we talked frankly: *No, it's not his original name but it's best to just get to know his current name. Yes, he prefers male pronouns. Whether he takes hormones or not shouldn't really matter—though he's open that he does.*

Shirley asked the grand finale: "Will he help us win against casinos?" When I nodded, Shirley sat back in her chair and smiled the serene smile of Buddha. "That's all we really need to know."

That was it. High-ground organizing invites a high-ground culture. When he arrived, Nico found CFP one of the easiest spaces for him to work. People were open about questions, relaxed when they made pronoun mistakes, and clear about our shared goals.

By early June, it felt almost eerie to be meeting in the CFP offices. Ghosts of Philly's Ballot Box lay scattered around. We were a movement between campaigns—our own empty-nest syndrome. I longed for the clarity and momentum of our past campaign, yet felt slow, stuck, with no creativity pouring from my pores.

Paul showed all the energy I didn't have. He ran breathlessly into the room and dropped into the empty seat on the couch. He nearly shouted. "People are energized! We need to create another Philly's Ballot Box!"

I stopped myself from rolling my eyes. I looked at Paul's boyish grin and wondered if he was addicted to the rush of campaign adrenaline. It's literally addictive, and, like skydivers or bungee-jumpers, activists can become consumed by seeking the next high. I wondered if Paul needed to take more walks or run to release the adrenaline pent up in his system.

Kathy did roll her eyes. "Paul, you're late."

Paul smiled on, ear-to-ear like a muppet. "I'm here now! I've got big news—"

"There's always news," Shirley cut him off. She turned to face the sitting team. "Daniel thinks it would help if all of us build our facilitation skills. So we're going to start rotating facilitation, and I'm facilitating this meeting. I even made an agenda like Daniel, but unfortunately without the pretty colors." She unrolled a newsprint with the agenda and made a big show of checking off the first item: *agenda review.*

We whipped through updates on how to pass the buffer zone at the state level. We had a dozen co-sponsors, including the bulk of the Philadelphia delegation, but none of the major Philly power players like Dwight Evans, who was walking back his support of the bill post-election.

Unable to wait any longer, Paul burst, "The DRNA met with Fumo last night!" He avoided Shirley's chastising stare for interrupting. "The Fumocrats were fawning over him as usual. And Fumo, of course, played the 'I'm powerless' card and told us the deal was beyond his control. He nearly ordered us to spend the summer negotiating with the casinos."

Kathy pretended to gag.

"Don't worry, everybody stayed strong," said Paul. "They kept pushing until Fumo..." He paused dramatically. "Until Fumo agreed to introduce the 1,500-foot buffer at the state level."

Shirley dropped her marker in shock. "The senator who introduced this whole debacle..."

Karim stuttered. "What? That's great... No, that can't be... Wait. *What exactly did he say?*"

"He promised to introduce a copy of the 1,500-foot buffer into the Senate, *just like House Bill 1477.*"

Shirley spoke our minds first. "It must be a trick. What's the catch?"

I clapped. "Now you're thinking like an activist, Shirley! Love that fresh skepticism."

Shirley whipped her head toward me. "I am not an *activist!*" She almost spat the words.

Surprised, I stifled a laugh. "Organizing with a radical grassroots group for over six months? Yeah, sorry Shirley, you're what an activist looks like."

Shirley shrugged her shoulders in passive acceptance. Oblivious to that dynamic, Paul blurted, "I fear he's two steps ahead of us and is trying to own the legislation. If it's his bill, he can hold it, table it, all without consulting us. Then he can pull the rug out from underneath us."

"It *could* be a trick," said Jethro cautiously. "But it's also true we just organized 7,000-some voters in his district—"

"7,911 voters," I interrupted, fresh from wading through district-by-district statistics. "Of whom 7,508 voted for the buffer zone."

"Point is," continued Jethro, "the vast majority wanted the buffer zone. He'll do what it takes to win next year's upcoming election."

"I still think it's a trick," said Paul.

"I think you're right to think it's a trick," said Jethro. "But we're not tricked if the DRNA holds strong and doesn't let go of him."

Shirley looked around, as if suddenly remembering there was an agenda. "So, what do *we* do?"

It was relieving to not be facilitating and holding the group to its task—because I felt no more sense than anyone else about what was next. Our list of targets had grown exponentially. On top of all our past targets, we had an even more hostile mayor, crumbling civic associations, the planning commission, and—Jethro kept reminding us—Ramos, too!

"We need to return to door-to-door organizing and go citywide," said Jethro. "I fear we get crushed by other parts of the city clamoring for casino jobs without realizing their own neighborhoods will suffer when people go bankrupt at the casinos."

I pulled out my calendar with my own worries and quietly drew a big circle around October 4—the earliest SugarHouse could get its zoning. *If we spend too much energy at the state level with Fumo, will we lose City Council?*

Kathy matter-of-factly turned to Jethro and me. "We're here to win. What do we have to do to pass the 1,500-foot buffer at the state?"

Jethro and I looked like deer in headlights. "We're making this up as we're going along," Jethro admitted.

Nico filled in the subsequent awkward pause. New to the team, he was unconnected to our feeling of being stuck. His voice hit us like a gong. "You all sound more down than I think you need to be. I mean, I can see why you feel pretty downcast. But people outside this meeting don't see you that way. People really respect you, and everyone I've talked with feels pretty hopeful. It really seems like you need to get back to doing what you do best, which is actions. I'm not saying you don't keep lobbying or do other stuff, but it seems like you all feel really worried, when what people need from you is direction on who they should target—they're ready to go!"

Nico's words struck a chord in me. I took a breath and said with conviction, "To win, we need to pick a bigger target than just the mayor or Ramos   we have to set our sights higher."

"Senator Fumo makes a lot of sense," said Jethro. His voice was noncommittal and casual, like an evening stroll. "He's clearly up to something."

I spoke quickly, with decisiveness. "But targeting Fumo will only raise the ire of the DRNA, which is second-guessing our motivations. They'll think we're trying to outplay them—and besides, Fumo needs the space to walk back his previously completely pro-casino position. He's too vindictive. Targeting him might make him harden his current stance." I shook my head. "No, the person to target is who we've tried to position so he wouldn't have to openly oppose us, hoping he'd play the hero. But he keeps maneuvering against us and making it impossible to win at the state level, no matter how effectively we lobby. It's time to use the summer to engage him as a public opponent." Heads nodded emphatically, knowing where I was going.

"It's time to get Governor Rendell," I said.

We just needed to figure out how.

CHAPTER 13
Governor Rendell's Picnic

JUNE 24, 2007 — JULY 31, 2007

*going up the political ladder, picking bigger targets • when in doubt, do something •
open sharing to set free buried anger • using times of creativity to inspire good planning •
sometimes you're lucky • negotiating with wheeler-dealers •
letting some fires burn on their own •
fear is a natural reaction to trauma, but fighting the injustice is healthier •
surfing the wave of people's emotions • getting an engaged opponent •
letting people do their (crazy) best thinking*

AFTER TWO WEEKS OF DISCUSSION, we had not found a way to get to the governor. It felt tricky. Governor Ed Rendell was a masterful fundraiser and experienced politician, with a fleet of public-relations specialists whose sole goal was to protect his image. He carried an 88% approval rating from Philadelphians—many who had loved him since he was mayor of the city and turned around a massive debt crisis—so it was difficult to coalesce our allies to challenge him directly. Even the media loved him—because he was loud and brash, and his big mouth was always quotable.

But we felt certain it was time to engage him. We had worked our way up the political ladder. Exposing the PGCB made it possible to win over City Council. That made it possible to move Fumo. We believed we had finally grown powerful enough to take on the governor.

Yet at our June executive meeting, even Jethro sounded unusually uncertain. "With Rendell and the Senate entering their annual fight over budget priorities, can we somehow connect us to the budget negotiations?"

Karim sighed. "It's way too late to insert ourselves. And he's been at such arm's length on this, he's been able to dupe people so they don't see how pro-casino he's been. To pull him out of the woodwork, we have to make this personal."

I kept quiet as people threw out considerations. I noted vaguely that we weren't really getting into Rendell's head—but stuck in our own. *It's okay, I guess, since this is just an opening sally. We don't know that much about him. We really need to do an action to stay in the mix, since we haven't proactively planned any action since Philly's Ballot Box, almost two months ago—that's an eternity for a direct action group!*

Yet as quickly as I thought of ideas, I threw them out. *Take over his office?* Media see that all that time—and so does he. It's so cliche it would likely just get ignored. *Bird-dog him, following him at every public event and harassing him?* Takes more energy then we have. *Letter-write?* Too minimal. *A citizen's arrest?* Too risky and too likely to isolate us.

Surprised at myself for getting stuck at finding a tactic, I slowed myself down. *If I can't think of the right tactic, then maybe I just need to think about what our people already want to do. Those who are ready to challenge Rendell are dead serious about it—wanting us to expose him as a gambling addict—and are ready for anything wild. But others? Well, others want to do community-building activities, like some folks wanted a picnic, and others thought of a big party to celebrate our earned summer lull.*

That opened me up. The tactic hit me.

"Members have been urging us to have a community picnic," I told the team. "So *let's do it*—but at Governor Rendell's house. We'll station ourselves on the sidewalk outside of his house. It's nonthreatening, because we'll be armed with picnic baskets and napkins. But there's a clear undertone that we're making this personal and willing to escalate further."

Jethro clapped his hands. "We'll ask him if he wants a casino near his home."

"I like that—it'll be community-building," said Kathy, nodding.

"And it's not *too* confrontative for our first shot at him directly," I said, dimly aware that some members would still discredit the tactic as "risky," "unnecessarily accosting," and "just plain stalking."

Nico immediately stepped into logistics—first finding Rendell's house and then finding nearby places to hold a picnic. We set a date almost a month away.

It wasn't a complete strategy, and we knew it. But we also knew: *When in doubt, stay active.* If people stopped participating in actions, it would be too easy for them to accept the prescriptions of despair offered by pundits or slide into useless negotiations as per councilmembers' recommendations. We needed to stay in the mix to not lose momentum.

But we had absolutely no idea how big next month's action would become.

The summer slid by quietly. It's a natural lull for organizing, as elected officials take time off and many people plan trips to the shore or elsewhere. The executive team knew we needed to plan what to do next, so after regular meetings netted us no clear longer-term strategy, we decided to hold a focused weekend strategy retreat in early July.

Armed with a dizzying array of foods—strawberry shortcake, mozzarella-tomato salad—we holed up just a few blocks from the Jersey shore in a quaint beach house, filled with knick-knacks of sea shells and beach-ball-shaped towel holders.

By the afternoon of the second day, the room was littered with newsprint. As if to decompress our brains, we had downloaded our analyses onto paper. The morning's pages of SWOT analysis—a listing of organizational strengths and weaknesses alongside external opportunities and threats—were hung delicately around the sheer curtains in the bright front room.

There were so many facets to track: Senator Fumo's new moves, foundations continuing to reject us as "too controversial," presumptive-mayor Nutter's eventual inauguration, the 1,500-foot buffer stalling in committee in the state house. What stood out to me was the scrawled five pages of opportunities, which showed how much our environment had changed. For example, last month the Delaware River community planning process, PennPraxis, had agreed to abandon its solidly pro-casino plan and design two plans: one with and one without casinos. It marked the first signal of mainstream planners joining our side.

"We've always had so many ways to lose," I commented. "For the first time, we have so many ways to win!"

With the catharsis of seeing our analyses on paper—and seeing why we felt so crazy busy—we turned our focus squarely to the next steps of CFP.

"I think it's great we ran these past campaigns on transparency or creating a buffer zone," said Paul. "But I want CFP to be clear that we don't just want to move these casinos—we oppose their predatory nature and the government's role in backing them."

"So what do you suggest?" asked Kathy.

"We need to completely rescind Act 71."

"A political impossibility," I said without thinking about it, causing Jethro to gasp.

"No, I'm serious," said Paul. "Just like the tobacco industry was exposed for its millions in health care costs for smokers, we need to show the harm to gambling addicts is a hidden social cost. Then politicians will flee the issue when they see it's really an economic drain."

Anne shook her head as if talking to political novices. "Opening Act 71 is a political nightmare, and it won't happen even if we had all the Philadelphia politicians behind us. It's the 1,500-foot buffer zone that's winnable, at least as a compromise position."

Paul's jaw stiffened. "I don't want them moved, I want them killed." He looked around for support.

"I agree with everyone," I said. "Seems like these casinos are financially vulnerable. They're leveraging huge debts to finance building. They still owe the state $50 million for the licensing fee. I think we can build a strategy that can stop them by costing them too much. Every day they're not open, nearby casinos are concreting their customer bases. The longer this goes on, the more the casinos turn on each other."

Like a splash of cold water, Jethro spoke in his deep voice. "What happens if all our strategies fail, and the law doesn't change, and we can't make them unprofitable? SugarHouse gets built? What will we do then?" He glared around the room.

A heavy silence fell on the group. None of us wanted to face that despair—and coming from Jethro, it was all the more depressing.

Nico turned to Jethro. His small size and quiet voice nearly hid the steel in his voice. "Then you shut them down."

Jethro grinned. The heaviness wasn't gone. But Nico's words sparked a new mission statement: *Stop casinos from coming to Philadelphia, and close any that open*. It matched our gnawing fear that Casino-Free Philadelphia might fail, while freeing us up to focus on stopping casinos as if we would win.

We took the evening off, following Shirley's urging that we stop overworking ourselves.

After dinner, we prepared to head to the beach—until Paul yelled from the living room.

Perched on the couch, Paul waved us to join him quietly around the TV.

There, behind a raft of microphones, Governor Rendell spoke with unusual sheepishness. "We made tremendous progress yesterday toward reaching an agreement on the state budget. Regretfully, we were not close enough to stop the furloughs."

The announcer explained that since last-minute state budget negotiations had broken down, the state had no money allocated for the new budget cycle. That meant the state would be temporarily giving unpaid leaves to approximately 24,000 state employees deemed as "nonessential" workers. Hundreds of state programs would close: parks, department of motor vehicles, libraries—and casinos.

Paul's boyish face looked gleeful. "You hear that? Casinos around the state will be closed!"

Casinos required revenue department workers to monitor their cash flow.

"Wait," said Kathy, counting on her fingers. "They'll still be in negotiations on Monday. Rendell might not even be back home by Tuesday! Do we cancel our picnic?"

"I guess we go ahead," I shrugged, to nods around the room. "Emails are already sent."

That night we walked along the beach, amazed at the sheer stupidity of politicians to cause havoc on our state over party gamesmanship.

I opened up on the Sunday morning of our retreat. "Today we'll start with Open Sharing. Yesterday reminded me that in addition to all our strategic work, there's a lot of stress and strain for each of us. Unless we address the emotional toxicity, we'll have trouble moving forward on strategy. So for now, each person will get a chance to share whatever is in their hearts."

The sharing was light and easy, until Jethro spoke. His voice was choked and halting. "I'm... sorting out this business with FACT..."

I caught Jethro's eye. "Be real with us."

"I'm really, *really* pissed!" His face contorted and turned flaming red. "We're suffering up North! I feel like the last Fishtown neighborhood meeting we barely pulled out a win. I mean it's good we were able to at least slow down FACT's push for negotiations—but it won't hold forever. Fishtown Neighbors Association is going to be the first civic to break with the DRNA commitment to non-negotiation. And then, and then... FACT swarms the meeting and keeps saying *they* are the largest membership organization—and what does FNA leadership do? They just sit there and take it." He sighed heavily.

Weeks ago when we had talked about that meeting, I had tried to convince Jethro that they should take solace that they were able to turn out more people and declare success over the tough strings attached to negotiation, like nothing getting approved without a two-thirds vote, and negotiation starting with talks *only* about re-siting. But Jethro hadn't been convinced and merely grunted in acquiescence. Rather than talking him out of his feelings, this time I'd get him to air them out. "And?" I said quietly, urging him on.

"I don't get why we're allowing a corporation to buy a neighborhood. We're getting constant direct mails and even calls from SugarHouse executives. SugarHouse has even stolen information on how to write a letter to the editor from our website and used it on theirs. It's a full press and I'm feeling isolated. Councilmembers keep calling us stuck and intransigent, and it's wearing all of us down. But, look around this room—I'm the only one here living in the North. And... and I just need more support."

"And you rarely express your anger," I prodded.

"No! I don't!" He whirled up again. "SugarHouse is outflanking us! DRNA is missing an opportunity to re-site, and FNA is getting co-opted and not being strategic. We could have stopped negotiations, but the tide has turned up there. All of us could use some real help, but all I can come up with is getting mad and breaking things." He took a breath. "I have too much on my plate! I'm the one who has to face my neighbors. Charlie Hocker is a 70-year-old veteran of the Battle of the Bulge—it's total crap that he has to fight against a casino outside his window. He's scared. All of us on Allen Street are scared... I'm scared." His face flushed. "I haven't said that to anyone but my wife. I guess I really need to say it to folks."

He sat back in his chair, adding, "There's my check-in... you're last, Daniel."

I grinned at Jethro's honesty, and knew I couldn't help but pour out my own frustration. "I am sick of getting nasty emails from allies attacking us for not doing everything—oh, and I hate *unsubscribe* emails, that drains me more than anything else. And I'm working way too much, and I need you all to step up more. More than anything, I'm dreading every time my phone rings, worried that it'll be press. They're wearing me down, and I can't take it."

The group held the anger and pain of their two co-directors. We made easy fixes, like Nico taking over handling unsubscribe requests and organizing some events up North to help Jethro. But mostly it was a huge relief that the team had our backs.

"We can't work on problems unless you say them, guys. So thanks for your honesty," said Shirley brightly.

We slid smoothly into future campaign ideas.

Over the night, we had apparently coalesced with clarity that Paul was wrong about eliminating Act 71 as the goal, but right about opening up the economic argument. "Whenever they say revenue," said Jethro, "we should be talking about the local businesses that are going to get hit hardest: restaurants, movie theaters, as well as businesses that lose customers to problem gambling: car companies, furniture stores."

"We need to openly attack the chamber of commerce," said Shirley. "They should represent us. I'm a member, but they never asked me what I thought. They're even less democratic than our civic associations."

With increasing speed, we had growing clarity and energy for organizing small businesses.

I stood up. "Time for a break." The team looked confused—why quit when we were energetic? "Take thirty minutes and, since we're all excited use that energy to assemble pieces into coherent actions, one storyline. Do whatever gets you in a spirit of creativity, and see you in thirty minutes. We each think differently. Rather than a group process to talk it through, I suggest we each let the gush of energy flow into new ideas and see where it takes us."

As others took walks or journaled, I went upstairs and paced... *small businesses... hitting the casino's bottom line... changing the tenor of the conversation...*

When we returned, Paul argued that businesses could move recalcitrant elected officials. Jethro suggested organizing businesses and customers for a boycott on anything SugarHouse- or Foxwoods-related. But Kathy vociferously shot it down, saying, "We need a strategy to *stop* these things, not admit they're coming."

"Kathy's right we need to give people something to do that's meaningful now," I said. "We can't build campaign momentum off people *not* doing anything. So we do a *pro-cott!*" Jethro snickered. "No, I'm serious. I heard of it near where I grew up in Fort Wayne, Indiana. Instead of boycotting bad companies, they buy from good ones—a positive boycott or *procott*. We get people to commit to *not* going to a casino and *instead* promise to support local anti-casino businesses. We'd inherently be the pro-business people. Our action would speak that message, *and* we challenge the storyline of casinos being pro-business."

Shirley clapped in her chair. "Yes!"

And over the next hours, Philly's ProCott was born. In our vision, the campaign had an easy, low bar, with a vow to support participating ProCott businesses. That meant it didn't require anti-casino buy-in. But the ProCott could grow anti-casino converts. With increasingly confrontational public actions, our aim would be to focus on the harm of casinos as a predatory industry.

We left our shore weekend pumped with a draft timeline and campaign, and with the time to build it slowly and without being rushed. We came back just in time for our picnic.

Anne Dicker drove me to the picnic, while outside the sun shined brightly, past bright patches of puffy clouds.

I chatted idly about the morning's *Philadelphia Inquirer*. It had published an article headlined, "Gambling Revenue: The New Mother's Milk." Jeff Shields's piece covered two groups challenging the state's classification as nonessential: casinos and AFSCME, Pennsylvania's largest state employee union. In a swift motion that even took the veteran reporter by surprise, the courts hurried along a ruling that sided against state employees but with casinos. Courts agreed that closing casinos would harm the "health, safety, and welfare" of the state and "most importantly" lose an estimated $1.7 million in profits. State employees were not essential and lost an estimated $3.5 million in wages. In the state of Pennsylvania, casinos were now *essential*, a view upheld by commonwealth judges.

"But the important thing is, they reached an agreement late Monday night. So Governor Rendell should be home just in time for our visit," I said.

Unexpectedly, my cell phone rang. I dug into my pocket. It was an unknown number. I assumed press. Instead, a brash, fast-talking voice answered. "It's John Dougherty."

It took me a moment to register: this was the powerful leader of the electricians' union, IBEW Local 98. *Calling me.*

John spoke quickly, like someone who believed time was money. "I understand that you want to make a point, but this is not the way you want to do it." His voice was forceful and intimate, sounding like the long-lost best friend I never knew I had—or needed.

"Uh..." My mind whirled from the unexpected criticism. "We're doing this picnic because the governor has avoided addressing the issue for so long."

"Of course, you're well within your rights." His words dripped. "But you don't wanna do this. I've had people come to my house before, and believe me, it's an experience you'll never forget. And maybe never forgive. I know the governor, and he's tired from all the budget negotiations, and he can't be forgiving to what you're about to do. Call this off, and I'm sure you can work this out."

I felt sheepish, lost in his conviction. Yet it dawned on me that our timing could not have been luckier: we were meeting an exhausted, depleted governor.

"We're not calling this off," I said. "We have an action planned, it's perfectly reasonable and has been planned for weeks. We are going ahead." I struggled not to ask, *Why are you really calling now?* I knew he wouldn't have told me.

He urged me to reconsider, trying every avenue to convince me to not do it. "This will only inflame the governor more, when a meeting might be possible." Or, in desperation, "As a young person, you need to be worried about your political future."

When I remained impervious, he abruptly hung up.

"What was *that?*" I turned to Anne. "Why would a political player of Doc's league call us about such a small action? And if he opposed our tactic, why call now? Why not a month ago?"

"The governor is using him as a go-between," she said. Sensing my confusion at that, she explained more. "He's sending you an indirect message to back off. It's a negotiation position." She paused at the stop sign and looked at me. "Why he's using Dougherty to do it, I'm not sure. I bet Dougherty is trying to score points—showing that he can reign in the anti-casino activists. Rendell, naturally, doesn't want us at his house, especially after intense budget negotiations. He's probably stayed up late night after night and doesn't want us in his hair."

I felt at sea in political subtext and nuance. *How would I know what Dougherty was doing if Anne weren't here?* "Did I handle it okay?"

"Oh, you did great," she said, swerving to narrowly miss a car. "This is an opening. Now we can ask for something."

Juggling my phone, I gathered opinions from the executive team. Eventually, we developed a winning option: ask for a meeting with the governor—with two caveats urged by Jethro. First, the meeting must be public. Years ago in Boston, he watched a community leader jump when the mayor asked in the middle of a crisis for an emergency meeting. There, the leader made a host of agreements, only to return to a hostile community. They hadn't agreed to any compromises and resented the leader for allowing the mayor to decide who represented their democratic group—and manipulate his position at that.

Second, we get a commitment for a meeting in writing, by fax or email, so that we can hold the governor to such an agreement. Jethro insisted on both, knowing that a nonpublic meeting would isolate our members from the process and, while it may be "fruitful," would not strengthen our collective hands.

"You should call him back," said Anne, "and make the deal."

"No way," I said. "This is some sick, insider ball game. You have the political instincts and know what's going on."

"Doc called you, not me," she said. "It's yours to do."

I breathed heavily and called back Dougherty's cell phone. It rang only once.

"Uh, hi, it's Daniel Hunter." The words toppled out. *Not a strong start.*

His voice was quick and alert. "Will you call it off?"

"No, we can't call it off just because." *How is this done?* I searched for my own style, instead of trying to match his. "It hurts our reputation to arbitrarily call off actions and is not consistent with how we operate. But..." I forced my voice to go slowly. "If the governor agreed to a meeting with us, we could call it off." Dougherty listened carefully as I added the two caveats.

"Give me five minutes," he said. "Don't do *anything.*"

Anne parked the car near the park, watching me as we waited anxiously.

"Is this how things are run in Pennsylvania?"

"Yes," she said. "Lots of politics are done by trading cards and favors. It's pretty gross, isn't it?"

I nodded, stomach clenching. This back-door negotiating was why we didn't have a state budget and how we got casinos in the first place. But, getting to Rendell would mean occasionally playing his game—even as we taught him how to play ours.

My cell phone made a piercing ring.

Dougherty's voice was quick. "Okay, it's done. The governor will meet with you."

"What about the two conditions?"

"Look," said Dougherty, "we'll figure out the details, okay? Don't worry about it."

"It's my job to worry! If we don't get it in writing, we don't have any reason to be assured the meeting will necessarily happen."

"You have *my* word. My word is *my* reputation." Doc sounded both charming and menacing. "The governor is not going to fax you something saying he'll meet. But if he tells me he will meet with you, then he's going to meet with you. I'll make sure it happens."

I pressed and pressed but got no affirmation of either caveat.

I got off the phone, shaken, having agreed that we would call off the march to the governor's house. I faced Anne. "Is that okay? Did I do all right?"

"You did fine," she said. "Your points are going to get relayed."

Yet I was immediately having buyer's regret. I hadn't gotten confirmation of our caveats. I called Jethro.

"It's okay," said Jethro quickly. "I'm not happy we didn't get them, but we haven't lost anything. We can always go back another time. We just tossed together this picnic, and now it's a whole new avenue for us: a meeting with the governor!"

Anne and I jumped out of the car and presented the plan to supporters—"because, if you say you disagree," I told them, "I can call Dougherty up and tell him the deal is off." For people who had traveled thirty minutes or more to arrive at the picnic, they took it in great stride. One advocated going anyway but was talked down by others who were delighted our mere picnic threat had so intimidated the governor.

Thinking it was intentional, several people expressed admiration for our brilliant timing. I freely admitted that sometimes you're tactically brilliant, and sometimes you just have lucky timing. Press were disappointed, but they covered the governor acceding to meet with us.

Then, under the blue sky at McMichael Park, we had a genuine picnic, eating macaroni salad, munching chips and dip, and swapping stories for the most productive picnic any of us had ever had. As one news reporter said, "They're celebrating some victory tonight, but whether that's true or wishful thinking will only be decided by the passage of time."

The next morning, Paul's voice cracked with concern. "You remember DRNA delegate Joel Palmer? This must stay quiet for now, but Christopher Craig called him up attacking you."

I shuddered. Christopher Craig was Senator Fumo's vitriolic legislative counsel. He was like a porcupine—there never appeared to be a good way to handle him.

Paul continued, "Joel now thinks CFP lied in last night's newscast and set back the cause of the 1,500-foot buffer."

"Wait? Where? What did I say?"

"Action 6 news last night. You talked about the meeting with the governor and, almost off-handedly, mentioned Senator Fumo introducing the 1,500-foot buffer zone. You explicitly said Fumo would introduce the buffer zone for *both* casinos. Christopher's pissed."

"But Senator Fumo *did* say that. The DRNA has him on tape saying *exactly* that—that he'd take the same language as our bill sitting in the house of representatives. *Why is this even an issue?*"

Paul chose his words carefully. It occurred to me that he showed caution like a squirrel, his lawyer training always worried about an unforeseen circumstance jumping out and catching him unaware. "Yes... he did... But there are those who feel CFP shouldn't speak on this issue. I think Fumo is going to use your words as an excuse to *not* introduce the 1,500-foot buffer."

"Classic Fumo gambit!" I almost shouted the words. I experienced a refreshing feeling of seeing political machinations snap into place. Knowing what our opponents were up to was often half the battle. "Fumo always had some angle, but I think he promised too much to his constituents. Think about it, for days he's been doing the time-honored political tactic of 'walking it back'—what my church mothers would call 'backsliding between Sundays.' In the *Daily News*, he acted like he had never said he'd introduce the buffer zone. He doesn't want to be pinned down by his own words. Then later, he acts as though he may introduce a bill for Foxwoods but not SugarHouse. It's all to split up North/South, and now CFP/DRNA..."

I could picture Christopher Craig screaming: "Fumo is not some lowly councilmember. CFP can't blackmail him! He'll introduce appropriate legislation that he deems important!"

It was exactly as the Action News reporter had predicted. Off-camera, he had told me Fumo would sell us out and lie right to our face. At the time, I had shrugged off the suggestion, telling him, "If that's true—and I don't know if it is—it's all the more important to make that backtracking public. Because us giving him an opportunity to stick to his word is a win/win. If he's truthful, we win. If he lies, we win—at least so far as we make it public, expose him, and move his support base toward us."

But that meant the DRNA needed to play hardball.

The sound of Paul's fingers scampering over his keyboard jolted me back to the present. "Just got more emails," he said with urgency. "Christopher's taking his tirade to other DRNA members. This is the wedge the *anti*-anti-casino people need to distance DRNA from CFP. We gotta respond!"

"I'm not sure we do. Aside from us giving people the information to defend us, we can't force the DRNA's hands."

"But it's our reputation at stake. They're attacking *you*."

"Yeah," I said, "people love attacking me, and that's fine. But I don't think it's a good idea for us to get caught in this. For one, it's DRNA's internal mess. Christopher *wants* this to be about us to split us up. We can remind Joel and others that I've said nothing that isn't true. But past that, it's up to the DRNA to stiffen its resolve. Me running in to protect myself only feeds the flames. DRNA needs to figure out how to handle this fire."

Purely by coincidence, the DRNA was finishing a letter to Senator Fumo. Written at their previous night's meeting, held—again by coincidence—in CFP headquarters, the letter had been watered down and de-toothed by an obscure DRNA committee process until it reflected Philadelphia's classic civic association posture: respectful supplicant. "You stated that you would introduce the bill within a week of our June 13, 2007 meeting. We now understand from your office that you intend to submit buffer legislation at the end of this week"—a whole month late. The DRNA therefore "respectfully requests" the 1,500-foot buffer introduction, using the most passive language possible—and completely forgetting to urge that it's a buffer to both sites.

The senator's office was not about to be held responsible. It was free to attack the citizens who did speak truth: at this moment, me. Meanwhile, the internal divisions of the DRNA were about to explode.

The following morning, Ed Goppelt proposed to the DRNA that they release the thirty seconds of videotape that showed Fumo's promise for the 1,500-foot buffer. I agreed with every ounce of Ed's logic, who urged a vote by midnight, writing, "To wait until Fumo introduces a bill that applies only to one casino is to allow him to break his commitment to us and to all Philadelphia neighborhoods. Communities should never be pitted against each other. It is time to stand up for what we believe in. Our silence now will be interpreted later as acquiescence."

The response was swift and severe. Those who had heard from Christopher Craig yesterday urged caution and suggested Fumo may not really be backing out of his agreement. Others slammed Ed's "radical positions" that "jeopardize the standing of civic groups." Votes stacked up against Ed's proposal.

Alongside public letters, I was forwarded private, nasty messages from DRNA delegates, including one proposing a purging, so nobody inside DRNA could remain a member of CFP.

Jeremy Beaudry, still active in NABR, cursed and urged the DRNA to "use your power," comparing the DRNA's caution to DiCicco's shrugging shoulders and claims of powerlessness. "The DRNA *is* in a position of power, so why not use it?" By late evening, votes swung back in favor of releasing the tape.

Near midnight and the end of voting, Joel Palmer urged people to ignore the vote, saying "it borders on anarchy" without going through the proper procedures. "DO NOT VOTE," emails urged, insinuating a CFP takeover or attacking Ed's status as a delegate.

The rivalries and hidden tensions in DRNA were floating to the surface.

Queen Village President Jeff Rush rounded out the evening with a series of rapid-fire, combative emails. He called Ed's proposal the "start of World War III" and claimed Ed was acting like George W. Bush, saying his judgment was "unconscionable, discredits you, and your profession." He later added, "I know the senator. Nothing's lost by keeping our powder dry." Then, "We have a mission and I'm not sure either CFP or your tactics—one and the same?—is going to get us to Heaven." Finally, with no sense of irony, "We need to stop this back biting and blaming. Queen Village votes to put politics and vengeance aside."

It was clear the DRNA would not send out the tape—and distrust within the organization now looked permanent.

Jethro and I called each other late that night, amazed at the level of rancor.

"It's like a slow-motion train wreck," I told him.

Jethro laughed, "Tension and conflict are important, and I think the DRNA should embrace it. Coming to blows would be good, since Fishtown always wins in a fistfight."

I ignored his joke. "The DRNA is neutering itself, on this belief that having a politician mad at you is a bad thing. Politicians don't respect pushovers. Fumo is running for office—and if those corruption charges stick, possibly as a convicted felon! He *needs* them and their political cover!"

"Like you have said," said Jethro, "DRNA is a values-based organization. If it does not stand up for the 1,500-foot buffer, it will crumble. When nobody challenges Jeff Rush saying moving one casino—i.e., Foxwoods—would be enough, it makes me less inclined to trust DRNA. If the tables were turned, the Southern leaders would be in a tizzy, whereas the Northern leaders have been thoughtful and respectful in their response." His voice rose. "They're *so* stuck in fear. It's a natural reaction to being traumatized all these years by dominating politicians. Except instead of being in recovery, they're stuck in shock and *always* believe they are victims of circumstance."

"Instead of bringing key players together to move forward on re-siting," I said, "they may have shown Fumo that he can steamroll them. It shows a lot of weakness right before our meeting with the governor. It's gonna kill them internally. They're gonna get stuck in tighter and tighter circles, nursing conspiracy theories about each other. It's not open conflict, it's tossing grenades at each other behind emails."

"Just before you came to CFP, Fumo tried the same thing with us," Jethro said. "Fumo tried to take away city zoning, so we raised holy hell. Christopher Craig yelled at us then, even dropping the f-bomb in front of little kids. But when we didn't back down, Fumo blinked. Unfortunately, people have learned the wrong lessons. Instead of taking the path of more resistance and preparing to fight, they're closing their eyes and doing a little trust fall with the same guy who screwed them."

"We need to tell Paul to leave the DRNA," I said. "The two-hat thing isn't healthy, especially since the DRNA is slipping away from its core value of standing against casinos in neighborhoods. The psychological strain is showing, and people are going to get burned out at those traumatic meetings. Plus, the whole situation invites suspicion about whether Paul's really acting as a DRNA delegate or a CFP double agent. He needs one hat, and ideally the same would go for Caryn, Debbie, and everyone."

"Yeah," said Jethro. "You're right. I know lots of activists take it as a badge of honor to hold lots of hats. But the most powerful are those who do one thing and are able to connect their one hat to other issues. Have a single place to stand and stand there. So I'll talk to Paul."

"What's both disappointing and complimentary is that inside the DRNA, anything that smacks of strength and resolve is associated with CFP," I said. "Tonight I watched a clip from the civil rights movie *Eyes on the Prize*. The DRNA's fight reminds me of fights within Dr. King's circle. Maybe King's most amazing skill was facilitating the massive ego of his Baptist minister colleagues—yet even his meetings occasionally had fistfights! At least *we* haven't come to blows."

Jethro laughed, "Maybe you and I should wrestle!"

We got off the phone never having discussed releasing the tape ourselves. That would have only cemented the end of our alliance with many folks. Instead, as if daring to Fumo to attack us, we highlighted the controversial Action News report in our next email blast, along with sending consoling and encouraging emails to DRNA allies.

Amidst the growing controversy, Ed withdrew the resolution the next morning, making one-sided attempts to patch up relationships from the "sometimes nasty statements." The DRNA would never release the tape.

Just as Ed and others had predicted, days later Senator Fumo introduced a "buffer" bill—two bills, actually—perfectly timed on late Friday afternoon to avoid public reaction in the press. As if shaking off the accusation of vulnerability from the previous day's *Daily News* article, "Fumo Ripe for Defeat," Fumo described the bills as having "virtually no chance"—then trumpeted his twenty-nine-year record for keeping his word.

With tortured logic, one bill created a 1,500-foot buffer within a fourteen-mile radius from Philadelphia Park Casino, and a second bill covered the twelve-and-a-half-mile swath around Harrah's casino. This left large segments of the city untouched by the buffer zone. Aside from being an openly divisive set of bills, additional weaknesses turned up in Karim and Ed Goppelt's research: they were mutually exclusive, included previous casino sites like Donald Trump's East Falls/Nicetown site, and so on.

The DRNA had completely missed the boat. Almost a week later, it sent a tardy letter calling them "insufficient" bills. Not a single major media outlet picked it up. Fumo's political gambit had worked—he got positive press for introducing a pathetic bill. He had lied to his constituents, and the DRNA didn't have the backbone to stick up for itself.

*   *   *

Unwilling to suffer the same fate, CFP focused on our own political dances. At Anne's advisement, I called Dougherty to get dates for a meeting with the governor. "His scheduler is away this week," Doc told me, urging me to stay in touch.

We turned to preparations, inviting elder statesmen and allies to share nuggets about Governor Rendell's negotiation style and seek advice on requests that might get some headway. Whenever we asked if they might join us, they all shook their heads and smiled. "You're unwanted to the governor. I can't be saddled with that." That response left Jethro and me with a free hand to put together a team of citizens with nothing to lose.

As if to make sure we didn't have time to plan Philly's ProCott, the planning commission announced a hearing on the Foxwoods plan. All of us expected it to give Foxwoods the same green-light treatment it had given SugarHouse.

So with plenty of other things on my mind, I headed down the steps into the Philadelphia Free Library's low-ceilinged auditorium, annoyed at the last-minute, hastily assembled meeting and worried at being bored and only angry at another planning commission meeting. I sat next to DRNA and Society Hill leader Rosanne Loesch, dressed with consummate elegance. Over the past months, a deep camaraderie had developed between us, and Rosanne and I greeted each other with the generous smiles of people in the trenches.

I was relieved that there were no pro-casino union members, only a few rows of opposition in the front. I wondered if it was a result of today's news that the convention center was going forward even without "casino funding." That construction promised labor thousands of jobs, so the trade unions may no longer have needed the few devoted to the casinos. Maybe they'd stop opposing us now.

The meeting started blandly, with the planning director telling the darkened audience, "Let's not debate with one another, and respect the speakers." But that was not to be.

The crowd was restless, angry, and at every opportunity interrupted the proceedings. Since the last planning commission hearing, the supreme court had screwed us twice, the planning director had admitted both sites were not ideal, and pressure had built inside the movement over Fumo's recent moves.

When the city solicitor boasted of behind-closed-door meetings committing the city to a development agreement, the planning director's meek attempts to quiet the riled crowd—"There will be public input later"—backfired. One fed-up person stood up. "What's the point of our input if it's already decided?" A board member threatened to eject the crowd, but the crowd shouted him down.

When the Foxwoods speaker lost his notes, the crowd took over, chanting, "*Pay your taxes!*"—a reference to Foxwoods asking the city to declare its land worthless and thus allow it to avoid paying millions of dollars in taxes. They taunted when his laser point broke down. When he accidentally showed slides of future development plans, the crowd erupted with jeers—rather than building on land it owned, Foxwoods' proposals built on state riparian land. "*You don't own it, and we won't give it to you!*"

There was an intoxicating release in the outpouring of emotion. But I sat silent, my stomach queazy as the crowd's fervor fed on itself. It turned to soaring applause as Jethro slammed the board. "I have over ten years' experience in community-based planning. I'd rather be talking about planning, which is what we're not doing, because this development has been forced upon us."

The crowd punctuated Matt Ruben's lines with shouted praise as he slammed Foxwoods' lack of a traffic and development plan. "The front green space is not meaningful public space and will have to be fenced off with a twenty-foot fence when every one of those communities uses it to protest every day when the casino opens."

The crowd hollered support as State Representative Mike O'Brien's spokeswoman threatened to take Foxwoods to court and insisted they would not give SugarHouse the riparian, riverfront land.

The meeting dragged on, and the group seemed to grow undirected, out of control. Losing all sense of courtesy, the crowd shouted down the handful of citizens testifying—for the first time that I could recall—on Foxwoods' behalf. "A casino like this will be an engine that will make our community a better, stronger community where we can live." The crowd shouted: *"Where do you live? Casinos aren't an engine!"*

Another read from prepared notes, "Foxwoods would provide a chance for my neighborhood in South Philly (*Never seen you before!*) to make a living wage within a walking distance (*Walk back home then!*) of their houses."

By the time Frank DiCicco spoke, the crowd had hit a feverish pitch. His attempt to cast himself as hero in the tragic casino struggle was laughed down and booed so heavily DiCicco halted and said, "I will wait."

"You should wait, dog," shouted one heckler.

"I... I've been called many things in my career, but never a dog." DiCicco sputtered. "But... uh... I love dogs, so... maybe it's okay." He, like us, was off his game. He paused for the crowd to return to a simmer. "Before I came up to the stage, a BlackBerry was handed to me (*By Foxwoods' lawyers! We saw you!*) and there was a text message. The Supreme Court of Pennsylvania ruled against the lawsuit for the Riverwalk, which means there are no longer, as far as I know, any lawsuits pending as it relates to the gaming matter in front of the supreme court." The crowd booed, as DiCicco waited with exaggerated patience. He turned to the planning commission. "Of the Foxwoods CED, I am not going to ask you to approve it. Nor am I going to ask you to disapprove it."

"Whoaaaah," screamed Rosanne, standing in her seat.

The crowd angrily shouted through DiCicco's next sentences. "There are buffer bills introduced by Representative Josephs and Senator Fumo," he said. "We don't know how those are going to play out." His hair was tussled, and he looked stranded and alone among the seething crowd. "We may have to accept these sites." The crowd blew apart in jeers, and no banging gavels could stop the deafening sound.

The planning commission quickly voted unanimously to table Foxwoods' proposal so "staff can have time to get further information on the traffic study, the riparian rights issue, and community input." *Pathetic,* I spat with the crowd.

I pulled myself together enough to manage a thoughtful response to reporter Jeff Shields. He wondered if this signaled that we had finally lost DiCicco. Even I was proud of my line. "This is the first time an unelected political body has *not* chosen to vote against us."

But as I biked home, my mind focused on our people and their disrespectful behavior. I understood and shared the outrage. For months, we'd been disrespected in hearings. Councilmembers and board members walked out when we testified, put us last on the agenda to waste our time, hushed us, disregarded our expertise though we often knew the projects better than anyone else, or outright condemned our input. We had plenty to be mad about. But that gave us no excuse to lose the high-ground. And at least for that moment, we had lost it.

The papers universally condemned our behavior. The *Daily News* wrote we crossed "the line from civil to uncivil disobedience... over and over and over again." They called the voice of reason "Saint Francis of DiCicco."

Karim's op-ed defended us. "Instead of blaming the victims, the *Daily News* should join residents in asking for Gov. Rendell to bring all parties to the table to negotiate new sites that won't destroy city neighborhoods. Only then will civility and the civil process be upheld."

But I knew that wasn't sufficient. Despite hours of coaching on strategy and discipline, our people had lost their cool.

At the next executive team meeting, my voice was sharp. "We *can't* have another hearing like that. Of course they painted us as uncivil. When we're shouting down other citizen testifiers, we *are* being uncivil!" I urged for us to redouble our training efforts, adding, "We have to surf the wave of people's emotions, and we need to take responsibility for not doing it. The anger means we're not giving people actions that give them full expression."

Jethro glared at nobody in particular. "I *still* think we should agree to never go to hearings unless we're doing an action at them. Sitting through those hearings is just killing us."

"Let's just focus on Philly's ProCott," said Kathy. "We have a ton to write to get it ready."

We quickly set dates for some training sessions. There was so much to do—not the least of which was our meeting with Rendell.

By mid-July, our concern over that meeting began to peak. Dougherty kept putting me off, before finally giving me Rendell's scheduler's direct number. Many calls later, and both Dougherty and the scheduler had shoved me off.

It wasn't the first time I wished politicians would explain their subtext. *Is Dougherty yanking my chain? Or has Rendell reneged on his agreement?* It was a guessing game, the opposite of the clear speech we tried to model.

The clues began adding up when out of the blue, KYW Newsradio's Mike Dunn reported that the governor would meet with residents opposed to casinos on one condition. "If they say, we're worried about traffic, we're worried about people parking in our neighborhoods, we're worried about crime, I'm happy to work with city officials to alleviate those concerns. If they say, we don't want casinos in Philadelphia, I can't help them."

Supporters were angry and urged us to cancel the meeting. "We run this city, not the governor," wrote volunteer Marge Schernecke. "Tell him and Fumo and all the other elected officials that we refuse to be pushed or blackmailed."

Jethro saw it differently. "The negotiation has begun. I don't think the message should be that we won't meet," he wrote over email. "The message should be that the agenda of the meeting is not for the governor to determine." So, through the media and back-channels, we pushed back on the governor.

No longer worried the governor was a distant, unengaged opponent, Jethro enthusiastically marked our crossing a threshold. "The governor is in play."

Upon returning from a week-long vacation with family, I redoubled my self-care practices, with eight to nine hours of sleep a night, regular meals and exercise, and quality time with friends.

Meeting at the office, Jethro accepted a hug and immediately gripped me. "You look good, Daniel. Your emails are back to your saucy self."

He was commenting on my latest email. Responding to nervousness in the executive team, I had written: "Since DiCicco is increasing talk that this is over, only further lets us know it's not over. Has he ever been right? Time to step up. Rendell hasn't called us back? Then let's go back to his house. We're not going out like suckers!"

"I feel good, Jet. We're right on the cusp of this whole issue blowing up and for people to see this issue deeply."

"I know!" Jethro's voice boomed through the empty room. "You see the PICA report?"

I nodded enthusiastically. PICA was a state agency that oversaw the city budget. It had estimated that including the social costs of 10,000 new gambling addicts, casinos could cost Philadelphia upwards of $200 million per year. "It's the first real crack in the economic argument! It's all coming together." I paused. "Unless it's not—and Fumo forces DiCicco to cave, council votes against us, and we lose everything." I laughed.

Jethro shared my fears. But he had an almost superstitious caution against journeying down the road of what if we lose. He merely shrugged his shoulders.

I wondered if we'd talk a little about Philly's ProCott and my own nagging worry that it didn't speak to our movement's urgency. We had *immediate* targets to worry about—it was hard to see how Philly's ProCott would get us on the offensive.

But as if to sweep away dark fears, Jethro waved his hands energetically. "Oh! I came up with this idea, and I know it sounds crazy. First of all, did you know that Race Street is called that because it hosted horse races in the 1700s? Well, it is true... So, it turns out that the simplest way to protect Philadelphia from casinos is to build a racetrack on my street. There are horses nearby, and it will be a huge revenue generator. Unlike slots parlors, this is an outdoor, recreational activity that is fun for the entire family."

"It *does* sound crazy." I burst out laughing. "But you do your best thinking when you're not constricted by... uhm... anything." Jethro joined my laughter.

It was relaxing and good, but self-care and a positive organizational culture isn't a strategy. We were still blowing in the winds of others' moves. As we pulled out calendars to select possible dates for a return picnic at Rendell's house, we learned of a startling twist: Rendell was going to meet with the Delaware Riverfront Neighborhood Alliance.

CHAPTER 14

Return to Direct Action

being at the negotiation table without being in the room •
ignoring when politicians shift responsibility •
playing high-stakes media games to bait your target •
being stuck in defensiveness is equivalent to disempowerment • stopping a riot •
direct action discipline to strengthen messaging • negotiating quickly with police •
dilemma demonstrations • coaching with questions

"I KNOW YOU'RE MEETING WITH THE GOVERNOR AND SENATOR FUMO TONIGHT," said the soft-spoken *Evening Bulletin* reporter, Jenny DeHuff. The paper was staunchly conservative and detested Democratic Governor Ed Rendell. "But I don't know what time, or where, or how long."

I had hoped it was friends calling about playing cards that evening. My heart sank at the prospect of another chat with a reporter. Despite our best efforts to find a replacement, I was still the major public face of CFP as media spokesperson—nobody wanted that job. "It's not our meeting, he decided to meet with the DRNA instead—"

"But that's your meeting! Why aren't you there?"

I took a breath. At first, we had been mad. But in the fast-moving whitewaters of our campaign, we buried that feeling and moved along. "We are there, in a way," I said. "It's rare for direct action groups to be at negotiation tables. So we influence the meeting by building context around it."

"What do you mean?"

In response, I asked, "What was the big issue in the news about casinos today?"

"You mean the news that PGCB chairman Tad Decker is stepping down?"

"Yes, and what we helped guide reporters to focus on is the fact that Decker— *Governor Rendell's appointment*—is returning to a big, fat $150,000 per year position at Cozen O'Connor after delivering casino licenses to two of their clients. As if to complete the circle, that law firm is now overseeing Senator Fumo's re-election campaign. We're encouraging reporters to dig deep into this story, because we believe there is real corruption going on. And while I believe reporters are generally bad at covering issues of economic injustice, they love sleaze. And this is nothing but sleaze. There's a scandal here, and you'll make front page for weeks if you uncover it."

"And you think today's coverage influences the governor?"

I chuckled, "Oh yeah. When even the tentative *Philadelphia Business Journal* is suggesting this doesn't sound right, it forces Rendell to the defensive. Rendell now has to explain to you about his appointee's gross appearance of corruption, right as he wants to put this whole debacle to rest. So we've earned a seat at the table, even if it's not official. And, besides, the DRNA is made up of civic leaders who, if they know one thing well, it's negotiation."

I could hear Jenny scribbling a few notes.

"Moving the casinos is the carrot, and we're the stick," I said. "But to answer your initial question, the location is being kept confidential." I paused dramatically. "So, 7 P.M. at the DiBona Conference Room at the Bellevue. Fumo will join. No taping. No cameras. Nobody will talk to press. Fumo made those stipulations after... you know... getting caught lying to his constituents. Oh, and Fumo told them they can't talk about re-siting—only traffic, parking, noise, and nuisance crimes."

"Wait, so nobody will talk to me if I go?"

"Show up," I said. "Again, you didn't get it from me, but I'm pretty sure somebody will be ready to speak to you on the record. But do this for me, give me a call after those interviews to update me. I don't want to talk on the record about the meeting, I just want to correct any mistakes asserted by our opposition."

She thanked me and promptly hung up.

I found some friends and played cards for several hours, until the reporter called back.

"The governor and Fumo wouldn't talk, but the DRNA did." She sounded surprised at their boldness. Given their previous history, I understood the sentiment. Jenny spoke quickly, her phone jangling as she walked, assumedly to her office to finish an article on this. "According to them, the governor vowed to veto the 1,500-foot buffer zone and insisted there will be two casinos in Philadelphia. But Caryn Hunt told me they *did* get the ear of the governor and that he's open to the idea of re-siting and challenged the DRNA to find viable sites."

"Do you believe them?" I asked. It sounded almost too good to be true.

"Well..." She gave me the skeptical voice only reporters and people who are used to being lied to can give. "They're definitely giving me positive spin. But I didn't think Rendell would even entertain them. Sorry, I gotta go write a story. Go get some sleep."

I headed home, uncertain and cautious as ever. If we'd learned one thing during our campaign, it was to be constantly on our guard.

A few days later, I emerged from the front room at CFP's offices and stretched from hours of staring at a computer screen and holding a phone to my ear. "Karim, you ready to meet?"

Karim was getting his third cup of coffee and nodded energetically. We plopped down on the couches and swiftly reviewed the past few days.

Because we weren't in the room, we didn't own the spin on the DRNA/governor meeting. The DRNA had chosen an upbeat take, framing the governor as honestly considering re-siting. Having been out-played by Fumo, they were stepping up to play hardball, slipping juicy details to *City Paper* journalist Bruce Schimmel—one of the Philly Phourteen—who lambasted the governor's "secret slots talk."

Schimmel wrote of the governor wagging his fingers at civic leaders and saying, "What are you afraid of? That elderly women will become addicted and commit crimes, and that people are going to be pissing on your doorstep? ... Bullshit." When the DRNA pushed that casinos would actually cost the city money, citing the $200 million from the latest PICA report, Rendell said he hadn't seen the PICA report. "At which point one of the activists handed him a copy"—though days later, PICA would mysteriously backtrack and claim its numbers were merely a gross approximation.

Other attendees were less enthusiastic. Fumo reluctantly called the meeting "useful." DiCicco shrilly said, "Our toolbox is pretty empty at this point," and declared, "Re-siting will not happen," while the casinos reiterated that they would never move and called the meeting mere "window dressing."

"But the real question is, what is the governor doing?" I said.

Like the reporters he spoke with so frequently, Karim's voice rushed along, a fast-flowing river. "I don't get why he's been silent for so long. Why didn't he just say what everyone thinks he's going to say: that re-siting is over?"

"I'm not sure. You heard his quote on KYW radio, right?" Karim nodded.

The governor had said, "We couldn't, under the law, force the licensees to move to another location. But we would try to do it, and we might even incentivize their move."

Thinking out loud, I said, "Rendell's quote is a classic politician move, trying to appear sensible by shifting responsibility, as though you have no control. And I agree with you—why didn't he just say it's over?"

Karim leaned back and sipped his coffee. "I think we're creaming him publicly with this Decker controversy. He wants it to calm down. Who wants to give bad news when you're being brought into a possible story of corruption?"

"The problem is, unless real corruption is uncovered, this news cycle is going to end soon," I said. "Reporters don't have the time to really dive into this story and expose corruption. Already, we've burned out a bunch of reporters with issue fatigue. I don't know if I mentioned a couple of papers are assigning new reporters to cover this issue. The *Weekly Press*, *Plan Philly*... Even Jeff Shields is taking himself off the casino beat, after joking with me, 'Can't you just lose already so we don't have to keep writing about this?' Did you know his beat includes the growing number of gun murders in the city, writing a daily blog, covering some state politics and *all* city politics—plus casinos!"

"It's all those staff cuts at the *Inquirer*," said Karim. He sounded angry, but I couldn't tell if it was just the hours of work or that he was actively decrying the state of journalism. "Nobody has time to cover this. So who is replacing Jeff?"

"He'll do some and share the issue with Jennifer Lin," I said. "But it's the same story with other papers—there's a lot of fresh reporters covering this issue. I've had to bring them up to speed on the basics of the situation—and even inoculate a couple from Dan Fee trying to convince them that we're really funded by Atlantic City all over again. Ugh!"

"Well," said Karim, trying to return to the discussion, "I think you're right this Decker storyline is either going to explode or fizzle in a few days."

"It just pisses me off," I said. "I've got this new reporter saying the recent supreme court ruling is 'likely the end of the road for casino opponents.' They don't yet get that we don't give up."

Karim looked at me quizzically, before understanding what I was talking about. The supreme court had *finally* given a rationale for removing the ballot referendum, saying the state "does not intend for the electorate of Philadelphia to be given the opportunity to disapprove, nullify, or otherwise affect the board's decision." The court's minority opinion was condemnatory: "There is no justification for the Court's unnecessary, paternalistic and remarkable prior restraint... Today's decision represents a dramatic departure from this Court's respect for the democratic values underlying our system of government."

"You've got to let it go," Karim said, with feeling. "You're too reactionary to reporters these days. You're brilliant at framing and being positive. Be that. Don't get into fights with reporters." He looked at me to make sure I heard him, then continued. "So how to wrap Rendell permanently into the casino storyline? His fingerprints need to be all over this mess."

"I agree, he's given us a dangerous gift, because it's not a red light."

As if to prove my point, at that moment, DiCicco was switching positions and saying re-siting was possible, even drafting a list of possible *other* locations for the casinos to move—including near my neighborhood at Bartram's Garden and back at the old Pinnacle site, just a short jaunt north of Jethro's house.

"So Rendell is giving us a little hope," I said, "even though we know it's just for a short time. He's going to *eventually* announce re-siting is over and try to sink all our hopes with it. It's why we have to keep preparing Philly's ProCott even in the midst of this."

"And we can use this opportunity to fully engage Rendell. I propose we play a high-stakes media game with him. And I think Decker is the right way to get to him—because there's the off-chance a reporter will uncover real stuff, and, if not, I think he has to defend his choice. But because it's the topic of corruption, we can almost guarantee positive coverage in the media. They *want* to look like they're on the side of the people, even though they detest regular people."

"How shall we do it?"

Karim grinned. "Put together a full report of Decker's tenure: Show how Pittsburgh papers exposed misspent PGCB funds, unearthed the current PGCB's executive director's past indictment for stealing money from Louisiana's gaming board, two staff lawyers and a licensing investigator arrested for separate barroom brawls, another licensing investigator charged with five counts of falsifying credentials on his job application, a press aide charged with third-degree murder—plus an investigation into alleged mob ties to Mount Airy Casino Resort, which was represented by Cozen O'Connor—the same law firm involved in Fumo's re-election campaign. Where Decker was returning. Who represented SugarHouse. We need to feed new angles to them on this story."

"Oh!" I clapped. "And Ed Goppelt had an idea that I had dismissed until now—to *expand* our charges on Decker by filing a formal complaint against him with the supreme court's disciplinary counsel, who oversees lawyers. Ed's right that they *ought* to investigate such apparently clear breaches of their rules of professional conduct."

"But doesn't Richard Sprague—*SugarHouse investor* Richard Sprague—oversee that counsel?"

"We think so!" I grinned. "It's just more grist for the apparent corruption storyline."

"Does that open us to a legal challenge?"

"Not if we do it right," I said. "We're just filing a petition and we only say what we believe."

Karim cracked his knuckles. "Let's get to work!"

We started sending press releases on Decker almost daily, with newly unearthed details that we or reporters had kicked up. For example, two days after that conversation, we sent a carefully packaged press release encouraging Rendell to select Jethro as a replacement candidate. We knew the humor would get a few new reporters to glance at it, which gave us a chance to update them on other news: that we had confirmed that Rendell had been rejecting Decker's resignation for months, wanting him to finish getting the Philly casinos built. Rendell's buckling was further credence that our pressure on Decker had forced Rendell to accept the PGCB chairman's premature departure.

The end result was a daily gush of editorials condemning Decker. The *Inquirer* celebrated the end of Decker's "reign" in their editorial: "Slot King Steps Down," which quoted us attacking Decker for overseeing "the worst-run and most anti-democratic regulatory body." In a sign of the media's reluctance to call it corruption, press used nasal images: the *Lancaster News* called it a "rank smell"; the *Daily News* offered the headline, "How Can We Get Rid of the Odor?"; and the *Inquirer* wrote that his departure "smelled terribly."

By the time we were ready to announce our formal complaint with the supreme court's disciplinary counsel, press were hyped, and our announcement immediately exploded onto every major news outlet.

As we expected, it outraged Decker's law firm, Cozen O'Connor, who—in language that sent chills down our lawyers' backs—called our "statements of innuendo... false, defamatory and scurrilous" and "subjects them to causes of action for libel and defamation." But despite their saber rattling, I felt fairly comfortable. We never acted as though we knew they were involved in illegal wrongdoing. We strenuously avoided statements like "Decker is corrupt" or "we know he's doing shady illegal dealings." We raised questions and spoke our minds—"we believe Decker is acting corruptly" or "it seems like corruption when you oversee a process to pick casinos that your old law firm represents, then return to them for a fat check." We were on firm legal ground.

What we didn't expect was some fortuitous timing. Apparently, our attacks on Decker had already so affected Rendell that he felt forced to defend his appointee's reputation with a rare gubernatorial op-ed in the *Philadelphia Inquirer,* calling Decker a man of "impeccable ethical standards and outstanding leadership skills" who "faced formidable challenges in establishing a new industry in Pennsylvania that would create thousands of jobs, foster millions of dollars of economic development across the commonwealth, and reduce taxes statewide."

Unfortunately for Rendell, it was printed the same day we released our complaint. So while Rendell was defending his appointee, news sources were widely quoting us with our details over the appearance of corruption.

We had successfully baited Rendell all the way into the casino issue.

That led to a full press war. Rendell doubled down with another op-ed in the *Daily News*. We immediately hit back with an *Inquirer* op-ed, causing Rendell's team to retaliate with an op-ed from the incoming PGCB chairwoman, who was replacing Tad Decker—only to be double-whammed by a meticulous point-by-point rebuttal by Ed Goppelt and an op-ed from me. Even the *Daily News* piled on and condemned another planning commission that would "all but shut out the public."

Through the media, we were playing ball with the governor of the state of Pennsylvania.

Even Decker was forced to defend himself in the *Legal Intelligencer*, arguing "to accuse me of that is slanderous" and "McCarthyism at its worst."

But that didn't stop the articles exposing the connections—though most merely repeated what had already been printed. No reporters had time for investigation.

As if accepting defeat, Rendell quietly dropped any public defense of Decker. He dampened hope for re-siting, calling his remarks as reported by the DRNA "overblown." But he was fully wrapped into the Philly casino drama, draped with the weight of poor planning and reeking with the stench of Decker.

I hoped this would be the thing that would free up my energy. But it wasn't. CFP was about to take several steps back.

Early Thursday evening, CFP's executive team prepared for the first presentation of Philly's ProCott to members. Anne and Kathy flew around the office setting up the projector, Karim silently reviewed notes, and Shirley deposited handouts on chairs, occasionally muttering, "We needed this presentation to be *professional*." Jethro and I nonchalantly arranged chairs.

"I'm not sure it's ready yet," Jet whispered to me.

I looked at him in surprise. "We've been talking about this for months, meeting with small-business leaders. What do you mean?"

"I'm just not sure it speaks to our anger. People are pissed," he said. "DiCicco's made himself a high-priority target for direct action, and Rendell, of course. People want to get *them*, not do some long-term business thing that I'm not sure I even understand."

"But..." I shook my head. Jethro was never attached to ideas, but I was. "We need a campaign to hold people together. Why are you bringing this up *now*?"

At that, he merely shrugged.

"*We need a campaign*," I said. "Gandhi had a word for staying on the defensive: powerlessness. Even if it doesn't speak to the urgency, we *can't* be urgent all the time. This allows us to graduate from wasting our time on DiCicco's re-siting suggestions and get our eyes on a bigger, real anti-casino position. Whatever faults the ProCott has, it's better than nothing."

Jethro shrugged again. "I just think it's missing the *oomph* factor." He left me, mouth hanging, to chat with the crowd of arriving members.

About fifty supporters listened to Anne explain the campaign. We had hand-picked representatives from the North and South and from our growing connections to citywide groups, both directly involved in this issue and working in others.

"What do we mean by a *ProCott?*" Anne asked rhetorically. She gestured toward the projected PowerPoint at the front of the room. "While a boycott is about not purchasing from some businesses, a ProCott encourages people to actively purchase from businesses." The slide flipped. "In this campaign, the messengers of our economic argument are those potentially cannibalized by casino development: owners of small businesses. Those businesses who join will be featured on PhillysProCott.org. Individuals who join commit to patronizing local ProCott businesses—and to protect them by promising to not go to SugarHouse or Foxwoods." The slides continued until Anne was finished.

Karim moved to the center and sat on a chair. "Questions?"

Two dozen hands went up. "Does this attack the political jugular of the mayor or governor in any way?" "How does this stop Foxwoods or SugarHouse?" "Do you all assume that at least one of these casinos is now inevitable?" "How does this have a direct political connection?"

Happy not to be in the front of the room, I watched Karim struggle to defend the campaign. "This will change the media narrative about jobs, and so make it harder for anybody to support casinos. We can always include other actions, like secondary boycotts of investors or handing over copies of our business deeds to the governor, to show he's okay with destroying *those* jobs."

The questions kept pouring. "What about the governor's re-siting process?" "Why not make this about Fumo and his re-election next year?" "How does this challenge the governor?"

It was as if a spotlight descended over Karim. He broke into a sweat. I didn't need to look to know the faces of executive team were drooping, like a deflating balloon.

When stalwart supporter Richard DeWyngaert edged his way out, I grabbed him as he opened the door to the outside. "You own a small independent bookstore. What do you think?"

He half-turned. "I'm not sure. But if you all think it's a great idea, I'm with you all the way."

He closed the door with a thud.

That was our answer. Nobody else really thought it was a good idea.

It was hard to give up. But to truly be a movement organization, we had to follow the will of our people. We couldn't force anything down their throats. We were democratic by the virtue that unless we matched what people sought, they wouldn't show up, and the campaign wouldn't fly. And Philly's ProCott wasn't going to fly.

The next executive team meeting was depressing. All of us responded differently to the realization that the ProCott idea was sunk. I had tried to argue the benefits of the campaign, but Jethro snapped decisively, "We need to switch." He didn't look sad, just matter-of-fact about it.

Paul was different. Feeling lost brought him conviction. "We *need* another Philly's Ballot Box. Let's do another big petition challenge." He looked around eagerly.

Nobody looked up.

Nico slowly responded. "I think we need a strategy that really addresses our current moment. How do we regain the offensive with the governor, Fumo, and all? What would the petition be about?"

"Let's lobby them," said Kathy flatly. She was unflappable. But I could sense her worry in the edge of her voice.

She wasn't the only one worried. CFP die-hard Morgan Jones's email stayed with me: "If I didn't know you better, I'd assume you had lost steam and were running out of options as the casinos closed in on starting construction at the end of the summer."

I *felt* out of options. But the truth was, while I knew we were losing strategic direction, we had been effective at using *every* moment to advance our cause. Each piece of news we leveraged. Each move our opponents made we used for our own ends. We had modeled something most movements only dream of: improvisational dancing with the news cycle and events to steadily gain an advantage. We just hadn't *made* news—and that meant we were at the mercy of what was happening outside of us.

Paul tried again. "Why don't we get a thousand people to descend on the state capitol to lobby for Bill 1477? We've only done one or two lobbying trips. Or a big rally?"

I started to rebut that doing *actions* isn't that same as being on the offensive, that we needed to settle down, pick a target, and develop a narrative around them to put on constant and increasing political pressure. I would have said all of that, but Anne interrupted.

"I'm sorry to have to do this, but I need to share bad news with the team." She took a deep breath. "In two weeks, I'm officially announcing my candidacy against Senator Fumo. I have to leave CFP to do it."

I'm sure we groaned, but I can't remember.

"It's hard to fault you," said Jethro quickly. We all knew that Fumo was vulnerable— what with 137 charges against him in what would no doubt be a wildly publicized trial. "But—well—we just can't replace your insider information and connections."

Shirley shrugged, as if unconcerned. "CFP has taken an eight-week hiatus to re-energize. We need to maintain momentum and continue to ponder what the best path to victory is and how to achieve it. Right now, we need to get back out into the community and show we continue to be a force in the city." I wondered if she was really feeling that solid. But she was a practical person—if Anne was leaving, that was just information to compute. As if to prove the point, she turned to me and stared. "And did we find a new fiscal sponsor?"

I dropped my head and shook it. "Nobody wants to touch us. 'Too political.' 'Too risky.' 'Too likely to be sued.' All that jazz."

"But we're still moving forward," she said. I again wondered if she was convincing herself—or all of us. "We're returning to picnic at Rendell's house on Saturday." She grabbed a marker and stood up at the newsprint. "Then later that day, Jethro, aren't you

Fishtown folks organizing an anti-casino barbecue near SugarHouse, in response to something SugarHouse is organizing?"

Jethro nodded, sulking. He hated feeling trivialized as the Northern representative, but such was our awe of him that we acted as though he could single-handedly sort through the tensions of working-class Fishtown and new hipsters moving into the neighborhood.

Shirley continued undeterred, writing up a list of events. "Then state hearings on the 1,500-foot buffer zone—"

"—which we're not going to turn people out for." I waved my finger at Paul, who was trying to interrupt me. "No, I think Jethro's right. No more mobilizing for hearings without direct action. It only sucks people's energy and wastes their time."

Shirley sniffed at being interrupted. "Then, Monday, Mothers Against SugarHouse has a rally!" She pointed at the lengthy list of activities. "Just in the next four days. That's a lot!"

I wanted to scream *"No!"*—that this wasn't a *campaign* and it wasn't *organizing*. We had gotten stuck *mobilizing* actions, where we turn people out but aren't building new recruits with face-to-face interactions. We were a darling of other movements, jealous of our media coverage and amazed at our ability to turn each loss into a win—but I was worried. Karim and I may have spent more time reading press reports then out in the field talking with people. It was an organizer's sin.

Yet there were good reasons. It felt tough enough to juggle the balls we already had, without building new relationships on top of that. I didn't feel I had the time to go door-knocking. Worried about losing completely, I refused to back down from each opportunity presented to us.

But Shirley *was* right that we were staying in motion—and that *was* something.

"And September 12 is going to be something, too," said Paul, looking up from his laptop. "Guess what? The PGCB set their next 'public' hearing. They're returning to Philadelphia!"

I clapped my hands. "I don't know what we're going to do. But it's gonna be spectacular," I said. "We're going to put into practice last week's direct action training!" I began brainstorming actions.

But another crisis was on the horizon—one not manufactured by the media or a politician's ploy. It would be the first time outright violence hit our movement.

The weekend felt packed. Saturday we returned for an anticlimactic picnic at the governor's house. Civil affairs threatened to stop us from going to Rendell's home, before our steadfast refusal bowled them over—and one officer whispered, "Go ahead. We know how important this issue is to you. Frankly, most of us agree with you."

Then Fishtown anti-casino group FAST held a quiet, community-building barbecue on Allen Street.

Jethro and I were dropping off materials from the picnic and barbecue when Jethro's cell phone rang. I stopped unloading when I saw Jethro's contorted face. "Just stay there," he snapped. "I'll be right over." He slammed his cell phone shut, shouting, "Ed Verral just got beat up at SugarHouse's barbecue. I'm heading over now. I'll be in touch."

Jethro sprinted to Ed's house.

Curious how SugarHouse was wooing his neighbors, Ed had gone to take pictures at SugarHouse's "Sweet Beginnings"–themed barbecue.

When Jethro arrived, he found Ed on his front stoop, nose smashed, eyes bulging, with traces of blood on his arms and face. Ed had tried to wash himself off and was waiting for a supervisor from the 26th Police District. He was fuming.

"I was just... I was taking pictures," Ed howled as Jethro listened, recording the conversation on his phone. Ed's voice was raw with frustration. "They had six city... six public works trucks down there setting the stage up, the DJ, and everything."

"Okay, so you were taking pictures, and then what?" asked Jethro, as neighbors stopped by to lend support.

Ed was shaking, still in shock from what had happened. He bellowed, "She came over—Donna—" he said. One of the pro-casino FACT organizers. "She came over and said, 'You're *one of those*.' She calls everyone over... and they circled me."

"How many people were surrounding you?"

"Like twenty or... like twenty people. And then, and then... he just hauls off and punches me. I had my hands on the handlebars. He kicked my back tire. My tire is all flattened... ninety-dollar tire... I had to drag it home."

"Who hit you?" Jethro asked.

"I don't remember," he said, describing some wide man, roughly 300 pounds. "I hit the ground, the bike hit the ground... then I don't... I don't really remember. I had blood all over me. They all circled me and smothered me. It was like a bloodfest."

Ed raged that the police arrived but refused to take testimony, letting the guy who hit him walk off.

"I want those who did this exposed," he said.

Jethro soon called me, in his own fit of rage. I listened as he ranted angrily. "This is SugarHouse's first public event! If they're prepared to attack a neighbor, they could escalate further. Those of us on Allen Street already didn't feel safe. What lengths will SugarHouse go to force a casino down our throats? This is strategic use of intimidation and violence."

"It's only intimidation," I said, matching my voice to meet his anger, "if we become scared by it. There's plenty for us to figure out, like did police really walk away? Why didn't SugarHouse executives intervene? Where did all the video footage go?"

I carefully kept some musings to myself. *Could SugarHouse have explicitly condoned the attack? Doubtful. They are the casinos backed by lawyers, who would avoid any explicit impropriety. But they did build the context, escalating the conflict, calling Casino-Free Philadelphia "elites" and "carpetbaggers" and much worse. Ed would have been a ripe local target—more isolated than Jethro, yet his status in the movement meant the story would move through the neighborhood quickly, with a sure-fire message intended to frighten.*

I felt little relief that we had built a high-ground movement and hadn't stooped to name-calling. CFP had never had anyone physically threatened—much less assaulted—at any of our actions.

As Jethro and Ed journeyed to the police station, I massaged a press release. "While we are not certain of the names of who was behind the attack and how it was planned, we believe organizers should take responsibility for violence done on their behalf and apologize for their role in fanning the flames of hatred and division in Fishtown. SugarHouse has repeatedly used heightened rhetoric to try to divide Fishtown."

We asked for an apology from SugarHouse and the barbecue organizers, adding that "Ed Verral is okay but recovering slowly. He wants everyone to know he will continue to be in the struggle and continue being vocal in opposition to SugarHouse. He also asks everybody from the anti-casino movement to keep the high moral ground and not return politically motivated violence with more violence."

Privately, I offered nonviolence training to FACT members, trying to bridge the divide and send a clear signal: we don't want violence. They declined, but it did open up a cordial email channel of communication.

Unfortunately for us, the press sensationalized the incident exactly as we dreaded they might: as a Fishtown versus Fishtown brawl. "Fishtown Boils over SugarHouse" one article blared. It was Ed's words—versus the other accounts, which said he took the first swing—that were the story.

Frustrated at the he-said/she-said portrayal, I yelled at one reporter, "Why don't you ask SugarHouse if they'll openly condemn the violence? We're trying to protect our members."

He replied, "But if one of *your* people were violent, would you condemn their actions?"

"*Absolutely*," I said. "I'd be the first."

The reporter agreed to try brokering a joint statement with SugarHouse that violence was unacceptable, but he got nowhere. Instead, press reaffirmed their narrative that the SugarHouse split was between old-timers versus new, working class versus middle class, and old people versus young people. It was one narrative that we completely lost. Maybe if we had done more ground organizing, we wouldn't have lost it.

But for that night, the tension was only increasing—especially when pro-casino FACT announced it would counter-protest tomorrow's anti-casino protest.

The next day, a bright sun shone on two very different-looking crowds. On the west side of the street were ninety anti-casino activists: babies in strollers donning colorful *casi*NO artwork, skinny-jeaned hipsters chatting with bulging-bellied old-timers next to fierce-looking mothers, waving 1,500-foot buffer placards. It was the first public action of Mothers Against SugarHouse (MASH) with Fishtowners Against SugarHouse Takeover (FAST).

On the east side of the street was a solid mass of thirty middle-aged, white, mostly men donning SugarHouse's "Pure Fun" T-shirts and caps. Their faces were grim. At a distance behind were SugarHouse executives, watching like generals removed from the front lines.

The air crackled. The attack on Ed whipped through the rumor mill, as Jethro and I chased it to stamp out any inklings of revenge. "Show up," we told people, "but be as light-hearted as you can be. Our target is *not* other Fishtowners, who have been historically disenfranchised. It's politicians."

Police arrived, crossing into the no man's land between the two groups.

Organizer Debbie King roared into the bullhorn. "They want to pretend this casino is just in Fishtown. But it's half in Northern Liberties! It's in our neighborhood and will affect us. And SugarHouse wants it to be just about Fishtown because from the start, we have been steadfast: *No casino!*" The crowd chanted "No casino!" back, as it moved through the anti-casino standbys: "Who wants democracy? We do!" And "Hey-hey! Ho-ho! Casinos have got to go!"

The crowd bobbed, marching across the street to SugarHouse's entrance, a dull, chain-link fence guarding the wasteland. Pro-casino marchers moved to intercept.

Organizer Hilary Regan, a fireball of high energy, flagged a police officer and waved her permit in his face. "*We* have a permit—they don't. You have to protect our right for them to not interfere."

When the officer kept shaking his head, she pulled me into the debate, looking to me for support.

I tossed up my hands. "It's a democracy. They have a right to express themselves, too." We had never sought a permit for a CFP action, on the belief that it was a right, not a request. I turned back to the cop. "We've had one of our members attacked recently, possibly by one of those folks. Will you help keep the groups separate, so nobody gets hurt?" The policeman nodded.

But when SugarHouse supporters—shouting *"Build them NOW!"*—headed directly toward us, the cops made no moves. Debbie grabbed the mike and drowned them out with our own chants: *"No casino! No way!"*

Each side ratcheted up their noise, creating loud, screeching dissonances. Truckers honked—to the cheers of each side.

Jethro pulled me aside, his teeth grinding. "Watch Ed. I can't do it—I'm too worked up myself. Make sure he's okay."

"I'm already on it," I said, as the first wave of SugarHouse supporters crashed into our lines. It was yelling right away.

"Get back to your neighborhood!"

"Where are you from?"

Chuck Valentine stepped forward to challenge two men who, by sight, could have been his blood brothers. He bellowed, "I am Fishtown! I am Fishtown!" Chuck described his church and neighborhood credentials like a pass.

The two pointed at the rest of the crowd. One shouted, "Where are *they* from? They're not from here."

Jethro, red-faced, shouted, "I live right over there. Where do *you* live?"

Chuck put a hand on Jethro's shoulder and hosted the debate like a pro. "We're from all over. If this is built, you and our neighbors will have to deal with the crime. I want everybody to care about Fishtown—no matter where they're from."

"It's about jobs! We need jobs! Everyone overlooks Fishtown. Not us. We live here."

"Let's talk about jobs," said Chuck. "How many jobs will go to Fishtown? They'll bring their own people."

"They made promises to us!"

Chuck squawked and chuckled, shouting back, "Harrah's casino made promises to the Chester community. How many locals are getting jobs? Not even half as many as promised! The casinos are gonna do whatever it takes to get your support."

With awe, I watched as Chuck created a sphere of dialogue around him, turning the taunts, epithets, and boastful swagger into serious arguments about casinos. But elsewhere, chants were dying down and turning to taunts: *elitist, sell-outs, carpet-baggers, ignorant brute.*

I took a breath and thought about what I know about crowd control. For one, dense crowds are more prone to act irrationally or even riot. Spread-out crowds breathe and feel less pressure. Moving quickly, hands to the side, I walked through the crowd, adjusting people with my presence to leave a wake of space wherever I went. I tried to project a calm spirit. I wasn't sure if it was making a difference. But unable to protect Ed before, I needed to do something.

The taunts continued. Someone shouted at Ed, "Come here for another ass-kicking?"

"*Shut up!*" shouted Ed, as he let me pull him away.

But someone took Ed's place and shouted back, "Come here to beat up some kids today, too?"

It's only ratcheting up.

There's a dangerous energy that happens when people stop to watch others yelling at each other. Bystanders feed the fight, because they're either immobilized or actively shouting from the sidelines—like a high-school fight, with people shouting, "*Fight! Fight!*" All the roles feed the conflict.

I realized I might not be able to engage the taunters, but I could help those whose immobilization made them feel powerless. Frozen people need to be loosened up, so they can make de-escalatory moves, like Chuck's respectful, passionate banter.

Holding Ed's shaking hand, I projected my voice so everyone directly around me could hear. "It's all good. People are just arguing passionately—that's what happens in a democracy. This is the first real debate this city has seen."

I yelled over to Jethro, "Remind everyone this is the first public debate." He passed the word along, as did organizers and others with cool heads. Slowly, the word spread, calming the crowds—or at least stopping the taunting.

Less tense, the crowds loosely mingled, until Hilary and Debbie led our part of the crowd to return to the west side for a short debrief.

I let my jaw relax. There had been no violence.

For the organizers: A great turnout, and with all the expansive media coverage—except *Daily News'* Chris Brennan—starting to refer to SugarHouse as in "Fishtown *and* Northern Liberties."

For Ed and Jethro: A healing re-integration, to see their community stand with them.

For me? Even that evening, I tossed right back into work after news that Michael Nutter, our presumptive mayor, was holding a $500-a-plate fundraiser at a private golf club. The headliner: disgraced ex-PGCB chairman Tad Decker.

It just never stops. We have to teach Nutter a lesson, too.

But not before teaching the PGCB a lesson.

*   *   *

The morning of the PGCB hearing, I biked over to Temple University, my heart pounding with anticipation. *Can a handful of us really shut down a hearing? Will we get enough people on a weekday morning? How will the new PGCB chairwoman respond to us? Will we be arrested? Did we organize it too hastily?*

It was a sunny day, and I arrived early, watching students bustling to and from classes. The Gittis Student Center towered up toward the sky, with a glass entranceway up to the second floor. This would be the first PGCB meeting in Philadelphia since it announced the casinos. Walking around, I counted at least ten police officers surrounding the perimeter of the building, plus a handful of plainclothes police with their characteristic cigarette, big build, and sunglasses, trying unsuccessfully to be incognito.

At the foot of the building, I put my backpack down and waited for only a minute before people started to arrive. All-star Andrea Preis was the first arrival, soon followed by fifteen others.

I reviewed the scenarios and possibilities for the day. *What if we're all immediately kicked out? What if they threaten all of us with arrest? What if the crowd grows hostile and boos us down? What if, what if, what if ... ?*

I held my tongue on my own biggest worry: a physical altercation. I didn't know if I was being irrational or—by not talking about it—overly protective of making them more fearful. But I couldn't shake the fear of a repeat attack, even when I reminded myself pro-casino folks weren't planning to be there.

"Tell me if I'm wrong, but the point here is to get our voices heard," said Chuck Valentine. "We're not challenging anyone's authority, just testifying."

"Yes," I said, "unless she tells us we cannot speak. Then she's just wrong. But we'll still be respectful. This action only works if we show clearly we're on the side of angels."

To press, we called it a *public filibuster,* built loosely on the principle of the Senate's procedural filibuster. Only it was with citizens. And without a law backing it up. We even made a handout for them to help support its framing.

Andrea caught the vision completely. "It can't be anything like that shouting session at that planning meeting."

"Exactly," I said. "To avoid becoming a howling mass, we each will speak individually and in an order. Who goes first?" Ed Goppelt pointed at me, then himself. We quickly created an order. "I know it's scarier for each person to do it alone, but our discipline avoids chaotic yelling. Plus," I grinned widely, "it takes more time for each person to be thrown out individually. We ready?"

Andrea, Chuck, and the other half-dozen folks nodded.

I led us the long way to the building entrance, hoping the walk would relax the knots in our stomachs. While walking, I said, "Relaxed direct actionists are the best. Unlike normal, highly scripted hearings, our actions introduce spontaneity. Everyone in the room suddenly becomes unwitting actors in our improvisational theater. Nobody's script is written. We, at least, know to prepare for it and have lead parts. But our opponents aren't prepared, so we have to stay relaxed and gracious as they figure out their new role."

We headed up the stairs and into the second floor. Immediately, two dozen civil affairs, city police, state police, and Temple University security guards turned their heads.

I wilted. Then impishly wondered: how long were *their* arguments over jurisdiction and who would arrest us?

On our left sat the PGCB board members, at a long table on the dark side of the square room, facing large windows. A hundred or so sitting spectators turned their heads as we filed in. Most were interested in the agenda before the PGCB, none of which related to the Philadelphia casinos. Standing behind them, intermingled with police, was a bevy of reporters.

Whether real or imagined, all their faces appeared hostile, and my heart leapt into my throat.

Trying to be devoutly quiet, we took our places on one empty, long row, halfway back. We had agreed not to interrupt anyone's testimony, so we listened to a presenter coo about the success of the PGCB's self-exclusion list, which allowed problem gamblers to sign up to be kept out of casinos.

The man boasted the list would seriously reduce problem gambling. Yet, so far, nobody had signed up, and unlike in other states, there was virtually zero money to advertise its existence. One of the few ways gamblers would be encouraged is if they called the 1-800-GAMBLER number, which was tucked away in fine print on casino billboards.

The gentleman concluded and started to get up. Andrea, practically shaking with rage, whispered to me, "Can I say something?"

"Sure," I replied, taken aback slightly at the request. "The point here is to speak our minds."

Andrea stood up, shoulders back. Her voice echoed like a gong. "Excuse me, sir. Is the solution to the increased gambling problem to build new casinos?"

Heads turned.

"I'm sorry," Chairwoman Mary Collins quickly cut her off. "We're not taking comments or questions from the audience."

Andrea sat back down. With horror, I suddenly realized I was supposed to go next. The words were out of my mouth before I could think. "My name's Daniel Hunter." I noted I was on my feet. "I'd like the opportunity to speak as allowed by the Pennsylvania Constitution. (*Sir, please have a seat, sir.*) We haven't had a chance to speak. (*I've addressed this issue. Have a seat, please, thank you.*) It's been fifteen months since the Pennsylvania Gaming Control Board had an opportunity for us to speak."

I sat down just as Ed Goppelt popped up. "Madam Chairwoman (*Sir, I spoke to you already*) please excuse this interruption, but I and others have asked (*Sir, sir, we are going to take a recess*) you in writing for a chance to address this panel (*We will take a recess*) pursuant to Article 1, Section 20 of the Pennsylvania Constitution."

The chairwoman pounded her gavel. A police officer wrenched at Ed's arm. Off-balance, Ed continued, "I ask for this opportunity to address this panel."

A second policewoman sidled up, speaking nonsense. "You'll have a chance to speak, just not now."

With admiration, I watched Ed—while being forcibly removed by the uniformed officers—yell out, "Article 1, Section 20 of the Pennsylvania Constitution!"

The crowd crawled toward recess. Karim shot up and began talking. "Madam, the process of casino slot parlors has been broken—"

A civil affairs officer materialized in front of me. "You all need to leave."

"*What?*"

"You all need to leave, *now*," she said, gesturing to our entire row.

"Nobody's asked us to leave."

"I'm asking you to leave."

"On what grounds?" I looked at her defiantly.

"I can tell you when to leave," she said.

"Not in a public hearing, you can't," I said.

She pulled another uniformed officer over to support her. "We will arrest you if you don't go," she insisted.

I hesitated, trying to calculate the situation in my head. *Is she bluffing? Does she have any what the law is in this situation? Will my arrest be better for us than another round of interrupting? Will she try arresting just me—or everyone?*

These were classic direct action questions, because police officers do not have to be legally right when they arrest you. They are often wrong. The law gives them incredible leeway to enforce "public order," even at the cost of your civil liberties.

I decided to try a compromise. "You can ask me and those of us who spoke to leave, but you can't tell people who did not do anything to leave. That's patently illegal."

She looked at me, then her partner, then back at me. She waved her hand dismissively in agreement.

As soon as she did, I wondered if I had given away too much by agreeing to leave. But the moment of self-reproach lifted immediately as I was thrust by the officers out of the room and into a line of microphones, along with Karim, Andrea, and Ed.

Chuck and Ramona watched through the glass windows but wisely chose not to leave the room, not certain they would be let back in.

Reporters asked the usual questions: "What do you hope to accomplish today?" "Do you think it will make a difference?" They scrambled back as the recess ended, while Karim, Andrea, Ed, and I were gently escorted outside by Temple security.

"You are not allowed back in the building," a guard said gruffly.

"On what grounds?" I asked.

"Mine." He smiled.

He was a lowly security guard, and we joined in a few minutes of playful banter about the abysmal pay of security-guard workers, initiatives to unionize their workforce—for which Jethro and I had done some consulting in the past few months—and a boast from me that I could race past him and get back into the meeting. "I'm quicker than I look," he joked back, pointing at his bulging belly and then breaking into laughter.

The four of us waited outside, hearts racing. But as our wait became nearly an hour, we fretted. *Have people chickened out? Are they getting arrested? Did they forget to call us?*

It took another half hour before Chuck emerged from the doors with a gigantic smile. He bellowed, "They shut the whole thing down!" Behind him, our crew erupted into cheers.

Chuck quickly told the story. "We kept trying to speak, again and again, but they kept not letting us. First they told us to be quiet, but we wouldn't. So they called another recess. Then they started again and tried to carry on the meeting in spite of us, but we just kept talking louder so they couldn't hear what was being said by the witnesses. Finally, they just shut the whole meeting down."

We were impressed.

Ramona Johnson looked up. "I think we really got to her. I just kept addressing the chairwoman, trying to convince her."

Andrea shook her head with an intense face. I looked at her questioningly. "It's just, I can't believe a dozen people just shut down the PGCB hearing. And they'd rather let that happen than just allow us to speak."

I nodded. For the next hour we basked, retelling details. Afterward, I laid out in a nearby field for a few minutes, relaxing and releasing the tension of an unscripted morning.

That night, my body still rippled with excitement. All day, I had talked with CFP members, using it as a moment to teach about the strategy of direct action. With Andrea, I explained, "We put the PGCB in a classic double-bind—where they're damned if they do allow us to speak and damned if they don't. In direct action parlance, we call this a *dilemma demonstration*—where we put our opponents in a dilemma where either way, they lose. We did it by modeling the behavior we wanted, rather than wait for someone else to do it for us."

To Chuck, I said, "Society has all sorts of myths, like that a public hearing means the public's voice matters. Through our personal risk, we exposed the injustice and that a widely shared value—public input—was being violated. People could then see the injustice with their own eyes, something a dozen rallies or a hundred meetings with newspapers' editorial boards would fail to have done."

To Jethro, I wrote, "Media need drama, and we gave them drama—but drama with *our* message. Our respectful shut-down of the PGCB has none of the blowback from that earlier planning commission hearing. Instead, the chairwoman was telling people, 'They're not violent people, they have sincere concerns. I don't think it would be appropriate to have the police remove them, absent any display of violence.' She may not know it, but that's an invitation to return."

Unable to sleep that night from a mix of adrenaline and excitement, I tip-toed to my computer. News was phenomenal. KYW calling us "soft-spoken, polite, and very determined" and the Associated Press and *Metro* reporting we "forced an early adjournment, signaling that the bitter grass roots battle against two city slots parlors is far from over." Even the unsympathetic *Daily News*—which gave us exclusively passive language in "our failure... to speak"—had to acknowledge our upbeat, positive tone.

It struck me to put clippings of the days' news into a single document. On my computer, I threw on logos from Fishtown's *Spirit* and NBC 10's coverage of the Northern Liberties rally. I added *Philebrity*'s blog coverage of the mountains of trash left on the SugarHouse site after its barbecue ("time to wake up and take out the trash") and the *Philadelphia Inquirer*'s coverage of the raging issues over how much land

SugarHouse and Foxwoods owned and how much was state land. And the *City Paper* and *Plan Philly*'s coverage of the 1,500-foot buffer hearings at the state level. And two editorials slamming justices "stained by the pay raise and slots." And extracts of articles from the *Wilkes-Barre Citizens' Voice, Patriot News, Legal Intelligencer*, and *Evening Bulletin*.

We were everywhere.

Not only had we achieved dense media coverage—this was just a sampling from the *past three days*—we were connecting to other movements. Our trainings brought out environmentalist, labor, and economic-justice activists, many of whom wanted to learn from our media, strategy, and direct action workshops how we did what we did.

Heading to sleep, I emailed the eight pages of press clippings to City Council members. It was better than a threat. It was evidence we knew how to create damaging press for those who stood against us. We were about to teach Mayor Nutter the same lesson.

Presumptive-mayor Michael Nutter had gotten little attention from us in recent months. His inauguration, to come in January, felt a year away. Though the DRNA was occasionally pressing him, CFP did next to nothing to target him, only building the context.

But news that disgraced PGCB chairman Tad Decker and his Cozen O'Connor cronies were headlining a major Nutter fundraiser caused a flood of emails expressing violation and distaste. Nutter was making himself a target.

Debbie King suggested dressing up like "Billionaires for Bush" and crashing the private party. Paul suggested passing out "dirty money"—fake money with Tad Decker's face on it, asking the question, "Why does Nutter accept dirty money from Decker, but not from us?"

None felt right to me. All a little too hokey. There's a big gap in my mind between street theater and direct action. One is play-acting. The other is acting out the society you want. Both may be staged, but only one operates on a principle of "Be the change you want to see." Too many groups spent time designing actions that were just "Tell people the change you want to see." I didn't want to be that.

Jethro didn't have ideas, but he grinned and said, "Just remember what my mom always said. 'There's a million ways to say *fuck you*.'"

We kept searching for the high-ground action.

A surprise call from Dot Yablin changed the equation.

I didn't know Dot as well as I wished. She'd never called me before. She was a regular attendee and seemed like one of those wise, retired women who never quite got the hang of staying silent.

Hesitantly, as if selecting her words delicately, she explained that Nutter's campaign office had just called her and told her that Michael Nutter wanted to speak with her.

My voice matched her shock. "He wants to talk to you? Why?"

"I think because of my letter to the editor that the *Inquirer* printed yesterday," she said. "He's calling me in an hour to talk. What should I say? I don't want to mess this up."

I went into coaching mode, using elicitive questions to help her steady herself. I had long ago left behind the idea that coaching meant telling people what to do. If they didn't see it for themselves, it would never stick as deeply. I asked: "What's his political interest in calling you?" "What do you want him to do after he hangs up?" "Why do you want him to not accept Decker's money?" Then, when she answered, I said, "Perfectly clear to me—sounds like you have it."

Together, we realized Dot's pithy letter to the editor was the first public attack on the likely new mayor. It was a gentle challenge over Decker's role in the fundraiser ("It's an understatement to say I am shocked and disappointed"). But angling for a broad mandate, Nutter wanted to avoid any public criticism—and most movements and groups, strangely, gave him the benefit of the doubt.

"I'm just anxious," she admitted shyly. "I don't want to come across as too assertive."

"I'd be nervous, too. But remember, he's *asking* to talk to you. What do you have to lose?"

"I just don't want to embarrass myself, or us..."

I laughed. "If it helps, I'm not worried one bit. You get to speak your mind, exactly as you see it. Nutter hasn't earned our trust simply with words. It's in his actions." I paused. "What generally helps you get less nervous?"

"Send me a copy of the fundraising letter with Decker's name on it, so I know I'm standing on solid ground," she said. She chewed on the question. "And I'll talk with my husband a little. Maybe take a walk."

"Excellent," I said.

We got off the phone. Like her, I took a short walk.

Two hours later, Dot called back. I could hear relief mixed with adrenaline. "He was respectful, but he said he didn't know about Tad Decker's involvement. When I explained it had been printed in the *Inquirer*, he insisted it was a media misrepresentation. Then, I told him I had a copy of the invitation. I insisted he must know what happens in his office. After that, Michael Nutter did most of the talking."

"Sounds like you made your point clearly," I said.

"I realize now, he didn't agree to do anything, though." Her voice started to deflate. "Maybe I should follow up with a letter, to make my point clear."

"That's a great idea," I said. "But don't beat yourself up. Politicians are masters at avoiding promises and commitments. You already got under Nutter's skin—in a good way. That's a big step forward. And it shows that Nutter clearly doesn't want to be pinned as a bad guy right now. That's something we can use to nudge him to do the right thing."

Surprising Karim, Paul, and others who expected me to support organizing direct action, I announced we shouldn't put Nutter's back up against the wall. His phone call meant he had wiggle room. We needed to offer him a way out.

Instead, we tried to crack the internal maze and power struggles inside Nutter's campaign office to open a direct line of negotiation to Nutter. Anne and Karim helped me reach high-level staffers, with whom I exchanged terse words, insisting that Nutter distance himself from Decker. "He doesn't want to be saddled with the stain of Decker," I told them.

Meanwhile, Debbie King, with Linda Soffer, Jeanne Kohl and others, kicked off a letter-writing campaign by the anti-SugarHouse mothers' group, MASH. The story was broken in the blog *Philebrity*—"Local Moms Set to Come Down Hard"—which spurred the *Inquirer* to cover the two dozen letters to Nutter.

Early the next week, Nutter caved.

Jeff Shields from the *Inquirer* alerted me that Decker was formally bowing out of the fundraiser, though Decker's reasons remained couched in vague statements about campaign contribution limits. Ignoring Karim's suggestion that we had gotten what we wanted, I told everyone to keep pushing. "We need this victory to be public, with anti-casino fingerprints all over it, not some quiet victory. We want Nutter to be our man."

Dozens more letters poured in, while we used relationships with reporters to keep hounding Nutter for a real explanation.

The next day, the Nutter campaign produced a form letter reasserting Michael Nutter's campaign promises: that he opposed the PGCB's selection process, intended to fight for greater local input, and opposed both casino sites. But I felt we could and should get more—we didn't want a repeat of his words, we wanted an active distancing of himself from Decker.

More MASH letters. More press calls.

By Wednesday, Jeff Shields got a direct quote from Michael Nutter admitting he had distanced himself because of "very public concerns about his recent service at the Gaming Board and his return to the firm."

Jeff wrote, "Nutter may have to get used to this. Casino-Free Philadelphia will try to delay the city's approval of SugarHouse and Foxwoods plans until Nutter gets in office, in the meantime trying to push Nutter to take up their cause in an active way."

Over email, Jethro crowed, "That is good for us and really bad for Decker. This is a real victory, and the governor's going to hear about it through meetings with Nutter now. Make sure MASH gets a real shout out for doing this—and let's celebrate!"

I felt ecstatic. We were moving major players. And though we didn't have a sexy, brand-new campaign to trot out, we were tightening back up and getting back to our storyline: democracy, good process, and politicians siding with the will of the people.

Soon, we would find out if City Council would keep siding with us, too. But murky rumors from council suggested its members might be ready to cave.

CHAPTER 15
Political Maneuvers

SEPTEMBER 13, 2007 — NOVEMBER 30, 2007

giving your opponents space to become allies • responsibility is a dangerous addiction •
don't target those who haven't done you wrong • negotiating a win •
direct action is a healing balm • about injunctions •
the rare online poll that makes a difference • upside-down triangle •
fighting the belief that ultimate power rests in lawsuits and politicians

IT FELT LIKE EVERYTHING I did was part of the movement. I dreamt about the campaign, walked down the street thinking about the campaign. Even when I was at the grocery store, I observed how products advertise themselves from the perspective of our campaign ("What can I learn about how to make short, punchy subject lines from this tomato sauce?"). I picked up tactic ideas while at the dollar store ("How could this squirt gun be used in an action?"). My life was breathing the details of our many—and growing—list of targets: Rendell, Fumo, Nutter, Decker, DiCicco, SugarHouse, Foxwoods, the PGCB.

So it was like a refreshing splash of cold water when volunteer Mary Reinhart asked me over email, "A while ago, you wrote us about a Movement Action Plan. What stage do you think we are in now?"

The email caught me by surprise because I had been so in the trees, missing the forest.

I returned to Bill Moyer's Movement Action Plan to read his description of the stages. I instantly recognized we had weathered Stage 4: Take-off (Philly's Ballot Box) and our own version of Stage 5: Perception of failure. Moyer's words were right on for the next stage: "Stage 6: Majority public opinion is often a difficult time for activists. The excitement, high hopes, big demonstrations, nonviolent actions, and media coverage of the take-off stage have subsided. The vibrant rebellion and the protest efforts have been replaced by a larger number of isolated organizations and events that many believe are not getting anywhere. Consequently, this can be a discouraging time, despite the beehive of activity and full calendar of events."

I wrote back to Mary, "I believe we are in Stage 6. We've proven the failure of powerholders to solve the problem, and moved a sizable set of the population—polling numbers now show a slight majority of Philadelphians oppose casinos outright. But that needs to expand. We need to build a critical mass of public opinion. As we do that, our next challenge is Stage 7: Success, where we have to respond to powerholders' attempts to advance minimal reforms, and groups fracture over different end goals."

Something about the big picture felt rejuvenating to me. With a flourish, I sent the email to Mary and created a larger analysis based on where we were for the whole movement.

At the next executive meeting, we'd learn that powerholders were starting to look for real solutions, a signal we were moving toward Stage 7. History rarely remembers that this is a long stage—and one in which, often, some things are won and some things are lost.

Shirley couldn't wait until we wrapped up our chit-chat and personal catching up. Before we could even get to our agenda, she blurted, "Fumo's offered money to the casinos to move!"

For once, our executive team had nothing to say. We listened quietly.

Shirley explained how she and Kathy DeAngelis had snuck into a talk given by Senator Fumo. "It was before a group of senior citizens at Temple," she said, laughing to let a few wrinkles show. "We thought we'd fit right in!" At the meeting, Fumo had complained of "South Philly, the worst site." Shirley turned to Jethro, "But—get this—he then said he's not happy with *any* of the siting. Then, he said he had offered Foxwoods $30 million to move. Then upped it to $50 million! And that he offered SugarHouse..." Shirley looked at her notes. "Something like $15 to 20 million to move."

"It's a long con," said Paul quickly. He would have said more, but Jethro interrupted angrily.

"Fumo's going to waste *taxpayer* money to fix a problem *he* created!" Jethro grimaced and bit down on his lip. "This is what's going to land him in jail!"

News reports had surfaced of Fumo coining a term, *OPM*, for "other people's money"—his favorite kind of money to spend. Jethro didn't just want to win on casinos—he wanted to help change the political culture.

I stared at Jethro with surprise. "This is how you take this news? Go ahead and be mad, but it's worth noting that Fumo might *really* be changing positions. Recall, Fumo opposed DiCicco's efforts forever. Fumo opposed the 1,500-foot-buffer. Fumo switched only enough to introduce a weak version, stating it could not work. *Now* he's offering money to get these casinos to move. That's a *real* change—he may really be playing ball."

"This is just another ploy," said Paul. His faced contorted into a lawyer's scowl. "Think about it. We all know Fumo is mucking about in the DRNA, where he's probably behind some delegates urging members to cut ties with CFP. It has Fumo's fingerprints all over it. This is another way to divide us up. If he wanted them to move, he'd *make* them move. He just wants to get re-elected and will screw us when the time is right."

"Maybe." But as I heard Paul, it made me even more confident in my first instinct. "But days ago, when DiCicco was saying the governor's meeting was fruitless, it was

Fumo telling the press it was a start. If it was just for votes, he'd have televised this offer of money like crazy so everyone could see it. It's not erratic behavior. He's a politically conscious man. I think he has an ulterior motive—"

"You may be right," said Jethro, coolly. His ability to switch emotions rapidly never ceased to amaze me. "Maybe things are falling apart behind the scenes between Fumo and his lawyer and SugarHouse investor Richard Sprague. That *would* explain why Fumo is asking the judge in his corruption trial to let him remove Sprague from his case—it's not just a ploy. It's a real falling out."

"Exactly," I said. "Can Richard Sprague be happy that his ex-client, the Honorable Senator Fumo, is even *talking* about re-siting his casino? They're going to war with each other, and I think this is just going to accelerate. It just proves the point that elites aren't all buddy-buddy. They're quite competitive with each other—and when direct action groups apply pressure, we can split them off from each other."

Nico inserted himself. "Sounds like we need to test Fumo somehow, to see where he's really coming from."

Heads nodded. Politicians can say anything; testing them comes from the crucible of action. We brainstormed actions to pull Fumo's real position out of the woodwork: Petition him to testify on our side in the upcoming council vote? Offer him chocolates in exchange for his support? Organize a hunger fast by his constituents? Ask the DRNA to host a public forum with him? Sit-in at DiCicco's office to flush out Fumo's real position?

None hit the mark.

We just couldn't decide whether to use the carrot or the stick. But we wanted options, in case something needed to be pulled together in hours if something did pop off. Because it always did.

As exciting as that news was, it felt ephemeral. After the meeting, as I walked toward my bike, I wondered if we had wasted our meeting. Instead of focusing on Fumo, shouldn't we be spending time thinking about the upcoming council hearing? We had little influence over Fumo. But in just a few days, the council Rules Committee could vote that bill introduced by Ramos months ago out of committee. If given a positive vote in full council, SugarHouse could start building by early October.

News on that front wasn't pretty.

Councilmembers kept telling us that they were unhappy that no civics had heeded their urgings or threats to negotiate with the casinos—aside from a half-hearted and eventually stalled attempt by Fishtown Neighbors. A few had shown unusual annoyance at Ed Goppelt's Hallwatch fax bank, targeting council with 926 emails and 774 faxes to each councilmember. They told us they were tired of being the target—they felt the state representatives who voted for Act 71 should be target.

I agreed, but we couldn't risk losing the city.

Most unnerving was a DiCicco staffer with whom I had frequently spoken abruptly saying he didn't want to talk with CFP anymore, telling me that "communication from CFP has been lacking, non-existent, or dishonest while we have done our best to be open and transparent." My gut said this smacked of Senator Fumo. He hated us, since we were out of his control, and must have urged DiCicco's office to distance themselves from us.

In response, I had let my irritation show. "If you're going to implode this relationship, I can't stop you from doing it—but it won't be our fault." I got the staffer to back down enough to admit we'd always been honest and transparent. But like all councilmembers now, DiCicco's staff kept their cards closer than usual. They told us nothing.

It was exactly what they would do if they were going to screw us.

Returning home, I sat on the carpet, my back up against my couch. I pulled out my cell phone and called an older political mentor, Antje Mattheus.

I knew Antje well enough that soon after our hello's, I exploded. "We're up against the wall! Months of effort could be wiped away as soon as council does something! We need to prepare civil disobedience against them." The taste of the PGCB shut-down was still in my mouth.

Distant from the campaign, Antje reflected none of the movement anxiety. Her voice felt slow, smooth. "Wouldn't the governor's talk of re-siting make council less likely to cave?"

Despite myself, I laughed out loud. There are so many levels to campaigns. Those of us on the inside knew that not a single politician trusted the governor's public word on this matter. Yet those further out took it at face value. It was a dynamic that stretched my patience, forcing me to re-explain our situation again and again. And yet, not doing it with patience would have quickly made us an insular campaign.

I filled her in on the political assumption that Rendell was just biding his time to announce that the search was over. "Maybe right before the council vote, to seal the deal," I fretted.

Antje put feeling behind her words, beneath a heavy, German accent. "You're more worried than usual."

"Yes." I took a breath. "What ideas can you give me about how we can shut down council's meeting with a few dozen people? We just did it with the PGCB and only a handful of people. But they weren't prepared, and council sees protests a lot. Could we use bullhorns? Whistles? Songs?"

I whipped out my notebook and—under the circled date for council's upcoming hearing—wrote in large print: "City Council Shut-Down."

Antje had been arrested on more than a few occasions. She had worked with César Chavez and a dozen direct action campaigns. I was certain she could help me think of a way to stop council's vote.

But instead of flowing with ideas, her voice was short. "Has City Council screwed you yet?"

"No."

"Then if you target them now, before they do something, you lose all your high ground."

"But—"

"I know. They *might* screw you. But direct action is not a stick to use because you have it. If you start targeting people who haven't done you wrong, people will see *you* as the problem. They'll say that you've wildly escalated, and who are these wide-eyed, crazy protestors? You lose the high ground, and that'll make any future organizing much harder."

"So what do I get us to do?"

"Maybe you'll have to lose the vote. But there's got to be other ways to get to them without trying to shut down a hearing from a body that's done you no wrong... or at least not grievous enough to make sense to those outside your movement."

I sat sulkily, knowing she was right. Her appeal was both moral and strategic. That alignment had never done me wrong. But it didn't help me see my way out.

She let the silence grow until adding, "Daniel, you sound like you're taking everything onto your shoulders right now. I know something about that. I was raised by the generation of Holocaust survivors who told me, 'Never again.' I took it personally, as if I had to stop *every* genocide. Every time I read a newspaper article, I felt like I had to personally do something. It's disabling—it kills us inside."

"And you think I'm doing that?" I asked.

"Are you?"

I leaned back on the couch, holding my legs close. "A little. But there's so much... I mean, yeah, I am taking a lot of pressure on."

"Share the load," she advised. "It'll make your planning easier."

"It's not getting easier. Karim, our communications director, is leaving to work for Anne Dicker's campaign." I sighed heavily. "But I guess we just have to fundraise to replace him... I need to just let go of more things—and stay true to the high-ground principles that have gotten us to this point."

I could hear Antje nod sagely.

Yet even as I said it, I worried I wouldn't be able to let go and find others. I wanted the work to be high quality, and we needed everything done quickly. But at least she had talked me out of orchestrating a massive direct action against City Council.

And days before the council meeting, her strategy was proven right. Instead of voting for the SugarHouse permits, council canceled the hearing. It turned out that SugarHouse was just as scared as we were. Worried it would get voted down without an agreement with local civic associations, the company asked for an indefinite postponement of its zoning permits.

Our press release blasted the good news: "SugarHouse Cries Uncle and Unwittingly Re-Asserts the Need for Community Support"—though, as a press release, it didn't matter. Issue fatigue meant almost no press would carry a non-story ("Council *Doesn't* Vote").

SugarHouse was officially mired.

It gave us a few more months' reprieve—just as we were gearing up to return to the PGCB.

Cognizant of Antje's reminder to keep the high ground, we sent letters to those who hadn't been able to speak at the last PGCB meeting due to our shutting it down: "Our intention never was to shut down the meeting, merely to advocate for our right to speak, too.... We request you write to the PGCB to settle this matter by allowing the public some time to speak at every hearing."

We also wrote to PGCB chairwoman Mary Collins, asking her to do the right thing and let us speak at the next PGCB public hearing. We hoped our pressure might help relieve her of her twisted legal rationalization to exclude us last time. "That's part of our ethics policy," she had told reporters, to not have people "commenting on matters pending before the board."

Her silence in response to our letter was disappointing, but expected.

So on October 2 we took a three-hour trip to towering Mellow Theater in Scranton. PGCB board member Ray Angeli was the college president here, having named the lavish theater in honor of powerful Democratic Senator Bob Mellow, who hand-picked Ray Angeli to be on the PGCB. As a reporter might have written, it all *stank*.

The theater was dark and sprawling. Assuming our opponents would be better prepared, we adapted our game plan and spread out, to avoid any chances of being kicked out en masse. Everyone had a buddy, for moral support.

There were very few police.

"Excuse me, sir." The chairwoman interrupted the current speaker. "I see that some members from the 'No Casino Free Philadelphia' coalition have just arrived." I laughed quietly at her mistake. "We understand you have some concerns, and we would like to talk with you. Please meet our representative in the back of the auditorium." Heads swiveled to watch pairs across the audience stand up and file to the back.

I wondered what this was about. My buddy—a straitlaced lawyer, George Kelly—and I headed to the back.

A PGCB representative swaggered up to us and grabbed our hands like old friends. "The PGCB is going to allow you to speak for five minutes at the end of the meeting today." His hands fidgeted, as if to add how little the PGCB wanted a repeat of the last meeting.

"Give us some time to discuss," Jethro announced, pulling us away for a group huddle.

George was ecstatic. "This is amazing! They're giving us what we wanted. We have to accept."

Jethro was mellow. "We aren't the only public group who has something to say. What about the poor groups in Pittsburgh who already lost their battle against a casino? Or folk from smaller towns in PA. Will they let others speak?"

"We can always return and teach others how to shut down a hearing," said Andrea. I grinned at her.

"You don't want to lose this chance," said George, hurriedly.

It was another civil disobedience quick-decision moment.

But Jethro kept the conversation slow. He encouraged us to take our time, before eventually agreeing on some preconditions.

The PGCB representative frowned as I explained. "We have two directors, and each of us will speak for ten minutes. And we need to be guaranteed that at every PGCB meeting, *any* person can speak." My voice was matter-of-fact.

"I can't commit right now," he said. "But we'll see if we can work something out."

"Not good enough." My voice was firmer than I expected, perhaps steeled from the lies of Dougherty and the governor. "We need something firm."

He wavered for a second before spinning around and talking to his people.

He returned a few short minutes later. "I promise you we'll allow the public to speak at future meetings. And we accept your time."

Two things flashed through my head: promises were worthless, and they were the most precious thing he would probably give us. Some childhood lesson about "Your word is your bond" caused me to stick out my hand. "You guarantee hearings are public in the future, and we'll speak for twenty minutes this session?"

He shook my hand.

"If not, we can always come back." I smiled as he slunk off.

We strutted into the auditorium and sat down.

Today's PGCB session included both Philadelphia casinos petitioning the board to give them an extension on their $50 million license payments to the state of Pennsylvania. Foxwoods said the interest alone would cost $400,000 *per month*. It was unwieldy, they claimed, given the unexpected delays caused by council and "anti-casino zealots." SugarHouse claimed it had spent nearly $12 million on these unanticipated disturbances.

All I could think of was our new fundraising pitch: we'd been outspent $200 to $1 by SugarHouse alone!

The PGCB ruled against them. They had to pay the state immediately.

I leaned over to Andrea to make sure she caught the significance. "We've carried this struggle long enough that, for the first time, the PGCB's interests and the casinos' are not perfectly aligned. The PGCB's interest of getting money for the state from casinos is no longer totally overlapping with the casinos' interests."

Andrea cocked her head. "But you know, ultimately, they're all in cahoots. They both want the casinos built."

"Yes and no." I whispered slightly above the din of the testimony in the front of the room. What did I care if everyone could hear us? "We ought not to lump the elites together as if they're all in it with the same interests. It's not strategic, and it isn't what we just saw. The longer we delay these things, the more that competition will show up. I believe SugarHouse and Foxwoods can be split from each other—each hopes the other doesn't get to build. Even other casinos in the area will get into the fight, trying to stave off their two Philadelphia competitors. This is a big step."

A boring hour later, and the press's video cameras flicked back on when the chairwoman told us it was time for us to talk.

George Kelly introduced us and, absent notes, Jethro and I talked through the campaign. I focused on falsehoods SugarHouse and Foxwoods had propagated before the board, crummy social-impact studies, and the disenfranchising process the PGCB had set up. Jethro spoke personally, describing SugarHouse calling his neighborhood a buffer zone: "The people in my neighborhood just could not believe that you would not even look at a map or learn the history of the place where you were siting the casino." He closed powerfully. "We believe strongly that we can lead a protracted delay forever in the construction of these casinos. We believe that if they are built, we can simply shut them down with no more than twenty-five people by blocking roads, because they are in such close proximity to our homes."

When we finished, the PGCB thanked us and abruptly left.

After almost two years of being ignored, it was something.

We celebrated two wins over Indian food: being able to speak directly to them, and SugarHouse and Foxwoods now being financially hit by any additional delays. Fork filled with rice in mid-air, George Kelly expressed his excitement. "This is a turning point! They could not have expected you to be so clear. I bet they thought you were some crazies, not so sharp, laser-focused."

Major coverage followed: the *Boston Globe*, the *New York Times*, and even an article in the UK. George Kelly persuaded the Society Hill Reporter to republish the testimony, adding to the substantial amount of ink from that paper on anti-casino reporting.

Because the PGCB did initiate the change, it was our first *policy* win—*two* years into our campaign. And our members rode the excitement, pouring out congratulations.

I couldn't stop talking about how direct action was a balm to heal the wounds of public abuse. "This abuse of the public leads to deep cynicism and distrust. Nonvoters rightly ask: why vote if it's one corrupt option or another? Our response has been to act more boldly, to publicly speak out, to shake off shackles of fear, and to take our demands beyond the ballot box."

I wrote an article to our members on this topic, drawing from a quote from Dr. King, who wrote of the need for "creative maladjustment" since, he wrote, "there are some things in our society, some things in our world to which we should never be adjusted." I urged everyone to teach the city the attitude and tactics needed to eliminate corruption and prevent public abuse—by standing up when it happens. "If you want to speak at a public meeting, do it whether they've said you can or not. If you want to ask a question at City Council, do it even if it interrupts the flow. It's not to be disruptive, but to implement the vision of a transparent, open city. If we don't take responsibility for corruption, it will continue to abuse us."

The article took on a life of its own and spurred a host of labor unions, groups fighting for historic preservation, and others to call and ask us to help them plan strategy. We set up a range of training events to keep up with the requests: *How to Not Rally*, *Effective Media Strategies*, *Organizing 101*, and *Strategic Planning*.

But not everyone was pleased.

Days later, Paul took Jethro and me out for lunch at a coffeeshop near our office. Jethro grabbed waters and sat down.

Paul was always upbeat, even when he was disgruntled. His voice didn't register anger, but his face was serious. "There's real danger in what you said before the PGCB."

Jethro and I looked at each other wonderingly but said nothing.

Paul continued, "If we say we can lead a protracted delay by blockading roads, we're giving them all they need to get an injunction."

I grinned and, as if to counter Paul's seriousness, wise-cracked, "That's right, Jethro. You know we need more than twenty-five people to pull off a blockade."

"I got caught up in the moment." Jethro tossed his hands in the air. "And maybe we can."

"I'm serious," said Paul, raising his voice. "You've got to stop. You've now got Mary Reinhart saying we may stand in front of bulldozers. What is so efficient about the injunction process is that one can get an *ex parte,* immediate, temporary restraining order—meaning we don't even have to be in the hearing. Then SugarHouse could stop an action, which is just one step toward getting a permanent injunction. As your lawyer, I need you to promise me you won't speak like that again. Plus, with this talk of delay, you're opening us to being accused of abusing the litigation process to delay—*vexatious litigation* is what it's called. SugarHouse could sue for attorney fees. That's a tactic the ACLU says is being used more and more by developers."

Jethro looked at me, nervously.

"I still believe we're in the clear, Paul," I said. "A lot of these are concerns I've heard before—that the cops will slam us with the worst charges, etc." I thought of the high schoolers who worried about me going to jail. "I don't need coaching from a zoning attorney about direct action law. Jethro and I know what we're doing. We've *never* said we're being litigious to delay. We're not. We're being litigious because we believe the casinos are legally in the wrong. Nowadays we're not doing any more litigation, anyways."

"I'm not criticizing, I'm just trying to be thorough," said Paul. "The ACLU and I both think saying we may block the streets may help them get an injunction. The courts—"

I cut him off. "I've always assumed the casinos are eyeing an injunction and the possibility of suing us. But the bar is fairly high: they generally need a pattern of behavior that reflects us doing illegal actions, preferably in secret. We have never acted illegally—check our record—and never acted secretly. Two, even if they win in the courts, it martyrs us and publicly validates the strength of our resistance. And three, they cannot get an injunction for every day of the week. Eventually it would happen."

"We just need to be prepared," said Paul. "What about RICO charges?"

RICO was shorthand for the Racketeer Influenced and Corrupt Organizations Act. Originally written to target the mafia and organized crime networks, judges' rulings expanded it into a wide net, including activist groups. Its expansion became codified, from merely criminal enterprises to political protests, like a case convicting PETA for infiltrating an animal-testing lab. But we had no such "pattern" of racketeering—things like gambling, murder, theft, extortion, money laundering, fraud, obstruction of justice, or the like.

"We're prepared," I said, before pausing. *Why am I treating this like an argument—a point to be won?*

In a flash, I recalled arguing with a labor leader years earlier. He'd badgered me that their bosses would obtain an injunction against the direct action I was organizing, wielding the legal argument like a club. But I could tell it wasn't legality that was driving him. He was fearful and acting out of terror, not a clear-headed strategic framework.

But Paul wasn't this labor leader. He wasn't merely being fearful. He was a lawyer who needed information and data to relieve his distress—not my boasting confidence.

I slowed myself down. "Injunctions are not typically used against informal organizations like us. Besides, we have no history of prior 'damage'—a pretty important bar. And it's not purely a legal question—it's also political. We keep the equation so they don't win enough by threatening us with frivolous garbage. But let's spend time getting our act together anyways."

Paul looked annoyed, but willing to trust me—at least until he got back to his office to do his own research.

I added, "And let's get you in contact with lawyers who are experienced with direct action."

The conversation slid on to other updates and strategy discussions. While it did, I wondered if I should apologize for my shortness.

As if sensing my concern, Paul looked into my face and gave me a big smile. "You're the best," he said, seemingly out of nowhere. "Always upbeat. Always high-ground. Always thinking and analyzing."

I could have hugged him right there—if he had been the kind of guy comfortable with public displays of affection. I grinned back at him, "I *do* appreciate your concerns. You keep us sharp. Thanks, Paul."

We needed a strong relationship, because the movement's speed was soon going to increase again. But not before we started to get a clear sense of where Rendell, Nutter, and even Fumo sat.

Governor Rendell's announcement so closely matched the script we expected for him that the afternoon I got it, I kicked myself for not writing a response press release ahead of time. For another evening, I tossed away plans in order to think on long-term campaign planning and respond. The press cycle is a beast that constantly needs feeding—and I no longer had Karim to help with last-minute edits.

Yet without a public challenge, I worried that our members would feel dispirited by the lengthy letter from the governor, addressed to the Philadelphia Neighborhood Alliance—the renamed Delaware Riverfront Neighborhood Alliance. "The commonwealth has no authority to require them to accept alternate sites. Therefore, I must reluctantly inform you that the issue of re-siting is over."

It was written to suggest only one option left: negotiations with the casinos. And I correctly suspected the PNA's unwieldy coalition would be unable to mount a response until days later—too late to counter the casinos' media response of thanking the governor for "putting this issue to rest." I knew that sentiment would be echoed by much of the political punditry.

I allowed my anger to show as I typed a public response to the governor, encouraging members to send their own letters. "I was not aware that we had elected the gambling industry to run Pennsylvania. You've tried to strip the city of authority. Now you strip yourself of authority? You are acting foolishly and recklessly. You should be pleased to know, however, that we will not keep hope dead, which seems to be your mantra. We will persevere and continue to fight for re-siting. We believe in the power of the commonwealth, even if you do not."

I reminded reporters who called of the $800,000 Rendell had received from casino investors.

I wasn't the only one angry. Within hours, our members sent a torrent of over a thousand scathing letters to the governor's office: "I'm disappointed that your motives have clearly shifted from the welfare of the people to your corporate friends and cronies. You've rarely been helpless, why now? Shame on you, sir!"

The governor was publicly harassed—and surprisingly, even the normally dour DiCicco insisted they still had tricks up their sleeves. ("I think Fumo is pulling DiCicco's strings and showing he's not finished yet. He's genuinely moved," I wrote to the skeptical executive team.)

That harassment apparently touched a nerve, because days later, the governor lost it when asked by a reporter about more people becoming addicted to gambling. "For every one person who falls addicted to gambling or loses their paycheck, I'll show you 500 mostly seniors who spent forty dollars at a casino and had the best day of their month," he said. "These are people who lead very gray lives. They don't see their sons and daughters very much. They don't have much social interaction. There's not a whole lot of good things that happen in their month. But if you put them on the bus they're excited. They're happy. They have fun. They see bright lights. They hear music. They pull that slot machine, and with each pull, they think they have a chance to win."

We hardly had to do anything for his words to spark outrage across Pennsylvania, with many openly wondering if the governor had a gambling problem himself. To defend himself, the governor explained his words were "taken way out of context." He clarified by repeating that seniors "do live in a very grey existence" and "don't get visited much." Press had a field day.

Just as we were about to strengthen support from presumptive-mayor Nutter.

Like everyone, I took Mary Reinhart vey seriously. She lived four blocks away from the proposed Foxwoods site—so close that Foxwoods' vision of a planned highway expansion would go right through her house. Above the fray of any formal organization, she had several hundred people on an email distribution list whom she gave constant updates.

Yet when she asked me to tell people about the CBS 3 poll, I immediately balked. Online polls are typically a waste of time. Many companies use them solely to drive traffic to their site—the results are completely meaningless. I had already urged people to ignore online polls in the *Philadelphia Business Journal,* the *Inquirer,* and a half-dozen other outlets.

However, unlike most polls, this one had a tangible result. Whichever question was submitted the most, promised CBS 3, they would ask it during a live mayoral debate between Michael Nutter and his long-shot Republican competitor.

"It is a quick and easy way to confront the candidates on this issue," Mary wrote.

I was convinced immediately, especially since Nutter was ignoring our letters, avoiding requests for meetings, and ducking media questions. Nutter's sole public response to the casino issue was to assert that he was not the mayor, and he'd let our elected officials speak to the issue. His attitude mirrored the analysis of The Next Mayor Forum and others in the political class who asserted that since the "casinos are coming to the waterfront" in months, Nutter would lose pro-casino support if he sided with us— especially since many held the new prevailing belief that our movement was gasping its last breath.

I discretely joined Mary in passing the poll to a few hundred of CFP's most active supporters. I didn't send it to our listserve, because I knew reporters—and opponents—

were on it. I wanted CBS 3 to feel the weight of our movement but not dismiss it as merely orchestrated.

Mary's work paid off.

Seven minutes into the live debate, the CBS 3 moderator said to the two candidates, "We asked viewers to submit questions to CBS3.com. The number-one issue that was asked about—we received more questions on this than any other question: Are you committed to preventing Foxwoods and SugarHouse casinos from building at the currently proposed sites or indeed within 1,500 feet of any Philadelphia neighborhood and, if so, what will you do—if elected mayor—to move them away?"

The moderator turned to the Republican challenger. "First of all," he said, "I think that when all the deals are made and all the things are done at the highest level and then the doors are shut and then people have no opportunity for redress, it is unfair and un-American." He argued for using "all legal means possible" to stop the casinos.

Nutter looked uncomfortable but found his footing. "I'm supportive of the legislation to prevent siting these facilities within 1,500 feet of any residence. That legislation is now sitting in Harrisburg. I've been supportive of it. The impact... the potential negative impact of casinos in Philadelphia, I think we've not fully come to grips with: traffic, congestion, gambling addiction, as well as crime. It was not the best idea. It's certainly not the way to try to develop our waterfront. And I would use every power within the mayor's office to prevent their siting."

The testimony was out on our email blast within hours. We had our strongest words to date to hold presumptive-mayor Nutter's feet to the fire. I wrote a big thank-you note to Mary.

Two hundred people packed the ballroom in the Warwick Hotel as Michael Nutter stood before the crowd. "They said Philadelphia is corrupt, and it will be politics as usual," he intoned. "They said that we're a city whose time has passed. Well, they were wrong. They didn't know you. But I did."

Holding hands with his wife, arms upraised in victory, Nutter announced what the crowd had assumed for months—that he had won against the Republican challenger, with a record-breaking 83% of the vote. A councilmember best known for passing ethics reform, same-sex partner benefits, and smoking-ban legislation, Nutter had moved from last place in the Democratic primary to becoming the mayor of Philadelphia.

As Michael took to the stage to convince Philadelphians he stood against pay-to-play politics and usher in a new day, we weren't there. Even though we were.

Physically, I was walking along Market Street in the cold, talking on the phone with Jethro and a young organizer who'd met us first at our nonviolence training over the summer. Calling from Virginia, she was preparing to be part of her first direct action to challenge mountaintop removal, a nefarious practice of blowing up the top of a mountain and dumping it into the river to get coal. I told her, "We can't offer you much pay, and we can't offer you a clear job description—this is a constantly flowing campaign, where every week we get news that changes our game plan, and each month our strategy completely changes in light of events."

"But you'll learn a lot, and you'll have the chance to help the city of Philadelphia in a special way," Jethro offered.

She wasn't the experienced media-savvy organizer we wanted to replace Karim with—but none of those in the city were interested in joining a direct action group. She was energetic, brimming with that optimism. More than the issue of casinos, she was attracted to joining a campaign where she could learn more about direct action, organizing, and strategy.

Lily Cavanagh accepted without hesitation. She would start in early December, assuming she was out of jail from her upcoming action.

Waves of relief swept over me. We had someone capable to help us. Just as we were vacillating more than ever between electoral politics, lobbying, lawsuits, community organizing, mobilizations, and direct action. Jethro and I could step back and let others step forward.

As crowds cheered Michael Nutter, our strategy had put us in the room. His acceptance speech borrowed liberally from the themes our movement had pushed to the forefront of the city: transparency, the people having their say, smart riverfront planning, and a fighting stance against the state trumping the city. He touted the riverfront planning process, which had grown sizably after creating a no-casino plan to achieve our movement's endorsement.

Nutter stood in opposition to the kind of sneakiness that brought casinos, with a full agenda tasked with reducing gun violence, creating a culture of transparency in government, and reducing pay-to-play.

The ball was in Nutter's court. The logic of the narrative we had crafted for months meant Nutter had to put some transparency and ethics reform in the casino mess. We weren't sure how far he would go, but it would be a different city without Mayor Street and the city's unflinching support for casinos.

Still, we wouldn't be safe from Mayor Street's clutches until Nutter's inauguration in January. That would be three long months.

It was a crisp, fall day and I was happy to be outside on the stoop waiting for Jethro. I wouldn't have to wait long. Jethro was always exceedingly punctual. I had learned to show up ten minutes early just to be on time for him.

He strode up, his neck tight from stress. He smiled and accepted a hug from me. "Can we take a walk?"

"Sure," I said. I jumped up and proceeded to follow his pace.

As if midstream in a conversation, Jethro said, "You know, while my dad was alive, he used to walk everywhere. It's a good habit and helps clear the mind."

I thought of Gandhi and his love of walking. Then noted how tight Jethro was as he strode along. Keeping up two jobs was really getting to him—small wonder that he wasn't sending out early morning letters to the team anymore or meeting his fundraising goals. He looked preoccupied.

"Well, you were right!" He didn't smile, but his tone was playful. "Fumo came out big at the commerce department meeting."

"I heard pieces," I said, encouragingly. "But I wanna hear from you what happened."

The hearing had been a last-minute gambit by lame-duck Mayor Street, orchestrated with all the ninja-like silence of Philly's pay-to-play politics. SugarHouse had dusted off a hundred-plus-year-old law that gave the city control over riparian land—land that used to be under the river but was now filled in. It was a significant portion of both casinos' plans. Mayor Street obliged by rushing to set up a hearing, where he advocated giving away the land for a song.

"It was crazy, man!" Jethro took a deep sigh. "We were all ready to do the filibuster, like you and Nico trained us. But when we went in, the building trades workers were there in almost every seat. Maybe 200 of them."

"You mean—"

Jethro nodded, then turned right. "Yeah. They turned out too because their number-one political opponent would be there: Senator Fumo."

It was the old Dougherty-and-the-building-trades-versus-Fumo fight. "So Fumo—"

"Yep." Jethro shook his head in disbelief. "The man who created the gambling law blasted away at SugarHouse's 'land grab.' He filed a lawsuit to block it, arguing legislators struck it down when it was last used in 1987. But, man, those construction trades guys hate him. They booed and hissed at every moment, chanting 'Allenwood! Allenwood!' and 'They'll love you in Lewisburg.'" Seeing my blank face, he added, "names of federal prisons." He continued, "But Fumo was just as nasty and yelled back to some of his people, 'Don't applaud, it just upsets the animals.'"

"I think Fumo's evolving stance means he really is trying to stop these things. It represents a major falling out between Fumo and his now ex-lawyer, Richard Sprague. We might have split them completely apart. So how did the filibuster go?"

"It was hard and fun and crazy," he said. "It was too loud for us to be heard when we stood up. And it was really tough to be booed by building trades workers."

For a second, I thought Jethro's eyes were tearing up, as if the yelling had gotten to him. But the moment passed.

He continued, "They escorted us into the frigid November cold. I had to be interviewed by Jennifer Lin through a crack in a glass doors, locked behind us so we couldn't return. We staggered our talking, so we were thrown out once every ten minutes. But, man, we missed you."

"Well, it sounds like you did good, Jet."

"Any advice on what we could have done differently?"

I halted for a second. "Well... maybe using buddies for support. Or you could have refused to leave when escorted out. Or just sit down when the director gavels you down, so you can pop up later." The scenario seemed unwieldy. Hundreds of people yelling against us. "Or just leave when you're that outnumbered."

For a few minutes, all we heard was street noise and the sound of our feet continuing to pad along. Jethro seemed proud of his action, though the filibuster didn't stop the hearing and made only a blip on news stories. Instead, the director had simply announced she'd rule "in the near future"—code for ruling in SugarHouse's favor before Mayor Street's term was up.

As if surprised that he hadn't asked about me or my vacation before, Jethro turned to me. "And what's new with you?"

A thousand new things flashed before me, but what rose to the top was my conversations with Rosanne Loesch.

She was an ally in the PNA, someone who had helped her civic Society Hill raise money for Casino-Free Philadelphia. She was the kind of lady who I'd have suspected of owning pearl earrings passed down from generation to generation. She had a fresh strategy in mind, consistent with her unbridled determination: a federal lawsuit against the PGCB concerning Decker's apparent conflicts of interest.

"It's not that I disagree with Rosanne's strategy," I said. "But the introduction was pretty bitter. After telling me she'd raise a quarter of a million dollars for the lawsuit, she shrugged off my shock over the pricetag. That was more than CFP had raised in our entire existence. Then... as if all that we had done before was play-acting, she told me, 'You've done good work. But we're now in the big leagues.' It felt like a pat on the head." I added quickly, "I really like her, but she doesn't seem to appreciate our expertise in organizing and direct action."

Jethro sighed. "I'm getting tired of people in this city not appreciating our skill. People keep thinking that the *ultimate* power is still lawsuits and politicians. They don't get that laws aren't written on behalf of the little guy—the law is a tool of the wealthy. They don't understand that power resides in our willingness to comply—and to believe in the system as it is."

We turned the corner and headed east.

"They still have a belief in the old pyramid of power," I said, "that a few people at the top have the real power, a few more in the middle have some power, and those at the bottom have none—"

"But that's not it, is it?" interrupted Jethro excitedly. "It's the *upside-down triangle*."

I smiled and almost chuckled to myself. Jethro was learning through this campaign, too, getting more into the direct action model. He had become exposed to the upside-down triangle, a model that took the pyramid and flipped it on its head. When a pyramid is on its head, it's unstable. It requires pillars of support on each side to keep it from falling. A CEO's power is dependent on their managers, stockholders, secretaries, tech workers, and janitors all doing what they say.

The lesson being that power is unstable. And rather than feeding that stability—believing more in courts that are corrupt or a political system that's unprincipled—we wanted to starve it. To withdraw support away from it and reduce   "It's   tough sometimes, being on the cutting edge!" Jethro sighed heavily, again looking preoccupied. He pulled at his chin. "So what's eating you about it now?"

I felt seen by Jethro, as though he could always tell how I was really doing. "She's somehow raised the money to hire a lawyer, and she's pulled together four civic associations, despite all the back-biting and in-fighting. But they're not ready to play hardball with Richard Sprague. And... I guess I'm just pissed! She's going to put a ton of money into this effort. Maybe it will work, but it's doubtful. *But* when she wants press, she asks me for our press lists and help sending out the release. I just sent out their announcement that they just filed."

"Maybe you shouldn't have done it," he said. It was as much a question as a statement.

Jethro suddenly stopped walking. "I need to tell you something." His stubbled face looked serious. "My wife and I are having a baby. Don't tell anyone yet. We'll announce once we're through the first trimester."

"Congratulations!" I shouted. "That's great!"

He smiled, a little weakly.

That explains his stepping back, his working hard to save up a little money... and then my heart sank. *Are we going to lose Jethro, too?*

That night, a late call from Fox News would fracture Rosanne and my relationship.

On the face of it, it looked insubstantial. A friendly Fox News reporter interrupted my evening plans, begging for someone to get interviewed on the casino issue for a ten o'clock story. "We have the casinos' side taped, and we need a statement from you. I need it in one hour."

"I'll get back to you," I said curtly and immediately tried to reach anyone and everyone to take the interview: Jethro, Nico, Paul, Shirley, Kathy, Rosanne...

Nobody was available, so I called the reporter back and reluctantly agreed to an interview—if they sent a truck over to my house. She came right away and performed a short interview.

The next day, Rosanne sent an angry message, the longest she'd written yet. "I think it goes without saying that the filing of the lawsuit was the only news that should have been focused on that day. In my mind, saying that you tried to reach me—doesn't do it. You could have called back. You could have called Hilary who you knew was working on the story. I don't want to have to fight with you for coverage on the federal lawsuit. When developments happen on it, I want your cooperation in directing reporters to our spokesman—who is me at the moment. If reporters want comments on the case—and they call you first—I am requesting that you direct them to me, or if I cannot be reached, Paul, Hilary, Debbie King, or Richard D. who would then handle it from there."

A gnawing in the pit of my stomach turned into a sharp pain. *Who is she to tell me what to do?* I had helped the lawsuit, introducing it to Fox 29 news, who did two pieces on it the next morning. I had helped just like I always helped.

I raged silently at the email. It felt like she was dictating to me—like a boss to a worker—telling me to call five people for the sake of *her* strategy. It wasn't enough to support. She wanted a clean sweep on the TV, and any other news stories were in violation of it.

I immediately wondered if I was getting misdirected fury. She had worked awfully hard to corral increasingly hostile civics. Some involved PNA delegates were so nasty and fearful of her influence, they exchanged emails suggesting they back-stab her so "there will be no teeth left at all in that old bitches mouth for her to bite with."

Angry as I was, I wasn't going to fight over email. I wrote back: "I hear your frustration and I'm sorry that you've lost some trust in me. It was a very stressful situation for me and I'd appreciate you getting to hear from me about it before rushing to judge me. I want to sit down and talk with you soon; but in the meantime, maybe you and I can talk on the phone sometime today."

It was a tough disagreement, because we both felt a sense of violation from our allies in a stressful moment. Violation from opponents is one thing, but the most tender hurts come from allies.

We made up enough to move forward, but, as she said, "something has diminished there for me" in our otherwise bright relationship. Like many ally relationships during the course of tough campaigns, we continued working together, battling it out, licking our wounds, and moving on. Because, despite our tension, it was a drop in the bucket compared to the internal stress her legal committee would have.

In late November, Richard Sprague would send a scare letter to the lawyers and plaintiffs. "Inasmuch as you and your law firm were counsel in the state court proceedings, your bad faith in this blatant forum-shopping exercise is patent." Calling their actions "vexatious and obdurate" with "bad faith," he demanded a withdrawal of their complaint in ten days "in order to mitigate the substantial damage that you have already caused." He threatened that after his win in court he "*will* bring an action against each of you and your law firm for malicious use of process and abuse of process" and that he might sue "any and/or all of your clients."

The legal committee was shocked and went into a tailspin. Individual plaintiffs dropped out. Then their lawyer asked to withdraw from the lawsuit. Then their communications team wouldn't make Sprague's letter public—fearful of scaring off a potential new lawyer.

I had to bite my fingers not to just leak it myself. I even ghost-wrote a press release for them, but it sat quietly while Rosanne's committee fought bitterly over strategy steps.

Ultimately, the federal lawsuit faded into the abyss. The committee was unable to find another lawyer willing to take the case, for fear of a lawsuit against them by the legendary Richard Sprague. Our movement had kowtowed to Sprague—and I was pissed.

Mostly I was frustrated, as Kathy said, that they silently let "a high-powered, well-connected wealthy lawyer to threaten middle-class and working people trying to protect their homes." Without a media strategy, the committee's months-late release of Sprague's letter resulted in a shabby three paragraphs tucked beneath a larger story about casinos.

Afterward, I hoped they would see the wisdom of supporting grassroots organizing work, because a few hundred thousand dollars would go a long way in hiring organizers and resourcing our still ragtag operation. True to their upper- and professional-class backgrounds, they refused to support our grassroots, winning strategy and chose to hire a national public-relations firm. No serious PR came from it.

Jethro and I railed against the classist assumptions behind their money strings. Casino-Free Philadelphia was based on actions, not words, and was more effective than any PR firm. We were swifter—and cheaper, too.

But organizing is not valued in mainstream society. Skills we had shown for months were not seen as worthy enough to give serious financial support: crafting innovative media-capturing and public-sympathy-framing actions, aligning political leadership with a grassroots strategy, and all the elements of pulling disparate segments of society into a shared enterprise.

Instead of money going to support successful organizing, it went to those the professional class trusted most: lawyers and public-relations firms.

＊　　　　＊　　　　＊

Days after my walk with Jethro, I mused that we had earned tangible wins with the nearly solid stance of Michael Nutter and the suspicious but increasingly positive moves of Senator Fumo and his protégé, Councilman DiCicco. Our grueling pace of educational events, religious meetings, town halls, and a constant parade of email, phone, and face-to-face communication with our movement's activists was paying off.

Further proof that Fumo might be scared of our organizing his constituency came in the form of an email from Ed Goppelt: "The supreme court has dismissed the Foxwoods' zoning case 88 EM 2007." For the first time since our movement began, a casino lost in a court system. Given the courts' record, we all assumed Fumo had pulled strings.

It wasn't a ruling against Foxwoods per se, but, as Paul explained, "kicking down the case to the lower courts on an expedited basis. Foxwoods had been asking for all of its permits to be given through the courts, bypassing the city completely. It's not a final nail in the coffin."

I asked Paul, "Still, it's our first win in the supreme court, right?" I wanted him to join my excitement.

"Yes," he said cautiously. If lawyers were given a gift, they'd examine it closely. "It appears like a good thing."

DiCicco became teisty. "You want to get these things built? Let's talk about re-siting, because if not, we're talking about another year or so before a final decision is made."

It gave credence to our hope that politicians, willingly or not, were being forced to veer toward us—and that if we kept up the pressure, we could get them to kill these casinos. Or at least move them, which would give us time to reopen the entire casino process.

When SugarHouse received the riparian land permit from the city a week later, it didn't dampen our spirits. Fumo was already throwing lawsuits at it. He even added an extensive legal brief to SugarHouse's lawsuit, the one that mirrored Foxwoods' now kicked-down lawsuit.

We felt the tide turning. We had a new mayor coming in soon, a supreme court streak suddenly broken in our favor, and a complete turnaround from Fumo. Lily was coming on board to expand our staff capacity.

Of course, tides come and tides go. Ours was about to go back out.

CHAPTER 16
Practice Site Occupation

DECEMBER 1, 2007 — DECEMBER 31, 2007

organizing down instead of upward • breaking the law isn't just for activists •
feeling both defeated and powerful • positioning politicians in your storyline •
following your conscience • a threat that's never fulfilled • enforcing action guidelines •
handling fear is an organizer's job • when up against a huge force, go small •
training builds confidence • educating reporters on social movements •
thanking allies with direct action

"WHAT A DIFFERENCE A YEAR MAKES!"

I typed out our latest email blast's subject line, lounging in CFP's offices. I joined in the loose banter of Lily, Jethro, and Paul. We casually talked about our next upcoming strategy session and preparing for a one-year celebration since the December 20 licensing. Paul tossed to Lily a purple squeeze toy that he had brought into the office. Lily batted it at Jethro, who barely caught it.

Just a year ago, the *Inquirer* had urged us to not fight casinos—a "done deal." Its recent editorial now called the casinos "long shots." It was sharing the new political viewpoint: "Neither Foxwoods nor the SugarHouse casino has any immediate prospect of getting city approvals to build any time soon."

Then Jeff Shields called.

Even before he spoke, my heart sank. It was too late for him to be calling.

"Heads up," he said, matter-of-factly. "The supreme court ruled a few minutes ago. SugarHouse was given a green light to all their city permits. I'll call back in a few minutes for a quote."

My head drooped. *Now this.* I took a deep breath. *Another long couple of nights.*

I turned to Paul, "The supreme court ruling came in..." Lily and Jethro stopped laughing and quietly folded their hands in their laps. We watched Paul scurry his fingers across his laptop.

"It was a six-to-one ruling..." He cursed and practically spit his words. "SugarHouse was given *everything* they asked for, even some things they *didn't* ask for! This is outrageous! How can a court hand out permits?"

I sharply inhaled.

With a narrow reading of technical law, the supreme court had deemed the city needlessly obstinate against SugarHouse. It had used the exact opposite logic in the Foxwoods case.

Once again, the court was spitting in the eye of Philadelphians—and all the city's planners and agencies. Now, the judges on the supreme court were in the business of approving sewer plans, environmental plans, architectural plans. Without professional external review, they were accepting a corporation's plans and ordering the city to abide.

It had even over-ruled the application of the 2002 law prohibiting adult entertainment facilities, which we had hoped for a long time might be a silver bullet against SugarHouse.

"Jeff Shields is calling back in a few minutes, and other press can't be far behind. We need a response. Now." I looked around the room.

Jethro's face was motionless. "Let's call it a high-ground victory—at least the highest law of the land had to be consulted on this issue."

I waved my hand dismissively. "That takes us nowhere."

Paul stared at his laptop, reading. "I just don't see any way to appeal..." He shouted, "There's no precedent! They are virtually making up law as they're going along. People need to know this."

"You're right, but being right doesn't help," I said. "The supreme court looks done now, at least with respect to SugarHouse." I stretched my body, feeling tense and tight in every part.

Lily looked around. She had the build of a competitive swimmer and the mindset to match. From her first day on the job just yesterday, she had shown she wanted to help us *win*—a key attitude for an organizer. At this news, she looked around nervously. "Have we... just... lost?"

All of us reflected internally for a moment, then I spoke. "No... but maybe we should declare a massive loss and tell everyone we're going to negotiate terms of surrender with the opposition forces—"

Paul interrupted. "Your sarcasm would never sufficiently drip off the page."

Something about our moment of hopelessness sparked me to remark, "When you can't go up, organize down."

"Yes!" Paul sat up. "And *who* implements the licensing process?"

It took us a moment to understand what Paul was asking. When we did, we rushed to call members to test a bold idea. Nico immediately liked it—and began crafting an email with a new subject line: "What a Difference Four Hours Make."

When Jeff Shields called me back, my hands immediately started shaking. If we tried something this brazen and failed, it would seriously deteriorate our reputation for getting things done. I stuttered while trying to explain it. "You know... the permits... SugarHouse's city permits still have to be handled by people in the Department of Licenses and Inspections offices. They can go quickly, or they can take their time, as anyone who has applied for a permit knows... So we're asking the folks who work there to... uhm... take their time."

As a professional reporter, Jeff had spent hours studying and understanding the inner workings of City Hall. It also meant he had lost a little vision along the way. "You can't do that," he said flatly.

"We are... this is what we're doing... we're urging people to take direct action." I kicked myself for not being crisp.

"You just can't do that, it's not... city workers can't just dismiss the highest court in the state," said Jeff, as if we had asked the world to rotate backwards.

Jethro yelled from the other side of the room. "It's *our* job to say what we're going to do, and Jeff's to report it!"

Jeff wrote it down but sounded unconvinced. He seemed worried our sanity may have been lost with the ruling, too.

Truth was, we *were* initiating a desperate move, asking city officials to join us in direct action. Yet it felt like the logical conclusion of having nearly every option closed to us.

The next morning, I woke up early and laid my laptop on the breakfast table. My ears still echoed with the angry chants from last night. Anne Dicker had organized a nine o'clock rally—to catch the eleven o'clock TV news cycle. Seventy-five of us had paced on the sidewalks outside of Foxwoods' site, as Paul, Caryn, Debbie, and others took turns leading chants: "Lame-duck deal!" "No casino! No way!" and—causing me to cringe— "Street! Rendell! Go to hell!"

We directed our anger at everyone. We mocked DiCicco's impotent diatribe that "the city of Philadelphia has no power. We can't make decisions." We expressed cynicism and frustration that the *Metro*, which last week proclaimed "the city's two casino projects aren't a done deal," today blared on its front page: "Done Deal: Casino All But Starting to Build."

Angry, impatient messages poured into my inbox. Like us, people wondered about the options available to us: "Obtain an injunction in the federal courts?" "Force the attorney general to investigate the court's corruption?" Or, "Arrest the supreme court justices for corruption and/or incompetence?" Strategically, none were viable. The federal courts were slow, expensive, and largely uninterested in taking on these kinds of cases. The attorney general was a joke. And a direct action to arrest the judges would do little to change the material outcome.

SugarHouse could start building. Soon.

The courts had screwed us—worse then ever before.

Turning each newspaper page heavily, I scrolled though SugarHouse's chest-beating, almost sarcastic message, "City Council did all it has to do, and we thank them." With the court ordering the city to hand over zoning permits, SugarHouse announced it would begin building by Christmas.

"How cynical is *that* Christmas gift," said Jethro caustically.

Adding salt to the wound, Foxwoods signed a secretly negotiated community-benefits agreement with Mayor Street. Armed with that, Foxwoods asserted that its case was now the same as that of SugarHouse and it would follow with a "me, too" filing of a mirror lawsuit. It would ask for the same treatment as SugarHouse.

To make things worse, Councilman DiCicco's aide called me with the news that he was drafting an award for CFP and the PNA for "all your efforts, even if they weren't successful." I was surprised at how much scorn slipped out of my mouth as I expressed disbelief that he was going to give us an award as if it were over.

"A meaningless resolution is nothing to us," I shouted. "Not when the courts are slapping you and me in the face. You had better do better than that. If you dare introduce the award with that attitude, we'll turn it down publicly and grandstand at City Council." I relished a sense of feistiness as he backed off and vaguely apologized for sounding like he thought it was over.

But there wasn't a lot of good news. I ran my fingers through my hair in frustration while reading the vague public sentiments from "ally" Senator Fumo. *It's not over. I've got a strategy. But I won't share it.*

Behind the scenes, Jeff Rush tried to clarify Fumo's stance. "The overweight lady's mouth is shut tight, and contrary to the posturing coming from SugarHouse, this thing is far from done.... The word is, the entire delegation on the state level is outraged and on the same page with coordinated planning occurring in real time. There is a developing sense of direction and strategy in the works that understandably will not be immediately articulated." It had not been a priority for Fumo when citizens' rights were violated, but now the supreme court had violated state legislators' rights to give out land.

Michael Nutter's voice on the radio shared the vague, strategically empty outrage of other politicians. "I am perplexed to understand how the courts are now in the zoning and permit issuance business. I thought that was the primary purview of local municipal governments." Broadcasters called these "harsh words."

Amidst the varied responses, our direct action strategy had gotten mere mentions in the newspapers.

Lily wondered why.

"We have to get distance from the current news cycles. Press would rather quote Fumo or Nutter," I coached. "So we need to plan events on days when nothing else is happening and we're not competing with our press. It's a lesson many groups could take to heart, since they often plan actions on the day of trade meetings or corporate conferences. Then they're in competition, instead of what we need to do, which is design our own action to dramatize our ask to government workers. Maybe Thursday—long enough to get our act together and for this current news cycle to slow down, but soon enough to be on the heels of the court's judgment.

Lily wrote it down, noting which things she would need to do to make it happen.

"But our people also need to do something together," I said. Then, recalling a tactic we had talked about for months, I added, "I'm not excited about the prospect of starting a long-term occupation during the winter, certainly not *before* building trucks arrive. So let's call it a practice site occupation."

We picked Saturday for that. Jethro agreed to bottom-line logistics, including the training session and action design.

We were in the flow and back to designing two actions ahead of time.

With our actions, we'd flush out where politicos really stood. With DiCicco and Nutter, we asked that they come out strongly and get their respective bodies—City

Council and the city administration—to openly flout the supreme court ruling. With Fumo, whom we trusted even less, we asked that he do direct action *with us*.

We would pull off two out of three—though neither in the way we had imagined.

Early Wednesday morning, I creaked out of bed. *What happens if Nutter slips through our fingers? Are we going to lose Jethro completely to his baby? What if SugarHouse counter-protests our practice site occupation?* The worries kept coming: *Is Lily getting enough support in her first week on the job? Are we finally going to get our new fiscal sponsorship? How can we tamp down petty attacks coming from PNA in jealousy of our media attention?*

It all swept out of my head when I opened the *Inquirer.*

The initial sentences reported that CFP had asked "city officials to defy the court ruling and refuse to issue permits." But the next few sentences were shocking: "City Councilman Frank DiCicco obliged yesterday. In a hearing on the joint city-state agreement to run the convention center, DiCicco asked council members to support an amendment to block casino building permits until the state releases $700 million in convention center funding. Refusing to issue building permits to SugarHouse at this point would fly in the face of the court's ruling, all acknowledged."

I couldn't believe it. DiCicco! *DiCicco is urging the city to break the law.*

Nor could others.

> *Richard A. Sprague, part-owner of SugarHouse, yesterday blasted council and casino opponents for failing to recognize the court's authority. "When there's a call to absolutely violate and ignore a ruling by the Supreme Court of Pennsylvania, that is something that is wrong," Sprague said.*
>
> *Gov. Rendell, at an unrelated news conference, also criticized the tactic. "Any time you hear rhetoric saying the law should be defied is a matter of concern," said Rendell, the leading proponent of slots gambling in Philadelphia and the state. "The citizens who are talking like that should think about what that does to the overall image of Philadelphia."*

Inside, I cheered. This felt like a perfect teachable moment for the whole city and state. I sprang to my computer, excited for a public debate about civil disobedience. I grabbed Dr. King's "Letter from a Birmingham Jail," in which he talked about the difference between *just laws* and *unjust laws* "out of harmony with the moral law."

My fingers blazed across the keyboard, writing to the executive team. "*This* is what it means that direct action polarizes and clarifies, focusing on action over people's positions. Notice that Rendell is at an unrelated news conference. It means we're under his skin. And he's trying to embarrass us, like SugarHouse when they repeated claims that we would lie in front of bulldozers. But times have changed. Rendell is out of step. Our bold action is just showing how wrong he is—something a thousand press releases or rallies would not have achieved. He's defending an unjust court."

Within hours, he would hear our members' scorching replies in phone calls, emails, quotations in every newspaper, and letters to the editor: "Could we imagine a worse image for Philly than as home to rebels willing to risk for freedom? First the Liberty Bell, now this!" Or, "A city known nationally as Killadelphia that is wildly corrupt, has a higher drop-out rate than graduates—and we're the bad guys?"

I was back in the swift-moving waters, rushing from emails to phone calls to writing and back again.

Timed perfectly to catch my own instinctual speeding up, my sister sent me an e-card. "Sorry the courts are corrupt," it blared, to the mismatched tune of Happy Birthday.

Droplets formed at my eyes. "Thanks for calling and for the card." My fingers shook slightly as I typed a reply. "It's a rough time and I'm feeling both defeated and beaten up and proud and powerful. It's a swirl of emotions, and we're all reeling from the supreme court decision. I don't know what is next. I don't want to lose and I fear we will. I also fear we'll have to step into even more power before this fight is through."

I took a deep breath and jumped back into the quick-moving campaign. Paul was already looking up each individual permit SugarHouse needed. Aside from the court's authorized city permits, they also needed a raft of federal permits. Lily and Nico picked up pieces of logistics that Jethro was dropping, including Lily's investigating our email blast system to announce this evening's emergency training session.

I spent the afternoon focused on Nutter. With only one month left of Mayor Street, Nutter seemed in prime position to *act* against the supreme court. Yet his office had gone completely silent since yesterday. Privately, his office told us, "We're looking at all options." But by contrast, he had created transition teams to prepare for every aspect of governance—except casinos. This paralleled a rumor slipping out of his office—that he wanted the casinos to begin building by the time he became mayor, so it would be a dead issue. He didn't want to touch the fight.

With the hand of an experienced media storyteller, I laid out a path of least resistance for Nutter. I knew people were in love with Nutter, which meant direct attacks on him would backfire with our people. Even making "demands" on him was met with resistance from members. So we needed a way to move him that was couched softly and non-confrontationally.

Behind the scenes, I launched attacks. I leaked to the *Evening Bulletin* that one of Nutter's key advisors was Tad Decker's friend Stephen Cozen, founder and chairman of Cozen O'Connor. I made sure dozens of press outlets covered a confrontation with Debbie and Hilary, in which Cozen unwisely suggested his close relationship with Nutter meant they saw eye-to-eye on casinos. The *Bulletin's* exposure forced Nutter to— for the second time—publicly distance himself from Cozen O'Connor, urged on by letters from the PNA.

Publicly, I positioned Nutter with a simple storyline: "To get rid of the stench of corruption, the city has to stop going along with corrupt decisions," I wrote in a column in the *Metro*. "Nutter should disregard the supreme court ruling and fight every step of the way."

That night, an anxious, angry bunch of supporters arrived in our offices for a training session for the practice site occupation. An experienced facilitator, Nico had to work hard to corral the group. "So, Saturday we'll walk onto the site, with picnic materials and blankets."

One participant blurted, "Hey! Is it true that Representative Mike O'Brien is seeking a restraining order on the commerce department, to fight them over who has riparian rights?"

"Yes," said Nico. "But for now, let's focus on the Saturday action. We're trying to model something light, so bring along things like beach balls—you know, the stuff the SugarHouse site should be used for."

"I heard Rendell attacking us this afternoon," said another participant. "He said that people shouldn't defy the law and that it'll hurt development in the city."

I couldn't help myself. "Guess who came to defend us?" I grinned. "DiCicco." Several people gasped. "He talked about how, years ago, the supreme court ruled that the state owed us millions to fund the city's court system. DiCicco said, 'Well, the precedent's been set. It's been ten years, and they have not fully funded our court system. Why should we pay any attention to them as well?'"

Nico rolled his eyes pointedly at me. Then he continued in his mellow, understated way. "This is all interesting news, and I'm sure there's more. But for now, how about we move into a role-play on how this action might go."

By the end of the role-play, attention had refocused. "Our goal is not to get arrested," he said. "We think there's too much going on to bail people out and go to court, too. But anyone who does this has to be prepared for arrest. Who's willing?"

Thirty people's hands shot into the air.

Lily organized the next day's press conference. For her first week on the job, I admired how confidently she jumped into the deep end—so much so that I felt relaxed in taking the morning off.

The action started at the underground entrance to the Municipal Services Building, where a handful of CFPers handed out 500 flyers to passing city officials. The flyers read, "Mayor Street wants you to expedite the processing of casino plans, but you don't have to do that. You can take your time, or you can turn to other business. You can do everything possible to make sure that permits do not get issued until February, March, or even April. You have the power." (Later, Morgan Jones and I would email the same flyer to 20,000 workers.)

When the flyers were gone, the group trooped up to City Hall's fourth floor, their backs facing the Pennsylvania Supreme Court's chambers. Our message was delivered quickly. Marj Rosenblum reminded press we wanted a 1,500-foot buffer. Jethro soft-balled a demand that Nutter create "an open, transparent" site re-selection committee. And Paul crafted a brilliant lawyerly phrase for the whole event. "We are not asking people to break the law. In this matter, we are asking people to *follow their consciences*."

The press could barely contain themselves. With a disparaging tone, the *Daily News'* Chris Brennan asked, "What is it you, Paul, think the new mayor could actually do—not what you hope he could do—but what could he actually do?"

Paul twirled his fingers as if reading tea leaves. "If the mayor moved the Democratic party to go to Rendell and say, 'You're hurting Philadelphia with these two casinos— you've got to change the law, and you've got to prevent this from happening.' Then it can be done."

Even the *Evening Bulletin*'s Jenny DeHuff seemed taken aback. "On what grounds are you asking a municipal body to reject the decisions of the supreme court?"

Jethro swayed before giving a one-word answer, "Conscience." The press chortled.

Despite the media's reticence, the impact was noticeable.

KYW Newsradio gave us the first optimistic press about our odds of winning in a week, arguing "opponents say Philadelphia casinos are going nowhere fast." They quoted Paul's pointing out that SugarHouse still needed to abide by the Clean Water Act and obtain federal regulatory and historical permits, and it still needed major earth-moving permits—"so they cannot legally begin building by Christmas."

To continue engaging Nutter, Lily suggested a hefty letter sent by email, with a request for him to create a blue-ribbon committee with four core values: a transparent process, full economic cost/benefit analysis, re-siting only with community support, and community expertise. Caught up in our feisty mood from the morning, I urged that we slide in our demand in my favorite "if-then" ultimatum style: "If you choose not to announce the formation of a committee meeting by December 13, we intend to try to pull together the committee ourselves, politely using your campaign office as a base."

Minutes after the message was sent, Lily's phone rang.

Lily's voice was uncertain. "Uh, yeah... we want to convene this committee in, like, Nutter's office."

"*Mayor* Nutter's office," snapped Nutter's aid, before abruptly hanging up.

Lily turned to Jethro and me. "Oh my goodness. Did that just happen? Did I do okay?"

I nodded, "You did great. We're clearly getting to him. You said what needed to be said."

"He's just going to sell us out," said Lily.

Jethro nodded affirmatively. "That's why he's ducking reporters on this. He doesn't want to admit what he's going to do."

I shook my head. "I think they genuinely don't know what they're going to do and are struggling internally right now. Some pressure is good."

As we told folks of the interchange, hoping to prod them to action, many held their mouths in horror. "Nutter is our ally, our friend," repeated one supporter over and over again. We had outpaced our supporters and—veering unsteadily, driven by exhaustion and concern—we had put forward the first threat that we would never fulfill.

By Friday, our call to conscience had kicked a debate on direct action into high gear, with players across the board joining the media fray. Rendell doubled down on his assertions that we were out of line. Letters to the editor from anti-casino activists defended our actions: "What does attracting casinos that are clearly ready to fight and bankrupt families say about the image of Philadelphia? It says our governor and mayor sold out the city, sold out historic neighborhoods, and now our neighbors might be sold down the river. And, Governor, if you want to improve the city's image, start by letting us make our own decisions." Editorials took shots at us, as did some community groups and civics, while others argued that sometimes civil disobedience is the right choice.

The stakes were raised innumerably over our practice site occupation.

I tracked all the worry in our movement: stress over our image, fears of getting beaten up, wild concerns over arrests. It wasn't just the normal worries—it was a litany of worst-case scenarios.

In the afternoon, Jethro showed he was joining that sentiment. He started shouting even before he got into the office. Bolting in, he looked haggard, his face even more unshaven than usual. "SugarHouse is going to counter-protest us!"

Once inside, he directed Lily and me to an email from SugarHouse. SugarHouse's statement deplored CFP's efforts to "continue fighting against our construction" even if it breaks the law. It mentioned the time and date of our Practice Run of a SugarHouse Site Occupation.

"You know this means they're gonna have people at the site occupation, right?" Jethro looked at me, then Lily, then back to me.

"It's definitely the case that everybody has something to say about our site occupation," I said. Having spent all morning handling people's fears, I wasn't going to join Jethro's urgency or concern. "I guess it's likely SugarHouse's people will show up... wouldn't you if you were them?"

Jethro thought about that for a second, then threw his hands up. "We can't let them push us around!"

At that, I laughed. Jethro looked offended for a second, then saw my smile. "Nobody's ever said that's gonna happen. Look, we've got to help people stayed disciplined and keep cool heads in this moment... You see this?"

I tossed over an op-ed from an anti-casino person—not someone I knew—that challenged a pro-casino person: "My sincere wish for you, sir, is that you're the first casino robbery victim." It was one of the many signs that people were scared.

Jethro took it in his hands and read slowly, moving his fingers across the lines. "Why is all this happening now?" He flopped onto the couch.

"Because we're not just proposing direct action for us. We're asking *other* people to do it, too. And direct action violates society's rules," I said, looking between him and Lily. "Naturally, people wonder how far will you go outside those rules. I've already written to the author to cut it out. But I'm worried that tomorrow, hyped by the energy of the week plus all of our frustration, one of our people might attack a counter-protestor."

I explained to Jethro that years ago, I had been part of an unsuccessful handling of this type of situation. During a high-profile civil disobedience action, protestors had earned a high ground and found the police initially restrained to initiate violence. The tide turned quickly when several people committed a few acts of property destruction and violence. Whether from protestors or paid government *agents provocateurs*, the few incidents of cars being smashed, property defaced, and alleged incidents of violence against police were lifted as the dominant media narrative.

That's when a key thing happened. Leaders refused to condemn the acts, despite them being against their own stated action guidelines. They argued the incidents were minor and sporadic—which was true—but that appeared to be defending them. They were quickly reduced to a stereotyped caricature in the media and rendered ineffective at talking about their issues, isolating them from a whole slew of allies.

"That's not going to happen to us," I said. I had already resent copies of our nonviolent action guidelines with press releases:

> **In our actions, we will...**
> * use humor and visuals to make our point;
> * adopt a dignified, open and friendly attitude towards anybody we encounter;
> * demonstrate our creativity in the use of new slogans, songs, and props;
> * keep our calm, and our eyes on the prize.
>
> **In our actions, we will not...**
> * bring weapons;
> * use verbal or physical violence;
> * use drugs or alcohol;
> * hide our identity behind hoods or masks;
> * run, as it contributes to heightening tensions for everybody.

I continued, "Whatever people's philosophy, we need a clear, strategic message sent out: democratic actions require trust in each other's behaviors. That is only achieved when we agree to do an action in unison."

"In my calls to supporters, everyone I hear is really, really concerned," said Lily. "We should send it to our folks to let them know, too."

"Yes, and we'll create a plan to address the counter-protestors," I said.

Jethro lightened. "If nothing else, we're having a good debate in public over whether people should do civil disobedience or not." He looked at his watch. "Sorry, I've gotta run to work, guys!"

The rest of the afternoon, I tried to keep my head level in the face of worried emails. It was all happening so quickly. With surprise, Kathy came to me half-laughing and half-nervous. "You know, just a few months ago, it would have been *my* job to arrest people like us! I remember when I saw people throwing red dye on themselves, calling it a die-in. Only now do I understand why they were doing it. You sure this is a good idea?"

Unusually, Kathy was more relaxed than Shirley, who fretted about whether donors might get turned off by us seeming too radical. I asked her if she thought that was the case. She nodded, then shrugged and said, "But if they don't see why we're escalating at this point, they just haven't been paying any attention."

But it was Paul Boni's letter that finally sent me overboard.

In no uncertain terms, he counseled us against doing anything illegal, distancing himself in every way from the action. "Indeed, as CFP's outside counsel, I do not believe it is appropriate for you to list me on any email blasts."

I sat stunned, as if slapped. All week he had shown strong, courageous leadership. Now this.

I tried to understand the concern, to empathize with his need to protect himself as a lawyer. But the rush and blur of everything made it feel impossible.

I called up a fellow organizer, Jennine Miller from Project H.O.M.E.

For a good ten minutes, she listened to me patiently as I vented.

Then, finally, she spoke. "A big part of your job right now is helping members deal with their fear. That's hard work and frustrating, especially when their fear is getting in the way of all the other things you need to do *and* is not helping your own morale. It sucks. But you have the experience. You have to calm people down."

It struck a chord.

I had known that Paul needed to protect himself as a lawyer—Paul had even told me. But I was worried the crew was going to back out, leaving me alone. That was just my own fear.

I headed home and jumped onto my computer, to find my eyes wet while writing:

> *We've carried ourselves with real grace for the past many months. As I was calling people today, so many understand why we are doing what we're doing and respect and appreciate us for doing it.*
>
> *Why? Because we're not telling people to stop being corrupt. We're trying to make it happen. We're not telling someone else to go protect our riverfront—we're enacting the world we want to see. That's inspiring and an optimistic vision of citizens' engagement.*
>
> *We are part of a long legacy of actors engaged in civil disobedience to protect their neighborhoods—from those who are well-known to those who are not.*
>
> *With our actions come risk and fear, too. Yesterday I was very in touch with my own fear—wondering what would happen Saturday and what would we be giving up to be part of it. But I remembered a quote from a friend who says, "Wherever there is fear, there is power."*
>
> *If it wasn't scary to stand up to corrupt authority, people would do it all the time. We show our courage by doing what scares us—not by being unafraid. More than anything else, to me, it's our integrity and courage that we're modeling to the city. I'm proud of all of us for what we've accomplished simply to be here in this struggle. The fight is long from over and it's been a joy working with all of you. Can't wait to see you tomorrow and modeling that spirit of optimism, personal integrity, and courage.*

The next morning was the practice site occupation. I walked into the offices, and immediately Jethro ran me down. "I've been getting calls all morning! The SugarHouse site has busloads of police *everywhere* around it."

Uneasily, I glanced at my cell phone. Sure enough, I had missed a dozen calls while on my bike ride.

It wasn't a surprise that police were tipped off to our action, but their huge show of force was.

"This is a major monkey wrench," said Jethro, pacing back and forth as Lily and Nico watched anxiously from the couch. "With so many police, we don't have time to get onto the site and practice an occupation. We'll get arrested before even getting onto the site."

"Then let's swarm onto the site," I said. "Small affinity groups." As I said it, I caught myself. "But we haven't trained people for that."

"We could just have people get arrested, without a successful occupation," said Nico.

Lily cradled her legs. "Or a large march could distract police away from a smaller group going onto the site."

"Chain ourselves to the fence," said Jethro.

We looked at each other uneasily. None of these ideas would work. Our people weren't experienced direct action technicians. It was already such a stretch for many of them to even consider such an action. Trying some advanced flanking formation was only going to add to their worries and make the action dangerous.

"I'm gonna go see for myself," said Jethro. "I'll be in touch." He ran out of the office to the SugarHouse site.

Lily, Nico, and I eyed each other worriedly. We sat in silence as I thought to myself: *For the first time, they're amassing a huge force. They're going hard. All our ideas are ways we could go harder...*

... Or, we could underplay our hand.

I nearly jumped from my chair. "I've got it!"

Nico, Lily, and I met up with Jethro and sixty CFP activists at the corner of Delaware and Spring Garden, just two blocks from the SugarHouse site. It was a bone-chilling day, the bright sun only teasing us. At first, I saw only a handful of police across the street, eyeing us warily.

"There are more cops around the corner," said experienced organizer Chuck Valentine with a spring in his step, greeting me with a handshake. "There are forty cops stationed at intervals around the site. There's at least 150 cops in total."

Our activists were wringing their hands nervously in stalled, tense chit-chat.

It only deepened when the civil affairs captain walked over and immediately began yelling at me. "We're going to throw everything at you. Any infraction, any laws broken, anything that we can throw at you we'll do it. We will hold you in jail all weekend."

"That's what he gets paid the big bucks to do: scare protestors." I grinned, trying to shake off his spell. "It's probably not even true." But I wasn't certain.

Only when the captain walked back and shook the hand of the city's police commissioner did it hit me that this was a full-court press to intimidate us. They had pulled the commissioner and all these cops from overseeing a controversial rally for Mumia Abu-Jamal, probably at Mayor Street's request, if not that of the governor. They were more frightened of us!

I pulled everyone into a huddle. "So here's the plan. We meet their force with lightness." I was interrupted by a busload of police flying by with sirens blaring. "That's just a scare tactic they do," I told the crowd. "Wave to them and smile."

People did. Someone shouted, to people's laughter: "Hey, come join us!"

At that, people's faces relaxed slightly.

I continued, "We never promised to anybody what a practice site occupation looks like. Lily, Nico, and I are proposing we conduct a training right *outside* of the SugarHouse site. If the plan works, we make their moves for force look stupid. For today, our presence at the site is more important than the actual arrest."

Jethro nodded positively. Others looked relieved to hear a clear plan.

We assembled our march to the site.

Jethro asked if anyone knew any good chants, before leading, "Okay, we're going to chant, 'Casinos—corruption!'" He was merely reading the words of our banner, donated the previous night by Mike McGettigan. Like it was delivering a dirge, the crowd chanted, shuffling toward the SugarHouse site until Hannah Sassaman grabbed the bullhorn and pumped up the crowd. "Casinos in neighborhoods? No way!" Then, "What we do want?" "No casinos!" "When we do we want them?" "Never!"

Off to the side, Nico and I rapidly used trainer shorthand to emergently design our nonviolence training.

We arrived on the south side of the SugarHouse site, where the fence veered inward, making a small peninsula perfect for a stage. On all its edges were police officers.

As if choreographed, we marched in to fill the peninsula, walking right up to the facing police. Then, in a single motion, we turned around and faced the media and SugarHouse officials, who had come to tell us to get off their land.

But we weren't on their land. Instead, we had photographic gold: a condensed 130 protestors, smiling, surrounded by police officers in full gear.

"We are going to be training in nonviolent peaceful resistance," said Jethro on the bullhorn, "in preparation for future actions." Nico and I laid out a large tarp in front of the crowd. Our training space.

"First," I said, "thanks to the police officers for joining us during this practice site occupation. It's good to see you here." A few police officers reluctantly cracked smiles. "We're going to role-play two scenarios today. We need some volunteers to be a bulldozer." I held up a hastily drawn cardboard dozer blade. Lily, Norma, Scott, Morgan, and Zach tossed up their hands and stepped forward. Others played the role of protestors: Anne, Zoë, Michelle.

Alongside cheers and interruptions from the amped crowd, I got the bulldozer moving slowly. It continued toward the sitting protestors until it stopped, hovering just above Dicker's head.

I stopped the action to debrief and learn from the experience. "What happened?"

One protester, who had chosen to literally lie down said, "I couldn't see anything! I couldn't tell if the thing was going to stop." The group laughed.

"Yes," I admitted, "lying down is actually a bad idea. Sit up, stand up, but make sure to be seen."

Training in front of police and media made it the most real role-play I had ever led. The group was pulsing with terror and excitement.

We ran through other lessons: making eye contact, trying to not appear threatening, having people communicating with media, and planning ahead with different support roles.

Nico stepped in with the second, more likely scenario: arrests on-site. Turning to the police, Nico asked if any of them would help play the role of police. They shook their heads. "Next time," Nico joked.

With volunteers, he ran the role-play and debriefed.

The debrief centered on one protestor going "limp," lying like a dead heap instead of walking with the arresting officers. "Media love the shot," I said, "but it can be more risky for protestors—and police. Police suffer from back injuries more than any other injury, and none of them look forward to having to pick up people." Several police nodded affirmatively. "It's risky for protestors, since sometimes police will manhandle folks unnecessarily. Let's talk more about techniques that can help reduce those risks..."

After the training, Nico leaned over to me, amazed. "This was a real chance to personalize ourselves to the police officers and explain clearly why we were doing what we were doing, showing the police who we really are: long-time residents, retired school teachers, parents, students, and professionals who care about protecting their community—not the mob of crazies that others in the city are trying to make us out to be."

The training complete, we held a speak-out as police and SugarHouse employees looked on. There was so much buzz in the air, people took over an hour, testifying against the casinos, drinking hot apple cider donated by Pennsport supporters Joe Callan and Kathy DeAngelis, and joking with the police officers that they hoped they got paid overtime.

After I finally biked homeward, I spent a rare evening not thinking about Casino-Free Philadelphia—and slept the most soundly I had all week.

We had weathered a tough, tough week.

The days after our practice site occupation, I worked in a post-action daze. There were the highs of talking to excited supporters and cozily huddling underneath blankets reading waves of articles, letters to the editor, and watching *Plan Philly*'s three-and-a-half minute online video—a heartfelt interview by Jethro, with the last thirty seconds devoted to walking down a row of a dozen police vehicles, as if to say, "What a waste."

There were lows, like realizing that regular beat reporters didn't work on weekends, so the skeleton crews of the *Inquirer* and *Daily News* had missed our event entirely. Or the new media framing. "Isn't it unfair that only a few hundred people are stopping this project?" asked one reporter from the *Weekly Review*. "You're just the vocal minority."

A recent *Inquirer* article had spurred the new narrative. With the headline, "Delays of Casinos Costing Millions," it asserted that each day of delay was costing the state $900,000. Of course, the reporter had pulled that number from pro-casino figures and steadfastly refused to give us a chance to rebut. I fumed over that article and wrote a blistering, line-by-line critique—but she and her editor ignored me.

It was still hard for me to hide my fury when talking with the *Weekly Review* reporter. In response to his question, I snapped, "Do *you* know how many people were in the US abolitionist movement to abolish slavery?"

"I dunno, maybe half the population?"

"It's hard to know for sure," I said, "but if you add up every petition signed, every meeting, every public action—you won't get close to 1% of the population. Your view of what makes a social movement is confused. The amount of displacement people have suffered to fight these casinos is huge. People are taking time off of work, setting aside home life—for months, even years. If we win, we'll win because we're convincing and indeed speaking for a majority. In fact, if you cared to look at any polling data, you'd see most people no longer want casinos in this city. Seventy-nine percent support the buffer zone."

But media were deeply fractured. While a host of reporters and editorials came out defending us, *Inquirer* columnist Tom Ferrick was one of several who did not. "We don't get to follow the laws we like and ignore the ones we don't." He rebuffed us, arguing that casinos "won't ruin the waterfront."

Feeling back-stabbed by the normally pro-civic columnist, civic activists filled his email box. A handful of the sometimes caustic responses were printed, like Pennsport resident Patty Griffin's letter to the editor vexing that he'd mention the pluses but "leave out any mention of the increased costs. At the very least, there will be an increase in police costs to maintain safety around the casinos, and a greater need for social services to deal with the rise in alcohol and gambling addictions."

But the most worrying new narrative was that SugarHouse was prepared to build. Day after day, SugarHouse kept telling press it was going to start in weeks—a clear tactic to scare the opposition into feeling waves of defeat.

"Don't Believe the Hype," I wrote to our supporters, inspired by Public Enemy's song with that title. "In the words of founder Jethro Heiko, 'They declared we lost months ago. But they were wrong. We cannot believe them now, either.' On December 20, 2006, the gaming control board announced its licensing decisions. Foxwoods said they would begin building by February 2006. But they misread the environment—we are no longer the city that will stay silent. Come celebrate our successes for our one-year anniversary."

At that celebration, Shirley asked the question that was on many people's minds. "Are we winning or losing?" With so many things going on, it was dizzying.

Jethro folded his arms. "It is never as simple as winning or losing. We're doing both. We have put a lot of pressure on everyone. Even our new mayor seems ready to start a 'New Day' in Philadelphia. But I am not relying on him for victory. I would never trust anyone but ourselves to win."

We couldn't help but reflect on an exhausting year of moving dozens of political players. DiCicco was off slamming the supreme court. A suddenly fierce Fumo had led the legislative body to file another lawsuit challenging SugarHouse's claim to riparian land, while Foxwoods lost its "me, too" brief in the supreme court. Mike O'Brien, William Keller, and other state representative allies got unanimous support for a bill asking the state attorney general to stop the riparian lands being handed to SugarHouse.

With Mayor Street nearly gone, the governor was now alone in open opposition.

He was not going to give up. Last weekend, he had spoken to an elite gathering of politicians, judges, lawyers, and business people at the Pennsylvania Society—held, ironically, in New York City, a twist of history stemming from a century ago when New York rail, steel, and coal barons exploited the state. The governor called us names, saying, "In my office, we don't call them NIMBYs, we call them BANANAs, meaning 'Build It Never And Nowhere.'"

Of all our political allies, it was council who had most surprised us. At our celebration party, we decided that we should thank them—but our way.

So the last week of December, we filed into City Council, just as Cardinal Rigali was getting pictures with the councilmembers. Like most Catholic leaders, Rigali had steadfastly refused our efforts to recruit him to the anti-casino issue. Word had it the Catholic church made so much money on bingo and other forms of gambling, they would never come out against slot-parlor gambling.

Yelling for attention into the packed audience, our small crew stopped the proceedings. Norma Van Dyke headed over to Councilman DiCicco, as others went to the sitting councilmembers. "Here is your *Standing with the People* award," she said, thrusting into his hand a bright orange certificate with Frederick Douglass' quote "Power concedes nothing without a demand." She placed on his desk an award statue made of people-shaped cardboard cut-outs. He awkwardly accepted it, like each of his colleagues—except Ramos, who received no award.

Our Award Ceremony/City Council Slow-Down ended with the friendly security guard grabbing my arm. "Come on," he nudged.

Even in thanking councilmembers—and State Representatives Mike O'Brien and Babette Josephs—we were going to do it *our* way—interrupting the pomp and ceremony of council sessions with our own fun direct action. It was a reminder of Jethro's mom's advice: "there's a million ways to say fuck you."

In our case, it signaled our intention that we would not back down and that we were teaching Philadelphians a new relationship with council—not one that was based on subservience, but the opposite. Council meetings were *the people's* meetings and we would treat it as such.

As the year ended, we hoped that in a few months we *could* give that award to Mayor Nutter. We were about to find out.

CHAPTER 17

Operation Hidden Costs

JANUARY 1, 2008—APRIL 10, 2008

surviving stage seven • creating goals with spice and subtlety •
move politicians like chess pieces • doing what feeds you •
finding your power in opponents' insults •
in a war of attrition, small measures add up to victory •
steering politicians via the media • the challenges of a numbers campaign •
letting go of old boogeymen • facing greatest fears in an action

THE COLD AIR AROUND CITY HALL felt crisp and fresh. Jethro and I stood in line waiting to shake hands with the new mayor. The line stretched three full city blocks. Even more unusual was the friendliness of the line, filled with optimistic and even joyous faces. Nutter had somehow convinced cynical Philadelphians that he might really carry out his anti-corruption campaign slogan: "A New Day."

Jethro had talked me into coming, telling me, "It'll be fun, and everyone will be there!"

I didn't want to come. But I missed getting time with Jethro. And something urged me to be there. It was the same thing that kept me committed to CFP even when I felt I needed a break. It was more than just my competitive nature driving me to win, or my now-dogged desire to root out the incestuous ties between casinos and government. It was my own sense of commitment, as if by agreeing to be a face of CFP I had vowed to finish with it and see the movement through to the end, despite my own growing weariness.

So I stood in line, my back tired and my legs sore. My voice cracked in the cold. "Nutter certainly started strong!"

Mayor Nutter's first moves in office involved calling for a review of SugarHouse's riparian land permit, ordered by Mayor Street's administration on its last day in office. Nutter also removed the pro-casino city planning commission director and city solicitor.

Jethro rubbed his arms to keep warm. "It's a big win that with Mayor Street totally in bed with casinos, SugarHouse only walked away with minor permits." He paused, and we shuffled slowly as the line inched forward. Abruptly, he threw his arms in the air. "But Nutter's not an anti-casino guy!"

"We don't know that," I said sharply. Within our movement there were two camps: either Nutter was hero or enemy. I was disappointed Jethro seemed stuck in a camp, rather than being more nuanced. "He's not signaled where he really stands yet. We can't assume he's *not* with us."

Jethro huffed. "If he was really anti-casino, he would have been fighting for a long time on this issue. He doesn't want this issue. Everything he's done was because he was forced to do it. I think he's gonna cave—he wants the casinos in the ground so he can claim powerlessness like a good politician. Look around. He understands how to get rock-star treatment. He knows he only wins with public goodwill. He's just playing us."

"I think you're wrong," I said. "Look at today's *Metro* front page: 'Can Nutter Be Savior to Philly Casino Foes?' Nobody *knows* where he stands. But I agree with you that Mayor Nutter is a *smart* politician. This huge line of people waiting to meet with him shows he's inspired people—and that he knows everything moves quicker through City Hall with a public mandate. He ignores us at his own peril. Every day in the past week, we've gotten articles directly challenging him. He wants public goodwill, and we're gonna give him an easy win: stop the casinos and prove it's a new day."

Jethro shrugged. "We'll see..."

We continued taking steps silently, each trapped in our own thoughts.

Mine drifted to how months ago nobody wanted to touch the casino issue. Now seemingly everyone did, moved by the issue now being mainstream and polls now suggesting most Philadelphians did not want casinos. The riverfront planning process PennPraxis's director had found his voice on the issue, saying casinos "don't fit" on the riverfront. A councilmember had made a publicity-seeking attempt to revoke the ten-year tax-free deal for the new casinos. DiCicco had tried a new gambit to slow up Foxwoods by introducing their zoning—but with a shackling ten points of restrictions, including a revised traffic plan, almost a dozen more hearings, and an economic analysis—the latter tossed in to appease CFP's unhappiness at his last-minute maneuver. Political players now saw an issue on which they needed to appear to be on the side of people. That meant we had to figure out which moves were phony and which had some legs.

It was exactly what Bill Moyer's Movement Action Plan says happens in Stage 7: Managing success. Movement histories normally glance over this period of time. They ignore its complications.

Stage 7 tends to be prolonged. Opposing powerholders offer false solutions and cheap concessions, while energy among movement activists splits and dissipates in response to the varied options. None of our current examples of this were more apparent than PNA's willingness to accept relocated casinos versus our more firm stance against any casinos in the city.

The ways to win had increased: SugarHouse's permits were being slowed by environmentalists' evidence of endangered red-bellied turtles, research by historian Ken Milano showing the site likely housed a redcoat army fort from the American Revolutionary War, and a Native nation—the Lenni Lenape—discovering evidence of possible artifacts on SugarHouse's land. The problem was, with the different options,

CFP had no idea where to put our energy. Movement energy branched between those and many other possible solutions. These were the classic challenges of Stage 7.

It was late into the evening and dark when we shuffled passed exhausted officials and overwhelmed volunteers to reach the mayor's cavernous, bare reception room. Jethro reached to shake Mayor Michael Nutter's hands. "I hope you'll stop these casinos. They're trying to build one in my neighborhood."

Michael Nutter gripped Jethro's hands tight and flashed a politician's smile. "We'll do the best we can," he said, his voice indeed sounding like—to quote one reporter—"Steve Urkel, if Urkel had chilled out and gone to the Wharton Business School."

Nutter turned to me and grinned. "I've seen you a lot on TV."

"Yes, Mayor Nutter, I've been active with Casino-Free Philadelphia. Thank you for halting the riparian rights permits for a review. We hope you'll go further."

"We'll do the best we can," he said in the same muppety sing-song voice. Then he turned away. There were thousands more hands to shake that night.

As we walked away, I really hoped he would—not only because I wanted us to win and the movement to succeed, but because I wanted us to do it quickly. I was ready to be done.

At the next executive team meeting, Lily announced brightly, "The action last weekend was amazing! JJ took tons of pictures, and CBS 3 News trailed us and reported on our action. Isn't that amazing?" She looked over to me for affirmation.

It was a real accomplishment that Lily—still only four weeks on the job—had organized her first action from start to finish: talking to the suburban casino investors' neighbors—neighbor-to-neighbor. But all I could do was shrug, hoping my face didn't show frustration. Unless we believed investors might give up millions of dollars due to neighborly embarrassment, the action didn't put much pressure on anyone.

But I didn't have an alternative vision for what was next. I looked around for Jethro, before remembering he was missing another meeting.

"I'm just a little distracted," I said, pulling myself out of my internal dialogue.

We quickly turned our attention to the major item: building another campaign. We all believed if we could move the governor, everyone else would move. But we felt stuck on *how* to do that.

"What's our campaign ask, our goal?" I asked, waiting for Paul to be the first to jump in.

He did not disappoint. "We need him to oppose all casinos, not just re-site them."

Kathy and Shirley nodded in agreement, while I grinned at Paul. Ever since he'd left the PNA, he brought more energy and enthusiasm—if that was possible—and felt freed up to be truly against state-sponsored gambling.

"A good campaign goal doesn't just say what we want," I said, "it helps rally new people toward us and makes it easier when we do organizing in the streets. It should speak to people—not just those agreeing with us. Just asking him to get rid of casinos is too much—too much of a complete turnaround."

Paul's brain whirled. "Then let's get him to agree to stop the two Philly casinos first."

"Or," said Kathy, "why not get him to sign a pledge to eliminate the casinos if a cost/benefit study shows they'd cost the city? They still haven't done a single study on these two casinos, right?"

I nodded slowly. "Everything you're suggesting is really just restating the same goal in different ways. Good campaign goals have spice, subtlety, and often unusual demands. *Asking for documents. A 1,500-foot buffer.* Or Gandhi saying that he'd liberate his people by *making salt.* What's another angle on this?"

The few more suggestions were all variants on asking Rendell to stop the casinos. I clutched my marker tightly.

"Back it all up," I said. Kathy looked taken aback by my voice carrying rare impatience. "Our goal doesn't have to be a statement of what we want to reach. What stands in our way of Rendell doing what we want? Let's not just think politically, but broadly speaking. What are the pillars of support?"

"It's all economics," said Paul.

"If media talked about the true costs of casinos, we wouldn't have these things," said Kathy. "These things are going to take money from the poor and hand it to rich investors."

"If the public had the facts," said Shirley, "we wouldn't even consider them. We need a real debate in this city."

I clapped. "Yes! A debate!" Shirley cocked her head.

"Many of the best campaigns get built around taking a metaphor seriously," I said. "Acting it out to its completion. So we ask Governor Rendell for a public debate. If he declines us, then we hold a debate at his office."

"We get a public debate based on the facts," said Kathy.

"A debate-in," I cried out.

Shirley huffed and eyed all of us. "Why can't we just approach the media and get them to talk about these issues?"

It surprised me a little that Shirley still believed the media would be our savior. Then, as I opened my mouth, she turned toward me. "But that's not realistic, is it?" She sighed softly. "It's just a shame that we have to make the case that professionals should be making. Even when we get economists to testify, it always falls on deaf ears. The media just don't do their jobs."

I beamed at Shirley, "Exactly. That's why we're activists. To expose the lies and myths of society."

I watched Shirley nod in agreement and silently accept the title.

Kathy pointed back at the newsprint. "So that's our goal: He shows us his facts, we show ours. His will never stand up to our better research."

"Sound good?" I asked the group. They nodded quickly, our loose test for consensus. We didn't need a formal process—we had learned to feel the energy shift in the group. I wrote up our goal: *Engage Governor Rendell in a public debate.*

It would need refinement. But as Nico hastily assembled a draft of our Citizens' Cost Challenge, it was a way for us to keep trying to build the political context.

Meanwhile, Nutter finally gave us an undeniable sign.

*　　　*　　　*

Reporter Jeff Shields' call was an unwelcome intrusion. I was having fun hanging out with Anne, Jethro, Paul, and Lily at a local diner. I walked outside into the cold, listening to something rare—a shocked reporter.

"Well, it looks like Nutter gave you what you wanted. It's not my place to say, but I think he may be doing this knowing he might be breaking the law. I wouldn't have guessed it, but between this and his passing gun control legislation that's definitely illegal, he's actually heeding your call for direct action."

I stayed quiet and just listened.

"Isn't that amazing?"

I muttered something of vague agreement. "What *exactly* did he do?"

"He pulled SugarHouse's riparian licenses, calling Mayor Street's last-minute handing them over an abuse of discretion and based on fundamental errors."

SugarHouse now didn't have a big chunk of the land it needed. "That's great." I was still trying to play out all the angles, wondering what was around the corner.

Jeff continued, a bit surprised by my cool demeanor. "He's basically doing exactly what you asked him to do, saying that a 'legitimate review will ask, what are the real costs? What are the real benefits?' It's as if you wrote the text for him."

"We did," I said, brightening a little bit. "At least, we built the doorway for him to step through."

Good activists don't merely attack politicians—they move them, like chess pieces. In some cases they use sheer force of political will, in Nutter's case by finding what the politician cherishes most and showing how their movement aligns with it. We had made our movement attractive to anyone wanting to prove they were against corruption, for transparency, and pro-neighborhoods.

"I assume SugarHouse is running to their parents and asking the supreme court to strike that down?"

"Yep," said Jeff quickly.

"But SugarHouse might actually be killed by this?"

"As much as ever," said Jeff. "But I'm not putting bets on anyone at this point."

I smiled. "Thanks, Jeff."

It wasn't until after I shared the news with the team and we didn't see any downsides to Nutter's moves that I felt joy. Nutter *had* taken a risk for our movement, causing even the cautious *Daily News* to announce: "Casino Forecast: Foggy as Ever"—which probably egged Governor Rendell on to make outlandish comments just a few days later.

"GUTLESS!"

The *Metro's* front-page article blared the words, "Gov. Ed Rendell blasted City Council yesterday, saying they have 'no guts,' for delaying the city's two casinos and for keeping Pennsylvanians from greater property tax reductions. Perhaps the governor's strongest statements about opposition to the slots parlors, Rendell referred to a 'City Council with no guts that can be extorted by community groups.' He said the delays were also blocking 7,000 jobs for a city 'dying for jobs' and wage-tax reductions for city residents."

When Lily called me with the news, it chilled me even as I reacted with angry words. "Gutless? *Extorted?* Isn't that slander? This shows the governor absolutely doesn't want to move on this issue. He's escalating this and sending a clear signal to Mayor Nutter to back off the issue."

"Shirley suggested a petition drive," said Lily calmly. The edge to her voice wasn't angry, just crisp. She had been a competitive swimmer for years, and losing just wasn't in her vocabulary.

"We have to hit back hard!" I felt blinded with indignation.

"We need something simple. There's way too much already with us getting together a new campaign."

"Okay," I said. "A petition drive sounds fine. But I want it to be brutal."

"I'll get a draft by noon," she said quickly.

"Maybe we should do a sit-in. Or... or I don't know... it's not really slander because he didn't call us out by name. But maybe we could call a citizen's arrest on him?"

Lily said nothing. It wasn't that she didn't enjoy the ideas, but she wanted to know what was her job. She didn't need ideas, she needed actionable items.

It had been enough that Jethro hadn't been able to supervise her daily. She came from a disciplined, numbers-driven style of organizing and was struggling to assess herself in our flexible, open-ended style of organizing. I tried to think of how to bridge the gap. *What would Jethro do?*

He would credit Lily for organizing the last-minute event outside the governor's speech, wafting signs in his face: "Don't Betray Us, Ed Rendell."

"I bet your action helped get to Rendell. Good work on that," I said. I hoped I didn't sound too calculated.

Lily stayed quiet. Then, "Yep. Thanks."

She got off the phone, and together we put together an outraged letter, entitled "Rendell Gone Wild." *Extorted by community groups? Give us a break! We call it democracy, Rendell!* It was our most scornful to date.

Over the next days, the governor's words struck a chord, and our letter was signed by over a thousand people. The PNA set up its own fax bank and sent a couple hundred letters on its own.

Yet our letter went virtually unnoticed outside our own circles. In a fit of frustration, I wondered if the letter should have been more sarcastic. I knew that a petition alone rarely would make a mark—but our campaign had earned stature such that for months we could snap our fingers and draw public attention to our issue. Maybe we had lost an edge.

But the tone of the letter—sarcastic as it was—was not the problem. Times had changed. With politicians vying to score points on the casino issue, DiCicco earned his by slamming Rendell's "tantrum," saying, "I would rather be called gutless than irresponsible." In this new phase we were competing with political players for attention—even Nutter's silence and a few statements from Fumo made the news. Reporters instinctually gave preferential treatment to elected officials.

Doesn't matter. We have to act publicly to show politicians they can't let up now.

Between two training workshops that took me out of the state with Training for Change, the executive team set up several sessions to figure out our campaign plan.

"Hey guys, we need a sexier campaign name then Citizens' Cost Challenge. It's a meaningless phrase."

I hoped I wasn't being too critical. It felt difficult to know when I was being helpful, too severe, or when I should just shut up when facilitating our executive team's planning sessions. But I knew that with Jethro and me giving less attention to CFP, now more than ever we needed to decentralize strategic thinking. And that would mean the outcome would take a lot longer.

Nobody looked annoyed at my statement.

In fact, the executive team was unusually focused. Kathy wouldn't let us talk about any news. Nothing about the sixty-one-page report by local historians forcing SugarHouse to dig for historical forts. No words about our hand in making public CFP activist Patty Griffin's alleging that she was fired for her anti-casino views by no less than Tierney Communications, whose founder was an investor in TrumpStreet, the *Inquirer*, and the *Daily News*. We didn't even talk about the comments from Rendell last week.

I fiddled with a marker, still worried. "What about Operation... Operation Loyalty? You know, asking Rendell to be loyal to us?"

Nico laughed. "We could give Rendell those, you know, Valentine's candies? Ones saying something like *Be Loyal* or *Be Mine*."

Lily turned to me. "You certainly love campaigns named Operation."

"It's just an idea." I surprised myself with the defensiveness in my voice. *What am I really defending myself from?*

"It's not bad." Lily frowned uncertainly. "I just don't know about loyalty."

With great guilt, I realized I didn't want to be there. I didn't want to plan another campaign—and I certainly didn't want to run another one. It wasn't just that I was going without pay, now that I felt obliged to scrape together enough to keep paying Lily, too. It wasn't that this left me doing more paid work outside of CFP. It wasn't even just that the funding world seemed out to get us, with two local foundations turning us down—then privately telling me they were worried about us being so "political," before whispering that they had board members with relationships to Rendell or the casino investors.

I need to renegotiate my relationship with CFP. I hate constantly getting press calls—but nobody wants to take on that role, so I keep doing it. I don't want to be the face of CFP, but I keep saying yes when I don't really want to do it.

"Let's play out the loyalty idea," said Jethro whimsically. "If the campaign is about loyalty, what do you do with someone who is disloyal?"

This was how Jethro moved at his best. He took a concept and felt around it, underneath it, let his mouth savor it. When he was present, he was incredibly present. You couldn't tell that he was going through all the worries of a soon-to-be first-time dad—except for his increasing absences from our meetings.

Paul piped up. "We could kick the governor out of office. I don't know if there's a provision for that."

"Even if there is, Pennsylvania is a big state. It'd be tons of signatures to get," said Kathy. I could have kissed her for her realism.

"Don't you shoot disloyal people?" Jethro met my eyes. "Is there a nonviolent way to shoot someone?"

I furrowed my brow. "Nothing comes to mind."

My words hit a chord in me. *I want to have energy for the stuff that feeds me—not doing administrative and management work. I'm not good at those. I should be freed up to be thinking of tactics and strategy. But its more than just that. Even when I am thinking tactics nowadays, I'm not in my creative center*—as had been shown by my flat-footed reaction to the governor.

That realization had been sparked by a letter from my plumber. He had written me about our harsh letter to the governor, "It's beneath you to be that belligerent and name-calling, though I agree with the position against casinos completely." It woke me up. Instead of being offended, we could have been appreciative. Rendell was telling everyone that community groups hold sway and power.

That perspective brought to mind a host of better actions we could have taken: holding a "community extortionist" fashion show so people could see what a community extortionist looks like. *Hint: it looks like you and me.* Or, turning ourselves in to Rendell's office, demanding to be arrested—if community extortion is a crime, we *are* guilty. Or, hiring a gambling addiction counselor for our clearly in-need and addicted governor—just one more cost of bringing casinos.

If we had done that, we would have gotten in the mix better *and* stayed within our integrity.

So what about now? How do we creatively respond to someone being disloyal?

"What about arresting them for treason?" I offered. "Or maybe we snip off 'governor' on his placards and refuse to call him that anymore?" Even as I said it, I knew they weren't great ideas. But at least I was thinking again.

"You shoot them—you don't hold a debate-in with them," said Jethro with a sigh. "I think we might have an *ugly baby*."

Everyone looked at Jethro wonderingly.

Jethro smiled. "You know. When you see an ugly baby, nobody is willing to say it. We need to let bad ideas go. I think Lily's right that loyalty isn't the right direction."

"That sounds right, and I think we can find something more in our integrity," I said, something vaguely snapping into place. "We're not trying to assassinate the governor's character by challenging his loyalty. We're challenging his stupidity for not offering a real cost/benefit analysis."

"Operation 'It's the Economy, Stupid,'" smiled Paul.

"Operation Real Debate," said Shirley.

"Or Operation Real Numbers?" offered Paul.

Jethro pulled at his chin. "Operation Name the Costs?"

"Costs! That's right," I said. "That's the ground we're trying to run on."

"Right," said Jethro. "These are hidden costs, so... Operation Hidden Costs!"

Heads nodded enthusiastically. We had a new campaign name.

I put a big checkmark on the name as I wrote it up. "Now we just have to select tactics and dates and strengthen the arc. Let's open our calendars..."

By February 27, we were ready.

We squished into an elevator destined for Governor Rendell's Philadelphia office. Lily pressed the button for the eleventh floor.

I breathed shallowly, wondering how Lily would do at her first campaign launch. "I want this to be *my* campaign," she had told me at our last staff meeting—something that thrilled me and made me wonder if she was ready.

Already she'd designed a "soft launch" action at the first Pennsylvania Gaming Congress held in Harrisburg. Somehow she had convinced Shirley Cook, Kathy Dilonardo, and Scott Seiber to join her in wearing outrageously oversized cardboard calculators on their heads. Instead of numbers as on a calculator, their red cardboard buttons were the names of different social and economic hidden costs.

Kathy had told curious leaders of Pennsylvania's nascent gambling industry, "What we want to do is calculate the hidden costs—for addiction, suicides, bankruptcies, job loss, higher divorce rate. Governor Rendell is putting only 0.001% of casino revenue to help problem gamblers. That's $15.50 spent for each expected problem gambler. We want a real accounting. So we brought calculators to help."

Inside the elevator, the double-sided campaign document was still warm. It had a calendar of events for the two-month campaign, laying out the arc of its questioning: "Governor Rendell says casinos will create 7,000 jobs in Philadelphia. SugarHouse Casino sometimes claims 12,000 new jobs. The actual number of employees at a casino would be 1,100. And the only independent study shows a net loss of up to 5,900 jobs.

"Where do these numbers come from? Studies funded by the casino industry assume that all of the jobs will be completely new. They assume casinos will not compete with other businesses. Those studies assume tourists will visit Philadelphia for the casinos and, each time, spend an average of $135 per person after spending $60 in a casino. That's an economic leap of faith that economists don't make. Economists conclude casinos will result in a net loss of jobs—from 3,000 to 5,000 per casino. Losing jobs and blowing a hole in the city budget makes one wonder: why are we really introducing casino gambling to Philadelphia?"

Lily looked at her hands, as if reviewing her notes. I figured Lily was facing all the same nervousness I had during the launch of Operation Transparency almost a year and a half ago. I didn't know if she was prepared to do it—but was I ever ready? *Is there any way to know if you're ready to lead a direct action campaign except by doing it?*

Lily held the door while Kathy and I stepped out of the elevator.

Folks approached me with questions. Norma asked, "Why are we here when the governor isn't in his office?" Andrea wondered if this campaign would impact Mayor Nutter. Deferring questions to Lily felt like a luxury.

Lily turned to the dozen milling activists in the surprisingly bright, pale hallway. "We're here!" Her voice barely rose above the hum of the incandescent lights. She raised her voice a fraction. "Hello! People! Let's get started!"

Her smiled look plastered on, as if to conceal her anxiety. I almost stepped forward to gather the crowd. *Lily looks so young to be leading a group of mostly retirees—but isn't that what I look like, too?*

Kathy grabbed a few people next to her and quieted the crowd.

Lily continued without appearing to notice. "We're outside the governor's office to tell him to create a *serious* cost/benefit analysis and then hold a public debate on the costs and benefits of casinos. He's never done it, and he's scared to do it!"

Lily explained the "if this, then that" component of the campaign. *If* the government did not create an analysis, we would "be forced" to create our own report. Then, *if* the governor did not hold that debate, we would just have to lead Philadelphia's first-ever debate-in at his offices.

Lily was interrupted by the governor's office manager blundering out of the office.

Lily and Kathy recognized him at once. Just two weeks earlier, they had dropped off the 1,333 signatures responding to the governor's "gutless" comments. We called it a "Valentine's Day delivery." The office manager had happily posed for cameras with anti-casino Valentine's Day cards complete with doilies and messages: "Governor Rendell: Have a heart," "Eddie, you broke my heart!" and "Love us, not the greedy." It was a frolicking good time for all, with upbeat front-page coverage in the *Metro*.

Today the manager was not smiling. "What do you guys want?" He threw his large arms around and glared as if we had interrupted him. Nobody moved.

The manager's eyes darted around. "Well! Who is leading this?"

Lily took a tiny step forward, her thin frame dwarfed by his linebacker build. "We're just preparing our action..." Her voice melted a little. "We aren't quite ready yet."

"Well I'm ready," he barked.

Lily tensed up. "Well, we're not." She dismissively walked away from him toward a corner and motioned for the group to join her. He sighed heavily, returned to the governor's office, and slammed the door shut.

I was glad to only be on the outside of our huddle, while Lily and Kathy discussed if his new tone warranted any change of plans. Clearly, the manager had gotten word from the governor not to treat us so nicely again—maybe he'd been unhappy about a front page with his staffer and us smiling together.

Lily and Kathy agreed to go ahead as planned—knowing they might have to be a little more pushy.

With quick strides from her long legs, Lily barreled into the governor's offices and walked past the secretary. Over-ruling the frustrated office manager, she told him that everyone was going to cram into his back office.

"There's not space," he exclaimed.

Lily ignored this and explained our demand to the governor. "We're giving him homework."

"You're not his teacher," the office manager quipped.

"He needs one," she said. "First, we want him to name *at least* seven hidden costs, since he's not acknowledged a single one publicly. We want a cost/benefit analysis followed by him holding a public debate on casinos."

Her voice had found its grounding. Lily was one of those people who do their best when they're challenged—a born competitor. She then handed the manager a calculator, magnifying glass, and ruler. "These are to help the governor do some measurements."

The manager's voice boomed. "I can't use a magnifying glass. But I can use a calculator, so I'll keep that."

"It's *not* for you," said Lily indignantly, staring him down. "It's for the governor. All of it."

"This ruler is cheap plastic," the manager said.

From behind Lily, Kathy exploded. Her face was red, and she wagged her finger at the manager. "We're here to visit the governor's office and be treated properly. I've been a government officer for years, and I would never treat someone the way you have treated us. You are being disrespectful, and it's completely unnecessary."

As anyone would do facing an explosive Kathy, the manager quieted down.

At a slower pace, Lily handed him a two-page report that I had written earlier that week. "This shows the lack of cost/benefit analyses done in the state." It was a review of all studies on the Philly casinos. It showed how the city's commissioned report ignored lost property taxes from driven-down property rates, criminal justice costs, and the massive social impact costs of problem and pathological gambling. It was still better than Foxwoods' study—widely cited by press and the PGCB—that ignored all those costs, plus those of policing and counseling. None calculated the money cannibalized from other industries.

"We'll be back in a few weeks to see what the governor has done on his homework." Lily turned to leave.

The office manager managed to fold his arms and glare, but under Kathy's wary eye, he remained silent.

On the elevator ride down, Norma barked. "This is how they have always treated the citizens. But now they have to do it to our faces."

Mary Stumpf turned to me. "So what's next?" I nodded toward Lily—it was her campaign.

"I'll be in touch," she said.

True to our current stage, no major media covered the action. But an *Inquirer* reporter used the phrase "hidden costs." A minor start. Our campaign was warming up.

I stayed attentive to the political atmosphere, involving myself swiftly and subtly. I was trying to live up to what a Greenpeace activist once told me, "In a messy war of attrition, a host of small measures can add up to victory."

Following our launch, reporters mostly stayed away from our framing of hidden costs and instead talked of "casino delays." Under that framework, it was only natural that they latched onto a proposal from Western Pennsylvania representative Bob Godshall. His proposal stripped Philadelphia from any tax cuts as punishment for its delay in opening up its two casinos, saying, "Philadelphia is not contributing anything, and yet they're siphoning off money."

The bill had no real chance to pass. But when Governor Rendell foresaw the bill "picking up steam," reporters interpreted it as a possible green light for the bill. So they ran with the story that it might pass.

I wasn't sure how to shoot the bill down—or more importantly, how to redirect the conversation about the bill, which was merely a distraction. But I had a good idea that reeked of political intrigue.

I asked for a lunch meeting with Queen Village civic leader Jeff Rush, a crony of Senator Fumo.

At a Middle Eastern restaurant in Center City, Jeff greeted me with enthusiasm and we quickly lapsed into an easy, cordial conversation. At a quiet moment I slipped in, "You know where I stand, Jeff. I hate these casinos. But for PNA to win, it needs to keep repeating the phrase, *"The only reasonable solution is for Rendell to move them."* Say it again and again until it's true. As for the bill, I think someone should say they'd happily support Godshall's legislation, provided the two casinos went to his district."

"That'd get him," Jeff laughed.

The rest moved as I had hoped.

Jeff talked to Fumo, who loved that kind of slapshot argument. The next day, Senator Fumo sent out a press release quoting my lines and adding, "Senator Fumo would be happy to introduce legislation to transfer one of Philadelphia's two licenses into his district." The quote reverberated into the media, Jeff's letter to the editor, and eventually the *Inquirer's* own editorial board—all using identical language.

Without risking Casino-Free Philadelphia's name, the bill was eviscerated and pressure returned to Rendell. Nobody continued to talk about the bill.

Not bad for a single, very choice meeting. But I didn't know if that small measure would make any difference.

Days before the Operation Hidden Costs Meet-and-Greet action, Lily and I had discussed the challenge of CFP's first campaign based on numbers. Numbers are faceless and boring. Reporters hate wading through numbers, because each side has their own. Lily pointed out that CFP had let the casinos make claims unchallenged for months— making it all the harder now to fight the "jobs and revenue" argument.

With a sense of regret, I acknowledged we had made a mistake in not leading with the victims of casinos, having them be spokespeople and out front. It was always a challenge given we were fighting something *before* it had caused damage, where the victims were in the future. But that made her idea for the Meet-and-Greet action even better.

At first, we were going to do some media action at Rendell's house, maybe dressing up as the costs and parading around Rendell's house. But, in my absence, she picked a wiser, less confrontational, easier to do, and more educational event.

The faces of the hidden costs were presented as a panel before the packed audience in our offices, backdropped with red Philly's Ballot Boxes.

First up, bald-headed Jim Paylor, the ILA president. His sharp turtleneck hid his bulging muscles. As he had done at a dozen hearings, he repeated how casino development along the port threatened his profession and the thousands of laborers on the shore.

Gambling counselor Tina DiSanto went next. Her voice was light and inviting, as one would expect from a therapist. "Every gambler I've ever met, they describe their relationship to the act of gambling just like they would describe a drug that they shoot into their arm. It's the same high. It's the same chase." She described how gambling addiction is hidden from view, much the same way that alcoholism had been completely shunned and not talked about. Ninety percent of a casino's income came from 10% of its customer base, exposing that casinos' major purpose was to get people hooked on their product, like a heroin dealer—except the suffering was more subtle, and institutionally backed by the government, which was giving its seal of approval and would provide its resources to promote casinos. Pulling out a large stack of "supporting literature," she recited statistics: pathological gambler costs between $10,000 and $30,000 a year for the state; as many as a quarter of *recovering* gambling addicts attempt suicide.

Tina was followed by a well-known real estate saleswoman, Kathy Conway. "Since Foxwoods' selection—but before the national housing market meltdown," she said, "all the developers started to drag their feet. They were concerned about Foxwoods and its impact on the community. Every single development with the exception of one was canceled—that one had a developer in New York who didn't know what was going on." She described houses sitting vacant, unable to sell when people heard about Foxwoods. "I'd say it hurt property prices by at least 20%."

Economist and professor David George, wearing his professor's garb of brown sweater and glasses, debunked the idea of casinos as just an individual's personal responsibility. "Government and business policy makes many things more or easy to access, for example, smoking. Many people who *choose* to smoke don't *want* to smoke. If policy makes it easier, then more people do it—even if it's not what they say they want. The accessibility and addictive nature of gambling makes it a social issue, not merely a personal choice."

But of all the speakers that night, Joe was the one who moved me most.

He had just emailed me a week earlier saying he wanted to use his story to help save others from casinos. After my initial call with him, I faced an organizer's dilemma: feeling absolutely horrified and saddened by his story *and* elated to find the first person willing—wanting—to tell their story. Most Gamblers Anonymous meetings encourage confidentially and eschew anything political. While helping the community heal, the policy keeps gamblers out of the spotlight and rarely speaking up on their own behalf.

Laid-back in his chair with a baseball cap and leather jacket, Joe drawled in a raspy voice. "I'm a compulsive gambler," he began. "I lived in New Jersey for seven years and never had a problem. It was too inconvenient, with a two-hour drive."

But when Harrah's Casino in Chester opened up, things changed for Joe. "Now I live in Chester. It's fifteen minutes from me." He shared how his wife had died and he sought solace and entertainment in Harrah's.

With intense eyes behind glasses, he leaned forward, looking down as if to avoid eye contact. "Now, being a widower and living alone, grief has a lot to do with depression. People who are depressed seek excitement. And that's what I did. I have two lights in Chester and I'm there at the casino. Started going on Saturdays. Started going on

Sundays. I'd win and it was exciting—I'm happy, I'm having a good time. I'm eating there for nothing, drinking there for nothing. It's a progressive disease.

"What happens is you have three stages. You know, you have winning stage, losing stage, and desperation stage. By the time you have that desperation stage, you're heading into bankruptcy. You've already lost your house, maxed out your credit cards, and probably pissed off a lot of relatives and friends.

"Before I knew it, I had devastated myself. I had lost my house, went bankrupt, lost my 401K—anything, you name it, I've done. Only good thing is that I stopped myself and admitted I had a problem. Luckily I had good friends and they saved me. Because the ones who don't stop either commit suicide, end up in jail... or go insane. And that's what you're going to have, especially because it's close to your neighborhood." He sat back quietly. "I just wanted to say that."

I could only think that Joe's story echoed those of thousands of to-be addicts at SugarHouse and Foxwoods. Following his words, I mechanically handed out the Operation Hidden Costs document. "Thanks, all, for coming," I said, dropping a few flyers and encouraging people with, "You now have more information than most politicians. Go ask Nutter for an economic analysis." People stood up and clapped for the panelists, breaking some of the tension.

Glaring at me, Kathy reminded me to encourage people to donate—especially since a major donor had agreed to match up to $10,000.

I mouthed the words, but Joe's story had deeply resonated with me. It was also the story of a Chester woman who had embezzled $573,000 from the city government to feed her addiction. It was the story of one parent, then two, then three parents at the casino north of Philly, leaving their children trapped in the car while they gambled inside. It was the story of a woman who told a casino attendant she had "stomach aches" before literally birthing a baby, all while sitting glued to the slot machines.

Three days later, a meeting occurred in the mayor's office. There, Foxwoods brought chairman Michael Thomas and a South Philly ward leader, Nike Maiale, "hired to break the deadlock that Nutter had helped create."

The meeting came on the heels of a mayoral aide's testimony that "Foxwoods casino will certainly create some new casino jobs, and will induce some construction jobs. However, we have not done any independent economic impact analysis of how many jobs or the likely impact. For this reason, the Nutter administration supports City Council's requirement for an outside economic impact study." She explained that the mayor's budget would not include casino revenue, nor would it assume the economic spin-off income the casinos boasted. "We need to be careful we don't mix up new spending with substitution spending. The Gaming Task Force model determined that 75 to 90% of all casino spending is new—that is, money that would not have been spent on movies, sporting events or other things in Philadelphia. We need to understand that number and test some of the assumptions that went into it. Conversely, we need to study whether there might be a negative impact on existing businesses, as has occurred at many other places with casinos."

The debate was on.

The aide's words echoed further than any of ours in challenging casino economics. It certainly set a chilly tone for the meeting in the mayor's office, which we wouldn't read about until six months later in the *Inquirer*:

> *"I realize I'm coming into this in the middle of the game," Nutter offered.*
> *"Actually, Mr. Mayor, it's the eighth or ninth inning," said Maiale, according to one of the meeting's participants.*
> *"Then this game is going into extra innings," Nutter replied.*

Michael Thomas offered a PowerPoint showing the benefits and plans for the $670 million Foxwoods casino. Nutter countered that he was unhappy with the casino and its location, citing community concerns.

Nothing was agreed upon. Neither side was happy.

Placed between a rock and a hard place, Nutter was spurred to keep escalating.

I didn't know about that meeting, or maybe it would have been easier to keep going. But I did get the bad news from the *Inquirer*'s Jeff Shields—which is why I was pedaling hard with a grimace on my face.

Just earlier that day, I had a pleasant bi-weekly meeting with Lily. She and Nico had reported on the Hidden Cost Easter Egg Hunt, an egg hunt with candies for the kids and "hidden cost" factoids stuck into the pastel plastic eggs for the adults. As usual, Lily was filled to the brim with positivity—"It went great! Debbie King is the best! Everyone had fun!"—and Nico with understated certainty: "It wasn't our biggest turnout—less than a dozen people. But it was mostly families who don't normally come out to our events."

The event had been covered by Fishtown's local newspaper, the *Spirit*. And two more newspapers began using the phrase "hidden costs" in their articles. Our campaign was slowly but steadily turning attention.

But that didn't stop the supreme court.

"Foxwoods gets SugarHouse treatment," texted Jeff Shields. "City blown out, is now out of the equation. Give me a call."

I don't want to call him. He'll just ask how we overcome another impossible hurdle. Now Foxwoods is just like SugarHouse, with only a few federal permits and the city's foot-dragging slowing it down.

I despaired silently as I headed into another meeting I wasn't sure I wanted—this time with a reporter trying to discern the details of how once-dear friends Senator Fumo and SugarHouse investor Richard Sprague had turned into bitter rivals. My money said our organizing had ripped them asunder.

I paced outside the coffeeshop, not wanting to head in just yet. I called Paul, who picked up immediately.

I began as if in midstream, "I need you to talk to Jeff Shields. I'm just too wound up."

"Sure thing," he said.

I heaved a sigh. "Thanks."

I hung up my phone and walked into the coffeeshop—just as my phone started ringing.

I could have ignored it. I should have—and even knew it. But my instincts were too fast.

"Yes?" My fingers had accepted the call, and my mouth was already speaking.

Jeff's voice was on the line, asking for a quick quote.

Just one quote. "This is going to be a major tug of war over a number of months, or years," I told him. I barely even thought about the words—though if I had, the prospect of more years would only have filled me with dread.

"What options do you have left?" The question was like a well-stabbed wound.

"You're going to write that Foxwoods now has the same court-ordered permits as SugarHouse. And what does SugarHouse have but a single earth-moving permit from the city? I'd say we have plenty of options."

Jeff was satisfied and got off. *Quick. Simple.*

I willed myself for another meeting. I was limp and tired, like a squeezed out rag. But instead of pushing work away, it kept gravitating toward me and I was unable to get the breaks I knew I needed.

The next day surprised me.

I headed downstairs and opened up my laptop, expecting the old boogeyman: the done deal. Jethro clearly had expected it, too. His quotes in the newspapers quietly raged, "Not only will we break the law to stop these—but we will do so repeatedly. I have a family. I have no interest in spending time in jail. I have an interest in protecting my city." I wondered if he, too, felt some kind of responsibility to present a bold face.

Yet that boogeyman wasn't anywhere. Nutter hinted vaguely at his own plans. Fumo blew off the court ruling. Even Foxwoods' lawyer refused to give a date they would begin building, because, "I never want to underestimate the resources of our foes." Not a single reporter suggested it was—as they had written in the past—"the end of the line."

Even the *Inquirer* editorial board—once openly hostile to us was quick to chastise the supreme court, saying that on casino issues they should keep a "rubber stamp handy that said 'APPROVED'" because it "would save time, trouble and the pretense of impartiality."

I stared at my computer screen, amazed. *Our opponents respect us. Past opponents are now acting like allies. Yet nothing has actually been won. Is this disappointing feeling the feeling of winning? Or is it just losing in a high-ground way?*

I gathered my stuff and headed downtown for the first trip back to City Council chambers since our awards delivery. The mayor was giving his first formal testimony before council, and I wanted to hear it myself.

It began rockily. "I have not stated opposition to casinos in Philadelphia," he lied, as my fingers clenched with worry, surrounded by anti-casino activists filling the first floor. "But, I want to be very direct about this. It is clear that the proposed Foxwoods site is the wrong site for Philadelphia and for the Commonwealth of Pennsylvania. If... If... If we are to have gaming in Philadelphia. There is a way to do it and there is a way to do it right." He looked angry, driving home his points with fingers flying through the air. "There are additional costs of infrastructure with no idea about where those dollars are coming from. The additional police and fire and other personnel costs—none of which are outlined in our budget or our five-year plan. None of which *we* should have to pay for as the City of Philadelphia. *If* there is to be casino gaming in Philadelphia, it needs to be done respectfully and thoughtfully, and we cannot allow ourselves to be run over by the various interests who have *their interests*, not our interests, at heart. Thank you, Madam Chairwoman."

From the next seat over, Paul and I looked at each other wide-eyed. Nutter had done the connecting that *we* should have been doing. I sat back in my chair, shaking my head. I had just been out-hustled on our issue by the mayor!

No. Not out-hustled. It's just that he's not fighting the done-deal storyline. He's present to the new political phase, which is about re-siting and economics. I'm still acting like we're a marginalized movement. Instead, I should be connecting the past months' twists and turns to hidden costs: Rendell calling us 'gutless.' Godshall's bill. Actions in investors' neighborhoods. Casinos asking the courts to force Nutter to stop his foot-dragging. Our buffer bill stalling completely at the state level. Everything could have been woven into Operation Hidden Costs, like a good campaigner does. But I didn't. I only bring those talking points to scheduling CFP actions.

Whenever reporters thrust microphones in my face, I'm back to the issues of being pro-transparency, pro-good process, even pro-buffer. I'm calcified and unable to switch to the hidden costs framework. It's probably because I've given the same answers for so long to reporters.

I looked over at Paul. He's the future. He has the hang of Stop Predatory Gambling's framing, that it's about being against a predatory industry. After all, isn't that what we've seen? Isn't that already the story being told about Philadelphia outside Philadelphia? That this is exactly how to not *do development, driven by a ferocious outside industry? From its introduction to its implementation across the state, casinos are showing themselves to have teeth, to bite communities and rip out huge pockets of wealth and social networks.*

Interrupting my self-reflection, reporters approached Paul and me to ask us what we thought.

I watched Paul answer smoothly. "Mayor Nutter is finally coming to the conclusion that citizens have come to months ago: that casinos are just not worth it. His police department just documented that the city would have to pay a minimum of $14 million for expanded policing. It's just one of the many hidden costs, and we're glad he's talking about them now."

I tried my hand. "A few days ago, a bankrupt patron north of here took his car and slammed it into a wall, trying to kill himself. He said he was just a compulsive gambler and needed mental help. Financially speaking, the municipality had to pay for the state and city police troopers who arrived on the scene, his ambulance trip to the emergency room, and his stay at the county jail. Costs for his court trial, possible rehabilitation, or prison will be additional expenses for the city. The cost is spread out, so no single department is hit alone. Times that story by 4,000 for the number of pathological gamblers in Philly and you can see why this is a major cost."

I was proud of what I'd said. But I knew that when I got tired, I'd still resort to the old storyline.

✻   ✻   ✻

Lily kicked off the debate-in with a handheld bullhorn at City Hall, under a warm spring sky surrounded by seventy CFP activists. It was our largest turnout in months.

"We're going to start here and march to Governor Rendell's office in the Bellevue." Nobody's voice ever sounded crystal through a bullhorn, but Lily's sounded distinct, grounded. Having to do paid work during the last two actions she had organized, I had missed how strongly she'd grown into the role.

No stutter interrupted as she reminded the assembled crowd of our history, asking for a public debate with the governor. She gave people a quick synopsis of the complex, twenty-six-page report—*You Pay Even If You Don't Play*—that we had delivered to the mayor the day before.

Rather than create new calculations, our report was a meta-analysis of the city, state, and independent analysis reporting of hidden costs. Our report noted the lowest costs, the highest costs, and then made reasonable mid-range predictions. For example, on the issue of addiction and criminal justice costs, the city's Gaming Advisory Task Force had calculated it would cost the city $0 (low estimate), PICA said $223 million (high estimate), and our calculation showed $82.3 million.

"You've got to read it! It gives you a sense of all the things nobody has calculated and gives estimates based on the best research out there. Two million dollars in municipal services. Four million lost in property taxes. Twelve million via what's called the substitution effect, money lost from the local economy by going to the coffers of wealthy investors. *The total net cost the city will lose each year a casino is in operation?* Fifty-two million dollars!"

As smooth as she was, I felt bad that I was still noticing what she wasn't doing well. Maybe it was the teacher in me. Or the perfectionist. But she wasn't relieving people's nervousness about what was going to happen today—several having been part of sour stand-offs at the governor's office and worried about the plan of action.

Lily led the crowd through the short four-block walk to Rendell's downtown office, along Broad Street, stopping along on the busy sidewalk outside of the regal Bellevue, a nineteen-floor building made of limestone and terra cotta. The tenants were a who's-who of Philly, including the governor, the chamber of commerce, and Tierney Communications (the same group that had fired anti-Foxwoods activist Patty Griffin), and it was managed by a company headed by a Foxwoods investor.

Lily stopped outside, before reaching the staircase to the lobby, and nodded at me.

I stepped to one side and asked the crowd to listen as I reviewed the action. "Rather than engage in a rational planning process, the governor has backed businesses over the people!" The mic was attached to a portable boombox donated by Mike McGettigan, who turned on music softly behind my voice. I found myself naturally rising with the music. "So today we are here with many allies—Anne Dicker! State Representative Babette Josephs! And the many neighborhoods here. Who's here?"

Faces crowed in pride: *"Hawthorn!" "Pennsport!" "West Philly!" "Fishtown!" "Northern Liberties!"*

"Today we will hold the *first* Philadelphia debate on casinos. This is the *closest* the governor has ever come to a public debate on casinos. In case the governor doesn't join us in person, he'll be represented by this puppet." To chuckles, someone brought forward a four-foot papier-mâché puppet of Rendell's head—donated by Spiral Q puppet theater.

"How many of you have been part of a debate-in?" I looked for hands jokingly. Nobody moved. "Ah, right. I don't think any of us have. This may be the first debate-in ever in the world. So here's the concept. We're going to go as far as we can to the governor's eleventh-floor office. There, we will set up and people can speak—whether you're pro-casino, or pro-re-siting, or anti-casino, or anti-re-siting, or believe casinos will cost $52 million per year, or believe casinos will be a major development for the city. The goal is to hold a public debate. Let's go do it!"

Inhaling collectively, the crowd surged behind as Kathy and Lily walked up the concrete steps. Two security guards materialized in the doorway, towering over Lily and Kathy's small frames. "You can't come in," one large man bellowed.

"Sir," asked Kathy as she nudged her way past his left side, "have you been told that I personally can't come in?"

"Your organization... none of you... it's not allowed!" His voice tried to boom.

Kathy's voice carried an edge. "Sir, of course it's allowed," she smiled as she wiggled her way past, pulling Lily in tow. "You can't tell people they can't come in because of their beliefs."

He looked over helplessly at his colleague as Kathy beelined toward the elevators. There, another team of security told her the elevators had been shut down and that the stairs were locked.

We had considered sending someone up hours earlier to secure access closer to the office. Maybe that person could manage some way to get to the eleventh floor through tricks and last-minute maneuvers. But that kind of scheming focused on the physical space and street turf—and we were far more interested in the more meaningful fight for political space.

Not setting a goal of getting into his office gave us a lot of freedom. If the governor locked his office, we would do the action in the outer offices. If we couldn't even get in, we'd do it in the hallway on the eleventh floor. Such an action design allowed us to be confrontational without risking arrest—an added bonus when we found out we could only scrounge up seven people willing to get arrested. But more importantly, we told ourselves, this particular action design would speak more cleanly to the public, who could help us move the governor, just like we had moved Nutter.

Lily stationed herself on the bullhorn near the south side of the Bellevue's lobby, an echoing two-story lobby with mosaic tile floor, crystal chandeliers, and gold leaf detail. She arranged people to create a crowd of half-circles surrounding the bullhorn, while to her right Governor Rendell's giant four-foot papier-mâché head bobbed unsteadily. "Who's first?" she asked.

Lily waited, tapping her feet for what seemed an eternity, before Mary Stumpf grabbed the bullhorn. "Governor Rendell, what are you going to do to protect our neighborhoods and our families?" She looked at the giant puppet, making encouraging motions with her arm. "Governor? *Governor?*"

"He doesn't have an answer," someone shouted. Mary returned to the crowd.

Another few pauses.

JJ Tiziou strode up. "Governor Rendell, the city has been my home for the past ten years." The lanky photographer spoke quickly and passionately. "I've been an ambassador for this city and really excited to talk about the wonderful things in Philly. I'm wondering, what's the long-term vision of the city if we're going the route of Atlantic City? I think casinos are going to be a minus and cause more people to move out of the city. What do you say to that?"

The crowd cheered. The Governor Rendell puppet said nothing.

Paul Boni went next. "Governor Rendell, who are you listening to? I'd like to know, Governor, who do you listen to? Are you having conversations with the investors, and do they have your ear—and if so, why?"

There was something thrilling about watching people wonder if they should get up, get cheered. *This is a good action—and an even better training exercise. Here, everyone is asked to participate and go in front of media cameras to speak their minds. There's fear as people approach the bullhorn. But it's low risk and an encouraging environment, so it's an easy success.*

I recalled a study that once asked people their greatest fears. Above dying or being left friendless, the number one response was speaking in front of an audience with a microphone! And here we had people facing down that fear maybe something we should have done earlier to prepare people for speaking to the media more.

It's a brilliant design. I wish it were intentional.

As Lily had asked, I closed the action. "A piece of history: a couple of months ago we asked the governor's office for their economic cost analyses. They said they would not give them to us for two reasons: first, because they're part of the legislative request and two, because there are no such documents. I have copies of those conversations for reporters. But the fact is we've asked time and time again to be engaged in the legislative process. While part of democracy is representation, another important part is *participation*. Without both, democracy falls apart. Rather than engage in a debate and participating with us, he has shut down his office. Seventy people are so terrifying to his office that he'd rather shut down his office than deal with questions." Boos emanated from the highly animated crowd. Laughing, I closed, "So, if you did not know you are powerful today—you are—in the eyes of the governor."

I *was* happy to be there—watching people take risks, be bold, and feel confident that as we were speaking our voices mattered. I liked the camaraderie and connection. Without that, I probably wouldn't have been able to last the next few months.

CHAPTER 18

Re-siting Committee

APRIL 11, 2008 — SEPTEMBER 10, 2008

*campaigns need time • tasting liberation in the midst of overworking •
action logic • uncertainty of too many avenues pervade stage seven •
creating a crisis atmosphere to break deals • aligning opponents' interests with yours •
expect politicians to act right; plan for if they don't •
snatching defeat from the jaws of victory*

IF I HAD CALLED PHILIPPE DUHAMEL after Operation Hidden Costs, he would have congratulated me over the flurry of articles and how we had earned council's plan for an economic impact study, gotten reluctant reporters diving into the numbers, and started a citywide debate over the economics of gambling. In his infectious optimism, which had crafted Operation Transparency and inspired Philly's Ballot Box, he would have laughed, saying, "I just *loved* Operation Hidden Costs, it's a beautiful design. The fact that the governor is telling Fox News that the debate is over—just *brilliant!*"

But Philippe would also have hit a stern note. "My concern is that it seemed like it could have been worded to give Mr. Rendell some small chance, the benefit of the doubt, in terms of him coming through. I know this would have probably run against your own experience—I have no doubt this guy's attitude must be quite obdurate—but it would have lent a bit more cred to the operation."

He would then direct my attention to the timeline. "I don't think it gave him—or you—much time at all. The campaign angle is so great, so educational, so powerful in leveraging the issues neglected for too long in this campaign, that it seemed too bad you weren't building it for long enough to milk all the good stuff at a nice, slow pace. Operation Hidden Costs needs to be an eight-month campaign at least to seep into people's consciousness."

It's at that point that he would have heard me groan.

"You're winning, Daniel, so what's the big rush? Slow down and enjoy the ride!"

Around that point, I would have had to explain the challenges flying in my face. Of a renewed effort by SugarHouse to tie CFP with the Atlantic City casinos. Of me calming the fears of allies in other parts of the city that they were the new target for a casino—

fueled by speculation and debate among editorial boards and political pundits over what were the best sites for the new casinos: A *return to the TrumpStreet location? Navy Yard? Center City? Airport?* Of me getting attacked publicly by members of the PNA—who felt that *only* discussion of moving casinos mattered—when some editorial boards had begun suggesting we didn't need casinos at all!

But I didn't call Philippe to share all that.

Nor did I call George Lakey, with his wise voice, stabilizing me in times of crisis.

He would have spent the first part just listening to me vent.

"Paul's doing everything to make sure SugarHouse dots every *i* and crosses every *t*, forcing SugarHouse's accrual of permits to slow to a crawl. Jethro's halfway out the door. Shirley keeps reporting disappointing funding numbers, since fewer and fewer people distrust Nutter and want to give to a feisty direct action group anymore."

George would have given me time to get to the heart of the matter. He wouldn't try to rush me to go to the core of the problems, but he'd nudge with a gentle "uh-huh" or a prodding "hmm."

"PNA's almost exclusively trying to play an insider ball game by pounding on the closed doors of Nutter and Fumo—but they're locked tight in their own relationships. We aren't going to move them by meeting with them—but that makes me feel like I'm left responding to each latest news cycle. I'm spending more time reading newspapers and talking to reporters than going out and hanging with members. Isn't that terrible?"

"Yes," he would have said. Then, "Go on."

"I just feel like my head is down and I'm trying to grin and bear it. To survive. To make it through. I feel like I'm stuck reacting and sliding toward the inevitable introduction of these casinos," I would have told him, sharing closely held words that I hadn't said to anyone. It would have been worse than heresy.

"Sounds like you've got a lot of pressure on you right now. You often love campaigning. Why are you merely surviving?"

"I made... I feel like a made this promise... not really. But I feel like I made a promise to everyone to see this through. But as I'm saying that, I'm realizing that I can't do it well in the current relationship I'm in with CFP. I can't be a full-time volunteer when I can't get out of things I don't want to do. But there's so much pressure to just keep going and keep going. I'm not even clear with anyone else—certainly not with Lily—about what I can and can't do. And then I have too many regrets. But at this point there's just too much I don't want to do."

George would have let that silence float, until maybe I would have made a decision or figured out how to renegotiate my relationship with CFP. Lacking a clear direction, he might have offered, "Your suffering has a kind of nobility, and I imagine a lot of people are feeding you encouragement to go ahead and keep suffering and overworking. There's plenty of rewards to your addiction to responsibility. But I hear that quiet voice inside you that says you also deserve the taste of liberation even during the struggle. Back in the day, we used to say that a movement should also live the revolution now."

He wouldn't have told me what to do—that's not his style. But given how long I had accepted work toward me, he would have been quick to remind me the organizer's job is to give work away—and that I had taken on so much that it was unhealthy not just for me but for CFP to rely on me in this way.

All of that could have happened.

But I didn't call Philippe. I didn't reach out to George.

I kept my head down and pushed through.

The crisis atmosphere wasn't just inside me. It was across the landscape, exploding into Senator Fumo's bombshell on April 30.

At the time, I was on the outskirts of Seoul, South Korea, in a large, bright training space filled with about forty union and environmental activists. While the group was on break, I checked email in the back of the room, where the interpreters huddled.

I had just told the group the story of Casino-Free Philadelphia's fight. Like so many other groups, they reveled in the creative adaptation of actions—something they very much wanted.

In South Korea, my co-facilitator and I had learned, Korean activists had regularly used marches to protest issues. Frustrated with diminishing media ignoring the ritualized actions, they escalated with an unusual tactic—public suicides. As expected, it got major media attention—but primarily on the tactic, not necessarily on their *issue*. But over time it, too, stopped getting press, to the disdain of South Korean activists.

What they saw in Operation Transparency and Philly's Ballot Box was part of what they had been missing: boldness mixed with action logic. Our direct actions were designed so that the logic was clear and obvious, because the action itself was the message. "Don't do a militant action for its own sake," I had urged them. "Do actions where your message is embedded in the behavior you do, so the public debates your message, not your tactics."

It sparked a helpful flow of ideas.

Now, in the back of the room, I struggled to maneuver through the Korean text to get to my email account, managing to find a series of excited emails from Paul. He reported that with much fanfare, Senator Fumo had introduced legislation in the Senate to re-site *both* Philadelphia casinos. Unlike his introduction of the buffer zone, back when he was still on speaking terms with his lawyer/SugarHouse investor, Fumo's press release spit fire. A "bombshell," wrote one reporter.

Even Paul's cynicism couldn't detect anything overtly fishy from Fumo. He might *really* be trying to move them. "How do we applaud an ally who might just be selling us out in the end?" Paul wondered. "Fumo said he offered the casinos even *more* money to move. It seems... I guess... a great start."

The freedom of a few thousand miles made it clear that I didn't have to do anything quickly. I couldn't calculate the time difference anyway. So I wrote slowly, deliberately. "This is good news, and we must reframe it away from it being between Fumo and the casinos. We ask Fumo to reimburse all his constituents who were forced to defend themselves from his casino debacle. He repay all the donors to CFP, PNA, NABR. It's an amazingly small amount—surely under $400,000 for all our costs. I, personally, don't want the money back, but government should not be bailing out corporations that are screwing us and have plenty of money, when politicians made the problems."

I smiled at my own message, content with its double-bind and high ground. I walked away and turned to my co-facilitator, "We've got a great addition to this morning's CFP story!"

My co-facilitator looked shocked when I explained. "You mean the guy who introduced casinos in the first place?"

I nodded, happy for another talking point to teach our group about how power truly resides in the grassroots—when we use it.

April stretched on into May. Reporters struggled to cram the myriad of avenues and updates into their columns. For the most part, they abandoned doing single stories on anything we—or anyone else—did, instead writing columns that read almost like long bullet-point lists of casino happenings. In turn, editors regularly put these columns on the front pages. They knew the casino issue had widespread interest.

I knew it in my own way. Walking down the street, random strangers would recognize me from TV and stop to cheer me on. Friends reported how weirdly invasive it was that they regularly woke up to my voice on their clock radio.

Fumo went quiet, causing the executive team to trade emails with hypotheses. *Maybe his recent heart attack has gotten to him. Or he's focused on his impending trial. Or his quitting his senatorial re-election race really was because he was tired. Or there's nothing to report. Or he's being sneaky.*

It was uncertain—just like everything was uncertain. Nutter, too, had gone quiet. Some people figured that meant he was fighting behind the scenes. So certain were they, that over a dozen volunteers figured re-siting was a done deal and decided to spend more time with their kids or move on to other issues. A few others gave up, figuring the opposite, that Nutter was selling us out or that the deal was so wired that anything stopped politically would just head to the courts who would give the casinos everything.

The fact was there were too many things going on. Even I couldn't keep track anymore. Our meetings were barely discussions—over half the time, we were just updating each other on what was happening. And each of us had our own obsessions.

After Jethro's baby was born, he didn't come to meetings, but he did become admittedly obsessed with revelations that one of Barack Obama's largest bankrollers was Neil Bluhm, the billionaire investor in SugarHouse. A *Washington Post* journalist had alerted us to Bluhm's $78,000 contributions as a bundler. That reporting touched off a firestorm in our movement.

First at Obama: "I know Democrats want to use casinos to generate revenue for social services and, too cowardly to raise taxes explicitly, are using casinos as a backdoor, highly regressive tax. But it is hard for me to be supportive of Obama given the connections to Bluhm," Jethro had written, annoyed given Obama's past statements that the "moral and social cost of gambling, particularly in low-income communities, could be devastating."

Then we learned Hillary Clinton had received almost twice as much money from casino sources and cavalierly described casinos as an "economic development tool." She had longstanding casino connections.

Then we learned that nationally, the gambling industry was equal-opportunity and had poured money into all the campaigns, nearly equally to Democratic and Republican candidates. (This was before casino magnate Sheldon Adelson unbalanced that in 2012 by pouring over $72 million toward Republican candidates, mostly via Super PAC donations.)

All this got under the skin of Hilary Regan, who saw the opportunity to send our issue national when Obama and Clinton came to Philadelphia to win the competitive Pennsylvania primary. She single-handedly grabbed attention on CNN and NPR, on which Obama coolly noted the large local opposition to gambling in Philadelphia but unsurprisingly took no stand on a local issue.

That was not my obsession. My obsession was the state politics. With help from our own volunteer lobbyist Hannah Sassaman and Lily, I tried to revitalize our long-dead 1,500-foot buffer bill. Weeks of meetings went nowhere, trying to unstick the committee chair, closely tied to Philadelphia's Democratic structure.

I also focused on writing and training to pass on lessons from the movement. CFP was gaining attention nationally, helped by casino trade magazines highlighting the Philadelphia casinos as examples of the danger of entering urban areas. Our story was an unmistakable warning signpost to the industry. So I followed requests from anti-casino activists in Massachusetts, Louisiana, and Ohio—even flying to Washington to help one group plan an action. Each place echoed our story: unwanted casinos forced into our cities and towns. CFP was becoming part of the national movement against predatory gambling.

It was unquestionably a hard time for me. I got frustrated easily—whether by students wasting my time but giving nothing in return, or more funding agencies turning us down (most frustratingly, one gave CFP an award but refused us funding). Like me, Shirley and Kathy alternated moods. Sometimes it was Shirley declaring, "We're going to win this!" Other times, Kathy spoke the despair, "They're going to screw us."

Paul's obsession was with permits—an area we easily ceded to him. By June, SugarHouse had gained some minor permits, but it would not be building anything substantial for months. It had spent nearly half a million dollars on archeological consultants searching for the British occupying troops' fort, leading to an uncovering of 182 Native American artifacts—some as old as 5,000 years, long before the Lenni Lenape were around.

The many avenues before us left us scattered. Aside from Lily's planning a few return trips to investors' neighborhoods, we didn't do any public actions. We were focusing on small battles, hoping we were picking the right ones. Worried we were picking the wrong ones.

It wasn't until our opponents reared their heads again that we refocused.

When my cell phone rang and I saw that it was Paul, I grew instantly annoyed. Not at Paul, but at being disturbed while on vacation—the day before the Fourth of July, no less.

I stole away from the dining table and headed off to a quiet corner. If Paul was calling me now, it must be important. "Hey, Paul."

Paul's voice was brusk. "Do you know either State Representative Dwight Evans or Curtis Thomas or Tony Payton?"

"Uh... All are African-American representatives from Philly. I think they represent Northeast districts. Tony is a progressive. The others are Democrat die-hards. Why?"

I could hear Paul deciding how much of the backstory to explain. "You remember State Representative Paul Clymer, right? How we asked him to introduce resolutions to stop Philly casinos from getting ten-year tax abatements, right?"

"Well, I remember Paul Clymer but not—"

"Doesn't matter," Paul interrupted feverishly. "Point is. Those other representatives— Evans, Thomas, Payton—they interrupted Clymer and said this was all a waste of time. Hold on, let me find it..."

Even though I couldn't tell where this was going, my heart leapt. New political players in the casino mix was only good for us—if only because it gave us fresh targets. It meant growing controversy, which suggested that past inside deals were breaking apart, causing new rifts. I had long believed that we could only win if we could break those deals, giving us the space to reopen discussions on the value of bringing casinos into our state.

Paul read from his notes. "Representative Evans said, 'It is unfair why these casinos are not online. I don't believe we should stand in the way of property tax reduction.' He went on to complain that any bill that gets introduced gets anti-casino bills tacked onto it. They're all pissy that it's slowing down the budgeting process."

"That's huge!" I clapped excitedly. Just a year ago, we hadn't been able to be in the budgeting process—now we were. My voice dropped. "But why would Evans and others wade into this political minefield when they don't have to? Don't they know they're going to become targets now?"

"I think Rendell is using them to circle the wagons," said Paul. "Rendell has to be truly frustrated to have this in the middle of a budget discussion. So he's asking them to get everyone in line."

"But Clymer's not going to listen."

"Nor are we," said Paul. I could hear his gears clicking, already thinking through how to apply pressure on those three. "We've got to get to them."

"Realize they are just the tip of a larger iceberg. This is a real opening to swing these representatives to become allies, if only because their interests align with us on at least one point: they, too, want the casino fiasco to end. We must convince them the answer is to force re-siting and reopen all the deals."

"I'll work on a draft email blast to our members," said Paul. I could hear his fingers already starting to type.

"I'll get a phone call with Payton," I said. "For now, let's play nice. Don't isolate them. We treat them like potential allies, knowing they're going to be stressed with the budget cycle coming up. We just explain to them with letters and personal phone calls that solving the casino problem means they have to get them unentrenched from their locations."

We knew it was big. We knew it was important. We didn't know exactly how. But the word "URGENT" in all caps appeared on our email blast's subject line for the first time. Members sent hundreds of letters within hours.

❊   ❊   ❊

The next day, Senator Fumo brought Dwight Evans into his office. It was almost exactly four years since Fumo and Rendell had orchestrated the late-night passage of casino gambling over the Fourth of July weekend.

It was another closed-door meeting.

Yet this time the public was very much present—not only in the sound of the fax machine dropping letters from CFP and allies. But in the political reality that pervaded their tense discussions.

With Senator Fumo dropping out of the Senate race, his once all-pervasive air of power was thinning. Instead, Larry Farnese—who had been active with our No Way Without Our Say petition drive—had been chosen by the voters over a disappointing race by Anne Dicker and a disastrously close-to-successful bid through hand-over-fist spending by John Dougherty.

Whereas two years earlier, Jethro had been cussed at by Fumo's right-hand man and told to get a bodyguard when the *Inquirer* published his editorial challenging Senator Fumo, there was now public revolt against Fumo in South Philly and elsewhere across the city. People knew that Fumo would be found guilty and would land in jail. But they had known that he was involved in corruption long ago. The freedom to speak out against Fumo had grown with the anti-casino movement.

In the other corner was Dwight Evans, a long-term Democratic leader who had given and taken his share of political hard knocks. He could see Fumo's limited options—and he could see a movement that was now casually challenging politicians who had previously been protected by Philly's political despair from something much worse than being told they were bad. We now expected politicians to do the right things and do good.

It took two hours before the deadlock broke and they came to an agreement.

Representative Dwight Evans and Senator Fumo stood before a raft of media cameras, joined by the bulk of Philadelphia's state representatives. "The entire Philadelphia delegation is now behind re-siting the casinos," said Senator Fumo. "We've been throwing spitballs. We will now start throwing atom bombs."

He explained they were sending a joint letter to the governor explaining that "the two proposed sites are no longer viable" and that continued reluctance to move them "will adversely impact the casino licensees' and developers' bottom line." They asked for a meeting to "begin this process in earnest," backed by promises of legislative delays and roadblocks if it were not.

We could taste the casinos moving. Even Rendell's cautioning, "Don't get too excited," seemed forced. Despite the courts, despite their powerful political and financial backing, the casinos might move. With them weakened, we even had the slim opening that maybe we could kill them for good.

That night, Fumo walked from the press conference to gingerly wave and speak words of goodbye on the floor of the Senate. After thirty years, it was his last day in the Senate. A few months later, his trial for 137 counts of conspiracy, fraud, and obstruction of justice would yield a guilty verdict. He would be sentenced to sixty-one months in prison.

That left only a summer before the Senate would reconvene with a replacement for Fumo. That was very little time to pressure Evans, Fumo, and others in what we termed—in a fit of hopefulness—the Re-siting Committee.

A month later, and there was no new news. Jethro and I had written a letter to the Re-siting Committee, asking for an open and transparent process with open, televised negotiations and involvement of neighborhoods. But neither Rendell, Fumo, Evans, or Nutter had anything to say—to anyone—for over a month. They held their cards so close even rumors didn't sneak out of their offices.

"So we return for a practice site occupation training," I exclaimed at the next executive meeting.

It was readily accepted. We needed something to energize the stalled feeling among our members. *Daily News* reporter Chris Brennan, in his nasty article entitled "Ten Reasons to Bet on Casinos Not Moving," had noted we had been "quiet since mid-April" and concluded that "community groups have taken their shot." Though I no longer believed a showdown with a prolonged site occupation was likely—this would be won or lost before a casino was actually building—I *did* believe we needed to show politicians we would continue to stir the crisis atmosphere surrounding the casinos.

I myself had my own doubts about our capacity. I had been worried for weeks over our empty office and quiet mailing lists. My direct action savvy, media work, and tactical creativity were poorly balanced without Jethro's community-organizing attitude of constant delegation, meeting new allies, and door-knocking. Our 5,000-person listserve was solid, but it wasn't growing. Our current movement seemed stuck at its size.

For the site occupation, we picked Gloria Dei (Old Swedes') Church, three blocks from Foxwoods' proposed siting and the oldest church building in Pennsylvania—second oldest in the United States. The room had large windows, overlooking the cemetery dating back to the 1700s.

There, George Lakey and I showed people how to create a blockade with linked arms—*sit close, link at the elbows, keep hands close to you*. We role-played scenarios, with lengthy discussions over how to interact with workers on the site, with the group's eventual conclusion to be polite but that acts of offering food or gifts to hostile workers were too likely to be misunderstood or deemed insulting.

The group—made up largely of older residents from the neighborhood—then walked three blocks to the sidewalk near Foxwoods' site to practice a "picnic-in." Our people carried beach balls and umbrellas, trailed by a dozen civil affairs officers carrying highly conspicuous video cameras, obtusely taking notes and snapping photos of the crowd.

Our action was smooth and bright. "In the very Casino-Free and democratic spirit of what this land *should* be used for," said George, "we will use Foxwoods' proposed site as an open green space where people can play by the riverside." He set up roles and led us through a role-play on the sidewalk.

Civil affairs tried a different intimidation tactic than last time. During my debrief of the role-play, an officer interrupted, shouting over my voice, "Nonsense—this is a total waste of time."

I laughed and pointed at him, "This is civil affairs 'doing their job.' (*You'll never just be able to walk onto the side!*) He wants control of the situation, because that's what he's paid to do. (*Not true! I'm just thinking of your future.*) But are we going to give it to him?" People shook their heads. "Then we continue—(*This guy doesn't know what he's talking about!*)—we finish the debrief and ignore him."

The message wasn't for him, as activist Valerie Killer explained to one reporter. "This wasn't just a training session. It was in itself direct action—this very public and well-publicized practice," she gestured toward the *Plan Philly* videographers and *Inquirer* reporter. "It was meant to show the casino builders and the members of city and state government who are behind the waterfront casino sites that we're not going away, we will continue to protest and object to their plans."

That was the message carried by news reports, telling of women "seventy-three and a half years old" considering risking further direct action.

The message was apparently heard. The day after our action hit news, Governor Rendell announced a meeting with Foxwoods for the next week.

Casino-Free Philadelphia finally organized a rally.

We needed something quick, something dirty, something simple. We were stretched thin as it was, so we simply stood outside City Hall the day before—and outside the upscale law offices of Ballard Spahr on the day of—the governor's meeting with Foxwoods. We carried signs ("Ed: Don't Ask, Just Tell"), hoisted a banner ("Casinos = Corruption"), and had a bullhorn with chants ("What do we want?" "No casinos!" "When do we want it?" "Now!").

The action was a basic workhorse, plodding us along to further our week-long framing to the press. "If there's a failure from this meeting," said Paul, "it's the *governor's* fault, not the casinos' intransigence."

If I had been there, I would have felt a lot riding on that moment. I would have joined Paul's frenetic chants and been excited to join with long-term activists outside on the sidewalk shaking our raised fists.

Instead, like Jethro who was in Denver, I was away working—this time at a training in Florida. But even if I had been in Philadelphia, issue fatigue may have kept me from coming, too. *Another rally, another crisis.*

Up in the law office sat elected officials familiar to us: Governor Rendell, Mayor Nutter, Senator Fumo, and several state representatives. This was a *political* meeting. The PGCB was not invited, nor DiCicco. It was the political heavyweights, the exact people we had moved up to target over the past months. Moderating was Rendell's former chief of staff. On the other end of the table sat two principal Foxwoods investors.

Foxwoods made a proposal. It was discussed, debated, and ultimately accepted.

They walked down silently and told the press nothing.

The next day, before a packed press conference, the deal was announced. I don't even know where I was when I heard, though I was probably traveling back from Florida. All I know is that I read the press headline with shock: "Foxwoods Agrees to Relocate in Principle."

They wouldn't say where they wanted to go. Or when.

Nutter said they *weren't* offered money to move—and that it wouldn't be on the waterfront.

But all those vague statements left even the most naïve in the movement wondering if it was just a ploy, a scheme to pretend to move, get attacked vociferously, and then, annoyed, stay at their current site—a Fumo-esque divide-and-conquer strategy. "Not time for celebration," urged DiCicco, "but it's time to be optimistic."

Or from the Philadelphia Neighborhood Alliance: "A good first step."

Despite the part of me trained to be cynical, I believed a public declaration of moving was too high-stakes to be a feint. That move would shake Foxwoods' investors and funders to the core. We had thrown everyone off their game plan for years—they, too, were now flying by the seat of their pants, spending nights worrying and wondering. A public misdirection that big was too likely to have blowback.

No, they were determined to try moving.

Helen Gym called me two weeks later. It was very late.

A community organizing legend, I was familiar with her leadership of Asian Americans United's successful campaign against the Phillies' baseball stadium moving into her neighborhood, Chinatown. In the anti-casino movement, we had retold her story of fighting done deals. Yet I couldn't see any reason she would call me.

I moved away from my friends playing cards and headed into a darkened room.

Her voice was constricted, but polite. "I'm sorry to be calling so late."

"No biggie," I said, downplaying my exhaustion.

"But I'm hearing disturbing rumors that they are planning a casino somewhere near Chinatown. I have great admiration for your work. I kinda feel like we should have been more involved to help you earlier. But I wanted to see what you think."

"I'm getting calls from people in lots of neighborhoods with rumors that Foxwoods is coming to their neighborhood."

"I think I have it on pretty good information," she said. "This is exactly the kind of thing they would do to our neighborhood—stick it to us because who cares about Chinatown anyways."

"You may be right." I sighed heavily. "But without any basis of information, I don't think neighborhoods should work themselves up into a frenzy."

We talked quietly a few more minutes before she thanked me and got off the phone.

I had barely walked back into the room with my friends when *Inquirer* reporter Jeff Shields called.

"We're both gonna have a late night," he said mournfully.

I looked at my clock. It was already past ten.

Jeff continued, "Foxwoods is moving to the Gallery, at Market East Station." Right next to Chinatown.

For a moment, I didn't say anything. Then, "You mean they're going to *try* building there."

"Yeah," he said, pausing. "I guess."

"You've got it for sure?" I didn't know why I was asking him. If it were just a rumor, he'd have told me.

"I'm printing it tomorrow. Thought you'd want to know. You gonna protest that one, too?"

"You know it." A thousand questions came to mind: *Why the Gallery? How far along is the deal?* But Jeff was working late, and I was now, too. I needed to call Helen back, and others in CFP. "You need a quote from me?"

"No, you gave me what I needed to know. I'll see you at the press conference tomorrow. Don't stay up too late."

"Yeah... you, too." My voice cracked.

I hung up the phone and sat in the dark. *A whole new fight. In brand-new territory. With a whole new group of people.* It took me a moment before I realized: we had *moved* a casino. This was one of the few large victories struck against a casino. And this win was gigantic, if only because nobody had ever won against a casino after it had so thoroughly lined up support with the courts, politicians, and media.

Yet even still, I was only aware of the daunted, exhausted feeling from the herculean task of moving it again, of killing it... I knew I should call Helen, but my arms felt like deadweight. Preparing to tell another neighborhood that they would have to fight what we fought felt too weighty a burden.

I let a few tears slip, then made the calls.

Helen was gracious, stumped, angry, prepared—just like the others in CFP. At the end of the night, I collapsed into a friend's arms. "I can't believe it. I just can't believe it."

The next day, I trudged into the mayor's ornate press room. Helen Gym and several of her neighborhood comrades sported a T-shirt that read "No Stadiums in Chinatown" in English and in Chinese characters. She half-smiled and pointed, "Same fight, different opponent. Thanks for being here and supporting our neighborhood." The T-shirts would soon be reprinted, except with the word "stadium" crossed out and "casinos" scrawled underneath.

I thanked her folks for their presence, taking seats next to two dozen CFP members.

It was weird to watch Governor Rendell, then the mayor, then Foxwoods give out their plans—with no statements or interruptions or action from us. Jethro grew grouchy as reporters gave the politicians softball questions ("How will this be a boon to the city?") and couldn't help but mutter loudly, "It's just *another* deal made in backdoors! Doesn't any reporter have a backbone?"

My own boldness to interrupt, despite Paul's poking me, was overshadowed by my shock.

It wasn't the Philadelphia paranoia felt by some members, who worried that it was all a ploy to make pressure on Foxwoods' riverfront site let up, then return to that site when Chinatown revolted. Several people grabbed on Rendell's statement that if the move to the Gallery failed, the site would return to its riverfront location.

Those people were stuck believing they were always being outplayed. One person even remarked to me that Rendell had *always* taken us into account and expected our movement—that he somehow really wanted a casino in Chinatown in the first place.

That was just Philadelphians' ability to snatch defeat from the jaws of victory.

My shock was different. I believed the win was even bigger than most people realized. I was filled with surprise that Foxwoods would really agree to accept a defeat by moving. Didn't they realize they were opening themselves up to us killing them? In shock, I pulled DiCicco's legislative aide aside and almost shouted, "This is unbelievable!" He stared at his BlackBerry, ignoring me. "Don't you understand? We can kill this thing now. It's never going to happen."

He shrugged me off.

But I felt confident that the forces were now aligned against Foxwoods. It had fallen into the trap we had set. The owners of the Foxwoods riverfront site would be against the move. Political insiders who had set up the first deal would be less motivated to do it again—and now they'd be making deals under a magnifying glass instead of in a backdoor. Those from Nutter's staff that were anti-casino would slow down each step. Wall Street investors would get jittery about a high-profile site move. A new slew of competing downtown businesses would fight them. And the PGCB would oppose the plan for never consulting them—the board believed what the courts had told them, that *they alone* held the sole right to decide location.

Yet I accepted the win, while rejecting any celebration. I felt the pain of a new neighborhood suffering the possibility of a casino in the neighborhood. Their worry. Their late night torments. I felt guilt over it, despite Helen's reassurance that she knew it wasn't *our* choice.

Still.

In my heart, I knew we could kill Foxwoods entirely.

I just wouldn't be there to do it.

CHAPTER 19
Casino Slayers

SEPTEMBER 11, 2008 — DECEMBER 19, 2010

a frozen moment of trauma and humanity • cracking open deals renews options •
humiliating a billionaire • retraining to slow oneself down •
unlearning paranoia • movements of values don't experience clean wins •
owning your wins when you are scrubbed from history

IN THE FOLLOWING MONTHS, Helen Gym and Ellen Somekawa from Asian Americans United fiercely mobilized Chinatown. They built the No Casinos in the Heart of Our City coalition with over fifty organizations, including the respected Black Clergy of Philadelphia. They received shaky support from the Philadelphia Neighborhood Alliance, which was ripped apart over whether it truly stood against casinos in neighborhoods or really just in *their* neighborhoods. With Jethro and I both stepping further back into mainly advisory roles, Casino-Free Philadelphia's support of AAU was staunch but with reduced capacity.

In October 2008, hundreds of concerned Chinatown residents pressed into Holy Redeemer Chinese Church. The gathering had been amped by a passionate youth speak-out, at which teenagers standing on the slides on the playground railed against the Foxwoods proposal. It took nearly half an hour of jostling to fit everyone into the room. Nobody looked pleased to be there, facing a table with DiCicco and Representative Mike O'Brien.

Councilman DiCicco feebly began, "This plan has some advantages." Hisses emanated from the mostly older crowd. He half-started sentences and tripped over words to explain that though he called this meeting, he didn't have much to tell them. The crowd punctuated his statements with the disquieting sounds of a seething mass trying to maintain politeness. "I made a mistake last time. Last time, I allowed civic groups to refuse to negotiate with Foxwoods. They had no deal with the casinos. I won't allow that to happen this time."

Jethro yelled along with others in the crowd, "Why dismiss a strategy that just worked? You're *trying* to lose!" Others hoisted signs with quotes from the Foxwoods chairman: "You call it a gambling addiction — I call it a client base."

The crowd was pissed at DiCicco, who wiped at his sweaty face and told them he was listening, would be open and transparent—but that he had no drawings of Foxwoods to present and no intention of trying to stop this casino. The crowd booed openly.

When DiCicco opened it up for questions, a torrent of angry words showered upon DiCicco and all the political representatives. DiCicco kept his sturdy toughness—until he faced the testimony of a raging Lai Har Cheung.

Face in tears, she raged in a high pitch how her family lost everything to casinos in Atlantic City. "My family lives with the scars from gambling addiction. *How can you bring this to us?*" When DiCicco told her to calm down, the crowd bristled at his callousness. Lai Har continued half-shouting, half-sobbing, "I'm scared! You don't know what it's like!"

At that, DiCicco snapped and interrupted sharply. "I understand!" His face was blood-red. "You know why I understand? My father took his life because of a gambling addiction."

If there were a single moment I could freeze from the entire campaign, it would be this one.

For years, we had worked alongside DiCicco, yet we never knew this. The silence of gambling addiction and its attached shame is so deep. Like alcoholism was decades ago, gambling addiction is almost never talked about. The scars are invisible. That silence makes it easy to pretend there's no social cost. No breakdown of families. No suicides. It's all about jobs and revenues. At best, the rest is just a personal responsibility. But DiCicco had no choice in his father's suicide.

State Representative Mike O'Brien turned to DiCicco and added, "I know, too. My father was a compulsive gambler. I know what it's like to go to bed hungry at night. I know the terror and anxiety a child can feel when left alone while his dad gambles." Mike, too, had no choice in his father's compulsive gambling.

Later, a therapist suggested to me that for these many years Frank DiCicco had likely avoided the pain and hurt of his father's gambling and suicide, the scar of a child unable to save his dad. Instead of coming to terms with the pain and therefore fighting harder so others wouldn't experience that pain, he distanced himself further. In his mind, if he couldn't save his dad from casinos, maybe at some level he couldn't save his constituents from them either.

That frozen moment as Lai Har and DiCicco stared at each other said it all. DiCicco, stuck in a belief of hopelessness, the pain kept locked tight. And Lai Har, passionately willing to speak of her own pain from her family's gambling addiction.

Both stories are our country's gambling problem. Only more people like Lai Har will break this issue open.

But as quickly as it happened—a united story of suffering—it broke apart.

Lai Har asked why, then, would DiCicco support casinos. DiCicco wiped his head, buried his grief, and turned back to the calculations of cheap political realism. "I'm not doing anything to you. I'm just bringing you the reality of what's happening here."

AAU didn't let up the pressure. Weeks later, they pulled together the largest anti-casino march—nearly a thousand people descending on City Hall.

Meanwhile, Nutter muttered vague words about his position on the new Foxwoods proposal, preferring to talk about his desired meeting with SugarHouse to get it to move, too. He admitted that Rendell had gotten him a brief meeting with billionaire investor Neil Bluhm at the Democratic National Convention. But he was clear, "This is not The Meeting. We still need to have The Meeting."

To force SugarHouse to the table, CFP escalated pressure, even heading to Chicago to protest outside Bluhm's offices. But the SugarHouse meeting never materialized.

By early 2009, Nutter had pushed for tough negotiations with SugarHouse over permitting details, keeping SugarHouse to its past promises and extracting a commitment for it to be more in line with the results of the PennPraxis riverfront plan. The success and influence of the PennPraxis plan was a corollary victory for us.

After many bruises, the PennPraxis director had solidified a public stance against casinos, and the PennPraxis plan offered a no-casino option, earning it public credibility. Through its process of participatory democracy, it had become a model of citizen input. Thousands had crowded to see its results—including its recommendation for a walkable riverfront, the prevention of future big-box development, and most of the values upheld by Neighbors Allied for the Best Riverfront years earlier.

Yet Nutter had switched to offering "unequivocal support" for Foxwoods' new location near Chinatown. In defending the shift, Nutter's spokesperson bizarrely differentiated Nutter's position as coming from "his time as mayor, not when he was a candidate" —back when Nutter had pledged to "keep casinos from being built within Philadelphia." His promise had become a heartbreaking lie, because while it's hard to get a politician to so brazenly lie, it's even harder to make them change their lie *again*.

Nutter was buoyed by elite city planners who saw a chance to "revitalize" Philadelphia's nearly abandoned downtown with an experiment that even Detroit wouldn't try—a downtown casino. Blogger Dan Urevick-Ackelsberg pointed out that a lengthy 1,400-word article from the *Daily News* titled "Casino May Save Market East" lacked a single piece of evidence that casinos had ever saved a city or an area.

But facts were never the guiding star of the casino enterprise.

Buoyed by Lily, Kathy, and Paul's vibrant energy plus a slew of new volunteers, Casino-Free Philadelphia stayed active with new campaigns: Declaration of Independence from Casinos and, later, In the Red: Bankrupting Casinos Before They Bankrupt Us. Aided by civic groups like Fishtown and Northern Liberties, CFP kept the pressure on SugarHouse, including by conducting a short-term blockade on the SugarHouse building. It wasn't a multi-day affair, but the fourteen arrested made a large splash: pastors and grandmas getting arrested to halt SugarHouse.

The collective pressure from that and the accumulated past pressure was sufficient to make SugarHouse increase its green space, reluctantly include a walking trail along the Delaware riverfront, green its building, and abandon a hideous, massive parking structure in favor of street-level parking. Its design conformed to most of the PennPraxis principles—except, most notably, for being an ugly big-box building. SugarHouse showered civic and neighborhood groups with money and put long-term pledges in writing.

But our biggest impact was on the size of the whole operation.

Mayor Street noted it, telling a group years later, "The governor was for gaming, the mayor was for gaming, the General Assembly was for gaming. But, in the end, the anti-gaming advocates kicked our collective behinds... They stopped something that none of us thought they could ever stop. We have a little facility down there, but we don't have anything near what all us big hot shots wanted."

Battered by years of delay, SugarHouse struggled to find funding. Even with strong financial connections, Neil Bluhm and company were forced to take a $180 million building loan at a whopping 12.9% interest rate. Moody's gave the loan "junk" status—too risky to justify investment—and, unusually, cited ongoing community resistance as part of the rationale. Lenders required SugarHouse to put up both the gambling license and the property as collateral.

In the words of *Inquirer* architectural critic Inga Saffron, the "original megaplan for the 21-acre site—a virtual city of condo towers and highway cloverleafs—was miniaturized into a single, modest box the size of a suburban supermarket." To reduce costs, it had a massively reduced footprint. Instead of 5,000 slots, the casino was forced to open with a mere 1,500 slots.

SugarHouse was a third its size, fit within the civic vision, and had deals with the neighborhood in writing. But it would be built.

Foxwoods' journey took a different route. For several months, Foxwoods developed site plans for the Gallery and, as Jethro and I had predicted, had long internal fights over land leasing and redesigning. It required a whole new set of deals, including a complex plan to relocate Burlington Coat Factory.

It didn't work, causing Foxwoods to try a second downtown location, in an old Strawbridge's building. Despite an outcry from AAU and CFP, Nutter and council fast-tracked all the zoning requirements for the new location. Consistent with his give-up attitude, DiCicco urged anti-casino activists to see that "it's over." His staff told them that Foxwoods' new location was a "done deal" and that they would never be happy.

But they would be.

Frustrated by months of delay, the PGCB turned outright combative—the first time it did so with a casino. It summoned Foxwoods to explain why every other casino in the state was running—except SugarHouse, which was partway through construction—while Foxwoods had not even started digging.

When Foxwoods officials explained their intent to move to a new location, the board erupted with contempt that they had never seen plans nor approved a change of location. The PGCB had been excluded from the deal and wasn't happy about it. They gave Foxwoods hard deadlines to report on its progress.

Months later, Foxwoods submitted its change of plans to the PGCB. But in late August 2009, the PGCB declared it unacceptable and ordered the PGCB back to the original South Philly site, largely worried about protecting its own legal hide—for years, the PGCB had trumpeted the site as the primary reason Foxwoods was selected.

It was a blow that would ultimately prove fatal.

Nutter threw up his hands in exasperation. Rendell had little to say, blandly telling people, "The law is the law."

Foxwoods was caught in our double-bind. The PGCB wouldn't let it move to a new location. Nutter wouldn't let it return to the old location.

We knew that either Nutter or the PGCB could crack, so angry citizens from Chinatown, Society Hill, South Philly, and elsewhere throughout the city kept up a barrage of protests and actions. We were able to pull Nutter's and the PGCB's strings enough to keep the Foxwoods deal in stasis.

At the next PGCB hearing, while anti-casino protestors chanted "Pull the plug!" the PGCB added $2,000-a-day fines for each day Foxwoods hadn't built on its original South Philly site.

All this accumulated delay took a financial toll, until its lead investor—suffering their own financial struggles—announced they needed outside money. Like the SugarHouse gang, they sought investor capitol—but few wanted to be part of that losing deal.

Eventually, Foxwoods got a rescue attempt from casino billionaire Steve Wynn. Amid a hero's welcome by politicians and officials, he promised to help turn the project around. Bringing his charming smile to his presentation before the PGCB, he was booed down by a boisterous crowd from Philadelphia. His smile faded. He turned to leave but was unnerved by young people from Chinatown filling the aisles and snuck out through the back.

Minutes later, he found himself in a testy interview by the *Inquirer's* Jennifer Lin, the video of which went viral. Cranky and snappy, he showed no knowledge of ongoing community opposition, the mayor's past opposition, or the PennPraxis project ("Are you familiar with the civic vision for the waterfront?" His response: "No! No! I answered you, no!").

Days later, he pulled out of the Foxwoods project.

Some speculated he withdrew because he was a buffered, ultra-rich billionaire from Vegas who had never been greeted so harshly. Others believed he was mad at Foxwoods officials for ill-preparing him. More still blamed the $127 million in racked-up debt from their fight with us.

I believed it was the combination of all of these—accentuated by the personal humiliation that, perhaps for the first time in his career, he was publicly shamed. Unlike his warm reception among Las Vegas citizens, retirees and young people were shouting down his every word—urging, pleading him to reconsider.

Unable to find funding or line up political consensus for either location, Foxwoods was irreparably weakened.

Though we had built the coffin, it took two more years for the final nails to be placed.

It was December 16, 2010 when I found out, while Christmas shopping at an Utrecht art store in Center City. My cell phone chirped, signaling a text message.

Over the past few years, I had trained myself to not react quickly. I willed myself to keep looking at paint supplies. I was not going to be reactive, no longer in a rush.

I took a breath and looked at the phone.

Lily's text message: "Fuck yeah. Thanks for all your hard work."

My heart fluttered. *Did the PGCB finally do it?*

I figured Lily would likely be handling a lot of press calls, so I called Jethro. He picked up on the first ring.

"Is it true?" My heart couldn't believe it was really happening.

"Yeah, they just ruled on it. I'm with my daughter right now, but it's something else."

"Incredible!" I looked around at the acrylic paints, trying to steady myself, convinced other customers were staring at me because my heart was beating so loudly. "I need to hear you say it, Jethro."

"The PGCB just revoked Foxwoods' casino license. Foxwoods is no more."

The freshest smile hit my face. We had killed a $670 million casino project.

George Lakey sat with me a few hours later. To my left and right were other close colleagues and friends. They had watched me over the course of my time with Casino-Free Philly and had assembled themselves to be with me in this exciting moment.

I sat shaking inside, unable to put my finger on my feeling. "I just can't believe it," I said. "It's been... just been years in the making..."

George smiled broadly. "But it's true."

"Yet something just feels wrong... it's just..." I caught my own inconsistent breathing, then noticed my stomach felt like it was on fire.

I had known that pit of stomach lava for years. We had become fast friends. It was my body tightening for the next hit—the next piece of bad news that inevitably followed any piece of good news.

I took a conscious breath. Then another.

"It's just that I've learned paranoia," I said. "Casino-Free Philadelphia has never had a success without getting bad news within a week. It's been bruising, and I'm still looking around my shoulder, even now. The supreme court—somebody is going to do something."

I demonstrated by turning around, only to realize how stiff my neck muscles were.

"You may be ready to let go," George offered. I looked up at him.

"I may need a hand," I said.

Spontaneously, one of my friends began clapping, rising to give a standing ovation. All rose from the table, clapping. I laughed hysterically. It was embarrassing, even as my stomach and neck muscles released under the intense tears of laughter and embarrassment.

"I get it, I get it," I laughed. "You know, it's funny. I've gotten so used to worrying about what's coming next. Yet when the unexpected happened to me, like the supreme court screwing us, some of our best thinking emerged, like Philly's Ballot Box. It takes so much energy to remain tight, braced for the next hit—yet I don't even think all that bracing helped."

One of my friends asked, "Is something right around the corner right now?"

I thought for a second, playing out the angles like I always did. Foxwoods was going to get embroiled in lengthy lawsuits challenging the PGCB ruling—they'd want their $50 million license fee returned. Would the PGCB look any more kindly on this than a drunk driver asking for their license application fee returned? *No.* The PGCB would fight them on it. Any resistance by Foxwoods would only embitter them more, making them even more likely to revoke the license, something so unexpected they didn't even have a process established for it.

With finality, I turned to my friends. "Foxwoods really is gone. It's no trick or ploy."

"Then stay in the present," said George. "Live the revolution now. There is no need to live braced. You truly won. You are surrounded by friends."

The next morning, I woke up early. I wanted to read the news in black and white.

I spent a few minutes dithering, uncertain if it was good to indulge my reactivity. But it was driven by excitement, not fear. I ran down the stairs and opened the *Inquirer*.

"After four years, the Pennsylvania Gaming Control Board finally ran out of patience with the Foxwoods Casino project. In a decision that shocked Foxwoods' attorneys and left anti-casino activists giddy with victory, the commissioners voted, 6-1, Thursday to strip the project of its $50 million slots license."

Foxwoods was gone. I took a moment to let that sink in.

As I let myself feel the win, I also felt the incompleteness. It wasn't a complete win if the license merely moved to another location. And SugarHouse was still going to open. I didn't want to admit it, even to myself, but I felt the failure easier than I felt the successes.

I remembered a training session I had led for Earth Quaker Action Team. They had waged a campaign against mountaintop removal, a dastardly way of getting coal by blowing off the tops of mountains and throwing them into nearby rivers. After months of pressuring PNC Bank, one of the largest investors in mountaintop removal, they had scored a major—though incomplete—victory: getting PNC to agree to exclude investment in companies undertaking mountaintop removal as a majority of their work. They asked me to lead their next planning session, to decide if they should press for a full exclusion or another demand entirely.

Sensing the emotional temperature of the room, I knew no good planning would come without addressing the psychological strain. I started with the group brainstorming on what their feelings were now, after hearing PNC's change in policy. The group of forty purred with a few positive feelings: *Happy. A bit surprised. Kinda shocked in a good way.* Then, as if a motor got turned on, the feelings poured out: *Disappointed that we didn't win more. Dissatisfied that PNC may continue the practice, using this just as a cover. Worried that people will leave the movement. Tired. Frustrated to not win more. Angry that PNC gets some good press. Screwed that people are acting like PNC did this on their own. Wanting to get to the bigger issues.* And so on.

After they had made that list, I smiled at them. "I'd like to introduce to you a theory about what happens after movements achieve a victory." They readied their pencils.

I moved my marker to the top of the list they had just made and titled it "Theory of Post-Movement Victory." Walking through the list, I explained how natural each reaction was to any movement victory. "Movement activists never have a completely clean win," I said. "Even in the rare cases when we win all our demands, we weren't running on a single policy or goal in the first place. We are running on a value, like transparency or environmental sanity—we do not see our values completely accepted into society. There's still a gap. And through the fight, we know even more how deep that gap goes. But we have to declare victory when we get it. Nobody else will do it for us."

George Lakey had been in that training room, and I remembered seeing his face relaxing, moving from fighting his feelings to accepting them.

I can give myself that same gift.

The reality is the PGCB is not a completely transparent institution. Casinos are still often trumpeted as a positive economic engine. Our state legislators did not suddenly start listening to the people. SugarHouse at one-third its size is still going to open. Foxwoods' license may be given to another casino.

Still, we killed a $670 million casino. For the years that nothing is in the ground, we've saved dozens of people from suicide, hundreds of people from gambling away their savings. I can relax. I don't have to brace for anything anymore.

Instead, we declare victory. Because as I reread the newspaper, I saw that it had completely ignored CFP, PNA, AAU, and any movement resistance.

The lengthy *Inquirer* article gave only mere mention to "fierce" local neighborhood and political opposition, "particularly from Nutter." Like that of other newspapers, its timeline of the failed Foxwoods project never mentioned *any* citizen action—unlike its timeline of the successful building of SugarHouse, which mentioned us a half-dozen times. Reporters who had seen our work up close completely ignored our force to make this win possible.

In victory, Casino-Free Philadelphia was scrubbed from history. It was infuriating!

Yet this is what they do. Reporters hand the power back to politicians, the PGCB, or the forces of the economy. Mainstream media don't tell the story of people power.

I recalled other direct action groups that had achieved wins—Disabled In Action, Pennsylvania's chapter of Health Care for America Now, Earth Quaker Action Team— and how the *Inquirer* and other newspapers steadfastly refused to even cover their actions—even while they won steady wins for people with disabilities or wins against mid-sized banks.

Pissed, I found myself opening up my email box—"like the old days," I mused. I pounded out a letter urging CFP supporters to claim this victory.

> *The power started with us. We know it and we will model what we've always done: when the politicians and elites won't do it, we'll do it ourselves.*
>
> *Foxwoods says you can't have their plans? Go take them. Supreme Court says you can't vote? Vote anyway. PGCB says you can't speak at their hearings? Speak anyway. Governor Rendell says you can't have a public debate on casinos? Have one anyway. And now: Philadelphia Inquirer says you aren't part of the history? Make yourself part of history anyway.*
>
> *Here's how: hold and treasure the victory. Did you sign a petition, participate in Philly's Ballot Box, get kicked out of a meeting, or write a letter or email to your representative? Then you are a casino slayer, too.*
>
> *Don't say it was Casino-Free Philadelphia's win. Or the anti-casino movement's win. Or the PGCB's "handing" us a victory. And don't follow DiCicco who's now idiotically saying it was "luck." No, no. Say it is your victory. Your win. Tell your friends. Write a note of congratulations to yourself. (Seriously.)*
>
> *Most importantly: own the title. Today you are officially a Casino Slayer.*

CHAPTER 20
Epilogue

DECEMBER 20, 2010—2012

OVER THE NEXT YEAR, SUGARHOUSE STRUGGLED to find its footing. Far from realizing its original plans to become the highest-grossing Pennsylvania casino, it moved from last place to only tenth out of the eleven Pennsylvania casinos in terms of revenue. As we foresaw, it was at a serious disadvantage in competing with statewide casinos, fighting heavily to capture 40% of its revenue from the other casinos.

SugarHouse worked hard to present itself as a good neighbor, pouring over $1 million per year into the neighborhood. But it knew it was being watched closely. Front pages screamed when someone was pistol-whipped in SugarHouse's parking lot. Media covered at least ten cases of winning gamblers being followed and robbed upon arriving at their house. Even a single employee arguing that their firing was because they were black and pro-union launched a series of articles. Press covered accusations from the union UNITE HERE that women at SugarHouse are 177% more likely to be fired, laid off, or quit than men and that racial and ethnic minority groups are 15% more likely than whites to be fired. SugarHouse responded with claims that "more than half of all promotions at SugarHouse last year were minorities or women."

To combat the bad press, the casino put up over 500 security cameras and even placed signs encouraging, "We care about your children's safety: Please don't leave them unattended in a vehicle"—a meager response to the closest casino's ten documented instances of children being left in cars.

Its heavy debt load and accrued expenses from the dragged-out fight reduced its earnings. Under the pressure, SugarHouse fought bitterly inside itself, spilling into the court, with Richard Sprague and his associates demanding that Neil Bluhm give them increased say in business operations.

Politicians, too, were bitter.

During the next election cycle, Councilman DiCicco unexpectedly left politics. Part of his reason, he explained, was that he was "burned out by the casino issue."

Unnerved by our years of badgering, Governor Ed Rendell was never the same on the issue of casinos. Asked by a veteran CBS reporter about the effect of casinos on addiction, he sputtered at her. "Let me answer this. You... you've... I've always... I've known, uh, for two or three decades, you're a very smart person," before finally waving his arms and grimacing angrily. "Those people would lose that money anyway. Don't you understand? You guys don't get that. You're simpletons. You're idiots if you don't get that." His embarrassing tirade was broadcast in full on *60 Minutes*, along with the show's carefully crafted argument against increasing state-sponsored gambling.

Mayor Nutter dramatically changed his tune. If he had any anti-casino inclinations, he violated every one of them. The Nutter administration abandoned its demand for a cost/benefit analysis—meaning no politician, academic institution, or research institution studied the impact of this unique introduction of casinos into an urban area. But Nutter went much further, welcoming and even fighting for a second casino in the city, a currently contested struggle.

It was an astounding change of heart. *City Paper* reporter Isaiah Thompson freely admitted frustration, echoing ours, that "on one side is data, on the other, vague half-answers and elusive responses." In an article entitled "My Gambling Problem," he wrote:

> *Part of the problem is that the more I learn about casinos in Pennsylvania, the more I see them lurking behind every political decision.*
> *Take the mayor's budget. Despite priding himself on refusing to forecast a possible windfall from Foxwoods and SugarHouse, the mayor is counting on $23 million in "host fees" from the casinos starting in 2012, as well as state casino revenue in the form of wage tax relief and economic redevelopment money. State lawmakers recently threatened to take that revenue away as a penalty for the slow progress on casinos. On Tuesday, the mayor met privately with SugarHouse investors. On Tuesday, those same lawmakers backed down from their threats.*
> *Suddenly, Nutter—who, as a candidate, pledged to fight casinos—now lists the slot parlors, along with the Barnes Foundation and the National Museum of American Jewish History, among the city's "incredible array of cultural and historical venues."*

Thompson criticized the Greater Philadelphia Tourism Marketing Corporation, "whose *With Love, Philadelphia XOXO* campaign recently included a 'love letter' about SugarHouse Casino: 'Dear Winning Streak, Is it hot in here or is it just you?' accompanied by a photo of a man and two women, all three Asian, at a Pai Gow table."

Nutter was now a protector and enabler to the casinos, using the power of the city to sponsor gambling.

While SugarHouse loudly reported the sums it gave to the state, its numbers shocked those of us who looked closely. After one year of operation, SugarHouse had given $11 million to Philadelphia in taxes and revenues—a mere pittance of the $232 million gamblers at its casino lost. According to CFP calculations, over $54 million was investor profit, with $34 million sent out of Philadelphia's economy to Chicago's Neil Bluhm and suburban investors.

Another year later, an *Inquirer* editorial noted that all the state's casinos combined had generated $426 million for all local municipalities and $3 billion for the state's coffers. But, it pivoted, "The rest of the story is not so pretty. It's found in the gaming board revenue report under two lines, 'wagers received' and 'amount won.' To date, gamblers have wagered $135 billion in the state's casinos, and won $123 billion. That means that they've lost [$12] billion. That's almost three times the amount of tax revenue that has been generated."

Soon after, a casino official stunned an audience by reporting that most of its regulars visit up to 200 times a year. SugarHouse confirmed similar numbers, saying a large percentage of its players come "three, four, five times a week."

It was consistent with what the widely ignored researcher Earl Grinols had shown, that 30% and 50% of all gambling revenues come from "problem" and "pathological" gamblers, respectively—largely made up of the poor, elderly, and people of color. Those people and their lives are the hidden costs, only breaching the news media over the most egregious problems.

Like the story of Raghunandan Yandamuri, who moved to the Philadelphia area in the spring of 2012. In desperation over his gambling debts, according to newspaper reports, the software engineer stabbed a sixty-one-year-old grandmother and gagged her granddaughter. Threatening to cut the baby into pieces, he wrote out a ransom note demanding $50,000—the amount he had lost gambling. He eventually drowned the ten-month-old. When caught, he boldly asked detectives to say his wife caught him—so she could get the $30,000 reward for his capture and reduce his family's debt.

It was a heartbreaking, tragic story that rocketed to the front pages. But the bulk of gambling stories would remain unknown, undetected among the public, and—from the perspective of politicians and casino investors—better left untold.

Politicians and casino investors were content to sit on their hands and let voices trumpeting personal responsibility apply moral judgment for his vicious crime.

But morality is not only individual. It is also social.

Casinos were a very conscious, calculated decision. Many people fought hard for them.

It wasn't the people who go to casinos.

It was casino investors who gave $4.4 million to the governor, legislators, and state supreme court justices between 2001 and 2008. It was the supreme court, which blithely interpreted law to give more authority to the casinos than city officials, city process, or the voters of Philadelphia. It was politicians who held onto despair and refused to fight against the industry. It was also the planners, civic leaders, reporters, and editors whenever they sided with the elites, whether out of malaise, callousness, or simply going with the flow.

The result made our government dependent on a new source of revenue, with its own interests. As businessman Warren Buffett opined, "It's a terrible way to raise money. It's a tax on ignorance... I don't like the idea of the government depending, for certain portions of its revenue, on hoodwinking citizens." Yet the government now had an investment in supporting the industry. It, too, was very much addicted to casinos.

Even before SugarHouse had finished building, the government of Pennsylvania decided to add table games and even passed a controversial bill to allow casinos to give lines of credit to gamblers.

Pitted against all that were the people.

Only a tiny percent were part of the fight. Yet they convinced the majority of Philadelphians.

When we started, over 80% supported casinos. Now, only a mere 33% of Philadelphians want a second casino, with a majority opposing any casino gambling outright.

None of that, of course, ended predatory gambling. Like any big issue, it will take longer than a few years to resist the injustice and havoc caused by a powerful, billion-dollar industry. Yet we accomplished some amazing things.

Casino-Free Philadelphia pulled together a new set of coalitions that taught a whole new generation of activists how to win in unwinnable situations. Many of those activists, like Paul Boni, continue to fight against SugarHouse expansion and the possibility of a second casino, concocting creative actions like the "Freedom Players" action, during which—to the consternation of casino managers—folks enter a casino with a simple plan: *to have fun our way*. Instead of inserting money into machines, the group sits down at slot machines and knits, read books, and chats with each other. Paul has joined the board of the Stop Predatory Gambling organization, a national group taking on the expansion of state-sponsored gambling, and is very much a thorn in the side of the industry.

Others from CFP have gone on to other fights, including Karim, Jethro, and Lily: against media conglomeration, preserving historic buildings, protecting the Delaware riverfront, as leaders in the Save the Libraries Coalition, halting climate change, and countless other social issues and movements, locally and nationally. Plus, a whole new set of politically wiser CFP activists became block captains and civic leaders.

Kathy Dilonardo was one of the changed. From someone who had been part of arresting activists in her past life, Kathy now gives full attention every time an activist knocks on her door. "Casino-Free Philadelphia was a marvel of working together—so many diverse people with different opinions."

When I asked about how CFP strategy had managed to stop a casino from being built in her neighborhood, she lit up. "We always planned ahead. We would talk about, 'If the supreme court does this, what are our options? What are we going to do if they say yes? What if they say no?' Often, those meetings were frustrating, because we weren't deciding anything. But, without realizing it, we were accomplishing something. It gave time for our plan to gel and for things to run around in our heads before it happened to us."

Those skills of planning and strategy continue to get passed on, with numerous movements citing Casino-Free Philadelphia as a model for them of good organizing, creative actions, and a spirited refusal to accept defeat. It wasn't just that we implemented effective organizing, creative tactics, or flexibility—we were showing a new model of democratic participation.

When I asked Karim what he'd learned, he turned to me with a serious face. "Something you need to take credit for: you always demanded that our elected officials and representatives should act right, that they should fulfill their roles to their constituents regardless of the evidence of corruption. You helped force them to do the right thing, always holding them to a high standard." Even then, he acknowledged it was a hard pill to see how deeply corrupt our politics were. "On the other hand, I've been involved with a few different nonprofits and I would say that it was a joy to work on one that functioned so well."

Or Shirley's reflection, "I learned so much about this new industry called activism. The process is slower because you are moving people's beliefs and perceptions. In business, you don't have to believe in it, you just have to go do it. At the end, it was much easier to look at our success. I walk away with a deep appreciation of that work. I spread my wings out of a few comfort zones for a lot of things. I realized I could stand up. I could do it for what was important for my community."

Of all the lessons she learned, she says the spectrum of allies and the upside-down triangle struck her the most. It moved her to see that groups win by drawing allies towards them—not winning over everyone at once, but by steadily winning over allies. And it was a brand new way of thinking to see that power doesn't flow downward but upward—that people are only governed by consent, and by withdrawing their consent the people have power.

As part of a panel of urban planning experts at the Academy of Natural Sciences, Jethro Heiko recounted the CFP story and spoke of its impact. "The results of our organizing approach are clear. Organized citizens, vastly outspent with little to no support from elected officials, have delayed and derailed highly juiced done-deal projects. We began to understand that we're all connected in the city, and our expectations have been raised when it comes to public process, public access to the river, and results. Casino-Free Philadelphia continues as an action-oriented force that engages citizens across a wide spectrum in nonviolent strategic means to shut down the wealth-extracting casinos. Meanwhile, the riverfront trail and new transit line along the riverfront are gaining traction. Millions of dollars of public and private money have been leveraged due to citizen push for riverfront planning. Many challenges remain. But it is clear that the more that citizens continue to put their ideas into action, the more likely you'll see great things happen and prevent bad things from getting in the way. I am excited to see how this approach will lead to real, smart, sustainable improvements in our city. It is the only realistic alternative to the tired, corrupt, and disempowering approach that has gotten us the riverfront we have now."

It's that spirit of power residing in our hands that defined Casino-Free Philadelphia. We clung to the notion that when the politicians and elites won't do it, we'll do it ourselves—that there is power from below. We knew we can move our neighbors, move media, move politicians, move corporations. That's why we call it a *move*-ment. It's what made it possible for us to decimate SugarHouse and kill Foxwoods—without a single court ruling in our favor or law passed in our favor.

That spirit has touched us—and I hope that it's touched you, too. You get to carry our story now, along with our loves and heartache—and also our lessons, emotional insights, strategy of people power, and the nuances of building a movement.

Index

Made in the USA
Lexington, KY
09 December 2014